WORDSWORTH CLASSICS
OF WORLD LITERATURE

General Editor: Tom Griffith MA, MPhil

METAMORPHOSES

Ovid

Metamorphoses

❖

Translated by John Dryden and others,
edited by Sir Samuel Garth

With an Introduction
by Garth Tissol

WORDSWORTH CLASSICS
OF WORLD LITERATURE

This edition published 1998 by Wordsworth Editions Limited
Cumberland House, Crib Street, Ware, Hertfordshire SG12 9ET

ISBN 1 85326 790 2

© Wordsworth Editions Limited 1998

Wordsworth® is a registered trade mark of
Wordsworth Editions Ltd

All rights reserved. This publication may not be reproduced,
stored in a retrieval system, or transmitted, in any form or by
any means, electronic, mechanical, photocopying, recording or
otherwise, without the prior permission of the publishers.

Typeset by Antony Gray
Printed and bound in Great Britain by
Mackays of Chatham, Chatham, Kent

CONTENTS

INTRODUCTION

Ovid

Ovid's *Metamorphoses* is a vast poem on the presence and prevalence of change in the world. If change is the only constant, it is easy to see how in one sense the *Metamorphoses* has always proved relevant to readers who have enjoyed and admired it over the centuries; and this was no doubt as true of its first readers as of their successors. During Ovid's early life the old Roman republic had reached its final stages of disintegration in civil war, and the Romans had found themselves ruled by a single individual, Augustus, whose power, vast and only partly definable, exceeded all recognisable limits. The republic had been officially restored, the senate and consuls still existed; but all institutions had been transformed, emptied of their former significance while superficially unchanged. When Ovid finished the *Metamorphoses* around AD 8, the date of his exile, the Augustan settlement had long been in effect. He, and the writers of the generation that preceded him, are commonly classified as 'Augustan': the poets Horace, Propertius and Virgil, and the historian Livy, are among the many who flourished during Augustus' long rule. They are a diverse lot, but have one notable feature in common: in their writings they all undertake to understand the events that had irrevocably altered their world and to interpret the unfamiliar peace that followed.

Publius Ovidius Naso was born in 43 BC at Sulmo in the Abruzzi region during the civil war that followed the assassination of Julius Caesar. In an autobiographical poem, *Tristia* 4. 10, written as a self-defence after his exile, he mentions, that he came from an old family of equestrian rank, and con-tinues with a serio-comic account of his education at Rome, where he was sent to receive the oratorical training necessary for a career at law and in public office. Poetry drew him instead, and when, by Ovid's account, his father objected to so unprofitable a pursuit, he tried to write prose – unsuccessfully, for his writing came out as verse of its own accord, passing into the appropriate metre (Alexander Pope was to adapt these lines to one of his own poems of self-fashioning: 'I lisp'd in Numbers, for the Numbers came,' *Epistle to Dr. Arbuthnot* 128).

Ovid insists that his beloved older brother, who was to die young, had a greater gift for eloquence than he. Yet Ovid derived much benefit from the legal training that they both received, which left traces in his diction and may well have contributed to the great sophistication and power of the argumentative speeches that abound in his work. Ovid had but a short legal career and held few judicial offices. The senate awaited him, but at this point he shifted all attention to poetry and the poets. He was already a member of the circle of poets who enjoyed the friendship of the aristocrat and soldier Messalla Corvinus, and he heard recitations by the great poets of his time. He mentions, among others, Propertius reciting his amatory elegies and Horace his lyric poetry. 'Virgil I only saw, and greedy fate did not allow Tibullus time for my friendship.' Ovid himself joined the roster of elegiac poets, fourth in the line of generic descent after Gallus, Tibullus and Propertius; and soon won a reputation.

Earliest among his works are the *Amores*, elegiac love-poems; there followed in uncertain sequence the *Ars Amatoria*, 'The Art of love', the *Remedia Amoris*, 'Cures for love', both mock-didactic poems; *Epistulae Heroidum*, 'Letters of heroines', elegiac complaints by abandoned women of legend; a collection of double epistles, in which three pairs of legendary lovers exchange letters; and a tragedy, *Medea*, now lost. While writing the *Metamorphoses*, Ovid was also working on the *Fasti*, a long elegiac poem that narrates, in the manner of Callimachus' *Aetia*, the origins of Roman festivals and rites.

When the *Metamorphoses* was apparently finished and the *Fasti* half-finished, Ovid's fortunes failed him; he was banished to Tomis (now Constanza) on the Black Sea, and was never allowed to return. By Ovid's account, Augustus himself pronounced the sentence. The causes of Ovid's exile are irretrievable. He mentions only *carmen* and *error*, a poem and a mistake. The poem was the *Ars Amatoria*. The mistake – which, one may infer, was accidental complicity in some scandal affecting Augustus's household – Ovid does not wish to explain. What he does want his contemporaries and posterity to know, in his many poems written at Tomis, is that his exile was sudden and unjustified.

In exile Ovid wrote five books of *Tristia* ('Sorrowful Poems'), four of *Epistulae ex Ponto* ('Letters from Pontus'), and the *Ibis*, a long curse-poem written against an unnamed enemy. His fortunes did not improve with the succession of Tiberius in AD 14, and he died at Tomis in AD 17.

The Metamorphoses

Ovid's *Metamorphoses* is a work of limitless fascination to readers, as its enduring popularity and influence make evident. Even so, one may well ask why so long a work, fifteen books in all, was needed to explain what could be summarized in two words, *omnia mutantur*, 'everything changes' – the very words, in fact, that Ovid gives to Pythagoras in a mock-philosophical discourse near the end of the poem (15. 165). One answer to the question is that only an immense and infinitely varied work could present its readers with an image of change adequate to the author's sense of its power and extent. The poem engages and entertains its readers because of, not in spite of, its size and scope, for variety and plenitude are its essential features – those qualities that grant its power of conviction as a representation of flux and transformation on a cosmic scale. Ovid brings all Greek and Roman myth within his theme, but not by attempting to re-tell all tales in the manner of a mythological handbook. Instead, he tells those that illustrate the transformation of human beings into trees, birds, animals, rocks, and other natural phenomena –

aetiological myths for the most part. Ovid offers a symbolic account of the origin of things, beginning with the creation of the world out of chaos. This creation-story includes the origin of human beings, but does not stop there. Throughout the rest of the work, metamorphosis continues the creation-story, as human beings become natural phenomena. Often Ovid traces the origin of a species to a disastrous event in the life of a person. Some of these aetiological tales were already famous when Ovid refashioned them, like the grim tragedy of Tereus, Procne, and Philomela (Book 6), who ultimately provide three new species of birds to the animal kingdom. Many became famous only after Ovid told them. He rescued many from the obscurity of catalogue-poems like Nicander's *Ornithogonia* and Boios's *Heteroiumena;* others he greatly altered, combining, for example, the tale of Narcissus with that of Echo (Book 3); others he searched out from sources that reach even beyond Greek and Roman tradition: an Anatolian origin appears likely for some tales, like that of Pyramus and Thisbe (Book 4). Although many of Ovid's tales were little-known before he transformed them, he includes reference and allusion to the traditionally more important cycles of narrative and more important figures, such as Hercules, Theseus, and Jason, often employing a well-known tale only as a frame for many others that more explicitly describe a metamorphosis. Although no single work could be literally all-inclusive, Ovid's appears so by the power of suggestion: his tale seems to embrace all tales, making them transformative and part of his own. The genres and specific works of his predecessors meet the same fate. Reading the *Metamorphoses,* we encounter anew Homer's *Iliad* and Virgil's *Aeneid,* for instance, but not on their own terms. Reduced to parodic summaries and extenuated into framing devices, they too become part of the *Metamorphoses* and illustrate, on more than one level, the power of transformation.

Ovid's *Metamorphoses* is more than a narrative description of change: the work embodies change in the experience of the reader. No sooner do we form an impression than that

impression shifts or abruptly disintegrates, whether we are trying
to follow a plot, to gauge the tone of a narrative, to form a just
impression of a character, or, at the beginning of the work, to get
a grasp on its generic affiliations. Is the *Metamorphoses* an epic? It
appears to be one at the outset, as the metre, dactylic hexameter,
would lead us to conclude; and Ovid loves to play with our
generic expectations of epic throughout the work. But these are
inevitably thwarted in one way or another. Dryden's translation
begins thus:

> Of bodies chang'd to various forms, I sing:
> Ye Gods, from whom these miracles did spring,
> Inspire my numbers with coelestial heat;
> 'Till I my long laborious work compleat,
> And add perpetual tenour to my rhimes,
> Deduc'd from Nature's birth to *Caesar's* times.

The translation is a free one: the original, for instance, did not
consist of 'rhimes' (a word borrowed from Dryden's predecessor
George Sandys). Yet in the words 'perpetual tenour' and 'deduc'd'
Dryden follows Ovid's vocabulary closely: *primaque ab origine mundi
/ ad mea perpetuum deducite tempora carmen* (*Metamorphoses* 1. 3–4), 'spin
out a continuous song from the first beginning of the world
down to my own times.' *Perpetuum* is a generically precise term to
describe traditional epic on the Homeric model, inviting us to
conclude for the moment that the present work is to be of that
type. But the very next word contradicts that impression, for
Ovid plays on a double sense of *deducite:* not only 'lead' or
'conduct' but 'spin finely' to produce a slender and refined work
on the model of Callimachus' narrative elegy. A *carmen deductum*
would have a place at one end of the generic spectrum, a *carmen
perpetuum* at the other. Although Ovid's paradoxical expression is
likely to leave readers at a loss about the nature of the work to
follow, it is in the event accurate; for Ovid's tales will prove as
fine-spun as any short narrative, while at the same time the whole
poem is indeed continuous in a new sense: all tales are linked by
transitions, succeeding each other in seamless progression. The

Metamorphoses proves to be generically original and unique, while it alludes to and incorporates many genres: epic (including Homeric epic, short epic and historical epic), elegy, didactic and philosophical poetry, tragedy, pastoral, and epigram, to name only the most conspicuous. To these must be added comic parody of all the genres listed.

Variety is as characteristic of the narrative style of the *Metamorphoses* as it is of any other feature. Yet to examine one tale will illustrate some general tendencies. Ovid begins his account of Meleager in Book 8 as a heroic exploit in epic style. The background of the story — how Oeneus, father of Meleager, neglects to make sacrifice to Diana, whereupon the goddess sends a huge and savage boar to devastate the fields of Calydon — Ovid presents in highly traditional fashion, with formal narrative structures and a serious tone, giving an initial impression that he plans to maintain such a style in the succeeding narrative. And so it continues in the catalogue of heroes who assemble to hunt the boar and win glory through their valour. By Book 8, however, we readers know better than to expect so serious and so heroic a story to continue uncompromised. Ovid has trained us to expect the unexpected. He always demolishes the heroic structures that he has built, transforming their fragments into something unpredictable and wondrous. In this case, the heroes prove comically incapable of wounding the boar. The style remains epic in the sense that Ovid passes from the actions of one warrior to those of the next, much as Homer describes a battle; but this event turns out to be a series of ludicrous failures. Further to debunk the valor of his heroes, Ovid adds cowardice to incapacity:

> *Nestor* had fail'd the fall of *Troy* to see,
> But leaning on his lance, he vaulted on a tree;
> Then gath'ring up his feet, look'd down with fear,
> And thought his monstrous foe was still too near.

The warriors' antics are better suited to slapstick comedy than to the epic treatment for which they originally seemed destined:

> But *Telamon* rush'd in, and happ'd to meet
> A rising root, that held his fastned feet;
> So down he fell, etc.

Ovid's buffoonish heroes appear even more so because he invites us to observe a disparity between their present behaviour and their later reputations. We may know Nestor as the wise and venerable counsellor of Homer's *Iliad*, but Ovid brings any such impression under assault by telling us of this undignified episode. The Calydonian hunt occurs before the Trojan War, and that fact gives Ovid an opportunity to upstage the later incident in comic fashion.

Atalanta, the only female warrior present, first wounds the boar, and Meleager kills it; but the main event of this tale is yet to come. Ovid speeds the narrative along as Meleager awards the spoils to Atalanta, his uncles object, and Meleager kills them. Ovid then focuses all attention on Meleager's mother Althea and her decision whether or not to avenge her brothers by killing her own son. The tone of the story shifts to a serious, even tragic intensity; tragic also is the form of utterance, a long soliloquy, in which Althea contemplates her hopeless choice. Ovid had developed this mode in his earlier masterpiece, the *Epistulae Heroidum;* here the soliloquy makes a powerful climax to the story of the Calydonian boar – a narrative shift that is unexpected and yet remarkably apt. Althea's inner conflict replaces heroic action as the focus of the story. To correspond to that change, battle-description now gives way to soliloquy, and the comic incapacity of the warriors to Althea's moral paralysis. That paralysis finds expression in paradox, the clash of contradictory abstractions. When, for instance, Althea forms an initial resolve to kill her son, she becomes, in Dryden's translation, a 'pious, impious wretch', and describes her approaching act in these terms:

> A crime I punish, and a crime commit;
> But blood for blood, and death for death is fit:
> Great crimes must be with greater crimes repaid,
> And second fun'rals on the former laid.

Ovid has a serious point to make in paradoxical expressions of this sort, which abound in this soliloquy and are scarcely less frequent elsewhere in the *Metamorphoses*. Contradictory terms embody the cleavage of identity that is taking place, as Althea separates into mother and sister, the two categories no longer reconcilable.

This tale of the boar-hunt and Althea is both unique and typical of Ovid's *Metamorphoses*. Althea is not the only heroine whose soliloquy becomes the central event of a narrative: the same is true of Scylla (Book 8), Byblis (Book 9), and Myrrha (Book 10). And in Book 13 a verbal engagement between Ajax and Ulysses becomes the central event in Ovid's re-telling of the Trojan War. Mock-epic and parodic features, so prominent in the boar-hunt, abound in the *Metamorphoses*. These are especially prominent in the later books, in which incidents familiar in the *Iliad, Odyssey* and *Aeneid,* as well as many events of Roman legendary history, receive richly serio-comic treatment.

Dryden and the Metamorphoses

In English there are three great translations of the *Metamorphoses,* those of Arthur Golding (1567), George Sandys (1626, 1632), and the present collaborative translation edited by Sir Samuel Garth (1717). Golding's work, in lumbering fourteeners, is well known because Shakespeare used it in adapting Ovid's Medea in Book 7 of the *Metamorphoses* to his own Prospero in *The Tempest.* Vigorous, homely in diction, and sometimes strikingly beautiful, Golding's translation is nevertheless hard going for present-day readers because of its long and obscurely elaborate sentences. Tastes had changed greatly in the half-century that intervened between Golding and Sandys, whose long-standard translation, composed in heroic couplets, did much to develop and refine that mode of verse. It reads like a reaction to Golding's rich Elizabethan style, for Sandys aimed at literal exactness and concision. He tried to keep his translation to the same number of lines that Ovid used, and achieved this feat of compression at some cost of clarity. To Dryden, writing some sixty years later, the work of 'the much admired Sandys' seemed obscure and prosaic. He asks his contemporaries to re-read their Sandys 'and see (if they understand the original) what is become of Ovid's poetry, in his version; whether it be not all, or the greatest part of it, evaporated.' (Dedication to *Examen Poeticum*, the Third Miscellany, 1693).

There was also another reason, besides its literalness, that made Sandys' translation obsolescent in Dryden's time. Late seventeen-century audiences were losing, or had lost, interest in the interpretive approaches to the *Metamorphoses* that earlier trans-lators had favoured. Both Golding and Sandys are late followers of a rich allegorical and moralising tradition that had flourished for centuries and had reached its most elaborate development in the vast *Ovide moralisé* of the fourteenth century. Golding equipped his translation with a long verse Epistle to the Earl of Leicester, whose first half shows book by book how Ovid's fables offer a 'myrror', 'image', or 'example' of various virtues and vices: Daphne is a 'myrror' of virginity, Narcissus of scornfulness and pride. Here Golding refits an old interpretive mode, making Ovid potentially acceptable to readers of some of his other translations; for he made English not only Ovid's Latin but that of the Geneva reformers John Calvin and Théodore de Bèze. In the second half of the Epistle Golding accommodates Ovid's tales as much as possible to scriptural history. On his view scripture, the source of all wisdom, lies at several removes from pagan authors like Ovid, who can offer only distorted and partial reflections of its truths. Yet its presence behind Ovid's account can be illustrated by numerous parallels, as for instance by the flood in Book 1. This flood reflects Noah's flood in Genesis, but Ovid 'in fablyng wise dooth make / It happen in Deucalions tyme, who reignd in Thessaly / Eyght hundred winters since Noyes flood or thereupon well nye.' (500–2)

Sandys led a life of adventure and enterprise, travelling to the Near East and to Jamestown in Virginia, where he com-posed part of his translation of the *Metamorphoses*. His completed translation of 1632 includes, appended to each book of the

Metamorphoses, a long discursive commentary, 'the greatest repository of allegorized myth in English' according to Douglas Bush. On a scale vaster than Golding's Epistle, Sandys undertakes to interpret pagan myth within scriptural history, extending this traditional viewpoint also to newly-discovered lands and peoples beyond Europe and the Near East. In his parallel of Noah's flood to Deucalion's, Sandys' own recent experience in America confirms the universal memory of the scriptural event: 'There is no nation so barbarous, no not the salvage *Virginians*, but have some notion of so great a ruine.'

Synoptic visions of antiquity like Sandys' would continue to thrive into the eighteenth century, but for Dryden and other readers of Ovid in the latter part of the seventeenth they had become no less old-fashioned than Sandys' rough couplets and awkwardly literal conception of the translator's task. In his preface to the complete translation of 1717, Garth commends Sandys' allegorical explanations, but offers, in place of their vast bulk, only a few pages of perfunctory moralising. Translation now arrives without elaborate commentary, and Ovid's poem thereby becomes more immediate and less familiar. Dryden is, on his own view, attempting 'to restore Ovid to his native sweetness, easiness, and smoothness'; his means, as in all his translations, is to aim at a middle way between the extremes of 'servile, literal translation', exemplified in Sandys' Ovid, and free 'imitation' of an author's manner.

Dryden makes these remarks in the preface to his earliest effort at translation, a collaborative version of the *Epistulae Heroidum* published in 1680 *(Ovid's Epistles, translated by several hands)*. After translating other authors, he returned to Ovid for his *Examen Poeticum* (Third Miscellany) of 1693. This included Book 1 of the *Metamorphoses* along with the tales of Iphis and Ianthe (Book 9) and of Acis, Polyphemus, and Galatea (Book 13). In his later years, as translation occupied more and more of his attention, Dryden recognised that he had found a rich vein in Ovid. He writes of these latest offerings, 'Whether it be the partiality of an old man to his youngest child, I know not; but they appear to me the best of all my endeavours in this kind. Perhaps this poet is more easy to be translated than some others whom I have lately attempted; perhaps, too, he was more according to my genius.' (Dedication to *Examen Poeticum*). Following his complete Virgil (1697), he gave Ovid's *Metamorphoses* a large share in his last collection, *Fables Ancient and Modern* (1700). In its famous Preface, despite critical objections to Ovid's 'Boyisms' and indecorous wit, Dryden admits that pleasure induced him to translate more of the *Metamorphoses* than he had originally intended. Including Book 1 of the *Iliad* among the *Fables*, Dryden declares an intention to complete a translation of that epic, for Homer is 'more according to my Genius' than Virgil, the author to whose works he had dedicated so much time and labour. The Preface mentions no further plans for Ovid, another author 'according to my genius'; yet there is evidence in letters and newspaper accounts that Dryden planned to compile a complete collaborative *Metamorphoses* in the 1690's.

In 1700 Dryden died after having translated at various times about a third of Ovid's *Metamorphoses*. His friends, his fellow-poets, and above all his publisher were not content to let the matter rest there, although twenty years were to pass before Dryden's original scheme could be realised. In 1717 a complete *Metamorphoses* in heroic couplets appeared under the editorship of Sir Samuel Garth, a friend and admirer of Dryden's in his later years. Garth assembled the sections of Ovid's work that Dryden had translated, filling out the rest with contributions, new or already published, from no fewer than seventeen other translators, including himself. The contributors range in reputation from the eminent (Joseph Addison, William Congreve) to the obscure (Stephen Harvey, William Stonestreet). The result of this remarkable collaboration – posthumous collaboration in Dryden's case – remains the best translation of Ovid's *Metamorphoses* ever made into English. It is more readable, more beautiful, and more faithful to the spirit of the original, than all competitors old and new.

Collaborative translation itself was not remarkable in those times, and this *Metamorphoses* came about as the result of a typical initiative of Jacob Tonson (1655–1736), the greatest of English publishers, 'Chief Merchant to the Muses' according to one contemporary (Edward Ward), 'a Pimp, or Gentleman-Usher to the Muses' according to another (William Wycherley). Tonson had been Dryden's publisher for the last twenty years of the poet's life, and had profited much from Dryden's plays, poems, and especially his famous translation of Virgil. Early in Tonson's career and his collaboration with Dryden he had published *Ovid's Epistles, translated by several hands* (1680), the preface of which has already been mentioned. Eighteen translators contributed to this translation of Ovid's twenty-three *Epistulae Heroidum*, Dryden among them. Dryden was again the editor, and Tonson the publisher, of Plutarch's *Lives* (1683–1686), a vast collaborative effort to which forty-one translators contributed. It remains the best and most widely-read English translation of the *Lives*. Another collaborative effort is the translation of Juvenal and Persius (1692) published by Tonson. Dryden edited the volume, and translated five of Juvenal's satires along with all six of Persius'; he also contributed his famous 'Discourse Concerning the Original and Progress of Satire'.

Early success with Ovid's *Epistles*, which Tonson reissued seven times, must have contributed to the decision to complete the *Metamorphoses*. Tonson had already published Dryden's translated portions of the work in the Third Miscellany (1693) and *Fables* (1700); in 1694 he published the tale of Salmacis (Book 4) translated by Addison and that of Byblis (Book 9) by Stephen Harvey. After Dryden's death appeared the remaining portions rendered by Addison, Tate and Stonestreet (Fifth Miscellany, 1704). To assist in getting the rest of the work translated Tonson called upon Garth, a successful physician, whose mock-epic *The Dispensary* (1699) had made him a successful poet as well (the poem remained popular throughout the eighteenth century and was to gain Garth a place among Johnson's *Lives of the Poets*). Garth had contributed the *Life of Otho* to Dryden's Plutarch. At Dryden's death in 1700, Garth arranged for his body to lie in state at the College of Physicians; he delivered a Latin encomium of Dryden and accompanied his funeral procession to Westminster Abbey.

Also around 1700 Tonson was instrumental in forming the Kit-Cat Club, a literary and political club with strong Whig leanings, named for Christopher Cat, a tavern-keeper whose mutton-pies the members favoured. Garth, prominent among the Kit-Cats, and Tonson engaged other members to assist in their collaborative *Metamorphoses.* These include the dramatist William Congreve (1670–1729) and Arthur Mainwaring (1668–1712), as well as Garth himself. The contributions of another member, the essayist Joseph Addison (1672–1719), were already available, as were those of the poet Nahum Tate (1652–1715) – like Dryden a posthumous contributor – and those of Harvey and Stonestreet.

Other contributors include John Gay (1685–1715), author of *The Beggar's Opera;* Samuel Croxall (d. 1752) and Alexander Catcott (1692–1749), both clergyman-poets; Temple Stanyan (d. 1752), later to write *The Grecian History;* the law reporter Thomas Vernon (1654–1721); and two poets-laureate, the dramatist Nicholas Rowe (1674–1718), who had edited Shakespeare for Tonson, and Laurence Eusden (1688–1730), who was later to be immortalised among the dunces of Pope's *Dunciad* (1728–1729, 1743). Also to share this fate were – along with Tate – the prolific translator John Ozell (d. 1743) and the poet Leonard Welsted (1688–1747).

Pope attacked the Ovidian enterprise in a satirical ballad, *Sandys' Ghost* (written around 1717, published 1727), in which the spirit of that eminent translator returns, filled with dismay upon learning that the task of translating Ovid has fallen to a band of 'Lords and Lordlings, Squires and Knights, / Wits, Witlings, Prigs and Peers,' all hastily mustered by Tonson and Garth: 'I hear the Beat of Jacob's Drums, / Poor Ovid finds no Quarter!' Yet Pope had his cake as well as ate it, for he was among the contributors to the new translation.

Welsted, to whom was entrusted the important task of bringing the *Metamorphoses* to its conclusion, is today remembered chiefly for Pope's later lines about him (a parody of Denham's famous lines about the Thames):

> Flow, Welsted, flow! Like thine inspirer, Beer,
> Tho' stale, not ripe; tho' thin, yet never clear;
> So sweetly mawkish, and so smoothly dull;
> Heady, not strong; o'erflowing, tho' not full.
>
> (*Dunciad* [1743] 3. 169–172).

Yet it would be a mistake to suppose that this translation consists of poor efforts by poetasters and dunces crudely stitched on to Dryden's noble but incomplete fabric. Minor as some of the contributors are, they all learned their craft from Dryden, whose writings defined their conceptions of poetic translation and had a determining influence on the style in which they wrote. Both they and the initiators of the project knew what they were about.

A style for translating Ovid

Dryden brought to his translations of Ovid a life of experience in writing for the theatre and in writing satire. Heroic drama in rhymed couplets, ribald comedy, and mock-heroic satire are far more than 'influences' on his style of translation. They trained the poet, developing in him modes of thought and expression whose full power he could bring to bear on the transmutation of Ovidian Latin into Ovidian English. Dryden's translations bring out the satirical, mock-heroic, and rhetorically manipulative aspects of Ovid's work. To these he adds the ability to achieve fast-paced narrative in heroic couplets; for, even more than in his *Aeneid,* speed and clarity are immediately noticeable virtues of this translation.

Some features of Dryden's style can be traced to his working methods. Open before him as he wrote were not only several Latin editions of Ovid with commentaries, but also Sandys' translation. To be sure, Dryden had a low opinion of Sandys' work and depreciates it in the dedication that precedes his own earliest translations from the *Metamorphoses,* claiming that 'I have never read him since I was a boy' (dedication to *Examen Poeticum*, 1693). This disingenuous remark belies the close study he made of Sandys' work and the many features that he lifted from it: rhyme-words especially, and many appealing turns of phrase, verbatim or revised. He also consulted or recalled other translators, Golding among them. These borrowings reflect a long-standard conception of the translator's duty, which was to produce not so much an original as a definitive translation. On this view, if earlier translators did anything especially well, their best features fittingly have a place in the later and more nearly perfect version. A glance at the opening lines of Book 1 in Sandys will show how much Dryden's lines, quoted above, owe to him:

> Of bodies chang'd to other shapes I sing.
> Assist, you Gods (from you these changes spring)
> And, from the Worlds first fabrick to these times,
> Deduce my never-discontinued Rymes.

Dryden takes over the first three words of Sandys' translation and the rhyme-words of both these couplets, along with the programmatically important word 'deduce'.

In its clarity and accessibility, Dryden's Ovid is a notable advance on Sandys. Among the features in which Dryden outdoes not only his predecessors but his successors as well is his transmutation into English of the ever-changing narrative surface of the *Metamorphoses*. Dryden comes to Ovid with a style perfectly fashioned to re-enact Ovid's paradoxical wit, his antitheses, his etymological wordplay, his mercurial shifts in tone, his exploitation of Virgilian epic and his debunking of it, his allusion to many genres beyond epic. The clash of abstractions in Althea's soliloquy, quoted above, offers an especially dazzling example of Dryden's antithetical mode in a context to which it is ideally suited. Yet examples can be chosen virtually at random to illustrate the match between styles. When, in the story of Daphne in Book 1, Ovid portrays the god Apollo smitten by desire, we witness a transformation of Apollo from the beneficent god of prophecy and healing to a single-minded embodiment of predatory lust in pursuit of its object. Although naive moralists of today sometimes claim that Ovid excuses rape by making it funny, in fact his serio-comic mode of debunking exposes to the thoughtful reader a process of culpable self-degradation in Apollo, a loss of divine identity that Ovid embodies in paradoxical wit. Dryden matches Ovidian paradox, as when Apollo complains of the diminution of his powers through love:

> To cure the pains of love, no plant avails:
> And his own physick, the physician fails.

Rhyme assists Dryden in intensifying balances and contrasts in thought, increasing the density of antitheses. By setting 'avails' against 'fails' he achieves a semantically self-cancelling witticism worthy of Ovid. The alliteration of f-sounds in the second line reinforces an eymological play in 'physick' and 'physician.' Dryden's etymological wordplay, like Ovid's, is thematically significant, embodying transformation in a verbal trope: for medical skill, 'physick,' to fail a physician compromises his identity. Earlier in the tale love-struck Apollo already lost his beneficent attributes as god of prophecy, 'by his own oracles mis-led'. Now the function of healer also slips away in a spate of witticisms. The spectacle of Apollo's diminution is suitably comic, even as its ugly and degraded nature is exposed to view. For this tale brings to light the workings of arbitrary power, whose possessor gives up his identity along with all noble qualities. As a victim of Cupid's shaft, Apollo becomes merely predatory — contemptible and ridiculous as well as dangerously threatening.

Ovid delights in balanced oppositions, and Dryden can bring antithetical features of Ovid's expression directly into his own verse-form. When in the debate in Book 13 Ajax maintains that he, unlike the feeble Ulysses, can make real use of Achilles' weapons, his English expression admirably matches the Latin: 'These arms want Ajax, more than Ajax them', *atque Aiax armis, non Aiaci arma petuntur* (13. 97).

Dryden is often faulted for adding to his original, yet his numerous small expansions make the translation clear and approachable as a literal translation cannot be, and they are guided by sure judgment of Ovid's narrative movement, tone and emphasis. Dryden's translation is successful because of its freedom, not in spite of it. He transmutes the *Metamorphoses* into an English poem, while expanding upon those features of his text that are especially significant. Disintegration of identity is a theme already touched upon, which Ovid characteristically embodies in the stylistic surface by a juxtaposed repetition of pronouns. When Ajax, for instance, having lost his rhetorical combat with Ulysses, resolves upon suicide, he first represents himself as a pronoun and divides it, so to speak, in two: *'hoc' ait 'utendum est in me mihi'* 'Against myself I must use this sword.' (13. 388) Dryden introduces this same self-cancelling play on pronouns into other contexts, as a few lines later when Ajax speaks of himself in the third person: *ne quisquam Aiacem possit superare nisi Aiax* (13. 390), 'None but himself, himself cou'd overthrow.' Here Dryden replaces Ovid's expression with another, equally Ovidian. Bolder is his addition of similar language to a comment on the death of Achilles near the end of Book 12:

> Yet great in *Homer*, still *Achilles* lives;
> And equal to himself, himself survives.

Dryden takes 'equal to himself' from Ovid (12. 819 *par sibi*), but makes Ovid's expression more Ovidian by adding the juxtaposed repetition of pronouns. Thus his words form an image on the page – a symbolic redoubling to represent the notion of surviving one's own death. Ovid may be the master of paradox, but here it is Dryden who transforms a relatively banal notion, that through fame a hero lives on, into a resonant paradox that links this passage thematically to its larger context.

Dryden's posthumous collaborators learned much from him about Ovidian style, to which they are often remarkably sensitive. Addison, for instance, can reproduce Ovid's favourite trope, later to be known as syllepsis, by which literal and figurative meanings of a single word are simultaneously registered. When in Book 2 the Sun-god begs his son Phaethon to give up his request, Addison alters only one word of Sandys to make the expression less literal, but paradoxically more Ovidian: *consiliis, non curribus utere nostris* (2. 146), 'And not my chariot but my counsel take' (Sandys wrote 'use'). Addison's translations of Ovid first appeared in 1704, and his expression here may have influenced Pope's more famous syllepsis in *The Rape of the Lock* (1714; Canto 3. 7–8):

> Here Thou, Great *Anna!* whom three Realms obey,
> Dost sometimes Counsel take – and sometimes *Tea*.

Eusden, adapting Sandys, succeeds at a comparable witticism in Book 10, when Venus rests on the ground with her beloved Adonis: *pressitque et gramen et ipsum* (10. 557), 'And swift at once the grass and him she prest.' Paradoxical wit, so impressively handled by Dryden, comes off well enough in the contributions of the others. In Book 2 personified Envy arrives at a peaceful and flourishing Athens, *vixque tenet lacrimas, quia nil lacrimabile cernit* (2. 796); and Addison manages Ovid's paradox with only a little less concision: 'Scarce could the hideous fiend from tears forbear, / To find out nothing that deserved a tear.'

   In a preface, 'written with more ostentation than ability' according to Johnson, Garth faults Ovid for verbal wit, including the 'boyisms' just mentioned. He is following Dryden's critical writings, especially the Preface to the *Fables* (1700), wherein Dryden attacks Ovid's paradoxical wit for its impropriety, its lack of accommodation to serious subject-matter: 'Wou'd any Man who is ready to die for Love, describe his Passion like *Narcissus?* Wou'd he think of *inopem me copia fecit* ['abundance makes me resourceless'], and a Dozen more of such Expressions, pour'd on the Neck of one another, and signifying all the same Thing? If this were Wit, was this a Time to be witty, when the poor Wretch was in the Agony of Death? . . . On these Occasions the Poet shou'd endeavour to raise Pity: But instead of this, *Ovid is* tickling you to laugh.' Fortunately for Ovid and his readers, Dryden's notions of decorum do not affect his practice as translator, which remains thoroughly indecorous like Ovid's practice; nor do such notions affect that of the other translators, like Addison, who similarly expressed disapproval of Ovidian wit. As translators they seem to recognise the significance and value of Ovidian wit — the very qualities they deny it in their more awkward and conventional role as literary critics.

Garth's collaborative *Metamorphoses* proved successful with the public and was often reprinted throughout the eighteenth and early nineteenth centuries. It passed from favour along with its poetic idiom, as readers of romantic sensibility lost interest in wit, satire, rhetorical exuberance and allusive sophistication. During the period of this translation's eclipse, Ovid's fortunes in general suffered; and the ascendancy of romantic Hellenism, whose backwash still stifles the appreciation of Roman literature, allowed him but few appreciative readers. In 1955 L. P. Wilkinson wrote that 'the translation of the *Metamorphoses* by Dryden, Congreve, Addison and others, issued in 1717, is the last great monument of his former glory.' Now that Ovid's reputation is gradually rising as his work becomes more widely appreciated, this translation can contribute to his recovered and ever-increasing glory.

GARTH TISSOL
Emory University
Atlanta, Georgia

FURTHER READING

Golding's translation (1567): *Shakespeare's Ovid, Being Arthur Golding's Translation of the Metamorphoses*, ed. W. H. D. Rouse (London 1961).

David Hopkins, 'Dryden and Ovid's "Wit out of Season" ' in *Ovid Renewed: Ovidian influence on literature and art from the Middle Ages to the twentieth century*, ed. Charles Martindale (Cambridge 1988) 167–190, 276–279: the best discussion of Dryden's translations of Ovid.

David Hopkins, 'Dryden and the Garth-Tonson *Metamorphoses*', *Review of English Studies* n. s. 39, no. 153 (1988) 64–74: on Dryden's plans for a complete *Metamorphoses*.

Samuel Johnson, Life of Sir Samuel Garth in *Lives of the English Poets*, ed. George Birkbeck Hill (Oxford 1905) 2. 57–64.

Kathleen M. Lynch, *Jacob Tonson: Kit-Cat Publisher* (Knoxville 1971).

L. Proudfoot, *Dryden's Aeneid and Its Seventeenth Century Predecessors* (Manchester 1960): on Dryden's working methods in translation and use of predecessors.

Sandys' translation (1632): *Ovid's Metamorphosis Englished, Mythologized, and Represented in Figures, by George Sandys*, ed. Karl K. Hulley and Stanley T. Vandersall (Lincoln 1970).

Tissol, Garth, *The Face of Nature: Wit, Narrative, and Cosmic Origins in Ovid's Metamorphoses* (Princeton 1997): on Ovid's style.

The method I propose in writing this preface, is to take notice of some of the beauties of the *Metamorphoses*, and also of the faults, and particular affectations. After which I shall proceed to hint at some rules for translation in general; and shall give a short account of the following version.

I shall not pretend to impose my opinion on others with the magisterial authority of a critic; but only take the liberty of discovering my own taste. I shall endeavour to show our poet's redundance of wit, justness of comparisons, elegance of descriptions, and peculiar delicacy in touching every circumstance relating to the passions, and affections; and with the same impartiality, and frankness, I shall confess the too frequent puerilities of his luxuriant fancy, and the too great negligence of his sometimes unlabour'd versification.

I am not of an opinion, too common to translators, to think that one is under an obligation to extoll every thing he finds in the author he undertakes: I am sure one is no more oblig'd to do so, than a painter is to make every face, that sits to him, handsome. 'Tis enough if he sets the best features he finds in their full, and most advantageous light. But if the poet has private deformities, tho' good-breeding will not allow to expose him naked, yet surely there can be no reason to recommend him, as the most finish'd model of harmony, and proportion.

Whoever has this undistinguishing complaisance, will not fail to vitiate the taste of the readers, and misguide many of them in their judgment, where to approve, and where to censure.

It must be granted, that where there appears an infinite variety of inimitable excellencies, it would be too harsh, and disingenuous to be severe on such faults, as have escap'd rather thro' want of leisure, and opportunity to correct, than thro' the erroneous turn of a deprav'd judgment. How sensible *Ovid* himself was of the uncorrectness of the *Metamorphoses*, appears from these lines prefix'd before some of the editions by the care of his commentators.

> *Orba parente suo quicunque Volumina tangis,*
>   *His saltem vestra detur in urbe locus.*
> *Quoque magis faveas; non sunt haec edita ab Illo.*
>   *Sed quasi de domini funere rapta sui.*
> *Quicquid in his igitur vitii rude carmen habebit,*
>   *Emendaturus, si licuisset, erat.*   [*Tristia* 7]

Since therefore the readers are not solemnly invited to an entertainment, but come accidentally; they ought to be contented with what they find: and pray what have they to complain of, but too great variety? where, tho' some of the dishes be not served in the exactest order, and politeness, but hash'd up in haste, there are a great many accommodated to every particular palate.

To like every thing, shows too little delicacy; and to like nothing, too much difficulty. So great is the variety of this Poem, that the reader, who is never pleas'd, will appear as monstrous, as he that is always so. Here are the hurries of battels for the heroe, tender emotions of soul for the lover, a search and penetration into Nature for the philosopher; fluency of numbers, and most expressive figures for the poet; morals for the serious, and plaisantries for admirers of points of wit.

'Tis certain a poet is more to be suspected for saying too much, than too little. To add is often hazardous; but to retrench, commonly judicious. If our author, instead of saying all he could, had only said all he should, *Daphne* had done well to fly from the God of wit, in order to crown his poet: thus *Ovid* had been more honour'd, and ador'd in his exile, than *Augustus* in his triumphs.

I shall now attempt to give some instances of the happiness, and vast extent of our author's imagination. I shall not proceed according to the order of the poem, but rather transcribe some lines here, and there, as my reflection shall suggest.

> *Nec circumfuso pendebat in aere tellus*
> *Ponderibus librata suis*

Thus was the state of Nature before the Creation: and here it is obvious, that *Ovid* had a discerning notion of the gravitation of bodies. 'Tis now demonstrated, that every part of matter tends to every part of matter with a force, which is always in a direct simple proportion of the quantity of the matter, and an inverse duplicate proportion of the distance; which tendency, or gravitating is constant, and universal. This power, whatever it be, acting always proportionably to the solid content of bodies, and never in any proportion to their superficies; cannot be explain'd by any material impulse. For the laws of impulse are physically necessary: there can be no αὐτεξούσιον, or arbitrary principle, in meer matter; its parts cannot move, unless they be mov'd; and cannot do otherwise, when press'd on by other parts in motion; and therefore 'tis evident from the following lines, that *Ovid* strictly adher'd to the opinion of the most discerning philosophers, who taught that all things were form'd by a wise, and intelligent mind.

> *Jussit et extendi campos subsidere valles,*
> *Fronde tegi sylvas . . .*

The *Fiat* of the *Hebrew* law-giver is not more sublime, than the *Jussit* of the *Latin* poet, who goes on in the same elevated, and philosophical style.

> *His super imposuit, liquidum et gravitate carentem*
> *Aethera . . .*

Here the author spreads a thin veil of *Aether* over his infant creation; and tho' his asserting the upper region to be void of gravitation, may not, in a mathematical rigour, be true, yet 'tis found from the natural enquiries made since, and especially from the learned Dr *Hally's* discourse on the *Barometer*, that if, on the surface of the Earth, an inch of quicksilver in the tube be equal to a cylinder of air of 300 foot, it will be at a mile's height equal to a cylinder of air of 2,700,000: and therefore the air at so great a distance from the Earth, must be rarify'd to so great a degree, that the space it fills must bear a very small proportion to that which is intirely void of matter.

I think, we may be confident from what already appears, as well as from what our author has writ on the *Roman* feasts, that he cou'd not be totally ignorant of astronomy. Some of the criticks wou'd insinuate from the following lines, that he mistook the annual motion of the sun for the diurnal.

> *Sectus in obliquum . . .*   [*Metamorphoses* 2]

Though the sun be always in one or other of the signs of the *Zodiack*, and never goes by either motion more northward, or southward, than is here describ'd, yet *Phaeton* being design'd to drive the chariot but one day, ought to have been directed in the *Aequator*, or a circle parallel to it, and not round the other oblique one of the ecliptick: a degree of which, and that by a motion contrary to the diurnal, he was obliged to go in that length of time.

I am inclin'd to think, that *Ovid* had so great an attention to poetical embellishments, that he voluntarily declin'd a strict observance of any astronomical system. For tho' that science was far from being neglected in former ages; yet the progress which was made in it, by no means equall'd that of our present time.

Lucretius, tho' in other things most penetrating, describes the sun scarce bigger, than he appears to the eye.

> *Nec nimio solis major rota, nec minor ardor*
> *Esse potest, nostris quam sensibus esse videtur.*

And *Homer*, imagining the seats of the Gods above the fix'd stars, represents the falling of *Vulcan* from thence to the isle of *Lemnos*, to continue during a whole day.

Πᾶν δ'ἦμαρ φερόμην, ἅμα δ'ἠελίῳ καταδύντι
Κάππεσον ἐν Λήμνῳ ...

The *Greek* poet aims here to give a surprising idea of the height of the celestial mansions: but if the computation of a modern astronomer be true, they are at so much a greater distance, that *Vulcan* wou'd have been more years in falling than he was minutes.

But lest I shou'd exceed the usual length of a preface, I shall now give some instances of the propriety of our author's similes, and epithets; the perspicuity of his allegories; the instructive excellence of the morals; the peculiar happy turn of his fancy; and shall begin with the elegance of his descriptions.

> *... Madidis Notus evolat alis,*
> *Terribilem picea tectus caligine vultum.*
> *Barba gravis nimbis, canis fluit unda capillis,*
> *Fronte sedent nebulae, rorant pennaeque, sinusque*
> ....
> *Sternuntur segetes, et deplorata coloni*
> *Vota jacent, longique labor perit irritus anni.*   [*Metamorphoses* 1]

These lines introduce those of the Deluge, which are also very poetical, and worthy to be compar'd with the next, concerning the golden age.

> *... Sine militis usu*
> *Mollia securae peragebant otia gentes.*
> *Ipsa quoque immunis rastroque intacta, nec ullis*
> *Saucia vomeribus, per se dabat omnia tellus.*
> *Contentique cibis, nullo cogente, creatis,*
> *Arbuteos foetus, montanaque fraga legebant,*
> *Et quae deciderunt patula Jovis arbore glandes.*
> *Ver erat aeternum, placidique tepentibus auris*
> *Mulcebant Zephyri natos sine semine flores.*

Virgil has also touch'd upon the same subject in the end of the second *Georgick.*

> *Aureus hanc vitam in terris Saturnus agebat,*
> *Nec dum etiam audierunt inflari classica, nec dum*
> *Impositos duris crepitare incudibus enses.*

And again

> *Primus ab aetherio venit Saturnus Olympo*
> . . . .
> *Aurea, quae perhibent, illo sub rege fuerunt*
> *Saecula: sic placida populos in pace regebat.*   [*Aeneid* 8, 319]

Some of the lines, a little foreign to the present subject, are omitted; but I shall make the most admirable author amends by transcribing at length his next description. 'Tis of a stag, which gave the first occasion to the war betwixt the *Trojans* and the *Rutulians:* I chuse this, because my design is to have these two great poets seen together, where the subject happens to be almost the same, tho' the nature of the poems be very different.

> *Cervus erat forma praestanti, et cornibus ingens,*
> *Tyrrheidae pueri, quem matris ab ubere raptum*
> *Nutribant, Tyrrheusque pater, cui regia parent*
> *Armenta, et late custodia credita campi.*
> *Assuetum imperiis soror omni Sylvia cura*
> *Mollibus intexens ornabat cornua sertis:*
> *Pectebatque ferum, puroque in fonte lavabat.*
> *Ille manum patiens, mensaeque assuetus herili*
> *Errabat sylvis . . .*   [*Aeneid* 7, 483]

The image which *Ovid* gives of the favourite stag slain accidentally by *Cyparissus*, seems not of less dignity.

> *Ingens cervus erat, lateque patentibus altas*
> *Ipse suo capiti praebebat cornibus umbras:*
> *Cornua fulgebant auro, demissaque in armos*
> *Pendebant tereti gemmata monilia collo.*
> *Bulla super frontem parvis argentea loris*
> *Vincta movebatur: parilique ex aere nitebant*
> *Auribus in geminis circum cava tempora baccae.*

> *Isque metu vacuus, naturalique pavore*
> *Deposito, celebrare domos, mulcendaque colla*
> *Quamlibet ignotis manibus praebere solebat.*
> *Gratus erat Cyparisse tibi, Tu pabula cervum*
> *Ad nova, tu liquidi ducebas fontis ad undam.*
> . . . .
> *Tu modo texebas . . . per cornua flores:*
> *Nunc, eques in tergo residens, huc latus et illuc*
> *Mollia purpureis fraenabas ora capistris.*

In the following lines, *Ovid* describes the watry court of the river *Peneus*, which the reader may compare with *Virgil's* subterranean grott of *Cyrene* the Naïad, mother to *Aristaeus*.

> *Est nemus Haemoniae, praerupta quod undique claudit*
> *Silva: vocant Tempe, per quae Penëus ab imo*
> *Effusus Pindo spumosis volvitur undis:*
> *Dejectuque gravi tenues agitantia fumos*
> *Nubila conducit, summasque aspergine sylvas*
> *Impluit; et sonitu plus quam vicina fatigat.*
> *Haec domus, hae sedes, haec sunt penetralia magni*
> *Amnis: in hoc residens facto de cantibus antro.*
> *Undis jura dabat, Nymphisque colentibus undas.*
> *Conveniunt illuc popularia flumina primum;*
> *Nescia gratentur, consolenturve parentem.*
> *Populifer Spercheös, et irrequietus Enipeus,*
> *Eridanusque senex, lenisque Amphrysos, et Aeas.*
> *Moxque amnes alii, qui, qua tulit impetus illos,*
> *In mare deducunt fessas erroribus undas.*   [Metamorphoses 2]
>
> *Tristis Aristaeus Penei genitoris ad undam*
> *Stat lacrymans . . .*
> . . . .
> *Jamque domum mirans genetricis, et humida regna,*
> *Speluncisque lacus clausos, lucosque sonantes*
> *Ibat; et ingenti motu stupefactus aquarum,*
> *Omnia sub magna labentia flumina terra*

> *Spectabat diversa locis, Phasimque, Lycumque,*
> *Et caput, unde altus primum se erumpit Enipeus,*
> *Unde pater Tiberinus, et unde Aniena fluenta,*
> *Et gemina auratus taurino cornua vultu*
> *Eridanus, quo non alius per pinguia culta*
> *In mare purpureum violentior influit amnis.*   [*Georgics* 4]

The divine poet goes on in pomp of numbers, and easy magnificence of words, till he introduces the story of *Orpheus* and *Euridice;* in the narration of which, he is as much superior to *Ovid,* as the reeds of his own *Mantuan* shepherds are less musical, than the lyre of *Orpheus.*

That I may not be too long on this article, I shall recommend to the reader, *Ovid's* admirable description of sleep

> *Est prope Cimmerios* . . .   [*Metamorphoses* 11]

That of hunger

> *Est locus extremis Scythiae* . . .   [*Metamorphoses* 8]

That of the plague

> *Dira lues* . . .   [*Metamorphoses* 7]

That of Fame

> *Orbe locus medio est* . . .   [*Metamorphoses* 12]

Virgil has also touch'd on the two last; in the one he had *Lucretius* in view; in the other *Homer:* and I think it will not be to the disadvantage of our author to appear at the same time.

There are many other descriptions scatter'd in the *Metamorphoses,* which for just expression of Nature, and majestick modulation of words, are only inferior to those already transcrib'd, as they are shorter; which makes the objection, that his diction is commonly loytring into prose, a great deal too severe.

The *Metamorphoses* must be consider'd, as is observ'd before, very uncorrect; and *Virgil's* works as finish'd: tho' his own modesty would not allow the *Aeneids* to be so. It seems it was harder for him to please himself, than his readers. His judgment was certainly great, nor was his vivacity of imagination less; for the first without the last is too heavy, and like a dress without fancy; and the last without the first is too gay, and but all trimming.

Our author's similitudes are next to be consider'd, which are always remarkably short, and convey some pleasing idea to the imagination. 'Tis in this branch of the poem, that he has discover'd as just a judgment, as any of the classicks whatever. Poets, to give a loose to a warm fancy, are generally too apt, not only to expatiate in their similes, but introduce them too frequently; by doing the first, they detain the attention too long from the principal narration; and by the latter, they make too frequent breaches in the unity of the poem.

These two errors *Ovid* has most discerningly avoided. How short, and significant are generally his comparisons! he fails not, in these, to keep a stiff rein on a high-mettled *Pegasus;* and takes care not to surfeit here, as he had done on other heads, by an erroneous abundance.

His similes are thicker sown by much in the fable of *Salmacis,* and *Hermaphroditus,* than in any other book, but always short. The nymph clasps the youth close to her breast, and both sensibly grow one.

> . . . *velut si quis conducto cortice ramos*
> *Crescendo jungi, pariterque adolescere cernat.*   [*Metamorphoses* 4]

Again, as *Atalanta* reddens in the race with *Hippomenes,*

> *Inque puellari corpus candore ruborem*
> *Traxerat; haud aliter quam cum super atria velum*
> *Candida purpureum simulatas inficit umbras.*   [*Metamorphoses* 10]

Philomela's tongue seem'd to move after it was cut out by *Tereus.*

> *Utque salire solet mutilatae cauda colubrae,*
> *Palpitat* . . .   [*Metamorphoses* 6]

Cadmus sows the dragon's teeth, and the sons of the Earth rise gradually.

> *Inde fide majus glebae cepere moveri;*
> *Primaque de sulcis acies apparuit hastae;*
> *Tegmina mox capitum picto nutantia cono,*
> *Mox humeri, pectusque . . .*
> *Sic ubi tolluntur festis aulaea theatris*
> *Surgere signa solent, primumque ostendere vultum,*
> *Caetera paulatim, placidoque educta tenore*
> *Tota patent, imoque pedes in margine ponunt.*   [*Metamorphoses* 3]

The objection to *Ovid*, that he never knows when to give over, is too manifest. Tho' he frequently expatiates on the same thought, in different words; yet in his similes, that exuberance is avoided. There is in them all a simplicity, and a confinement to the present object; always a fecundity of fancy, but rarely an intemperance: nor do I remember he has err'd above once by an ill-judg'd superfluity. After he has describ'd the labyrinth built by *Daedalus*, he compares it thus,

> *Non secus ac liquidus Phyrgiis Maenandros in arvis*
> *Ludit, ee ambiguo lapsu refluitque, fluitque;*
> *Et nunc ad fontes, nunc ad mare versus apertum*
> *Incertas exercet aquas*   [*Metamorphoses* 8]

He should have ended at the close of the second line, as *Virgil* should have done at the end of the fourth in his noble simile, where *Dido* proceeds to the temple with her court about her.

> *Qualis in Eurotae ripis, aut per juga Cynthi*
> *Exercet Diana choros, quam mille secutae*
> *Hinc, atque hinc glomerantur Oreades, illa pharetram*
> *Fert humero, gradiensque deas supereminet omnes:*
> *Latonae tacitum pertentant gaudia pectus.*   [*Aeneid* 4]

I see no reason for the last line: tho' the poet be justly celebrated for a most consummate judgment, yet by an endeavour to imitate *Homer's* similes, he is not only very long, but by introducing several circumstances, he fails of an applicable relation betwixt the principal subject, and his new ideas. He sometimes thinks fit

to work into the piece some differing embroidery, which, tho'
very rich, yet makes at best but glorious patch-work. I really
believe his excellent poem had not been the less so, if, in this
article, he had thought fit to have walk'd on in his own regular
and majestick grace, rather than have been hurry'd forward
through broken by-ways by his blind guide.

I shall transcribe one of his similes which is not cull'd out, but
exactly of the same texture with all the rest in the four last books
of the *Aeneids*. *Turnus* leaps in fury from his chariot.

> *Ac veluti montis saxum de vertice praeceps*
> *Cum ruit avulsum vento, seu turbidus imber*
> *Proluit, aut annis solvit sublapsa vetustas,*
> *Fertur in abruptum magno mons improbus actu,*
> *Exultatque solo, sylvas, armenta, virosque*
> *Involvens secum . . .*   [*Aeneid* 12, 684]

It does not seem to be at all material, whether the rock was
blown, or wash'd down by wind, or rain, or undermin'd by time.

But to return to *Ovid*; the reader may take notice how unforc'd
his compliments, and how natural his transitions generally are.
With how much ease does he slide into some new circumstance,
without any violation of the unity of the story. The texture is so
artful, that it may be compar'd to the work of his own *Arachne*,
where the shade dyes so gradually, and the light revives so imper-
ceptibly, that it is hard to tell where the one ceases, and the other
begins.

When he is going off from the story of *Apollo*, and *Daphne*, how
happily does he introduce a compliment to the *Roman* conquerors.

> *. . . et conjunx quoniam mea non potes esse,*
> *Arbor eris certe . . .*
> *Tu Ducibus laetis aderis, cum laeta triumphum*
> *Vox canet, et longae visent Capitolia pompae.*
> *Postibus Augustis eadem fidissima custos*
> *Ante fores stabis; mediamque tuebere quercum.*   [*Metamorphoses* 2]

He compliments *Augustus* upon the assassination of *Julius*; and, by way of simile, takes the opportunity from the horror that the barbarity of *Lycaon* gave.

> . . . *sic cum manus impia saevit*
> *Sanguine Caesareo Romanum extinguere nomen, etc.*

Julius is deify'd, and looks down on his adopted son.

> . . . *natique videns benefacta, fatetur*
> *Esse suis majora, et vinci gaudet ab illo.*   [*Metamorphoses* 15]

And immediately follows,

> *Hic sua praeferri quamquam vetat acta paternis;*
> *Libera fama tamen, nullisque obnoxia jussis*
> *Invitum praefert . . .*

The author in the two first lines shows the affectionate condescension of the father; in the three last, the pious gratitude of the son.

The compliments to *Augustus* are very frequent in the last book of the *Metamorphoses*; as those to the same emperor are in the *Georgicks* of *Virgil*, which also strike the imagination by their agreeable flattery.

> *Haec super arvorum cultu, pecorumque canebam,*
> *Et super arboribus; Caesar dum magnus ad altum*
> *Fulminat Euphratem bello, victorque volentes*
> *Per populos dat jura, viamque affectat Olympo.*   [*Georgics* 1]

Again on *Julius*,

> *Imperium Oceano, famam qui terminet astris*
> *Julius . . .*   [*Aeneid* 1]

The compliments have a great sublimity, and are worthy of the grandeur of the heroes, and the wit of the poet.

Ovid as much deserves praise for saying a great deal in a little, as censure for saying a little in a great deal. None of the classick poets had the talent of expressing himself with more force, and perspicuity. *Phaeton* desires some pledge of his father's tenderness, and asks to be trusted with his chariot. He answers,

> *Pignora certa petis; do pignora certa timendo.*   [*Metamorphoses 2*]

However, the latter complies with his importunity; the consequence is fatal, the world is set on fire, even the rivers feel the force of the conflagration. The *Tagus* boyls,

> *. . . fluit ignibus Aurum.*

The *Nile* retreats,

> *Occuluitque caput, quod adhuc latet . . .*

Zanthus is parch'd up,

> *Arsurusque iterum Zanthus . . .*

The poet's fancy is here full of energy, as well as in the following lines. *Apollo* courts *Daphne*, and promises himself success, but is disappointed.

> *Quodque cupit, sperat; suaque illum Oracula fallunt.*

And again, the river *Achelous* combats *Hercules*, and assumes several shapes in vain, then puts on at last that of a snake; the heroe smiles in contempt.

> *Cunarum labor est angues superare mearum.*

Ovid never excells himself so much, as when he takes occasion to touch upon the passion of love; all hearts are in a manner sensible of the same emotions; and, like instruments tun'd unisons, if a string of any one of them be struck, the rest by consent, vibrate. *Procris* is jealous of *Cephalus;* she endeavours to be confirm'd in her fears, but hopes the contrary,

> *. . . speratque miserrima falli.*

The next is not less natural,

> *. . . sed cuncta timemus amantes.*

Biblis is in love with *Caunus.* The struggle is betwixt her unlawful flame, and her honour. She's all confusion at the thoughts of discovering her passion.

> *. . . miserere fatentis amorem.*

She attempts to write,

> *Incipit et dubitat: scribit, damnatque tabellas,*
> *Et notat, et delet: mutat, culpatque probatque.*

In the end, inclination, as it does always, gets the better of discretion.

This last fable shows how touchingly the poet argues in love affairs, as well as those of *Medea*, and *Scylla*. The two last are left by their heroes, and their reflections are very natural, and affecting. *Ovid* seem'd here to have had *Virgil's* passion of *Dido* in his eye, but with this difference; the one had convers'd much with ladies, and knew they lov'd to talk a great deal: the other consider'd no less, what was natural for them to say, than what became them to say.

Virgil has, through the whole management of this rencounter, discover'd a most finish'd judgment. *Aeneas*, like other men, likes for convenience, and leaves for greater. *Dido*, like other ladies, resents the neglect, enumerates the obligations the lover is under, upbraids him with ingratitude, threatens him with revenge, then by and by submits, begs for compassion, and has recourse to tears.

It appears from this piece, that *Virgil* was a discerning master in the passion of love: and they that consider the spirit, and turn of that inimitable line . . . *Qui Bavium non odit* . . . cannot doubt but he had an equal talent for satyr.

Nor does the genius of *Ovid* more exert on the subject of love, than on all others. In the contention of *Ajax*, *Ulysses* his elocution is most nervous, and perswading. Where he endeavours to disswade mankind from indulging carnivorous appetites in his Pythagorean philosophy, how emphatical is his reasoning!

> *Quid meruere boves, animal sine fraude, dolisque,*
> *Innocuum, simplex, natum tolerare laborem?*
> *Immemor est demum, nec frugum munere dignus*

> *Qui potuit curvi dempto modo pondere aratri*
> *Ruricolam mactare suum . . .*   [*Metamorphoses* 15]

I think *Agricolam* had been stronger, but the authority of manuscripts does not warrant that emendation.

Through the whole texture of this work, *Ovid* discovers the highest humanity, and a most exceeding good nature. The virtuous in distress are always his concern; and his wit contrives to give them an immortality with himself.

He seems to have taken the most pains in the first, and second book of the *Metamorphoses*, though the thirteenth abounds with sentiments most moving, and with calamitous incidents, introduced with great art. The poet had here in view, the tragedy of *Hecuba* in *Euripides;* and 'tis a wonder, it has never been attempted in our own tongue. The house of *Priam* is destroy'd, his royal daughter a sacrifice to the *Manes* of him that occasion'd it. She is forc'd from the arms of her unhappy friends, and hurry'd to the altar, where she behaves her self with a decency becoming her sex, and a magnanimity equal to her blood, and so very affecting, that even the priest wept.

> *. . . ipse etiam flens, invitusque sacerdos, etc.*

She shows no concern at approaching death, but on the account of her old, unfortunate mother,

> *Mors tantum vellem matrem mea fallere possit.*
> *Mater obest, minuitque necis mea gaudia; quamvis*
> *Non mea mors illi: verum sua vita gemenda est.*

Then begs her body may be deliver'd to her without ransom,

> *. . . genetrici corpus inemptum*
> *Reddite; neve, auro redimat jus triste sepulchri,*
> *Sed lacrymis: tunc, cum poterat, redimebat et auro.*

The unhappy queen laments, she is not able to give her daughter royal burial,

> *Non haec est fortuna domus . . .*

Then takes the body in her decrepid arms, and halts to the sea to wash off the blood,

> *. . . ad littus passu processit anili*
> *Albentes laniata comas . . .*

The animated thoughts, and lively images of this poem, are numerous. None ever painted more to the life, than our author, tho' several grotesque figures are now and then seen in the same groupe. The most plentiful season, that gives birth to the finest flowers, produces also the rankest weeds. *Ovid* has shown in one line, the brightest fancy sometimes; and in the next, the poorest affectation. Venus makes court to *Adonis*,

> *. . . et ecce!*
> *Opportuna sua blanditur Populus umbra;*
> *Et requievit humo; pressitque et gramen et ipsum.*
>
> [*Metamorphoses* 10, 554]

Phoebus requests *Phaeton* to desist from his request.

> *. . . consiliis, non curribus utere nostris.*

Caeneus in the battle of the *Centaurs* wounds *Latreus* in several places.

> *. . .vulnusque in vulnere fecit.*

These are some of our poet's boyisms. There is another affectation, call'd by *Quintilian* Ὀξύμωρον, or a witty folly, which wou'd not have appear'd quite so trifling, had it been less frequent.

Medea persuades the daughters of *Pelias* to kill their father, in order to have his youth renew'd. She, that loves him best, gives the first wound,

> *Et, ne sit scelerata, facit scelus . . .*   [*Metamorphoses* 7]

Althea is enrag'd at her son *Meleager*, and to do justice to the *Manes* of her brothers, destroys him,

> *Impietate pia est . . .*

Envy enters *Athens*, and beholds the flourishing condition of the city,

> *Vixque tenet lacrymas, quia nil lacrymabile cernit.*

  Ovid was much too fond of such witticisms, which are more to be wonder'd at, because they were not the fashion of that age, as punns, and quibbles are of this. *Virgil*, as I remember, is not found trifling in this manner above once, or twice.

> *Deucalion vacuum lapides jactavit in orbem,*
> *Unde homines nati, durum genus . . .*   [*Georgics* 1, 63]

Juno is in indignation at *Aeneas* upon his arrival in *Italy*.

> *Num capti potuere capi? num incensa cremavit*
> *Troja viros?*   [*Aeneid* 7, 295]

The poet is so far from affecting this sort of wit, that he rarely ventures on so spirited a turn of fancy, as in these following instances. *Juno* upbraids *Venus* and *Cupid*, ironically, that two deities cou'd be able to get the better of one weak woman.

> *. . . memorabile nomen,*
> *Una dolo Divum, si faemina victa duorum est.*   [*Aeneid* 4, 95]

Euryalus, going upon an enterprise, expresses his concern for his surviving mother, if he shou'd fall, and recommends her to the care of *Ascanius*, who answers,

> *Namque erit ista mihi genitrix, nomenque Creüsae*
> *Solum defuerit . . .*

Venus is importunate in her sollicitations to *Vulcan*, to make armour for her son: he answers,

> *. . . absiste precando*
> *Viribus indubitare tuis . . .*   [*Aeneid* 7]

At the first kindling of *Dido's* passion, he has this most natural thought,

> *. . . Illum absens absentem auditque, videtque.*

But to return to *Ovid;* tho' I cannot vindicate him for his points, I shall endeavour to mollify his criticks, when they give him no quarter for his diction, and attack him so inflexibly for ending his lines with monosyllables, as . . . *si quis,* . . . *si non,* etc. And as I think he cannot be excus'd more advantageously, than by affirming, that where he has done it once, *Virgil* has twenty times

. . . *et cum*	[*Georgics* 1]
. . . *si quis*	[*Georgics* 2]
. . . *nec dum*	[*Georgics* 2]
. . . *si quam*	[*Aeneid* 1]
. . . *si quis*	[*Aeneid* 7]
. . . *jam bos*	[*Aeneid* 12]
. . . *nunc nunc* . . . *etc.*	

There are a great many endings of lines in this manner, and more indeed than seems consistent with the majesty of heroick verse. When lines are design'd to be *sermoni propriores,* this liberty may be allowable, but not so when the subject requires more sonorous numbers. *Virgil* seems to endeavour to keep up his versification to an harmonious dignity; and therefore, when fit words do not offer with some ease, he'll rather break off in an hemistick, than that the line shou'd be lazy, and languid. He well knew, how essential it was in poetry to flatter the ear; and at the same time was sensible, that this organ grows tir'd by a constant attention to the same harmony; and therefore he endeavour'd now and then to relieve it by a cadence of pauses, and a variation of measures.

Amphion Dircaeus in Aetaeo Aracyntho.   [*Eclogues* 2]

This line seems not tuneful at the first hearing; but by repetition, it reconciles itself, and has the same effect with some compositions of musick, which are at the first performance tiresome, and afterward entertaining.

The commentators, and criticks are of opinion, that whenever *Virgil is* less musical, it is where he endeavours at an agreement of the sound with the sense, as,

. . . *procumbit humi bos.*

It wou'd show as much singularity to deny this, as it does a fanciful facility to affirm it, because it is obvious, in many places he had no such view.

> . . . *inventa sub ilicibus sus.*   [*Aeneid* 3, 390]

> . . . *dentesque sabellicus exacuit sus.*   [*Georgics.* 3, 255]

> . . . *jam setis obsita, jam bos.*   [*Aeneid* 7, 790]

> . . . *furor additus, inde Lupi ceu, etc.*   [*Aeneid* 2, 355]

The places, which favour most the first opinion are,

> *Saxa per et scopulos, et depressas convalles.*   [*Georgics.* 3, 276]

> . . . *saepe exiguus mus.*
> *Omnia sub magna labentia flumina terra.*   [*Georgics* 4]

The last line is the only instance, I remember (except one in *Eclogues* 2) where the words terminate in the same vowel, and seem to represent the constant, and uniform sound of a sliding stream.

Those, that are most conversant in classick poetry, must be sensible, that *Virgil* has been much more sollicitous, than *Ovid*, to keep up his lines to an easy, and a musical flow; but tho' the criticks charge the latter with breaking through *Prosody* and *Grammar*, and allowing himself too often the licence of Graecisms, I take this censure to be only all arrogant pedantry in the grammarians, and groundless in it self; but tho' it were true, I dare be confident it is full as just upon *Virgil*,

> . . . *curru subjungere Tigres,*   [*Eclogues* 5, 29]

for *currui*, according to the grammarians.

Often adjectives for adverbs; and the contrary.

pinguia culta; [*Georgics* 1,]; an adjective for a substantive.

denso distinguere pingui [*Georgics* 1;]; the same.

seu languentis Hyacinthi [*Aeneid* 11, 69]; first foot of the dactyl short.

tulerunt fastidia menses [*Aeneid* 4]; the penultima of the verb short.

obstupui steteruntque comae; the same.

So, *Lucretius, prodiderunt, reciderunt,* etc.

pampineo gravidus autumno [*Georgics* 2, 5]; an iambick for a spondee.

fluviorum rex Eridanus camposque per omnes; an anapest for a dactyl, or a spondee.

nec Clytio genitore minor nec fratre Mnestheo [*Aeneid* 10, 129]; a trochee, unless the two consonants *M N* of the following word be allow'd.

fervere, non illa quisquam [*Georgics* 1, 456]; the penultima commonly short with *Virgil*, so *fulgere, stridere,* etc.

sine me furere ante furorem [*Aeneid* 12, 680]; a Graecism.

imponere Pelio Ossam [*Georgics* 1, 281]; a Graecism, where there is no elision, but the long vowel before another made short.

The learned and reverend Dr *Clark* has observ'd (as he tells me), that tho' there be several short vowels made long in *Homer*, yet there is no instance on the contrary, of any long vowel (such as the first syllable of τιμή, ψυχή, νίκη, and the like) ever made short, where no vowel follows. Which shows that there is no such thing as a *Poetica licentia*, properly so call'd.

Certainly no body can imagine but these two celebrated authors understood their own tongue, better than the scrupulous grammarians of after-ages, who are too dogmatical, and self-sufficient, when they presume to censure either of them for not attending strictly enough to syntax, and the measure of verse. The *Latin* tongue is a dead language, and none can decide with confidence on the harmony, or dissonance of the numbers of these times, unless they were thoroughly acquainted with their pauses, and cadence. They may indeed pronounce with much more assurance on their diction; and distinguish where they finish'd. There are certainly many lines in *Ovid*, where he has been downright lazy, and where he might have avoided the appearance of being obviously so, by a very little application. In recording the succession of the *Alban* kings, thus,

> *Epitus ex illo est, post hunc Capetusque, Capysque,*
> *Sed Capys ante fuit . . .*

There are also several lines in *Virgil*, which are not altogether tunable to a modern ear, and which appear unfinish'd.

> *Scilicet omnibus est labor impendendus, et omnes*
> *Cogendae in sulcum . . .*   [*Georgics* 2, 61]

> *Praesertim si tempestas a vertice sylvis*
> *Incubuit . . .*   [*Georgics* 2, 310]

> *Quasve referre parem? sed nunc, est omnia quando*
> *Iste animus supra . . .*   [*Aeneid* 11, 509]

> *Ista quidem quia nota mihi tua, magne, voluntas,*
> *Jupiter . . .*   [*Aeneid* 12, 808]

But the sun has its spots; and if amongst thousands of inimitable lines, there shou'd be some found of an unequal dignity with the rest, nothing can be said for their vindication more, than, if they be faults, they are the faults of *Virgil*.

As I ought to be on this occasion an advocate for *Ovid*, whom I think is too much run down at present by the critical spirit of this nation, I dare say, I cannot be more effectually so, than by comparing him in many places with his admir'd contemporary *Virgil;* and tho' the last certainly deserves the palm, I shall make use of *Ovid's* own lines, in the tryal of strength betwixt *Achelous* and *Hercules*, to show how much he is honour'd by the contention.

> *. . . non tam*
> *Turpe fuit vinci, quam contendisse decorum*   [*Metamorphoses*, 9]

I shall finish my remarks on our author, by taking notice of the justness, and perspicuity of his allegories; which are either physical, or natural; moral, or historical. Of the first kind is the fable of *Apollo*, and *Python;* in the explanation of this all the *Mythologists* agree; exhalations and mists, being the constant effects of inundations, are here dissipated by the rays of the sun.

Of the second kind, are *Actaeon* torn to pieces by his own pack of dogs, and *Erisichthon* starv'd by the disease of hunger. These two allegories seem to signify, that extravagance and luxury end in want.

Of the third, is the story of the rape of *Europa*. History says, she was daughter to *Agenor*, and carry'd by the *Candians* in a galley, bearing a bull in the stern, in order to be marry'd to one of their kings nam'd *Jupiter*.

This explanation gives an occasion for a digression which is not altogether foreign to the present purpose, because it will be of use to justify *Ovid* on some other occasions, where he is censured for being too free with the characters of the Gods. I was once representing the *Metamorphoses*, as an excellent system of morality; but an illustrious lady, whose least advantage above her sex, is that of being one of the greatest princesses in *Europe*, objected, that the loose and immodest sallys of *Jupiter* did by no means confirm my assertion.

One must consider, that what appear'd an absurdity in *Ovid*, is not so much his own fault, as that of the times before him. The characters of the Gods of the old heroick age represented them unjust in their actions; mutable in their designs; partial in their favours; ignorant of events; scurrilous in their language. Some of the superior hierarchy treating one another with injurious brutalities, and are often guilty of such indecencies and mis-behaviour as the lowest of mortals would blush to own. *Juno* calls *Diana*, the Goddess of chastity, κύον ἀδεές, brazen-fac'd bitch; Homer, *Iliad* 21, 481. *Jupiter* insults his daughter, the Goddess of wisdom, for rashness and folly; bids *Iris* tell her, he'll maul her coach-horses for her, like a surly bitch as she is; αἰνοτάτη κύον: *Iliad* 8, 423; then threatens in another place to beat his wife, that divine vixon, the immortal partner of the empyreal throne, καί σε πληγῇσιν ἱμάσσω; *Iliad* 15, 17.

The commentators may endeavour to hide those absurdities under the veil of allegories; but the reader that considers the whole texture of the *Iliad*, will find, that the author's meaning, and their interpretation, are often as unlike, as the imaginary heroes of his time, are to the real ones of ours.

Allegories should be obvious, and not like meteors in the air, which represent a different figure to every different eye. Now they are armies of soldiers; now flocks of sheep; and by and by nothing.

Perhaps the criticks of a more exalted taste, may discover such beauties in the antient poetry, as may escape the comprehension of us pigmies of a more limited genius. They may be able to fathom the divine sense of the pagan theology; whilst we aim at no more, than to judge of a little common sense.

It is, and ever will be a rule to a great many, to applaud and condemn with the general vogue, tho' never so ill grounded. The most are affraid of being particular; and rather than strive against the stream, are proud of being in the wrong with the many, rather than desirous of being in the right with the few: and tho' they be convinc'd of the reasonableness of dissenting from the common cry, yet out of a poor fear of censure, they contribute to establish it, and thus become an authority against others, who in reality are but of their own opinion.

Ovid was so far from paying a blind deference to the venerable name of his *Grecian* predecessor, in the character of his Gods, that when Jupiter punishes *Andromeda* for the crimes of her mother, he calls him *injustus Ammon*, *Metamorphoses* 4, and takes commonly an honourable care of the decorum of the Godhead, when their actions are consistent with the divinity of their character. His allegories include some religious, or instructive moral, wrap'd up in a peculiar perspicuity. The fable of *Proserpina*, being sometimes in Hell, and sometimes with *Ceres* her mother, can scarce mean any thing else than the sowing and coming up of corn. The various dresses, that *Vertumnus*, the God of seasons, puts on in his courtship of *Pomona* the garden Goddess, seem plainly to express the different and most proper times for digging, planting, pruning, and gathering the increase. I shall be shorter on this head, because our countryman Mr *Sands* has, by a laborious search amongst the mythologists, been very full. He has annex'd his explanations to the end of each book, which deserve to be recommended to those, that are curious in this figurative learning.

The reader cannot fail of observing, how many excellent lessons of morality *Ovid* has given us in the course of his fables.

The story of *Deucalion*, and *Pyrrha* teaches, that piety, and innocence cannot miss of the divine protection, and that the only loss irreparable is that of our probity, and justice.

That of *Phaeton;* how the too great tenderness of the parent proves a cruelty to the child; and that he, who wou'd climb to the seat of *Jupiter*, generally meets with his bolt by the way.

The tale of *Baucis* and *Philemon* is most inimitably told. He omits not the minutest circumstance of a cottage life; and is much fuller than *Virgil*, where he brings in his contented old Man *Corycius, Georgics 4. Ovid* represents a good old couple; happy, and satisfy'd in a cleanly poverty; hospitable, and free of the few things, that Fortune had given them; moderate in desires; affectionate in their conjugal relation; so religious in life, that when they observ'd their homely cabbin rising to a temple, all the bounty they ask'd of the Gods they had entertain'd, was, that they might do the office of priesthood there; and at their death, not survive one another.

The stories of *Lycaon*, and *Pentheus*, not only deter from infidelity, and irreverence to the Gods; but the last also shows, that too great zeal produces the same effects, as none at all; and that enthusiasm is often more cruel, than atheism.

The story of *Minos*, and *Scylla* represents the infamy of selling our country; and teaches, that even they who love the crime abhor the criminal.

In *Cippus* we find a noble magnanimity, and heavenly self-denial; he preferr'd the good of the republick to his own private grandeur; and chose, with an exemplary generosity, rather to live a private free-man out of *Rome*, than to command numbers of slaves in it.

From the story of *Hercules* we learn, that Glory is a lady, who, like many others, loves to have her admirers suffer a great deal for her. The poet enumerates the labours of the heroe; shows how he conquer'd every thing for others, but nothing for himself: then does him the poetical justice of an apotheosis; thinking it most fit that one, who had born the celestial orbs on his shoulders, shou'd have a mansion amongst them.

From the assumption of *Romulus*, that when war is at an end, the chief business of peace should be the enacting good laws; that after a people are preserv'd from the enemy, the next care shou'd be, to preserve them from themselves; and therefore the best legislators deserve a place amongst heroes, and deities.

From *Ariadne* being inhumanly deserted by *Theseus*, and generously receiv'd by *Bacchus*, we find, that as there is nothing we can be sure of, so there is nothing we ought to despair of.

From *Althea* burning the brand, that we shou'd take care lest under the notion of justice, we shou'd do a cruelty; for they that are set upon revenge, only endeavour to imitate the injury.

From *Polyphemus* making love to *Galatea* one may observe, that the most deform'd can find something to like in their own person. He examines his face in the stream, combs his ruful locks with a rake, grows more exact, and studious of his dress, and discovers the first sign of being in love, by endeavouring at a more than usual care to please.

The fable of *Cephalus*, and *Procrys* confirms, that every trifle contributes to heighten the disease of jealousy; and that the most convincing proofs can scarce cure it.

From that of *Hippomenes*, and *Atalanta* we may discover, that a generous present helps to persuade, as well as an agreeable person.

From *Medea's* flying from *Pelias's* court, that the offer'd favours of the impious should be always suspected; and that they, who design to make every one fear them, are afraid of every one.

From *Myrrha*, that shame is sometimes hard to be overcome, but if the sex once gets the better of it, it gives them afterwards no more trouble.

From *Cenis*, that effeminacy in youth may change to valour in manhood, and that as fame perishes, so does censure.

From *Tereus*, that one crime lays the foundation of many; and that the same person, who begins with lust, may conclude with murther.

From *Midas*, that no body can punish a covetous man worse, than he punishes himself; that scarce any thing wou'd sometimes prove more fatal to us, than the completion of our own wishes; and that he who has the most desires, will certainly meet with the most disappointments.

From the *Pythagorean* philosophy, it may be observ'd, that man is the only animal, who kills his fellow-creature without being angry.

From *Proteus* we have this lesson, that a statesman can put on any shape; can be a spaniel to the lyon, and a lyon to the spaniel; and that he knows not to be an enemy, who knows not how to seem a friend; that if all crowns shou'd change their ministry, as often as they please, tho' they may be called other ministers, they are still the same men.

The legend of *Aesculapius's* voyage to *Rome* in form of a snake, seems to express the necessary sagacity requir'd in professors of that art, for the readier insight into distempers: this reptile being celebrated by the ancient naturalists for a quick sight.

> *Cur in amicorum vitium tam cernis acutum*
> *Quam aut aquilae, aut serpens Epidaurius?* [Horace, *Satires* 1, 3]

The venerable *Epidaurian* assum'd the figure of an animal without hands to take fees; and therefore, grateful posterity honour'd him with a temple. In this manner shou'd wealthy physicians, upon proper occasions, practise; and thus their surviving patients reward.

If the *Metamorphoses* be attended to with a just application and without prepossession, one will be the less surpris'd at the author's prophetick spirit, relating to the duration, and success of the work.

> *Jamque opus exegi, etc.*

This prediction has so far prov'd true, that this poem has been ever since the magazine, which has furnish'd the greatest poets of the following ages with fancy, and allusions; and the most celebrated painters with subjects, and design. Nor have his poetical predecessors, and contemporaries, paid less regard to their own performances.

> *Insignemque meo capiti petere inde coronam,*
> *Unde prius nulli velarunt tempora Musae.*   [Lucretius 1]

> *Nemo me lacrumeis decoret, nec funera fletu*
> *Facsit; quur volito vivu' per ora virum.*   [Ennius. Frag.]

> *. . . temptenda via est, qua me quoque possim*
> *Tollere humo, victorque virum volitare per ora.*   [Virgil, *Georgics* 3]

> *Me doctarum Ederae frontium*
> *Dis miscent superis . . .*   [Horace, *Odes* 1]

Again,

> *Exegi monumentum aere perennius,*
> *Regalique situ Pyramidum altius,*
> *Quod non imber edax, non Aquilo impotens*
> *Possit diruere, aut innumerabilis*
> *Annorum series, et fuga temporum.*
> *Non omnis moriar . . .*   [Horace *Odes* 3, 30]

The whole ode is in a manner a continu'd compliment to his own writings; nor, in imitation of this celebrated author, want we poets of our present age, who have been pleas'd to rank themselves amongst their own admirers.

I have done with the original, and shall make no excuse for the length of the preface, because it is in the power of the reader to make it as short as he pleases. I shall now conclude with a word or two about the version.

Translation is commonly either verbal, or paraphrase, or imitation; of the first is Mr *Sands's*, which I think the *Metamorphoses*, can by no means allow of. It is agreed, the author left it unfinish'd; if it had undergone his last hand, it is more than probable, that many superfluities had been retrench'd. Where a poem is perfectly finish'd; the translation, with regard to particular idioms, cannot be too exact; by doing this, the sense of the author is more entirely his own, and the cast of the periods more faithfully preserv'd: but where a poem is tedious through exuberance, or dark through a hasty brevity, I think the translator may be excus'd for doing what the author upon revising, wou'd have done himself.

If Mr *Sands* had been of this opinion, perhaps other translations of the *Metamorphoses* had not been attempted.

A critick has observ'd, that in his version of this book, he has scrupulously confin'd the number of his lines to those of the original. 'Tis fit I should take the summ upon content, and be better bred, than to count after him.

The manner that seems most suited for this present undertaking, is neither to follow the author too close out of a critical timorousness; nor abandon him too wantonly through a poetick boldness. The original should always be kept in view, without too apparent a deviation from the sense. Where it is otherwise, it is not a version, but an imitation. The translator ought to be as intent to keep up the gracefulness of the poem, as artful to hide its imperfections; to copy its beauties, and to throw a shade over its blemishes; to be faithful to an idolatry, where the author excells; and to take the licence of a little paraphrase, where penury of fancy, or dryness of expression seem to ask for it.

The ingenious gentlemen concern'd in this undertaking seem to be of this opinion, and therefore they have not only consulted the reputation of the author, but their own also. There is one of them has no other share in this compliment, than by being the occasion of engaging them that have, in obliging the publick. He has also been so just to the memory, and reputation of Mr *Dryden*, as to give his incomparable lines the advantage of appearing so near his own.

I cannot pass by that admirable *English* poet, without endeavouring to make his country sensible of the obligations they have to his Muse. Whether they consider the flowing grace of his versification; the vigorous sallies of his fancy; or the peculiar delicacy of his periods; they'll discover excellencies never to be enough admir'd. If they trace him from the first productions of his youth, to the last performances of his age, they'll find, that as the tyranny of rhyme never impos'd on the perspicuity of the sense, so a languid sense never wanted to be set off by the harmony of rhyme. And as his earlier works wanted no maturity, so his latter wanted no force, or spirit. The falling off of his hair, had no other consequence, than to make his lawrels be seen the more.

As a translator he was just; as an inventer he was rich. His versions of some parts of *Lucretius*, *Horace*, *Homer*, and *Virgil* throughout, gave him a just pretence to that compliment which was made to *Monsieur d'Ablancourt*, a celebrated *French* translater: *It is uncertain who have the greatest obligations to him, the dead or the living.*

With all these wondrous talents, he was libell'd in his life-time by the very men, who had no other excellencies, but as they were his imitators. Where he was allow'd to have sentiments superior to all others, they charged him with theft: but how did he steal? no otherwise, than like those, that steal beggars' children, only to cloath them the better.

'Tis to be lamented, that gentlemen still continue this unfair behaviour, and treat one another every day with most injurious libels. The Muses should be ladies of a chaste and fair behaviour: when they are otherwise, they are Furies. 'Tis certain that *Parnassus* is at best but a barren mountain, and its inhabitants contrive to make it more so by their unneighbourly deportment; the authors are the only corporation that endeavour at the ruin of their own society. Every day may convince them, how much a rich fool is respected above a poor wit. The only talents in esteem at present are those of *Exchange-Ally*; one tally is worth a grove of bays; and 'tis of much more consequence to be well read in the tables of interest, and the rise and fall of stocks, than in the revolution of empires.

Mr *Dryden* is still a sad, and shameful instance of this truth: the man, that cou'd make kings immortal, and raise triumphant arches to heroes, now wants a poor square foot of stone, to show where the ashes of one of the greatest poets, that ever was upon Earth, are deposited.

SAMUEL GARTH

BOOK THE FIRST

O F bodies chang'd to various forms, I sing:
   Ye Gods, from whom these miracles did spring,
   Inspire my numbers with coelestial heat;
'Till I my long laborious work compleat:
And add perpetual tenour to my rhimes,
Deduc'd from Nature's birth, to *Caesar's* times.
   Before the seas, and this terrestrial ball,
And Heav'n's high canopy, that covers all,
One was the face of Nature; if a face:
Rather a rude and indigested mass:
A lifeless lump, unfashion'd, and unfram'd,
Of jarring seeds; and justly *Chaos* nam'd.
No sun was lighted up, the world to view;
No moon did yet her blunted horns renew:
Nor yet was Earth suspended in the sky;
Nor pois'd, did on her own foundations lye:
Nor seas about the shores their arms had thrown;
But earth, and air, and water, were in one.
Thus air was void of light, and earth unstable,
And water's dark abyss unnavigable.
No certain form on any was imprest;
All were confus'd, and each disturb'd the rest.
For hot and cold were in one body fixt;
And soft with hard, and light with heavy mixt.
   But God, or Nature, while they thus contend,
To these intestine discords put an end:
Then earth from air, and seas from earth were driv'n,
And grosser air sunk from aetherial Heav'n.
Thus disembroil'd, they take their proper place;
The next of kin, contiguously embrace;
And foes are sunder'd, by a larger space.
The force of fire ascended first on high,
And took its dwelling in the vaulted sky:
Then air succeeds, in lightness next to fire;

Whose atoms from unactive earth retire.
Earth sinks beneath, and draws a num'rous throng
Of pondrous, thick, unwieldy seeds along.
About her coasts, unruly waters roar;
And rising, on a ridge, insult the shore.
Thus when the God, whatever God was he,
Had form'd the whole, and made the parts agree,
That no unequal portions might be found,
He moulded Earth into a spacious round:
Then with a breath, he gave the winds to blow;
And bad the congregated waters flow.
He adds the running springs, and standing lakes;
And bounding banks for winding rivers makes.
Some part, in Earth are swallow'd up, the most
In ample oceans, disembogu'd, are lost.
He shades the woods, the vallies he restrains
With rocky mountains, and extends the plains.

And as five zones th' aetherial regions bind,
Five, correspondent, are to Earth assign'd:
The sun with rays, directly darting down,
Fires all beneath, and fries the middle zone:
The two beneath the distant poles, complain
Of endless winter, and perpetual rain.
Betwixt th' extreams, two happier climates hold
The temper that partakes of hot, and cold.
The fields of liquid air, inclosing all,
Surround the compass of this earthly ball:
The lighter parts lye next the fires above;
The grosser near the watry surface move:
Thick clouds are spread, and storms engender there,
And thunder's voice, which wretched mortals fear,
And winds that on their wings cold winter bear.
Nor were those blustring brethren left at large,
On seas, and shores, their fury to discharge:
Bound as they are, and circumscrib'd in place,

They rend the world, resistless, where they pass;
And mighty marks of mischief leave behind;
Such is the rage of their tempestuous kind.
First *Eurus* to the rising morn is sent
(The regions of the balmy continent);
And *Eastern* realms, where early *Persians* run,
To greet the blest appearance of the sun.
Westward, the wanton *Zephyr* wings his flight;
Pleas'd with the remnants of departing light:
Fierce *Boreas*, with his off-spring, issues forth
T' invade the frozen waggon of the *North*.
While frowning *Auster* seeks the *Southern* sphere;
And rots, with endless rain, th' unwholsom year.

　　High o'er the clouds, and empty realms of wind,
The God a clearer space for Heav'n design'd;
Where fields of light, and liquid aether flow;
Purg'd from the pondrous dregs of Earth below.

　　Scarce had the Pow'r distinguish'd these, when streight
The stars, no longer overlaid with weight,
Exert their heads, from underneath the mass;
And upward shoot, and kindle as they pass,
And with diffusive light adorn their heav'nly place.
Then, every void of Nature to supply,
With forms of Gods he fills the vacant sky:
New herds of beasts he sends, the plains to share:
New colonies of birds, to people air:
And to their oozy beds, the finny fish repair.

　　A creature of a more exalted kind
Was wanting yet, and then was Man design'd:
Conscious of thought, of more capacious breast,
For empire form'd, and fit to rule the rest:
Whether with particles of heav'nly fire
The God of Nature did his soul inspire,
Or Earth, but new divided from the sky,
And, pliant, still retain'd th' aetherial energy:

Which wise *Prometheus* temper'd into paste,
And, mixt with living streams, the godlike image cast.
Thus, while the mute creation downward bend
Their sight, and to their earthly mother tend,
Man looks aloft; and with erected eyes
Beholds his own hereditary skies.
From such rude principles our form began;
And earth was metamorphos'd into Man.

The golden age was first; when Man yet new,
No rule but uncorrupted reason knew:
And, with a native bent, did good pursue.
Unforc'd by punishment, un-aw'd by fear,
His words were simple, and his soul sincere;
Needless was written law, where none opprest:
The law of Man was written in his breast:
No suppliant crowds before the judge appear'd,
No court erected yet, nor cause was heard:
But all was safe, for conscience was their guard.
The mountain-trees in distant prospect please,
E're yet the pine descended to the seas:
E're sails were spread, new oceans to explore:
And happy mortals, unconcern'd for more,
Confin'd their wishes to their native shore.
No walls were yet; nor fence, nor mote, nor mound,
Nor drum was heard, nor trumpet's angry sound:
Nor swords were forg'd; but void of care and crime,
The soft creation slept away their time.
The teeming Earth, yet guiltless of the plough,
And unprovok'd, did fruitful stores allow:
Content with food, which Nature freely bred,
On wildings and on strawberries they fed;
Cornels and bramble-berries gave the rest,
And falling acorns furnish'd out a feast.
The flow'rs unsown, in fields and meadows reign'd:
And *Western* winds immortal spring maintain'd.

In following years, the bearded corn ensu'd
From Earth unask'd, nor was that Earth renew'd.
From veins of vallies, milk and nectar broke;
And honey sweating through the pores of oak.

But when good *Saturn*, banish'd from above,
Was driv'n to Hell, the world was under *Jove*.
Succeeding times a silver age behold,
Excelling brass, but more excell'd by gold.
Then summer, autumn, winter did appear:
And spring was but a season of the year.
The sun his annual course obliquely made,
Good days contracted, and enlarg'd the bad.
Then air with sultry heats began to glow;
The wings of winds were clogg'd with ice and snow;
And shivering mortals, into houses driv'n,
Sought shelter from th' inclemency of Heav'n.
Those houses, then, were caves, or homely sheds;
With twining oziers fenc'd; and moss their beds.
Then ploughs, for seed, the fruitful furrows broke,
And oxen labour'd first beneath the yoke.

To this came next in course, the brazen age:
A warlike offspring, prompt to bloody rage,
Not impious yet . . .
                    Hard steel succeeded then:
And stubborn as the metal, were the men.
Truth, modesty, and shame, the world forsook:
Fraud, avarice, and force, their places took.
Then sails were spread, to every wind that blew.
Raw were the sailors, and the depths were new:
Trees, rudely hollow'd, did the waves sustain;
E're ships in triumph plough'd the watry plain.

Then land-marks limited to each his right:
For all before was common as the light.
Nor was the ground alone requir'd to bear
Her annual income to the crooked share,

But greedy mortals, rummaging her store,
Digg'd from her entrails first the precious oar;
Which next to Hell, the prudent Gods had laid;
And that alluring ill, to sight display'd.
Thus cursed steel, and more accursed gold,
Gave mischief birth, and made that mischief bold:
And double death did wretched Man invade,
By steel assaulted, and by gold betray'd,
Now (brandish'd weapons glittering in their hands)
Mankind is broken loose from moral bands;
No rights of hospitality remain:
The guest, by him who harbour'd him, is slain,
The son-in-law pursues the father's life;
The wife her husband murders, he the wife.
The step-dame poyson for the son prepares;
The son inquires into his father's years.
Faith flies, and piety in exile mourns;
And justice, here opprest, to Heav'n returns.

　　Nor were the Gods themselves more safe above;
Against beleaguer'd Heav'n the giants move.
Hills pil'd on hills, on mountains mountains lie,
To make their mad approaches to the skie.
'Till *Jove*, no longer patient, took his time
T' avenge with thunder their audacious crime:
Red light'ning plaid along the firmament,
And their demolish'd works to pieces rent.
Sing'd with the flames, and with the bolts transfixt,
With native Earth, their blood the monsters mixt;
The blood, indu'd with animating heat,
Did in th' impregnant Earth new sons beget:
They, like the seed from which they sprung, accurst,
Against the Gods immortal hatred nurst,
An impious, arrogant, and cruel brood;
Expressing their original from blood.
　　Which when the king of Gods beheld from high

(Withal revolving in his memory,
What he himself had found on Earth of late,
Lycaon's guilt, and his inhumane treat),
He sigh'd; nor longer with his pity strove;
But kindled to a wrath becoming *Jove*:
  Then call'd a general council of the Gods;
Who summon'd, issue from their blest abodes,
And fill th' assembly with a shining train.
A way there is, in Heav'n's expanded plain,
Which, when the skies are clear, is seen below,
And mortals, by the name of Milky, know.
The ground-work is of stars; through which the road
Lyes open to the Thunderer's abode:
The Gods of greater nations dwell around,
And, on the right and left, the palace bound;
The commons where they can: the nobler sort
With winding-doors wide open, front the court.
This place, as far as Earth with Heav'n may vie,
I dare to call the *Louvre* of the skie.
When all were plac'd, in seats distinctly known,
And he, their father, had assum'd the throne,
Upon his iv'ry sceptre first he leant,
Then shook his head, that shook the firmament:
Air, Earth, and seas, obey'd th' almighty nod;
And, with a gen'ral fear, confess'd the God.
At length, with indignation, thus he broke
His awful silence, and the Pow'rs bespoke.
  I was not more concern'd in that debate
Of empire, when our universal state
Was put to hazard, and the giant race
Our captive skies were ready to imbrace:
For tho' the foe was fierce, the seeds of all
Rebellion, sprung from one original;
Now, wheresoever ambient waters glide,
All are corrupt, and all must be destroy'd.

Let me this holy protestation make,
By Hell, and Hell's inviolable lake,
I try'd whatever in the godhead lay:
But gangren'd members must be lopt away,
Before the nobler parts are tainted to decay.
There dwells below, a race of demi-gods,
Of nymphs in waters, and of fawns in woods:
Who, tho' not worthy yet, in Heav'n to live,
Let 'em, at least, enjoy that Earth we give.
Can these be thought securely lodg'd below,
When I my self, who no superior know,
I, who have Heav'n and Earth at my command,
Have been attempted by *Lycaon's* hand?

At this a murmur through the synod went,
And with one voice they vote his punishment.
Thus, when conspiring traytors dar'd to doom
The fall of *Caesar*, and in him of *Rome*,
The nations trembled with a pious fear;
All anxious for their earthly Thunderer:
Nor was their care, o *Caesar*, less esteem'd
By thee, than that of Heav'n for *Jove* was deem'd:
Who with his hand, and voice, did first restrain
Their murmurs, then resum'd his speech again.
The Gods to silence were compos'd, and sate
With reverence, due to his superior state.

Cancel your pious cares; already he
Has paid his debt to justice, and to me.
Yet what his crimes, and what my judgments were,
Remains for me thus briefly to declare.
The clamours of this vile degenerate age,
The cries of orphans, and th' oppressor's rage,
Had reach'd the stars: I will descend, said I,
In hope to prove this loud complaint a lye.
Disguis'd in humane shape, I travell'd round
The world, and more than what I heard, I found.

O'er *Maenalus* I took my steepy way,
By caverns infamous for beasts of prey:
Then cross'd *Cyllené*, and the piny shade
More infamous, by curst *Lycaon* made:
Dark night had cover'd Heaven, and Earth, before
I enter'd his unhospitable door.
Just at my entrance, I display'd the sign
That somewhat was approaching of divine.
The prostrate people pray; the tyrant grins;
And, adding prophanation to his sins,
I'll try, said he, and if a God appear,
To prove his deity shall cost him dear.
'Twas late; the graceless wretch my death prepares,
When I shou'd soundly sleep, opprest with cares:
This dire experiment he chose, to prove
If I were mortal, or undoubted *Jove*:
But first he had resolv'd to taste my pow'r;
Not long before, but in a luckless hour,
Some legates, sent from the *Molossian* state,
Were on a peaceful errand come to treat:
Of these he murders one, he boils the flesh;
And lays the mangled morsels in a dish:
Some part he roasts; then serves it up, so drest,
And bids me welcome to this humane feast.
Mov'd with disdain, the table I o'er-turn'd;
And with avenging flames, the palace burn'd.
The tyrant in a fright, for shelter gains
The neighb'ring fields, and scours along the plains.
Howling he fled, and fain he wou'd have spoke;
But humane voice his brutal tongue forsook.
About his lips the gather'd foam he churns,
And, breathing slaughters, still with rage he burns,
But on the bleating flock his fury turns.
His mantle, now his hide, with rugged hairs
Cleaves to his back; a famish'd face he bears;

His arms descend, his shoulders sink away
To multiply his legs for chase of prey.
He grows a wolf, his hoariness remains,
And the same rage in other members reigns.
His eyes still sparkle in a narr'wer space:
His jaws retain the grin, and violence of his face.
   This was a single ruin, but not one
Deserves so just a punishment alone.
Mankind's a monster, and th' ungodly times
Confed'rate into guilt, are sworn to crimes.
All are alike involv'd in ill, and all
Must by the same relentless fury fall.
Thus ended he; the greater Gods assent;
By clamours urging his severe intent;
The less fill up the cry for punishment.
Yet still with pity they remember Man;
And mourn as much as heav'nly spirits can.
They ask, when those were lost of humane birth,
What he wou'd do with all this waste of Earth:
If his dispeopl'd world he would resign
To beasts, a mute, and more ignoble line;
Neglected altars must no longer smoke,
If none were left to worship, and invoke.
To whom the Father of the Gods reply'd,
Lay that unnecessary fear aside:
Mine be the care, new people to provide.
I will from wondrous principles ordain
A race unlike the first, and try my skill again.
   Already had he toss'd the flaming brand;
And roll'd the thunder in his spacious hand;
Preparing to discharge on seas and land:
But stopt, for fear, thus violently driv'n,
The sparks should catch his axle-tree of Heav'n.
Remembring in the fates, a time when fire
Shou'd to the battlements of Heaven aspire,

And all his blazing worlds above shou'd burn;
And all th' inferior globe to cinders turn.
His dire artill'ry thus dismist, he bent
His thoughts to some securer punishment:
Concludes to pour a watry deluge down;
And what he durst not burn, resolves to drown.

   The northern breath, that freezes floods, he binds;
With all the race of cloud-dispelling winds:
The south he loos'd, who night and horror brings;
And foggs are shaken from his flaggy wings.
From his divided beard two streams he pours,
His head, and rheumy eyes distill in show'rs,
With rain his robe, and heavy mantle flow:
And lazy mists are lowring on his brow;
Still as he swept along, with his clench'd fist
He squeez'd the clouds, th' imprison'd clouds resist:
The skies, from pole to pole, with peals resound;
And show'rs inlarg'd, come pouring on the ground.
Then, clad in colours of a various dye,
Junonian Iris breeds a new supply
To feed the clouds: impetuous rain descends;
The bearded corn beneath the burden bends:
Defrauded clowns deplore their perish'd grain;
And the long labours of the year are vain.

   Nor from his patrimonial Heaven alone
Is *Jove* content to pour his vengeance down;
Aid from his brother of the seas he craves,
To help him with auxiliary waves.
The watry tyrant calls his brooks and floods,
Who rowl from mossie caves (their moist abodes);
And with perpetual urns his palace fill:
To whom in brief, he thus imparts his will.

   Small exhortation needs; your pow'rs employ:
And this bad world, so *Jove* requires, destroy.
Let loose the reins to all your watry store:

Bear down the damms, and open ev'ry door.
  The floods, by Nature enemies to land,
And proudly swelling with their new command,
Remove the living stones, that stopt their way,
And gushing from their source, augment the sea.
Then, with his mace, their monarch struck the ground;
With inward trembling Earth receiv'd the wound;
And rising streams a ready passage found.
Th' expanded waters gather on the plain:
They float the fields, and over-top the grain;
Then rushing onwards, with a sweepy sway,
Bear flocks, and folds, and lab'ring hinds away.
Nor safe their dwellings were, for, sap'd by floods,
Their houses fell upon their houshold Gods.
The solid piles, too strongly built to fall,
High o'er their heads, behold a watry wall:
Now seas and Earth were in confusion lost;
A world of waters, and without a coast.
  One climbs a cliff; one in his boat is born:
And ploughs above, where late he sow'd his corn.
Others o'er chimney-tops and turrets row,
And drop their anchors on the meads below:
Or downward driv'n, they bruise the tender vine,
Or tost aloft, are knock'd against a pine.
And where of late the kids had cropt the grass,
The monsters of the deep now take their place.
Insulting Nereids on the cities ride,
And wond'ring dolphins o'er the palace glide.
On leaves, and masts of mighty oaks they brouze;
And their broad fins entangle in the boughs.
The frighted wolf now swims amongst the sheep;
The yellow lion wanders in the deep:
His rapid force no longer helps the boar:
The stag swims faster, than he ran before.
The fowls, long beating on their wings in vain,

Despair of land, and drop into the main.
Now hills, and vales no more distinction know;
And levell'd Nature lies oppress'd below.
The most of mortals perish in the flood:
The small remainder dies for want of food.

  A mountain of stupendous height there stands
Betwixt th' *Athenian* and *Boeotian* lands,
The bound of fruitful fields, while fields they were,
But then a field of waters did appear:
Parnassus is its name; whose forky rise
Mounts thro' the clouds, and mates the lofty skies.
High on the summit of this dubious cliff,
Deucalion wafting, moor'd his little skiff.
He with his wife were only left behind
Of perish'd Man; they two were human kind.
The mountain nymphs, and *Themis* they adore,
And from her oracles relief implore.
The most upright of mortal men was he;
The most sincere, and holy woman, she.

  When *Jupiter*, surveying Earth from high,
Beheld it in a lake of water lie,
That where so many millions lately liv'd,
But two, the best of either sex, surviv'd;
He loos'd the northern wind; fierce *Boreas* flies
To puff away the clouds, and purge the skies:
Serenely, while he blows, the vapours driv'n,
Discover Heav'n to Earth, and Earth to Heav'n.
The billows fall, while *Neptune* lays his mace
On the rough sea, and smooths its furrow'd face.
Already *Triton*, at his call, appears
Above the waves; a *Tyrian* robe he wears;
And in his hand a crooked trumpet bears.
The soveraign bids him peaceful sounds inspire,
And give the waves the signal to retire.
His writhen shell he takes; whose narrow vent

Grows by degrees into a large extent,
Then gives it breath; the blast with doubling sound,
Runs the wide circuit of the world around:
The sun first heard it, in his early east,
And met the rattling ecchos in the west.
The waters, listning to the trumpet's roar,
Obey the summons, and forsake the shore.

  A thin circumference of land appears;
And Earth, but not at once, her visage rears,
And peeps upon the seas from upper grounds;
The streams, but just contain'd within their bounds,
By slow degrees into their channels crawl;
And Earth increases, as the waters fall.
In longer time the tops of trees appear,
Which mud on their dishonour'd branches bear.

  At length the world was all restor'd to view;
But desolate, and of a sickly hue:
Nature beheld her self, and stood aghast,
A dismal desart, and a silent waste.

  Which when *Deucalion*, with a piteous look
Beheld, he wept, and thus to *Pyrrha* spoke:
Oh wife, oh sister, oh of all thy kind
The best, and only creature left behind,
By kindred, love, and now by dangers joyn'd;
Of multitudes, who breath'd the common air,
We two remain; a species in a pair:
The rest the seas have swallow'd; nor have we
Ev'n of this wretched life a certainty.
The clouds are still above; and, while I speak,
A second deluge o'er our heads may break.
Shou'd I be snatcht from hence, and thou remain,
Without relief, or partner of thy pain,
How cou'dst thou such a wretched life sustain?
Shou'd I be left, and thou be lost, the sea
That bury'd her I lov'd, shou'd bury me.

Oh cou'd our father his old arts inspire,
And make me heir of his informing fire,
That so I might abolisht Man retrieve,
And perisht people in new souls might live.
But Heav'n is pleas'd, nor ought we to complain,
That we, th' examples of mankind, remain.
He said; the careful couple joyn their tears:
And then invoke the Gods, with pious prayers.
Thus, in devotion having eas'd their grief,
From sacred oracles they seek relief;
And to *Cephysus'* brook their way pursue:
The stream was troubled, but the ford they knew;
With living waters, in the fountain bred,
They sprinkle first their garments, and their head,
Then took the way, which to the temple led.
The roofs were all defil'd with moss, and mire,
The desart altars void of solemn fire.
Before the gradual, prostrate they ador'd;
The pavement kiss'd; and thus the saint implor'd.

　　O righteous *Themis*, if the Pow'rs above
By pray'rs are bent to pity, and to love;
If humane miseries can move their mind;
If yet they can forgive, and yet be kind;
Tell how we may restore, by second birth,
Mankind, and people desolated Earth.
Then thus the gracious Goddess, nodding, said;
Depart, and with your vestments veil your head:
And stooping lowly down, with losen'd zones,
Throw each behind your backs, your mighty mother's bones.
Amaz'd the pair, and mute with wonder stand,
'Till *Pyrrha* first refus'd the dire command.
Forbid it Heav'n, said she, that I shou'd tear
Those holy reliques from the sepulcher.
They ponder'd the mysterious words again,
For some new sense; and long they sought in vain:

At length *Deucalion* clear'd his cloudy brow,
And said, the dark *Aenigma* will allow
A meaning, which, if well I understand,
From sacrilege will free the God's command:
This Earth our mighty mother is, the stones
In her capacious body, are her bones:
These we must cast behind. With hope, and fear,
The woman did the new solution hear:
The man diffides in his own augury,
And doubts the Gods; yet both resolve to try.
Descending from the mount, they first unbind
Their vests, and veil'd, they cast the stones behind:
The stones (a miracle to mortal view,
But long tradition makes it pass for true)
Did first the rigour of their kind expel,
And suppled into softness, as they fell;
Then swell'd, and swelling, by degrees grew warm;
And took the rudiments of human form.
Imperfect shapes: in marble such are seen,
When the rude chizzel does the man begin;
While yet the roughness of the stone remains,
Without the rising muscles, and the veins.
The sappy parts, and next resembling juice,
Were turn'd to moisture, for the body's use:
Supplying humours, blood, and nourishment;
The rest, too solid to receive a bent,
Converts to bones; and what was once a vein,
Its former name and Nature did retain.
By help of pow'r divine, in little space,
What the man threw, assum'd a manly face;
And what the wife, renew'd the female race.
Hence we derive our nature; born to bear
Laborious life; and harden'd into care.

    The rest of animals, from teeming Earth
Produc'd, in various forms receiv'd their birth.

The native moisture, in its close retreat,
Digested by the sun's aetherial heat,
As in a kindly womb, began to breed:
Then swell'd, and quicken'd by the vital seed.
And some in less, and some in longer space,
Were ripen'd into form, and took a sev'ral face.
Thus when the *Nile* from *Pharian* fields is fled,
And seeks, with ebbing tides, his ancient bed,
The fat manure with heav'nly fire is warm'd;
And crusted creatures, as in wombs, are form'd;
These, when they turn the glebe, the peasants find;
Some rude, and yet unfinish'd in their kind:
Short of their limbs, a lame imperfect birth:
One half alive; and one of lifeless earth.

　For heat, and moisture, when in bodies join'd,
The temper that results from either kind
Conception makes; and fighting 'till they mix,
Their mingled atoms in each other fix.
Thus Nature's hand the genial bed prepares
With friendly discord, and with fruitful wars.

　From hence the surface of the ground, with mud
And slime besmear'd (the faeces of the flood),
Receiv'd the rays of Heav'n: and sucking in
The seeds of heat, new creatures did begin:
Some were of sev'ral sorts produc'd before,
But of new monsters, Earth created more.
Unwillingly, but yet she brought to light
Thee, *Python* too, the wondring world to fright,
And the new nations, with so dire a sight:
So monstrous was his bulk, so large a space
Did his vast body, and long train embrace.
Whom *Phoebus* basking on a bank espy'd;
E're now the God his arrows had not try'd
But on the trembling deer, or mountain goat;
At this new quarry he prepares to shoot.

Though ev'ry shaft took place, he spent the store
Of his full quiver; and 'twas long before
Th' expiring serpent wallow'd in his gore.
Then, to preserve the fame of such a deed,
For *Python* slain, he *Pythian* games decred.
Where noble youths for mastership shou'd strive,
To quoit, to run, and steeds, and chariots drive.
The prize was fame: in witness of renown
An oaken garland did the victor crown.
The laurel was not yet for triumphs born;
But every green alike by *Phoebus* worn,
Did, with promiscuous grace, his flowing locks adorn.

The first and fairest of his loves, was she
Whom not blind fortune, but the dire decree
Of angry *Cupid* forc'd him to desire:
Daphne her name, and *Peneus* was her sire.
Swell'd with the pride, that new success attends,
He sees the stripling, while his bow he bends,
And thus insults him: Thou lascivious boy,
Are arms like these for children to employ?
Know, such atchievements are my proper claim;
Due to my vigour, and unerring aim:
Resistless are my shafts, and *Python* late
In such a feather'd death, has found his fate.
Take up the torch (and lay my weapons by),
With that the feeble souls of lovers fry.
To whom the son of *Venus* thus reply'd,
Phoebus, thy shafts are sure on all beside,
But mine of *Phoebus*, mine the fame shall be
Of all thy conquests, when I conquer thee.

He said, and soaring, swiftly wing'd his flight:
Nor stopt but on *Parnassus*' airy height.
Two diff'rent shafts he from his quiver draws;
One to repel desire, and one to cause.
One shaft is pointed with refulgent gold:

To bribe the love, and make the lover bold:
One blunt, and tipt with lead, whose base allay
Provokes disdain, and drives desire away.
The blunted bolt against the nymph he drest:
But with the sharp transfixt *Apollo's* breast.

Th' enamour'd deity pursues the chace;
The scornful damsel shuns his loath'd embrace:
In hunting beasts of prey, her youth employs;
And *Phoebe* rivals in her rural joys.
With naked neck she goes, and shoulders bare;
And with a fillet binds her flowing hair.
By many suitors sought, she mocks their pains,
And still her vow'd virginity maintains.
Impatient of a yoke, the name of bride
She shuns, and hates the joys, she never try'd.
On wilds, and woods, she fixes her desire:
Nor knows what youth, and kindly love, inspire.
Her father chides her oft: Thou ow'st, says he,
A husband to thy self, a son to me.
She, like a crime, abhors the nuptial bed:
She glows with blushes, and she hangs her head.
Then casting round his neck her tender arms,
Sooths him with blandishments, and filial charms:
Give me, my Lord, she said, to live, and die,
A spotless maid, without the marriage tye.
'Tis but a small request; I beg no more
Than what *Diana's* father gave before.
The good old sire was soften'd to consent;
But said her wish wou'd prove her punishment:
For so much youth, and so much beauty join'd,
Oppos'd the state, which her desires design'd.

The God of light, aspiring to her bed,
Hopes what he seeks, with flattering fancies fed;
And is, by his own oracles, mis-led.
And as in empty fields the stubble burns,

Or nightly travellers, when day returns,
Their useless torches on dry hedges throw,
That catch the flames, and kindle all the row;
So burns the God, consuming in desire,
And feeding in his breast a fruitless fire:
Her well-turn'd neck he view'd (her neck was bare)
And on her shoulders her dishevel'd hair;
Oh were it comb'd, said he, with what a grace
Wou'd every waving curl become her face!
He view'd her eyes, like heav'nly lamps that shone,
He view'd her lips, too sweet to view alone,
Her taper fingers, and her panting breast;
He praises all he sees, and for the rest
Believes the beauties yet unseen are best:
Swift as the wind, the damsel fled away,
Nor did for these alluring speeches stay:
Stay Nymph, he cry'd, I follow, not a foe.
Thus from the lyon trips the trembling doe;
Thus from the wolf the frighten'd lamb removes,
And, from pursuing faulcons, fearful doves;
Thou shunn'st a God, and shunn'st a God, that loves.
Ah, lest some thorn shou'd pierce thy tender foot,
Or thou shou'dst fall in flying my pursuit!
To sharp uneven ways thy steps decline;
Abate thy speed, and I will bate of mine.
Yet think from whom thou dost so rashly fly;
Nor basely born, nor shepherd's swain am I.
Perhaps thou know'st not my superior state;
And from that ignorance proceeds thy hate.
Me *Claros*, *Delphi*, *Tenedos* obey;
These hands the *Patareian* scepter sway.
The King of Gods begot me: what shall be,
Or is, or ever was, in Fate, I see.
Mine is th' invention of the charming lyre;
Sweet notes, and heav'nly numbers, I inspire.

Sure is my bow, unerring is my dart;
But ah! more deadly his, who pierc'd my heart.
Med'cine is mine; what herbs and simples grow
In fields, and forrests, all their pow'rs I know;
And am the great physician call'd, below.
Alas that fields and forrests can afford.
No remedies to heal their love-sick lord!
To cure the pains of love, no plant avails:
And his own physick, the physician fails.

 She heard not half; so furiously she flies;
And on her·ear th'imperfect accent dies,
Fear gave her wings; and as she fled, the wind
Increasing, spread her flowing hair behind;
And left her legs and thighs expos'd to view:
Which made the God more eager to pursue.
The God was young, and was too hotly bent
To lose his time in empty compliment:
But led by love, and fir'd with such a sight,
Impetuously pursu'd his near delight.

 As when th' impatient greyhound slipt from far,
Bounds o'er the glebe to course the fearful hare,
She in her speed does all her safety lay;
And he with double speed pursues the prey;
O'er-runs her at the sitting turn, and licks
His chaps in vain, and blows upon the flix:
She scapes, and for the neighb'ring covert strives,
And gaining shelter, doubts if yet she lives:
If little things with great we may compare,
Such was the God, and such the flying fair,
She urg'd by fear, her feet did swiftly move,
But he more swiftly, who was urg'd by love.
He gathers ground upon her in the chace:
Now breathes upon her hair, with nearer pace;
And just is fast'ning on the wish'd embrace.
The nymph grew pale, and in a mortal fright,

Spent with the labour of so long a flight;
And now despairing, cast a mournful look
Upon the streams of her paternal brook;
Oh help, she cry'd, in this extreamest need!
If water Gods are deities indeed:
Gape Earth, and this unhappy wretch intomb;
Or change my form, whence all my sorrows come.
Scarce had she finish'd, when her feet she found
Benumb'd with cold, and fasten'd to the ground:
A filmy rind about her body grows;
Her hair to leaves, her arms extend to boughs:
The nymph is all into a lawrel gone;
The smoothness of her skin remains alone.
Yet *Phoebus* loves her still, and casting round
Her bole, his arms, some little warmth he found.
The tree still panted in th' unfinish'd part:
Not wholly vegetive, and heav'd her heart.
He fixt his lips upon the trembling rind;
It swerv'd aside, and his embrace declin'd.
To whom the God, Because thou canst not be
My mistress, I espouse thee for my tree:
Be thou the prize of honour, and renown;
The deathless poet, and the poem, crown.
Thou shalt the *Roman* festivals adorn,
And, after poets, be by victors worn.
Thou shalt returning *Caesar's* triumph grace;
When pomps shall in a long procession pass.
Wreath'd on the posts before his palace wait;
And be the sacred guardian of the gate.
Secure from thunder, and unharm'd by *Jove*,
Unfading as th' immortal Pow'rs above:
And as the locks of *Phoebus* are unshorn,
So shall perpetual green thy boughs adorn.
The grateful tree was pleas'd with what he said;
And shook the shady honours of her head.

An ancient forest in *Thessalia* grows;
Which *Tempe's* pleasing valley does inclose:
Through this the rapid *Peneus* take his course;
From *Pindus* rolling with impetuous force;
Mists from the river's mighty fall arise:
And deadly damps inclose the cloudy skies:
Perpetual fogs are hanging o'er the wood;
And sounds of waters deaf the neighbourhood.
Deep, in a rocky cave, he makes abode
(A mansion proper for a mourning God).
Here he gives audience; issuing out decrees
To rivers, his dependant deities.
On this occasion hither they resort;
To pay their homage, and to make their court.
All doubtful, whether to congratulate
His daughter's honour, or lament her fate.
Sperchaeus, crown'd with poplar, first appears;
Then old *Apidanus* came crown'd with years:
Enipeus turbulent, *Amphrysos* tame;
And *Aeas* last with lagging waters came.
Then, of his kindred brooks, a num'rous throng
Condole his loss; and bring their urns along.
Not one was wanting of the wat'ry train,
That fill'd his flood, or mingled with the main:
But *Inachus*, who in his cave, alone,
Wept not another's losses, but his own,
For his dear *Io*, whether stray'd, or dead,
To him uncertain, doubtful tears he shed.
He sought her through the world; but sought in vain;
And no where finding, rather fear'd her slain.

    Her, just returning from her father's brook,
Jove had beheld, with a desiring look:
And, Oh fair daughter of the flood, he said,
Worthy alone of *Jove's* imperial bed,
Happy whoever shall those charms possess;

The king of Gods (nor is thy lover less)
Invites thee to yon cooler shades; to shun
The scorching rays of the meridian sun.
Nor shalt thou tempt the dangers of the grove
Alone, without a guide; thy guide is *Jove*.
No puny Pow'r, but he whose high command
Is unconfin'd, who rules the seas and land;
And tempers thunder in his awful hand,
Oh fly not: for she fled from his embrace
O'er *Lerna's* pastures: he pursu'd the chace
Along the shades of the *Lyrcaean* plain;
At length the God, who never asks in vain,
Involv'd with vapours, imitating night,
Both Air, and Earth; and then suppress'd her flight,
And mingling force with love, enjoy'd the full delight.
Mean-time the jealous *Juno*, from on high,
Survey'd the fruitful fields of *Arcady*;
And wonder'd that the mist shou'd over-run
The face of day-light, and obscure the sun.
No nat'ral cause she found, from brooks, or bogs,
Or marshy lowlands, to produce the fogs;
Then round the skies she sought for *Jupiter*,
Her faithless husband; but no *Jove* was there:
Suspecting now the worst, Or I, she said,
Am much mistaken, or am much betray'd.
With fury she precipitates her flight:
Dispels the shadows of dissembled night;
And to the day restores his native light.
Th' Almighty *Leacher*, careful to prevent
The consequence, foreseeing her descent,
Transforms his mistress in a trice; and now
In *Io's* place appears a lovely cow.
So sleek her skin, so faultless was her make,
Ev'n *Juno* did unwilling pleasure take
To see so fair a rival of her love;

And what she was, and whence, enquir'd of *Jove*:
Of what fair herd, and from what pedigree?
The God, half caught, was forc'd upon a lye:
And said she sprung from Earth. She took the word,
And begg'd the beauteous heyfer of her lord.
What should he do? 'twas equal shame to *Jove*
Or to relinquish, or betray his love:
Yet to refuse so slight a gift, wou'd be
But more t' increase his consort's jealousie:
Thus fear, and love, by turns, his heart assail'd;
And stronger love had sure, at length, prevail'd:
But some faint hope remain'd, his jealous queen
Had not the mistress through the heyfer seen.
The cautious Goddess, of her gift possest,
Yet harbour'd anxious thoughts within her breast;
As she who knew the falshood of her *Jove*;
And justly fear'd some new relapse of love.
Which to prevent, and to secure her care,
To trusty *Argus* she commits the fair.

   The head of *Argus* (as with stars the skies)
Was compass'd round, and wore an hundred eyes.
But two by turns their lids in slumber steep;
The rest on duty still their station keep;
Nor cou'd the total constellation sleep.
Thus, ever present, to his eyes, and mind,
His charge was still before him, tho' behind.
In fields he suffer'd her to feed by Day,
But when the setting sun to night gave way,
The captive cow he summon'd with a call;
And drove her back, and ty'd her to the stall.
On leaves of trees, and bitter herbs she fed,
Heav'n was her canopy, bare earth her bed:
So hardly lodg'd, and to digest her food,
She drank from troubled streams, defil'd with mud.
Her woeful story fain she wou'd have told,

With hands upheld, but had no hands to hold.
Her head to her ungentle keeper bow'd,
She strove to speak, she spoke not, but she low'd:
Affrighted with the noise, she look'd around,
And seem'd t' inquire the author of the sound.

Once on the banks where often she had play'd
(Her father's banks), she came, and there survey'd
Her alter'd visage, and her branching head;
And starting, from her self she wou'd have fled.
Her fellow nymphs, familiar to her eyes,
Beheld, but knew her not in this disguise.
Ev'n *Inachus* himself was ignorant;
And in his daughter, did his daughter want.
She follow'd where her fellows went, as she
Were still a partner of the company:
They stroak her neck; the gentle heyfer stands,
And her neck offers to their stroaking hands.
Her father gave her grass; the grass she took;
And lick'd his palms, and cast a piteous look;
And in the language of her eyes, she spoke.
She wou'd have told her name, and ask'd relief,
But wanting words, in tears she tells her grief.
Which, with her foot she makes him understand;
And prints the name of *Io* in the sand.

Ah wretched me! her mournful father cry'd;
She, with a sigh, to wretched me reply'd:
About her milk-white neck, his arms he threw;
And wept, and then these tender words ensue.
And art thou she, whom I have sought around
The world, and have at length so sadly found?
So found, is worse than lost: with mutual words
Thou answer'st not, no voice thy tongue affords:
But sighs are deeply drawn from out thy breast;
And speech deny'd, by lowing is express'd.
Unknowing, I prepar'd thy bridal bed;

With empty hopes of happy issue fed.
But now the husband of a herd must be
Thy mate, and bell'wing sons thy progeny.
Oh, were I mortal, death might bring relief:
But now my God-head but extends my grief:
Prolongs my woes, of which no end I see,
And makes me curse my immortality!
More had he said, but fearful of her stay,
The starry guardian drove his charge away,
To some fresh pasture; on a hilly height
He sate himself, and kept her still in sight.

Now *Jove* no longer cou'd her suff'rings bear;
But call'd in haste his airy messenger,
The son of *Maïa*, with severe decree
To kill the keeper, and to set her free.
With all his harness soon the God was sped,
His flying hat was fastned on his head,
Wings on his heels were hung, and in his hand
He holds the vertue of the snaky wand.
The liquid air his moving pinions wound,
And, in the moment, shoot him on the ground.
Before he came in sight, the crafty God
His wings dismiss'd, but still retain'd his rod:
That sleep-procuring wand wise *Hermes* took,
But made it seem to sight a sherpherd's hook.
With this, he did a herd of goats controul;
Which by the way he met, and slily stole.
Clad like a country swain, he pip'd, and sung;
And playing, drove his jolly troop along.

With pleasure, *Argus* the musician heeds;
But wonders much at those new vocal reeds.
And whosoe'er thou art, my friend, said he,
Up hither drive thy goats, and play by me:
This hill has browz for them, and shade for thee.
The God, who was with ease induc'd to climb,

Began discourse to pass away the time;
And still betwixt, his tuneful pipe he plies;
And watch'd his hour, to close the keeper's eyes.
With much ado, he partly kept awake;
Not suff'ring all his eyes repose to take:
And ask'd the stranger, who did reeds invent,
And whence began so rare an instrument?

    Then Hermes thus: A nymph of late there was
Whose heav'nly form her fellows did surpass.
The pride and joy of fair *Arcadia's* plains,
Belov'd by deities, ador'd by swains:
Syrinx her name, by *Sylvans* oft pursu'd,
As oft she did the lustful Gods delude:
The rural, and the woodland Pow'rs disdain'd;
With *Cynthia* hunted, and her rites maintain'd:
Like *Phoebe* clad, even *Phoebe's* self she seems,
So tall, so streight, such well-proportion'd limbs:
The nicest eye did no distinction know,
But that the goddess bore a golden bow:
Distinguish'd thus, the sight she cheated too.
Descending from *Lycaeus*, *Pan* admires
The matchless nymph, and burns with new desires.
A crown of pine upon his head he wore;
And thus began her pity to implore.
But e'er he thus began, she took her flight
So swift, she was already out of sight.
Nor stay'd to hear the courtship of the God;
But bent her course to *Ladon's* gentle flood:
There by the river stopt, and tir'd before;
Relief from water nymphs her pray'rs implore.

    Now while the lustful God, with speedy pace,
Just thought to strain her in a strict embrace,
He fill'd his arms with reeds, new rising on the place.
And while he sighs, his ill success to find,
The tender canes were shaken by the wind;

And breath'd a mournful air, unheard before;
That much surprizing *Pan*, yet pleas'd him more.
Admiring this new musick, Thou, he said,
Who canst not be the partner of my bed,
At least shall be the confort of my mind:
And often, often to my lips be joyn'd.
He form'd the reeds, proportion'd as they are,
Unequal in their length, and wax'd with care,
They still retain the name of his ungrateful fair.
    While *Hermes* pip'd, and sung, and told his tale,
The keeper's winking eyes began to fail,
And drowsie slumber on the lids to creep;
'Till all the watchman was at length asleep.
Then soon the God his voice, and song supprest;
And with his pow'rful rod confirm'd his rest:
Without delay his crooked faulchion drew,
And at one fatal stroke the keeper slew.
Down from the rock fell the dissever'd head,
Opening its eyes in death; and falling, bled;
And mark'd the passage with a crimson trail:
Thus *Argus* lies in pieces, cold, and pale;
And all his hundred eyes, with all their light,
Are clos'd at once, in one perpetual night.
These *Juno* takes, that they no more may fail,
And spreads them in her peacock's gaudy tail.
    Impatient to revenge her injur'd bed,
She wreaks her anger on her rival's head;
With Furies frights her from her native home;
And drives her gadding, round the world to roam:
Nor ceas'd her madness, and her flight, before
She touch'd the limits of the *Pharian* shore.
At length, arriving on the banks of *Nile*,
Wearied with length of ways, and worn with toil,
She laid her down; and leaning on her knees,
Invok'd the cause of all her miseries:

And cast her languishing regards above,
For help from Heav'n, and her ungrateful *Jove*.
She sigh'd, she wept, she low'd; 'twas all she cou'd;
And with unkindness seem'd to tax the God.
Last, with an humble pray'r, she beg'd repose,
Or death at least, to finish all her woes.
Jove heard her vows, and with a flatt'ring look,
In her behalf to jealous *Juno* spoke.
He cast his arms about her neck, and said,
Dame, rest secure; no more thy nuptial bed
This nymph shall violate; by *Styx* I swear,
And every oath that binds the Thunderer.
The Goddess was appeas'd; and at the word
Was *Io* to her former shape restor'd.
The rugged hair began to fall away;
The sweetness of her eyes did only stay,
Tho' not so large; her crooked horns decrease;
The wideness of her jaws and nostrils cease:
Her hoofs to hands return, in little space:
The five long taper fingers take their place,
And nothing of the heyfer now is seen,
Beside the native whiteness of the skin.
Erected on her feet she walks again:
And two the duty of the four sustain.
She tries her tongue; her silence softly breaks,
And fears her former lowings when she speaks:
A Goddess now, through all th' *Aegyptian* State:
And serv'd by priests, who in white linnen wait.
    Her son was *Epaphus*, at length believ'd
The son of *Jove*, and as a God receiv'd;
With sacrifice ador'd, and publick pray'rs,
He common temples with his mother shares.
Equal in years, and rival in renown
With *Epaphus*, the youthful *Phaeton*
Like honour claims; and boasts his sire the sun.

His haughty looks, and his assuming air,
The son of *Isis* could no longer bear:
Thou tak'st thy mother's word too far, said he,
And hast usurp'd thy boasted pedigree.
Go, base pretender to a borrow'd name.
Thus tax'd, he blush'd with anger, and with shame;
But shame repress'd his rage: the daunted youth
Soon seeks his mother, and enquires the truth:
Mother, said he, this infamy was thrown
By *Epaphus* on you, and me your son.
He spoke in publick, told it to my face;
Nor durst I vindicate the dire disgrace:
Even I, the bold, the sensible of wrong,
Restrain'd by shame, was forc'd to hold my tongue.
To hear an open slander, is a curse:
But not to find an answer, is a worse.
If I am Heav'n-begot, assert your son
By some sure sign; and make my father known,
To right my honour, and redeem your own.
He said, and saying cast his arms about
Her neck, and beg'd her to resolve the doubt.

  'Tis hard to judge if *Clymenè* were mov'd
More by his pray'r, whom she so dearly lov'd,
Or more with fury fir'd, to find her name
Traduc'd, and made the sport of common fame.
She stretch'd her arms to Heav'n, and fix'd her eyes
On that fair planet that adorns the skies;
Now by those beams, said she, whose holy fires
Consume my breast, and kindle my desires;
By him, who sees us both, and chears our sight,
By him, the publick minister of light,
I swear that *Sun* begot thee; if I lye,
Let him his chearful influence deny:
Let him no more this perjur'd creature see;
And shine on all the world but only me.

If still you doubt your mother's innocence,
His eastern mansion is not far from hence;
With little pains you to his *Levè* go,
And from himself your parentage may know.
With joy th' ambitious youth his mother heard,
And eager, for the journey soon prepar'd.
He longs the world beneath him to survey;
To guide the chariot; and to give the day:
From *Meroe's* burning sands he bends his course,
Nor less in *India* feels his father's force:
His travel urging, till he came in sight;
And saw the palace by the purple light.

The End of the First Book.

THE Sun's bright palace, on high columns rais'd,
With burnish'd gold and flaming jewels blaz'd;
The folding gates diffus'd a silver light,
And with a milder gleam refresh'd the sight;
Of polish'd iv'ry was the cov'ring wrought:
The matter vied not with the sculptor's thought,
For in the portal was display'd on high
(The work of *Vulcan*) a fictitious sky;
A waving sea th' inferiour Earth embrac'd,
And Gods and Goddesses the waters grac'd.
Aegeon here a mighty whale bestrode;
Triton, and *Proteus* (the deceiving God)
With *Doris* here were carv'd, and all her train,
Some loosely swimming in the figur'd main,
While some on rocks their dropping hair divide,
And some on fishes through the waters glide:
Tho' various features did the sisters grace,
A sister's likeness was in ev'ry face.
On Earth a diff'rent landskip courts the eyes,
Men, towns, and beasts in distant prospects rise,
And nymphs, and streams, and woods, and rural deities.
O'er all, the Heav'n's refulgent image shines;
On either gate were six engraven signs.

    Here *Phaeton* still gaining on th' ascent,
To his suspected father's palace went,
'Till pressing forward through the bright abode,
He saw at distance the illustrious God:
He saw at distance, or the dazling light
Had flash'd too strongly on his aking sight.

    The God sits high, exalted on a throne
Of blazing gems, with purple garments on;
The Hours, in order rang'd on either hand,
And Days, and Months, and Years, and Ages stand.
Here Spring appears with flow'ry chaplets bound;

Here Summer in her wheaten garland crown'd;
Here Autumn the rich trodden grapes besmear;
And hoary Winter shivers in the reer.
  Phoebus beheld the youth from off his throne;
That eye, which looks on all, was fix'd in one.
He saw the boy's confusion in his face,
Surpriz'd at all the wonders of the place;
And cries aloud, "What wants my son? for know
My son thou art, and I must call thee so."
"Light of the world," the trembling youth replies,
"Illustrious parent! since you don't despise
The parent's name, some certain token give,
That I may *Clymenè's* proud boast believe,
Nor longer under false reproaches grieve."
  The tender sire was touch'd with what he said,
And flung the blaze of glories from his head,
And bid the youth advance: "My son," said he,
"Come to thy father's arms! for *Clymenè*
Has told thee true; a parent's name I own,
And deem thee worthy to be called my son.
As a sure proof, make some request, and I,
Whate'er it be, with that request comply;
By *Styx* I swear, whose waves are hid in night,
And roul impervious to my piercing sight."
The youth transported, asks, without delay,
To guide the sun's bright chariot for a day.
  The God repented of the oath he took,
For anguish thrice his radiant head he shook;
"My son," says he, "some other proof require,
Rash was my promise, rash is thy desire.
I'd fain deny this wish, which thou hast made,
Or, what I can't deny, wou'd fain disswade.
Too vast and hazardous the task appears,
Nor suited to thy strength, nor to thy years.
Thy lot is mortal, but thy wishes fly

Beyond the province of mortality:
There is not one of all the Gods that dares
(However skill'd in other great affairs)
To mount the burning axle-tree, but I;
Not *Jove* himself, the ruler of the sky,
That hurles the three-fork'd thunder from above,
Dares try his strength: yet who so strong as *Jove*?
The steeds climb up the first ascent with pain,
And when the middle firmament they gain,
If downward from the Heav'ns my head I bow,
And see the Earth and Ocean hang below,
Ev'n I am seiz'd with horror and affright,
And my own heart misgives me at the sight.
A mighty downfal steeps the ev'ning stage,
And steddy reins must curb the horses' rage.
Tethys herself has fear'd to see me driv'n
Down headlong from the precipice of Heav'n.
Besides, consider what impetuous force
Turns stars and planets in a diff'rent course.
I steer against their motions; nor am I
Born back by all the current of the sky.
But how cou'd you resist the orbs that roul
In adverse whirls, and stem the rapid pole?
But you perhaps may hope for pleasing woods,
And stately dooms, and cities fill'd with Gods;
While through a thousand snares your progress lies,
Where forms of starry monsters stock the skies:
For, shou'd you hit the doubtful way aright,
The bull with stooping horns stands opposite;
Next him the bright *Haemonian* bow is strung,
And next, the lion's grinning visage hung:
The scorpion's claws, here clasp a wide extent;
And here the crab's in lesser clasps are bent.
Nor wou'd you find it easie to compose
The mettled steeds, when from their nostrils flows

The scorching fire, that in their entrails glows.
Ev'n I their head-strong fury scarce restrain,
When they grow warm and restif to the rein.
Let not my son a fatal gift require,
But, O! in time, recall your rash desire;
You ask a gift that may your parent tell,
Let these my fears your parentage reveal;
And learn a father from a father's care:
Look on my face; or if my heart lay bare,
Cou'd you but look, you'd read the father there.
Chuse out a gift from seas, or Earth, or skies,
For open to your wish all Nature lies,
Only decline this one unequal task,
For 'tis a mischief, not a gift, you ask.
You ask a real mischief, *Phaeton*:
Nay hang not thus about my neck, my son:
I grant your wish, and *Styx* has heard my voice,
Chuse what you will, but make a wiser choice."

    Thus did the God th' unwary youth advise;
But he still longs to travel through the skies.
When the fond father (for in vain he pleads)
At length to the *Vulcanian* Chariot leads.
A golden axle did the work uphold,
Gold was the beam, the wheels were orb'd with gold.
The spokes in rows of silver pleas'd the sight,
The seat with party-colour'd gems was bright;
Apollo shin'd amid the glare of light.
The youth with secret joy the work surveys,
When now the moon disclos'd her purple rays;
The stars were fled, for *Lucifer* had chased
The stars away, and fled himself at last.
Soon as the father saw the rosy morn,
And the moon shining with a blunter horn,
He bid the nimble *Hours*, without delay,
Bring forth the steeds; the nimble *Hours* obey:

From their full racks the gen'rous steeds retire,
Dropping ambrosial foams, and snorting fire.
Still anxious for his son, the God of day,
To make him proof against the burning ray,
His temples with celestial ointment wet,
Of sov'reign virtue to repel the heat;
Then fix'd the beamy circle on his head,
And fetch'd a deep foreboding sigh, and said,
"Take this at least, this last advice, my son,
Keep a stiff rein, and move but gently on:
The coursers of themselves will run too fast,
Your art must be to moderate their haste.
Drive 'em not on directly through the skies,
But where the *Zodiac's* winding circle lies,
Along the midmost *Zone*; but sally forth
Nor to the distant south, nor stormy north.
The horses' hoofs a beaten track will show,
But neither mount too high, nor sink too low.
That no new fires, or Heav'n, or Earth infest;
Keep the mid way, the middle way is best.
Nor, where in radiant folds the serpent twines,
Direct your course, nor where the altar shines.
Shun both extreams; the rest let Fortune guide,
And better for thee than thy self provide!
See, while I speak, the shades disperse away,
Aurora gives the promise of a day;
I'm call'd, nor can I make a longer stay.
Snatch up the reins; or still th' attempt forsake,
And not my chariot, but my counsel, take,
While yet securely on the Earth you stand;
Nor touch the horses with too rash a hand.
Let me alone to light the world, while you
Enjoy those beams which you may safely view."
He spoke in vain; the youth with active heat
And sprightly vigour vaults into the seat;

And joys to hold the reins, and fondly gives
Those thanks his father with remorse receives.
    Mean-while the restless horses neigh'd aloud,
Breathing out fire, and pawing where they stood.
Tethys, not knowing what had past, gave way,
And all the waste of Heav'n before 'em lay.
They spring together out, and swiftly bear
The flying youth thro' clouds and yielding air;
With wingy speed outstrip the eastern wind,
And leave the breezes of the morn behind.
The youth was light, nor cou'd he fill the seat,
Or poise the chariot with its wonted weight:
But as at sea th' unballass'd vessel rides,
Cast to and fro, the sport of winds and tides;
So in the bounding chariot toss'd on high,
The youth is hurry'd headlong through the sky.
Soon as the steeds perceive it, they forsake
Their stated course, and leave the beaten track.
The youth was in a maze, nor did he know
Which way to turn the reins, or where to go;
Nor wou'd the horses, had he known, obey.
Then the sev'n stars first felt *Apollo*'s ray,
And wish'd to dip in the forbidden sea.
The folded serpent next the frozen pole,
Stiff and benum'd before, began to rowle,
And raged with inward heat, and threaten'd war,
And shot a redder light from ev'ry star;
Nay, and 'tis said *Bootes* too, that fain
Thou woud'st have fled, tho' cumber'd with thy wane.
    Th' unhappy youth then, bending down his head,
Saw Earth and Ocean far beneath him spread.
His colour chang'd, he startled at the sight,
And his eyes darken'd by too great a light.
Now cou'd he wish the fiery steeds untry'd,
His birth obscure, and his request deny'd:

Now wou'd he *Merops* for his father own,
And quit his boasted kindred to the sun.

  So fares the pilot, when his ship is tost
In troubled seas, and all its steerage lost,
He gives her to the winds, and in despair
Seeks his last refuge in the Gods and pray'r.

  What cou'd he do? his eyes, if backward cast,
Find a long path he had already past;
If forward, still a longer path they find:
Both he compares, and measures in his mind;
And sometimes casts an eye upon the east,
And sometimes looks on the forbidden west,
The horses' names he knew not in the fright,
Nor wou'd he loose the reins, nor cou'd he hold 'em right.

  Now all the horrors of the Heav'ns he spies,
And monstrous shadows of prodigious size,
That, deck'd with stars, lye scatter'd o'er the skies.
There is a place above, where *Scorpio* bent
In tail and arms surrounds a vast extent;
In a wide circuit of the Heav'ns he shines,
And fills the space of two coelestial signs.
Soon as the youth beheld him vex'd with heat
Brandish his sting, and in his poison sweat,
Half dead with sudden fear he dropt the reins;
The horses felt 'em loose upon their mains,
And, flying out through all the plains above,
Ran uncontroul'd where-e're their fury drove;
Rush'd on the stars, and through a pathless way
Of unknown regions hurry'd on the day.
And now above, and now below they flew,
And near the Earth the burning chariot drew.

  The clouds disperse in fumes, the wond'ring Moon
Beholds her brother's steeds beneath her own;
The highlands smoak, cleft by the piercing rays,
Or, clad with woods, in their own fewel blaze.

Next o'er the plains, where ripen'd harvests grow,
The running conflagration spreads below.
But these are trivial ills: whole cities burn,
And peopled kingdoms into ashes turn.

   The mountains kindle as the car draws near,
Athos and *Tmolus* red with fires appear;
Oeagrian Haemus (then a single name)
And virgin *Helicon* increase the flame;
Taurus and *Oetè* glare amid the sky,
And *Ida*, spight of all her fountains, dry.
Eryx, and *Othrys*, and *Cithaeron*, glow,
And *Rhodopè*, no longer cloath'd in snow;
High *Pindus*, *Mimas*, and *Parnassus*, sweat,
And *Aetna* rages with redoubled heat.
Ev'n *Scythia*, through her hoary regions warm'd,
In vain with all her native frost was arm'd.
Cover'd with flames the tow'ring *Appennine*,
And *Caucasus*, and proud *Olympus*, shine;
And, where the long-extended *Alpes* aspire,
Now stands a huge continu'd range of fire.

   Th' astonisht youth, where-e'er his eyes cou'd turn,
Beheld the universe around him burn:
The world was in a blaze; nor cou'd he bear
The sultry vapours and the scorching air,
Which from below, as from a furnace, flow'd;
And now the axle-tree beneath him glow'd:
Lost in the whirling clouds that round him broke,
And white with ashes, hov'ring in the smoke.
He flew where-e'er the horses drove, nor knew
Whither the horses drove, or where he flew.

   'Twas then, they say, the swarthy *Moor* begun
To change his hue, and blacken in the sun.
Then *Libya* first, of all her moisture drain'd,
Became a barren waste, a wild of sand.
The water-nymphs lament their empty urns,

Boeotia, robb's of silve *Dirce*, mourns,
Corinth Pyrene's wasted spring bewails,
And *Argos* grieves whilst *Amymonè* fails.
　　The floods are drain'd from ev'ry distant coast,
Ev'n *Tanais*, tho' fix'd in ice, was lost.
Enrag'd *Caïcus* and *Lycormas* roar,
And *Xanthus*, fated to be burnt once more.
The fam'd *Maeander*, that unweary'd strays
Through mazy windings, smoaks in ev'ry maze.
From his lov'd *Babylon Euphrates* flies;
The big-swoln *Ganges* and the *Danube* rise
In thick'ning fumes, and darken half the skies.
In flames *Ismenos* and the *Phasis* roul'd,
And *Tagus* floating in his melted gold.
The swans, that on *Caÿster* often try'd
Their tuneful songs, now sung their last and dy'd.
The frighted *Nile* ran off, and under ground
Conceal'd his head, nor can it yet be found:
His sev'n divided currents all are dry,
And where they row'ld, sev'n gaping trenches lye:
No more the *Rhine* or *Rhone* their course maintain,
Nor *Tiber*, of his promis'd empire vain.
　　The ground, deep-cleft, admits the dazling ray,
And startles *Pluto* with the flash of day.
The seas shrink in, and to the sight disclose
Wide naked plains, where once their billows rose;
Their rocks are all discover'd, and increase
The number of the scatter'd *Cyclades*.
The fish in sholes about the bottom creep,
Nor longer dares the crooked dolphin leap:
Gasping for breath, th' unshapen *Phocae* die,
And on the boiling wave extended lye.
Nereus, and *Doris* with her virgin train,
Seek out the last recesses of the main;
Beneath unfathomable depths they faint,

And secret in their gloomy caverns pant.
Stern *Neptune* thrice above the waves upheld
His face, and thrice was by the flames repell'd.
    The *Earth* at length, on ev'ry side embrac'd
With scalding seas that floated round her waste,
When now she felt the springs and rivers come,
And crowd within the hollow of her womb,
Up-lifted to the Heav'ns her blasted head,
And clapt her hand upon her brows, and said
(But first, impatient of the sultry heat,
Sunk deeper down, and sought a cooler seat):
"If you, great king of Gods, my death approve,
And I deserve it, let me die by *Jove*;
If I must perish by the force of fire,
Let me transfix'd with thunder-bolts expire.
See, whilst I speak, my breath the vapours choak
(For now her face lay wrapt in clouds of smoak),
See my singe'd hair, behold my faded eye,
And wither'd face, where heaps of cinders lye!
And does the plow for this my body tear?
This the reward for all the fruits I bear,
Tortur'd with rakes, and harrass'd all the year?
That herbs for cattle daily I renew,
And food for Man, and frankincense for you?
But grant me guilty; what has *Neptune* done?
Why are his waters boiling in the sun?
The wavy empire, which by lot was giv'n,
Why does it waste, and further shrink from Heav'n?
If I nor he your pity can provoke,
See your own Heav'ns, the Heav'ns begin to smoke!
Shou'd once the sparkles catch those bright abodes,
Destruction seizes on the Heav'ns and Gods;
Atlas becomes unequal to his freight,
And almost faints beneath the glowing weight.
If Heav'n, and Earth, and sea, together burn,

All must again into their chaos turn.
Apply some speedy cure, prevent our fate,
And succour Nature, ere it be too late."
She cea'sd, for choak'd with vapours round her spread,
Down to the deepest shades she sunk her head.

 Jove call'd to witness ev'ry Pow'r above,
And ev'n the God, whose son the chariot drove,
That what he acts he is compell'd to do,
Or universal ruin must ensue.
Strait he ascends the high aetherial throne,
From whence he us'd to dart his thunder down,
From whence his show'rs and storms he us'd to pour,
But now cou'd meet with neither storm nor show'r.
Then, aiming at the youth, with lifted hand,
Full at his head he hurl'd the forky brand,
In dreadful thund'rings. Thus th' almighty sire
Suppress'd the raging of the fires with fire.

 At once from life and from the chariot driv'n,
Th' ambitious boy fell thunder-struck from Heav'n.
The horses started with a sudden bound,
And flung the reins and chariot to the ground:
The studded harness from their necks they broke,
Here fell a wheel, and here a silver spoke,
Here were the beam and axle torn away;
And, scatter'd o'er the Earth, the shining fragments lay.
The breathless *Phaeton*, with flaming hair,
Shot from the chariot, like a falling star,
That in a summer's ev'ning from the top
Of Heav'n drops down, or seems at least to drop;
'Till on the *Po* his blasted corps was hurl'd,
Far from his country, in the western world.

 The *Latian* nymphs came round him, and, amaz'd,
On the dead youth, transfix'd with thunder, gaz'd;
And, whilst yet smoking from the bolt he lay,
His shatter'd body to a tomb convey,

And o'er the tomb an epitaph devise:
"Here he, who drove the sun's bright chariot, lies;
His father's fiery steeds he cou'd not guide,
But in the glorious enterprize he dy'd."

Apollo hid his face, and pin'd for grief,
And, if the story may deserve belief,
The space of one whole day is said to run,
From morn to wonted ev'n, without a sun:
The burning ruins, with a fainter ray,
Supply the sun, and counterfeit a day,
A day, that still did Nature's face disclose:
This comfort from the mighty mischief rose.

But *Clymenè*, enrag'd with grief, laments,
And as her grief inspires, her passion vents:
Wild for her son, and frantick in her woes,
With hair dishevel'd round the world she goes,
To seek where-e'er his body might be cast;
'Till, on the borders of the *Po*, at last
The name inscrib'd on the new tomb appears.
The dear dear name she bathes in flowing tears,
Hangs o'er the tomb, unable to depart,
And hugs the marble to her throbbing heart.

Her daughters too lament, and sigh, and mourn
(A fruitless tribute to their brother's urn),
And beat their naked bosoms, and complain,
And call aloud for *Phaeton* in vain:
All the long night their mournful watch they keep,
And all the day stand round the tomb, and weep.

Four times, revolving, the full moon return'd;
So long the mother and the daughters mourn'd:
When now the eldest, *Phaethusa*, strove
To rest her weary limbs, but could not move;
Lampetia wou'd have help'd her, but she found
Her self with-held, and rooted to the ground:
A third in wild affliction, as she grieves,

Wou'd rend her hair, but fills her hands with leaves;
One sees her thighs transform'd, another views
Her arms shot out, and branching into boughs.
And now their legs, and breasts, and bodies stood
Crusted with bark, and hard'ning into wood;
But still above were female heads display'd,
And mouths, that call'd the mother to their aid.
What cou'd, alas! the weeping mother do?
From this to that with eager haste she flew,
And kiss'd her sprouting daughters as they grew.
She tears the bark that to each body cleaves,
And from their verdant fingers strips the leaves:
The blood came trickling, where she tore away
The leaves and bark: the maids were heard to say,
"Forbear, mistaken parent, oh! forbear;
A wounded daughter in each tree you tear;
Farewell for ever." Here the bark encreas'd,
Clos'd on their faces, and their words suppress'd.

　　The new-made trees in tears of amber run,
Which, harden'd into value by the sun,
Distill for ever on the streams below:
The limpid streams their radiant treasure show,
Mixt in the sand; whence the rich drops convey'd
Shine in the dress of the bright *Latian* maid.

　　Cycnus beheld the nymphs transform'd, ally'd
To their dead brother on the mortal side,
In friendship and affection nearer bound;
He left the cities and the realms he own'd,
Thro' pathless fields and lonely shores to range,
And woods made thicker by the sisters' change.
Whilst here, within the dismal gloom, alone,
The melancholy monarch made his moan,
His voice was lessen'd, as he try'd to speak,
And issu'd through a long-extended neck;
His hair transforms to down, his fingers meet

In skinny films, and shape his oary feet;
From both his sides the wings and feathers break;
And from his mouth proceeds a blunted beak:
All *Cycnus* now into a Swan was turn'd,
Who, still remembring how his kinsman burn'd,
To solitary pools and lakes retires,
And loves the waters as oppos'd to fires.

  Mean-while *Apollo* in a gloomy shade
(The native lustre of his brows decay'd)
Indulging sorrow, sickens at the sight
Of his own sun-shine, and abhors the light;
The hidden griefs, that in his bosom rise,
Sadden his looks and over-cast his eyes,
As when some dusky orb obstructs his ray,
And sullies in a dim eclipse the day.

  Now secretly with inward griefs he pin'd,
Now warm resentments to his griefs he joyn'd,
And now renounc'd his office to mankind.
"Ere since the birth of time," said he, "I've born
A long ungrateful toil, without return;
Let now some other manage, if he dare,
The fiery steeds, and mount the burning carr;
Or, if none else, let *Jove* his fortune try,
And learn to lay his murd'ring thunder by;
Then will he own, perhaps, but own too late,
My son deserv'd not so severe a fate."

  The Gods stand round him, as he mourns, and pray
He would resume the conduct of the day,
Nor let the world be lost in endless night:
Jove too himself descending from his height,
Excuses what had happen'd, and intreats,
Majestically mixing pray'rs and threats.
Prevail'd upon at length, again he took
The harness'd steeds, that still with horror shook,
And plies 'em with the lash, and whips 'em on,

And, as he whips, upbraids 'em with his son.
The day was settled in its course; and *Jove*
Walk'd the wide circuit of the Heavens above,
To search if any cracks or flaws were made;
But all was safe: the Earth he then survey'd,
And cast an eye on ev'ry diff'rent coast,
And ev'ry land; but on *Arcadia* most.
Her fields he cloath'd, and chear'd her blasted face
With running fountains, and with springing grass.
No tracks of Heav'n's destructive fire remain,
The fields and woods revive, and Nature smiles again.

But as the God walk'd to and fro the Earth,
And rais'd the plants, and gave the spring its birth,
By chance a fair *Arcadian* nymph he view'd,
And felt the lovely charmer in his blood.
The nymph nor spun, nor dress'd with artful pride,
Her vest was gather'd up, her hair was ty'd;
Now in her hand a slender spear she bore,
Now a light quiver on her shoulders wore;
To chaste *Diana* from her youth inclin'd,
The sprightly warriors of the wood she joyn'd.
Diana too the gentle huntress lov'd,
Nor was there one of all the nymphs that rov'd
O'er *Maenalus*, amid the maiden throng,
More favour'd once; but favour lasts not long.

The sun now shone in all its strength, and drove
The heated virgin panting to a grove;
The grove around a grateful shadow cast:
She dropt her arrows, and her bow unbrac'd;
She flung her self on the cool grassy bed;
And on the painted quiver rais'd her head,
Jove saw the charming huntress unprepar'd,
Stretch'd on the verdant turf, without a guard.
"Here I am safe," he cries, "from *Juno's* eye;
Or shou'd my jealous queen the theft descry,

Yet wou'd I venture on a theft like this,
And stand her rage for such, for such a bliss!"
Diana's shape and habit strait he took,
Soften'd his brows, and smooth'd his awful look,
And mildly in a female accent spoke.
"How fares my girl? How went the morning chase?"
To whom the virgin, starting from the grass,
"All hail, bright deity, whom I prefer
To *Jove* himself, tho' *Jove* himself were here."
The God was nearer than she thought, and heard
Well-pleas'd himself before himself preferr'd.

He then salutes her with a warm embrace;
And, e're she half had told the morning chase,
With love enflam'd, and eager on his bliss,
Smother'd her words, and stop'd her with a kiss;
His kisses with unwonted ardour glow'd,
Nor cou'd *Diana's* shape conceal the God.
The virgin did whate'er a virgin cou'd
(Sure *Juno* must have pardon'd, had she view'd);
With all her might against his force she strove;
But how can mortal maids contend with *Jove*?

Possest at length of what his heart desir'd,
Back to his Heav'ns, th' exulting God retir'd.
The lovely huntress, rising from the grass,
With down-cast eyes, and with a blushing face,
By shame confounded, and by fear dismay'd,
Flew from the covert of the guilty shade,
And almost, in the tumult of her mind,
Left her forgotten bow and shafts behind.

But now *Diana*, with a sprightly train
Of quiver'd virgins, bounding o'er the plain,
Call'd to the nymph; the nymph began to fear
A second fraud, a *Jove* disguis'd in her;
But, when she saw the sister nymphs, suppress'd
Her rising fears, and mingled with the rest.

How in the look does conscious guilt appear!
Slowly she mov'd, and loiter'd in the rear;
Nor lightly tripp'd, nor by the Goddess ran,
As once she us'd, the foremost of the train.
Her looks were flush'd, and sullen was her mien,
That sure the virgin Goddess (had she been
Aught but a virgin) must the guilt have seen.
'Tis said the nymphs saw all, and guess'd aright:
And now the moon had nine times lost her light,
When *Dian*, fainting in the mid-day beams,
Found a cool covert, and refreshing streams
That in soft murmurs through the forest flow'd,
And a smooth bed of shining gravel show'd.

A covert so obscure, and streams so clear,
The Goddess prais'd: "And now no spies are near
Let's strip, my gentle maids, and wash," she cries.
Pleas'd with the motion, every maid complies;
Only the blushing huntress stood confus'd,
And form'd delays, and her delays excus'd;
In vain excus'd: her fellows round her press'd,
And the reluctant nymph by force undress'd,
The naked huntress all her shame reveal'd,
In vain her hands the pregnant womb conceal'd;
"Begone!" the Goddess cries with stern disdain,
"Begone! nor dare the hallow'd stream to stain":
She fled, for ever banish'd from the train.

This *Juno* heard, who long had watch'd her time
To punish the detested rival's crime;
The time was come; for, to enrage her more,
A lovely boy the teeming rival bore.

The Goddess cast a furious look, and cry'd,
"It is enough! I'm fully satisfy'd!
This boy shall stand a living mark, to prove
My husband's baseness and the strumpet's love:
But vengeance shall awake: those guilty charms

That drew the Thunderer from *Juno's* arms,
No longer shall their wonted force retain,
Nor please the God, nor make the mortal vain."
    This said, her hand within her hair she wound,
Swung her to Earth, and drag'd her on the ground:
The prostrate wretch lifts up her arms in pray'r;
Her arms grow shaggy, and deform'd with hair,
Her nails are sharpen'd into pointed claws,
Her hands bear half her weight, and turn to paws;
Her lips, that once cou'd tempt a God, begin
To grow distorted in an ugly grin.
And, lest the supplicating brute might reach
The ears of *Jove*, she was depriv'd of speech:
Her surly voice thro' a hoarse passage came
In savage sounds: her mind was still the same,
The furry monster fix'd her eyes above,
And heav'd her new unwieldy paws to *Jove*,
And beg'd his aid with inward groans; and tho'
She could not call him false, she thought him so.
    How did she fear to lodge in woods alone,
And haunt the fields and meadows, once her own!
How often wou'd the deep-mouth'd dogs pursue,
Whilst from her hounds the frighted huntress flew!
How did she fear her fellow-brutes, and shun
The shaggy bear, tho' now her self was one!
How from the sight of rugged wolves retire,
Although the grim *Lycaon* was her sire!
    But now her son had fifteen summers told,
Fierce at the chase, and in the forest bold;
When, as he beat the woods in quest of prey,
He chanc'd to rouze his mother where she lay.
She knew her son, and kept him in her sight,
And fondly gaz'd: the boy was in a fright,
And aim'd a pointed arrow at her breast,
And would have slain his mother in the beast;

But *Jove* forbad, and snatch'd 'em through the air
In whirlwinds up to Heav'n, and fix'd 'em there!
Where the new constellations nightly rise,
And add a lustre to the northern skies.
    When *Juno* saw the rival in her height,
Spangled with stars, and circled round with light,
She sought old *Ocean* in his deep abodes,
And *Tethys*, both rever'd among the Gods.
They ask what brings her there: "Ne'er ask," says she,
"What brings me here, Heav'n is no place for me.
You'll see, when night has cover'd all things o'er,
Jove's starry bastard and triumphant whore
Usurp the Heav'ns; you'll see 'em proudly rowle
And who shall now on *Juno's* altars wait,
When those she hates grow greater by her hate?
I on the nymph a brutal form impress'd,
Jove to a goddess has transform'd the beast;
This, this was all my weak revenge could do:
But let the God his chaste amours pursue,
And, as he acted after *Io's* rape,
Restore th' adultress to her former shape;
Then may he cast his *Juno* off, and lead
The great *Lycaon's* offspring to his bed.
But you, ye venerable Pow'rs, be kind,
And, if my wrongs a due resentment find,
Receive not in your waves their setting beams,
Nor let the glaring strumpet taint your streams."
    The Goddess ended, and her wish was giv'n.
Back she return'd in triumph up to Heav'n;
Her gawdy peacocks drew her through the skies.
Their tails were spotted with a thousand eyes;
The eyes of *Argus* on their tails were rang'd,
At the same time the raven's colour chang'd.
    The raven once in snowy plumes was drest,
White as the whitest dove's unsully'd breast,

Fair as the guardian of the Capitol,
Soft as the swan; a large and lovely fowl;
His tongue, his prating tongue had chang'd him quite
To sooty blackness, from the purest white.

   The story of his change shall here be told;
In *Thessaly* there liv'd a nymph of old,
Coronis nam'd; a peerless maid she shin'd,
Confest the fairest of the fairer kind.
Apollo lov'd her, 'till her guilt he knew,
While true she was, or whilst he thought her true.
But his own bird the raven chanc'd to find
The false one with a secret rival joyn'd.
Coronis begg'd him to suppress the tale,
But could not with repeated pray'rs prevail.
His milk-white pinions to the God he ply'd;
The busy daw flew with him, side by side,
And by a thousand teizing questions drew
Th' important secret from him as they flew.
The daw gave honest counsel, tho' despis'd,
And, tedious in her tattle, thus advis'd:
"Stay, silly bird, th' ill-natur'd task refuse,
Nor be the bearer of unwelcome news.
Be warn'd by my example: you discern
What now I am, and what I was shall learn.
My foolish honesty was all my crime;
Then hear my story. Once upon a time,
The two-shap'd *Ericthonius* had his birth
(Without a mother) from the teeming Earth;
Minerva nurs'd him, and the infant laid
Within a chest, of twining osiers made.
The daughters of king *Cecrops* undertook
To guard the chest, commanded not to look
On what was hid within. I stood to see
The charge obey'd, perch'd on a neighb'ring tree.
The sisters *Pandrosos* and *Hersé* keep

The strict command; *Aglauros* needs would peep,
And saw the monstrous infant, in a fright,
And call'd her sisters to the hideous sight:
A boy's soft shape did to the waste prevail,
But the boy ended in a dragon's tail.
I told the stern *Minerva* all that pass'd;
But for my pains, discarded and disgrac'd,
The frowning Goddess drove me from her sight,
And for her fav'rite chose the bird of night.
Be then no tell-tale; for I think my wrong
Enough to teach a bird to hold her tongue.

But you, perhaps, may think I was remov'd,
As never by the heav'nly maid belov'd:
But I was lov'd; ask *Pallas* if I lye;
Tho' *Pallas* hate me now, she won't deny:
For I, whom in a feather'd shape you view,
Was once a maid (by Heav'n the story's true)
A blooming maid, and a king's daughter too.
A crowd of lovers own'd my beauty's charms;
My beauty was the cause of all my harms;
Neptune, as on his shores I wont to rove,
Observ'd me in my walks, and fell in love.
He made his courtship, he confess'd his pain,
And offer'd force, when all his arts were vain;
Swift he pursu'd: I ran along the strand,
'Till, spent and weary'd on the sinking sand,
I shriek'd aloud, with cries I fill'd the air
To Gods and men; nor God nor man was there:
A virgin Goddess heard a virgin's pray'r.
For, as my arms I lifted to the skies,
I saw black feathers from my fingers rise;
I strove to fling my garment on the ground;
My garment turn'd to plumes, and girt me round:
My hands to beat my naked bosom try;
Nor naked bosom now nor hands had I:

Lightly I tript, nor weary as before
Sunk in the sand, but skim'd along the shore;
'Till, rising on my wings, I was preferr'd
To be the chaste *Minerva's* virgin bird:
Preferr'd in vain! I am now in disgrace:
Nyctimenè the owl enjoys my place.

On her incestuous life I need not dwell
(In *Lesbos* still the horrid tale they tell),
And of her dire amours you must have heard,
For which she now does penance in a bird,
That conscious of her shame, avoids the light,
And loves the gloomy cov'ring of the night;
The birds, where-e'er she flutters, scare away
The hooting wretch, and drive her from the day."

The raven, urg'd by such impertinence,
Grew passionate, it seems, and took offence,
And curst the harmless daw; the daw withdrew:
The raven to her injur'd patron flew,
And found him out, and told the fatal truth
Of false *Coronis* and the favour'd youth.

The God was wroth; the colour left his look,
The wreath his head, the harp his hand forsook:
His silver bow and feather'd shafts he took,
And lodg'd an arrow in the tender breast,
That had so often to his own been prest.
Down fell the wounded nymph, and sadly groan'd,
And pull'd his arrow reeking from the wound;
And weltring in her blood, thus faintly cry'd,
"Ah cruel God! tho' I have justly dy'd,
What has, alas! my unborn infant done,
That he should fall, and two expire in one?"
This said, in agonies she fetch'd her breath.

The God dissolves in pity at her death;
He hates the bird that made her falshood known,
And hates himself for what himself had done;

The feather'd shaft, that sent her to the Fates,
And his own hand, that sent the shaft, he hates.
Fain would he heal the wound, and ease her pain,
And tries the compass of his art in vain.
Soon as he saw the lovely nymph expire,
The pile made ready, and the kindling fire.
With sighs and groans her obsequies he kept,
And, if a God could weep, the God had wept.
Her corps he kiss'd, and heav'nly incense brought,
And solemniz'd the death himself had wrought.

But lest his offspring should her fate partake,
Spight of th' immortal mixture in his make,
He ript her womb, and set the child at large,
And gave him to the centaur *Chiron's* charge:
Then in his fury black'd the raven o'er,
And bid him prate in his white plumes no more.

Old *Chiron* took the babe with secret joy,
Proud of the charge of the celestial boy.
His daughter too, whom on the sandy shore
The nymph *Charicle* to the centaur bore,
With hair dishevel'd on her shoulders, came
To see the child, *Ocyrrhoë* was her name;
She knew her father's arts, and could rehearse
The depths of prophecy in sounding verse.
Once, as the sacred infant she survey'd,
The God was kindled in the raving maid,
And thus she utter'd her prophetick tale:
"Hail, great physician of the world, all-hail;
Hail, mighty infant, who in years to come
Shalt heal the nations, and defraud the tomb;
Swift be thy growth! thy triumphs unconfin'd!
Make kingdoms thicker, and increase mankind.
Thy daring art shall animate the dead,
And draw the thunder on thy guilty head:
Then shalt thou dye, but from the dark abode

Rise up victorious, and be twice a God.
And thou, my sire, not destin'd by thy birth
To turn to dust, and mix with common earth,
How wilt thou toss, and rave, and long to dye,
And quit thy claim to immortality;
When thou shalt feel, enrag'd with inward pains,
The *Hydra's* venom rankling in thy veins?
The Gods, in pity, shall contract thy date,
And give thee over to the pow'r of Fate."

    Thus entring into destiny, the maid
The secrets of offended *Jove* betray'd:
More had she still to say; but now appears
Oppress'd with sobs and sighs, and drown'd in tears.
"My voice," says she, "is gone, my language fails;
Through ev'ry limb my kindred shape prevails:
Why did the God this fatal gift impart,
And with prophetick raptures swell my heart!
What new desires are these? I long to pace
O'er flow'ry meadows, and to feed on grass;
I hasten to a brute, a maid no more;
But why, alas! am I transform'd all o'er?
My sire does half a human shape retain,
And in his upper parts preserve the man."

    Her tongue no more distinct complaints affords,
But in shrill accents and mis-shapen words
Pours forth such hideous wailings, as declare
The human form confounded in the mare:
'Till by degrees accomplish'd in the beast,
She neigh'd outright, and all the steed exprest.
Her stooping body on her hands is born,
Her hands are turn'd to hoofs, and shod in horn,
Her yellow tresses ruffle in a mane,
And in a flowing tail she frisks her train,
The mare was finish'd in her voice and look,
And a new name from the new figure took.

Sore wept the centaur, and to *Phoebus* pray'd;
But how could *Phoebus* give the centaur aid?
Degraded of his pow'r by angry *Jove*,
In *Elis* then a herd of beeves he drove;
And wielded in his hand a staff of oak,
And o'er his shoulders threw the shepherd's cloak;
On sev'n compacted reeds he us'd to play,
And on his rural pipe to waste the day.

As once attentive to his pipe he play'd,
The crafty *Hermes* from the God convey'd
A drove, that sep'rate from their fellows stray'd.
The theft an old insidious peasant view'd
(They call'd him *Battus* in the neighbourhood),
Hir'd by a vealthy *Pylian* prince to feed
His fav'rite mares, and watch the gen'rous breed.
The thievish God suspected him, and took
The hind aside, and thus in whispers spoke:
"Discover not the theft, whoe'er thou be,
And take that milk-white heifer for thy fee."
"Go, stranger," cries the clown, "securely on,
That stone shall sooner tell," and show'd a stone.

The God withdrew, but strait return'd again,
In speech and habit like a country swain;
And cries out, "Neighbour, hast thou seen a stray
Of bullocks and of heifers pass this way?
In the recov'ry of my cattle join,
A bullock and a heifer shall be thine."
The peasant quick replies, "You'll find 'em there
In yon dark vale"; and in the vale they were.
The double bribe had his false heart beguil'd:
The God, successful in the tryal, smil'd;
"And dost thou thus betray my self to me?
Me to my self dost thou betray?" says he:
Then to a *Touch stone* turns the faithless spy;
And in his name records his infamy.

This done, the God flew up on high, and pass'd
O'er lofty *Athens*, by *Minerva* grac'd,
And wide *Munichia*, whilst his eyes survey
All the vast region that beneath him lay.

'Twas now the feast, when each *Athenian* maid
Her yearly homage to *Minerva* paid;
In canisters, with garlands cover'd o'er,
High on their heads, their mystick gifts they bore:
And now, returning in a solemn train,
The troop of shining virgins fill'd the plain.

The God well pleas'd beheld the pompous show,
And saw the bright procession pass below;
Then veer'd about, and took a wheeling flight,
And hover'd o'er them: as the spreading kite,
That smells the slaughter'd victim from on high,
Flies at a distance, if the priests are nigh,
And sails around, and keeps it in her eye:
So kept the God the virgin quire in view,
And in slow winding circles round them flew.

As *Lucifer* excells the meanest star,
Or, as the full-orb'd *Phoebe*, *Lucifer*;
So much did *Hersè* all the rest outvy,
And gave a grace to the solemnity.
Hermes was fir'd, as in the clouds he hung:
So the cold bullet, that with fury slung
From *Balearick* engines mounts on high,
Glows in the whirl, and burns along the sky.
At length he pitch'd upon the ground, and show'd
The form divine, the features of a God.
He knew their vertue o'er a female heart,
And yet he strives to better them by art.
He hangs his mantle loose, and sets to show
The golden edging on the seam below;
Adjusts his flowing curls, and in his hand
Waves, with an air, the sleep-procuring wand;

The glitt'ring sandals to his feet applies,
And to each heel the well-trim'd pinion ties.

His ornaments with nicest art display'd,
He seeks th' apartment of the royal maid.
The roof was all with polish'd iv'ry lin'd,
That richly mix'd, in clouds of tortoise shin'd.
Three rooms, contiguous, in a range were plac'd,
The midmost by the beauteous *Hersè* grac'd;
Her virgin sisters lodg'd on either side.
Aglauros first th' approaching God descry'd,
And, as he cross'd her chamber, ask'd his name,
And what his business was, and whence he came.
"I come," reply'd the God, "from Heav'n, to woo
Your sister, and to make an aunt of you;
I am the son and messenger of *Jove*;
My name is *Mercury*, my bus'ness love;
Do you, kind damsel, take a lover's part,
And gain admittance to your sister's heart."
She star'd him in the face with looks amaz'd,
As when she on *Minerva's* secret gaz'd,
And asks a mighty treasure for her hire;
And, 'till he brings it, makes the God retire.
Minerva griev'd to see the nymph succeed;
And now remembring the late impious deed,
When, disobedient to her strict command,
She touch'd the chest with an unhallow'd hand;
In big-swoln sighs her inward rage express'd,
That heav'd the rising *Aegis* on her breast;
Then sought out *Envy* in her dark abode,
Defil'd with ropy gore and clots of blood:
Shut from the winds, and from the wholesome skies,
In a deep vale the gloomy dungeon lies,
Dismal and cold, where not a beam of light
Invades the winter, or disturbs the night.

Directly to the cave her course she steer'd;

Against the gates her martial lance she rear'd;
The gates flew open, and the fiend appear'd.
A pois'nous morsel in her teeth she chew'd,
And gorg'd the flesh of vipers for her food.
Minerva loathing turn'd away her eye;
The hideous monster, rising heavily,
Came stalking forward with a sullen pace,
And left her mangled offals on the place.
Soon as she saw the goddess gay and bright,
She fetch'd a groan at such a chearful sight.
Livid and meagre were her looks, her eye
In foul distorted glances turn'd awry;
A hoard of gall her inward parts possess'd,
And spread a greenness o'er her canker'd breast;
Her teeth were brown with rust, and from her tongue,
In dangling drops, the stringy poison hung.
She never smiles but when the wretched weep,
Nor lulls her malice with a moment's sleep,
Restless in spite: while watchful to destroy,
She pines and sickens at another's joy;
Foe to her self, distressing and distrest,
She bears her own tormentor in her breast.
The Goddess gave (for she abhorr'd her sight)
A short command: "To *Athens* speed thy flight;
On curst *Aglauros* try thy utmost art,
And fix thy rankest venoms in her heart."
This said, her spear she push'd against the ground,
And mounting from it with an active bound,
Flew off to Heav'n: the hag with eyes askew
Look'd up, and mutter'd curses as she flew;
For sore she fretted, and began to grieve
At the success which she her self must give.
Then takes her staff, hung round with wreaths of thorn,
And sails along, in a black whirlwind born,
O'er fields and flow'ry meadows: where she steers

Her baneful course, a mighty blast appears,
Mildews and blights; the meadows are defac'd,
The fields, the flow'rs, and the whole years laid waste:
On mortals next, and peopled towns she falls,
And breathes a burning plague among their walls.

When *Athens* she beheld, for arts renown'd,
With peace made happy, and with plenty crown'd,
Scarce could the hideous fiend from tears forbear,
To find out nothing that deserv'd a tear.
Th' apartment now she enter'd, where at rest
Aglauros lay, with gentle sleep opprest.
To execute *Minerva's* dire command,
She stroak'd the virgin with her canker'd hand,
Then prickly thorns into her breast convey'd,
That stung to madness the devoted maid:
Her subtle venom still improves the smart,
Frets in the blood, and festers in the heart.

To make the work more sure, a scene she drew,
And plac'd before the dreaming virgin's view
Her sister's marriage, and her glorious fate:
Th' imaginary bride appears in state;
The bride-groom with unwonted beauty glows:
For envy magnifies what-e'er she shows.

Full of the dream, *Aglauros* pin'd away
In tears all night, in darkness all the day;
Consum'd like ice, that just begins to run,
When feebly smitten by the distant sun;
Or like unwholsome weeds, that set on fire
Are slowly wasted, and in smoke expire.
Giv'n up to envy (for in ev'ry thought
The thorns, the venom, and the vision wrought)
Oft did she call on death, as oft decreed,
Rather than see her sister's wish succeed,
To tell her awfull father what had past:
At length before the door her self she cast;

And, sitting on the ground with sullen pride,
A passage to the love-sick God deny'd.
The God caress'd, and for admission pray'd,
And sooth'd in softest words th' envenom'd maid.
In vain he sooth'd: "Begone!" the maid replies,
"Or here I keep my seat, and never rise."
"Then keep thy seat for ever," cries the God,
And touch'd the door, wide op'ning to his rod.
Fain would she rise, and stop him, but she found
Her trunk too heavy to forsake the ground;
Her joynts are all benum'd, her hands are pale,
And marble now appears in ev'ry nail.
As when a cancer in the body feeds,
And gradual death from limb to limb proceeds;
So does the chilness to each vital parte
Spread by degrees, and creeps into her heart;
'Till hard'ning ev'ry where, and speechless grown,
She sits unmov'd, and freezes to a stone.
But still her envious hue and sullen mien
Are in the sedentary figure seen.

When now the God his fury had allay'd,
And taken vengeance of the stubborn maid,
From where the bright *Athenian* turrets rise
He mounts aloft, and re-ascends the skies.
Jove saw him enter the sublime abodes,
And, as he mix'd among the crowd of Gods,
Beckon'd him out, and drew him from the rest,
And in soft whispers thus his will exprest.

"My trusty *Hermes*, by whose ready aid
Thy sire's commands are through the world convey'd.
Resume thy wings, exert their utmost force,
And to the walls of *Sidon* speed thy course;
There find a herd of heifers wand'ring o'er
The neighb'ring hill, and drive 'em to the shore."

Thus spoke the God, concealing his intent.

The trusty *Hermes* on his message went,
And found the herd of heifers wand'ring o'er
A neighb'ring hill, and drove 'em to the shore;
Where the king's daughter, with a lovely train
Of fellow-nymphs, was sporting on the plain.
   The dignity of empire laid aside,
(For love but ill agrees with kingly pride)
The ruler of the skies, the thund'ring God,
Who shakes the world's foundations with a nod,
Among a herd of lowing heifers ran,
Frisk'd in a bull, and bellow'd o'er the plain.
Large rowles of fat about his shoulders clung,
And from his neck the double dewlap hung.
His skin was whiter than the snow that lies
Unsully'd by the breath of southern skies;
Small shining horns on his curl'd forehead stand,
As turn'd and polish'd by the work-man's hand;
His eye-balls rowl'd, not formidably bright,
But gaz'd and languish'd with a gentle light.
His ev'ry look was peaceful, and exprest
The softness of the lover in the beast.
   Agenor's royal daughter, as she plaid
Among the fields, the milk-white bull survey'd,
And view'd his spotless body with delight,
And at a distance kept him in her sight.
At length she pluck'd the rising flow'rs, and fed
The gentle beast, and fondly stroak'd his head.
He stood well-pleas'd to touch the charming fair,
But hardly could confine his pleasure there.
And now he wantons o'er the neighb'ring strand,
Now rowls his body on the yellow sand;
And, now perceiving all her fears decay'd,
Comes tossing forward to the royal maid;
Gives her his breast to stroke, and downward turns
His grizly brow, and gently stoops his horns.

In flow'ry wreaths the royal virgin drest
His bending horns, and kindly clapt his breast.
'Till now grown wanton and devoid of fear,
Not knowing that she prest the Thunderer,
She plac'd her self upon his back, and rode
O'er fields and meadows, seated on the God.

He gently march'd along, and by degrees
Left the dry meadow, and approach'd the seas;
Where now he dips his hoofs and wets his thighs,
Now plunges in, and carries off the prize.
The frighted nymph looks backward on the shoar,
And hears the tumbling billows round her roar;
But still she holds him fast: one hand is born
Upon his back; the other grasps a horn:
Her train of ruffling garments flies behind,
Swells in the air, and hovers in the wind.

Through storms and tempests he the virgin bore,
And lands her safe on the *Dictean* shore;
Where now, in his divinest form array'd,
In his true shape he captivates the maid;
Who gazes on him, and with wond'ring eyes
Beholds the new majestick figure rise,
His glowing features, and celestial light,
And all the God discover'd to her sight.

The End of the Second Book.

BOOK THE THIRD

WHEN now *Agenor* had his daughter lost,
He sent his son to search on ev'ry coast;
And sternly bid him to his arms restore
The darling maid, or see his face no more,
But live an exile in a foreign clime;
Thus was the father pious to a crime.

    The restless youth search'd all the world around;
But how can *Jove* in his amours be found?
When, tir'd at length with unsuccessful toil,
To shun his angry sire and native soil,
He goes a suppliant to the *Delphick* dome;
There asks the God what new appointed home
Should end his wand'rings, and his toils relieve.
The *Delphick* oracles this answer give.

    "Behold among the fields a lonely cow,
Unworn with yokes, unbroken to the plow;
Mark well the place where first she lays her down,
There measure out thy walls, and build thy town,
And from thy guide *Boeotia* call the land,
In which the destin'd walls and town shall stand."

    No sooner had he left the dark abode,
Big with the promise of the *Delphick* God,
When in the fields the fatal cow he view'd,
Nor gall'd with yokes, nor worn with servitude:
Her gently at a distance he pursu'd;
And as he walk'd aloof, in silence pray'd
To the great Pow'r whose counsels he obey'd.
Her way thro' flow'ry *Panopè* she took,
And now, *Cephisus*, cross'd thy silver brook;
When to the Heav'ns her spacious front she rais'd,
And bellow'd thrice, then backward turning gaz'd
On those behind, 'till on the destin'd place
She stoop'd, and couch'd amid the rising grass.

    Cadmus salutes the soil, and gladly hails

The new-found mountains, and the nameless vales,
And thanks the Gods, and turns about his eye
To see his new dominions round him lye;
Then sends his servants to a neighb'ring grove
For living streams, a sacrifice to *Jove*.
O'er the wide plain there rose a shady wood
Of aged trees; in its dark bosom stood
A bushy thicket, pathless and unworn,
O'er-run with brambles, and perplex'd with thorn:
Amidst the brake a hollow den was found,
With rocks and shelving arches vaulted round.
   Deep in the dreary den, conceal'd from day,
Sacred to *Mars*, a mighty dragon lay,
Bloated with poison to a monstrous size;
Fire broke in flashes when he glanc'd his eyes:
His tow'ring crest was glorious to behold,
His shoulders and his sides were scal'd with gold;
Three tongues he brandish'd when he charg'd his foes;
His teeth stood jaggy in three dreadful rowes.
The *Tyrians* in the den for water sought,
And with their urns explor'd the hollow vault:
From side to side their empty urns rebound,
And rowse the sleeping serpent with the sound.
Strait he bestirs him, and is seen to rise;
And now with dreadful hissings fills the skies,
And darts his forky tongues, and rowles his glaring eyes.
The *Tyrians* drop their vessels in the fright,
All pale and trembling at the hideous sight.
Spire above spire uprear'd in air he stood,
And gazing round him over-look'd the wood:
Then floating on the ground in circles rowl'd;
Then leap'd upon them in a mighty fold.
Of such a bulk, and such a monstrous size
The serpent in the polar circle lyes,
That stretches over half the northern skies.

In vain the *Tyrians* on their arms rely,
In vain attempt to fight, in vain to fly:
All their endeavours and their hopes are vain;
Some die entangled in the winding train;
Some are devour'd, or feel a loathsom death,
Swoln up with blasts of pestilential breath.

    And now the scorching sun was mounted high,
In all its lustre, to the noon-day sky;
When, anxious for his friends, and fill'd with cares,
To search the woods th' impatient chief prepares.
A lion's hide around his loins he wore,
The well poiz'd javelin to the field he bore,
Inur'd to blood; the far-destroying dart;
And, the best weapon, an undaunted heart.

    Soon as the youth approach'd the fatal place,
He saw his servants breathless on the grass;
The scaly foe amid their corps he view'd,
Basking at ease, and feasting in their blood.
"Such friends," he cries, "deserv'd a longer date;
But *Cadmus* will revenge or share their fate."
Then heav'd a stone, and rising to the throw,
He sent it in a whirlwind at the foe:
A tow'r, assaulted by so rude a stroke,
With all its lofty battlements had shook;
But nothing here th' unwieldy rock avails,
Rebounding harmless from the plaited scales,
That, firmly join'd, preserv'd him from a wound,
With native armour crusted all around.
With more success, the dart unerring flew,
Which at his back the raging warriour threw;
Amid the plaited scales it took its course,
And in the spinal marrow spent its force.
The monster hiss'd aloud, and rag'd in vain,
And writh'd his body to and fro with pain;
He bit the dart, and wrench'd the wood away;

The point still buried in the marrow lay.
And now his rage, increasing with his pain,
Reddens his eyes, and beats in ev'ry vein;
Churn'd in his teeth the foamy venom rose,
Whilst from his mouth a blast of vapours flows,
Such as th' infernal *Stygian* waters cast.
The plants around him wither in the blast.
Now in a maze of rings he lies enrowl'd,
Now all unravel'd, and without a fold;
Now, like a torrent, with a mighty force
Bears down the forest in his boist'rous course.
Cadmus gave back, and on the lion's spoil
Sustain'd the shock, then forc'd him to recoil;
The pointed jav'lin warded off his rage:
Mad with his pains, and furious to engage,
The serpent champs the steel, and bites the spear,
'Till blood and venom all the point besmear.
But still the hurt he yet receiv'd was slight;
For, whilst the champion with redoubled might
Strikes home the jav'lin, his retiring foe
Shrinks from the wound, and disappoints the blow.

The dauntless heroe still pursues his stroke,
And presses forward, 'till a knotty oak
Retards his foe, and stops him in the rear;
Full in his throat he plung'd the fatal spear,
That in th' extended neck a passage found,
And pierc'd the solid timber through the wound.
Fix'd to the reeling trunk, with many a stroke
Of his huge tail he lash'd the sturdy oak;
'Till spent with toil, and lab'ring hard for breath,
He now lay twisting in the pangs of death.

Cadmus beheld him wallow in a flood
Of swimming poison, intermix'd with blood;
When suddenly a speech was heard from high
(The speech was heard, nor was the speaker nigh),

"Why dost thou thus with secret pleasure see,
Insulting man! what thou thy self shalt be?"
Astonish'd at the voice, he stood amaz'd,
And all around with inward horror gaz'd:
When *Pallas* swift descending from the skies,
Pallas, the guardian of the bold and wise,
Bids him plow up the field, and scatter round
The dragon's teeth o'er all the furrow'd ground;
Then tells the youth how to his wond'ring eyes
Embattled armies from the field should rise.

He sows the teeth at *Pallas's* command,
And flings the future people from his hand.
The clods grow warm, and crumble where he sows;
And now the pointed spears advance in rows;
Now nodding plumes appear, and shining crests,
Now the broad shoulders and the rising breasts;
O'er all the field the breathing harvest swarms,
A growing host, a crop of men and arms.

So through the parting stage a figure rears
Its body up, and limb by limb appears
By just degrees; 'till all the man arise,
And in his full proportion strikes the eyes.

Cadmus surpriz'd, and startled at the sight
Of his new foes, prepar'd himself for fight:
When one cry'd out, "Forbear, fond man, forbear
To mingle in a blind promiscuous war."
This said, he struck his brother to the ground,
Himself expiring by another's wound;
Nor did the third his conquest long survive,
Dying ere scarce he had begun to live.

The dire example ran through all the field,
'Till heaps of brothers were by brothers kill'd;
The furrows swam in blood: and only five
Of all the vast increase were left alive.
Echion one, at *Pallas's* command,

Let fall the guiltless weapon from his hand,
And with the rest a peaceful treaty makes,
Whom *Cadmus* as his friends and partners takes;
So founds a city on the promis'd earth,
And gives his new *Boeotian* empire birth.

　　Here *Cadmus* reign'd; and now one would have guess'
The royal founder in his exile blest:
Long did he live within his new abodes,
Ally'd by marriage to the deathless Gods;
And, in a fruitful wife's embraces old,
A long increase of children's children told:
But no frail man, however great or high,
Can be concluded blest before he die.

　　Actaeon was the first of all his race,
Who griev'd his grandsire in his borrow'd face;
Condemn'd by stern *Diana* to bemoan
The branching horns, and visage not his own;
To shun his once lov'd dogs, to bound away,
And from their huntsman to become their prey,
And yet consider why the change was wrought,
You'll find it his misfortune, not his fault;
Or, if a fault, it was the fault of chance:
For how can guilt proceed from ignorance?

　　In a fair chace a shady mountain stood,
Well stor'd with game, and mark'd with trails of blood
Here did the huntsmen, 'till the heat of day,
Pursue the stag, and load themselves with prey:
When thus *Actaeon* calling to the rest:
"My friends," said he, "our sport is at the best,
The sun is high advanc'd, and downward sheds
His burning beams directly on our heads;
Then by consent abstain from further spoils,
Call off the dogs, and gather up the toils,
And ere to-morrow's sun begins his race,
Take the cool morning to renew the chace."

They all consent, and in a chearful train
The jolly huntsmen, loaden with the slain,
Return in triumph from the sultry plain.

   Down in a vale with pine and cypress clad,
Refresh'd with gentle winds, and brown with shade,
The chaste *Diana's* private haunt, there stood
Full in the centre of the darksome wood
A spacious grotto, all around o'er-grown
With hoary moss, and arch'd with pumice-stone.
From out its rocky clefts the waters flow,
And trickling swell into a lake below.
Nature had ev'ry where so plaid her part,
That ev'ry where she seem'd to vie with art.
Here the bright Goddess, toil'd and chaf'd with heat,
Was wont to bathe her in the cool retreat.

   Here did she now with all her train resort,
Panting with heat, and breathless from the sport;
Her armour-bearer laid her bow aside,
Some loos'd her sandals, some her veil unty'd;
Each busy nymph her proper part undrest;
While *Crocale*, more handy than the rest,
Gather'd her flowing hair, and in a noose
Bound it together, whilst her own hung loose.
Five of the more ignoble sort by turns
Fetch up the water, and unlade the urns.

   Now all undrest the shining Goddess stood,
When young *Actaeon*, wilder'd in the wood,
To the cool grott by his hard fate betray'd,
The fountains fill'd with naked nymphs survey'd.
The frighted virgins shriek'd at the surprize
(The forest echo'd with their piercing cries).
Then in a huddle round their Goddess prest:
She, proudly eminent above the rest,
With blushes glow'd; such blushes as adorn
The ruddy welkin, or the purple morn;

And tho' the crowding nymphs her body hide,
Half backward shrunk, and view'd him from a side.
Surpriz'd, at first she would have snatch'd her bow,
But sees the circling waters round her flow;
These in the hollow of her hand she took,
And dash'd 'em in his face, while thus she spoke:
"Tell, if thou can'st, the wond'rous sight disclos'd,
A Goddess naked to thy view expos'd."

This said, the man begun to disappear
By slow degrees, and ended in a deer.
A rising horn on either brow he wears,
And stretches out his neck, and pricks his ears;
Rough is his skin, with sudden hairs o'er-grown,
His bosom pants with fears before unknown:
Transform'd at length, he flies away in haste,
And wonders why he flies away so fast.
But as by chance, within a neighb'ring brook,
He saw his branching horns and alter'd look.
Wretched *Actaeon*! in a doleful tone
He try'd to speak, but only gave a groan;
And as he wept, within the watry glass
He saw the big round drops, with silent pace,
Run trickling down a savage hairy face.
What should he do? Or seek his old abodes,
Or herd among the deer, and sculk in woods!
Here shame dissuades him, there his fear prevails,
And each by turns his aking heart assails.

As he thus ponders, he behind him spies
His op'ning hounds, and now he hears their cries:
A gen'rous pack, or to maintain the chace,
Or snuff the vapour from the scented grass.

He bounded off with fear, and swiftly ran
O'er craggy mountains, and the flow'ry plain;
Through brakes and thickets forc'd his way, and flew
Through many a ring, where once he did pursue.

In vain he oft endeavour'd to proclaim
His new misfortune, and to tell his name;
Nor voice nor words the brutal tongue supplies;
From shouting men, and horns, and dogs he flies,
Deafen'd and stunn'd with their promiscuous cries.
When now the fleetest of the pack, that prest
Close at his heels, and sprung before the rest,
Had fasten'd on him, straight another pair,
Hung on his wounded haunch, and held him there,
'Till all the pack came up, and ev'ry hound
Tore the sad huntsman grov'ling on the ground,
Who now appear'd but one continu'd wound.
With dropping tears his bitter fate he moans,
And fills the mountain with his dying groans.
His servants with a piteous look he spies,
And turns about his supplicating eyes.
His servants, ignorant of what had chanc'd,
With eager haste and joyful shouts advanc'd,
And call'd their lord *Actaeon* to the game.
He shook his head in answer to the name;
He heard, but wish'd he had indeed been gone,
Or only to have stood a looker-on.
But to his grief he finds himself too near,
And feels his rav'nous dogs with fury tear
Their wretched master panting in a deer.

   Actaeon's suff'rings, and *Diana's* rage,
Did all the thoughts of men and Gods engage;
Some call'd the evils which *Diana* wrought,
Too great, and disproportion'd to the fault:
Others again, esteem'd *Actaeon's* woes
Fit for a virgin Goddess to impose.
The hearers into diff'rent parts divide,
And reasons are produc'd on either side.

   Juno alone, of all that heard the news,
Nor would condemn the Goddess, nor excuse:

She heeded not the justice of the deed,
But joy'd to see the race of *Cadmus* bleed;
For still she kept *Europa* in her mind,
And, for her sake, detested all her kind.
Besides, to aggravate her hate, she heard
How *Semele*, to *Jove's* embrace preferr'd,
Was now grown big with an immortal load,
And carry'd in her womb a future God.
Thus terribly incens'd, the Goddess broke
To sudden fury, and abruptly spoke.

"Are my reproaches of so small a force?
'Tis time I then pursue another course:
It is decreed the guilty wretch shall die,
If I'm indeed the mistress of the sky,
If rightly styl'd among the Pow'rs above
The wife and sister of the thund'ring *Jove*
(And none can sure a sister's right deny);
It is decreed the guilty wretch shall die.
She boasts an honour I can hardly claim,
Pregnant she rises to a mother's name;
While proud and vain she triumphs in her *Jove*,
And shows the glorious tokens of his love:
But if I'm still the mistress of the skies,
By her own lover the fond beauty dies."
This said, descending in a yellow cloud,
Before the gates of *Semele* she stood.

Old *Beroë's* decrepit shape she wears,
Her wrinkled visage, and her hoary hairs;
Whilst in her trembling gait she totters on,
And learns to tattle in the nurse's tone.
The Goddess, thus disguis'd in age, beguil'd
With pleasing stories her false foster-child.
Much did she talk of love, and when she came
To mention to the nymph her lover's name,
Fetching a sigh, and holding down her head,

"'Tis well," says she, "if all be true that's said.
But trust me, child, I'm much inclin'd to fear
Some counterfeit in this your *Jupiter*:
Many an honest well-designing maid
Has been by these pretended Gods betray'd,
But if he be indeed the thund'ring *Jove*,
Bid him, when next he courts the rites of love,
Descend triumphant from th' etherial sky,
In all the pomp of his divinity,
Encompass'd round by those celestial charms,
With which he fills th' immortal *Juno's* arms."

    Th' unwary nymph, ensnar'd with what she said,
Desir'd of *Jove*, when next he sought her bed,
To grant a certain gift which she would chuse;
"Fear not," reply'd the God, "that I'll refuse
Whate'er you ask: may *Styx* confirm my voice,
Chuse what you will, and you shall have your choice."
"Then," says the nymph, "when next you seek my arms,
May you descend in those celestial charms,
With which your *Juno's* bosom you enflame,
And fill with transport Heav'n's immortal dame."
The God surpriz'd would fain have stopp'd her voice,
But he had sworn, and she had made her choice.

    To keep his promise he ascends, and shrouds
His awful brow in whirl-winds and in clouds;
Whilst all around, in terrible array,
His thunders rattle, and his light'nings play.
And yet, the dazling lustre to abate,
He set not out in all his pomp and state,
Clad in the mildest light'ning of the skies,
And arm'd with thunder of the smallest size:
Not those huge bolts, by which the giants slain
Lay overthrown on the *Phlegrean* plain.
'Twas of a lesser mould, and lighter weight;
They call it thunder of a second-rate,

For the rough *Cyclops*, who by *Jove's* command
Temper'd the bolt, and turn'd it to his hand,
Work'd up less flame and fury in its make,
And quench'd it sooner in the standing lake.
Thus dreadfully adorn'd, with horror bright,
Th' illustrious God, descending from his height,
Came rushing on her in a storm of light.

  The mortal dame, too feeble to engage
The lightning's flashes, and the thunder's rage,
Consum'd amidst the glories she desir'd,
And in the terrible embrace expir'd.

  But, to preserve his offspring from the tomb,
Jove took him smoaking from the blasted womb:
And, if on ancient tales we may rely,
Inclos'd th' abortive infant in his thigh.
Here when the babe had all his time fulfill'd,
Ino first took him for her foster-child;
Then the *Niseans*, in their dark abode,
Nurs'd secretly with milk the thriving God.

  'Twas now, while these transactions past on Earth,
And *Bacchus* thus procur'd a second birth,
When *Jove*, dispos'd to lay aside the weight
Of publick empire and the cares of state,
As to his queen in nectar bowls he quaff'd,
"In troth," says he, and as he spoke he laugh'd,
"The sense of pleasure in the male is far
More dull and dead, than what you females share."
Juno the truth of what was said deny'd;
Tiresias therefore must the cause decide,
For he the pleasure of each sex had try'd.

  It happen'd once, within a shady wood,
Two twisted snakes he in conjunction view'd,
When with his staff their slimy folds he broke,
And lost his manhood at the fatal stroke.
But, after seven revolving years, he view'd

The self-same serpents in the self-same wood:
"And if," says he, "such virtue in you lye,
That he who dares your slimy folds untie
Must change his kind, a second stroke I'll try."
Again he struck the snakes, and stood again
New-sex'd, and strait recover'd into man.
Him therefore both the deities create
The sov'raign umpire, in their grand debate;
And he declar'd for *Jove*: when *Juno* fir'd,
More than so trivial an affair requir'd,
Depriv'd him, in her fury, of his sight,
And left him groping round in sudden night.
But *Jove* (for so it is in Heav'n decreed,
That no one God repeal another's deed)
Irradiates all his soul with inward light,
And with the prophet's art relieves the want of sight.

   Fam'd far and near for knowing things to come,
From him th' enquiring nations sought their doom;
The fair *Liriope* his answers try'd,
And first th' unerring prophet justify'd.
This nymph the God *Cephisus* had abus'd,
With all his winding waters circumfus'd,
And on the *Nereid* got a lovely boy,
Whom the soft maids ev'n then beheld with joy.

   The tender dame, sollicitous to know
Whether her child should reach old age or no,
Consults the sage *Tiresias*, who replies,
"If e'er he knows himself he surely dies."
Long liv'd the dubious mother in suspence,
'Till time unriddled all the prophet's sense.

   Narcissus now his sixteenth year began,
Just turn'd of boy, and on the verge of man;
Many a friend the blooming youth caress'd,
Many a love-sick maid her flame confess'd:
Such was his pride, in vain the friend caress'd,

The love-sick maid in vain her flame confess'd.
    Once, in the woods, as he pursu'd the chace,
The babbling *Echo* had descry'd his face;
She, who in others' words her silence breaks,
Nor speaks her self but when another speaks.
Echo was then a maid, of speech bereft,
Of wonted speech; for tho' her voice was left,
Juno a curse did on her tongue impose,
To sport with ev'ry sentence in the close.
Full often when the Goddess might have caught
Jove and her rivals in the very fault,
This nymph with subtle stories would delay
Her coming, 'till the lovers slip'd away.
The Goddess found out the deceit in time,
And then she cry'd, "That tongue, for this thy crime,
Which could so many subtle tales produce,
Shall be hereafter but of little use."
Hence 'tis she prattles in a fainter tone,
With mimick sounds, and accents not her own.
    This love-sick virgin, over-joy'd to find
The boy alone, still follow'd him behind:
When glowing warmly at her near approach,
As sulphur blazes at the taper's touch,
She long'd her hidden passion to reveal,
And tell her pains, but had not words to tell:
She can't begin, but waits fot the rebound,
To catch his voice, and to return the sound.
    The nymph, when nothing could *Narcissus* move,
Still dash'd with blushes for her slighted love,
Liv'd in the shady covert of the woods,
In solitary caves and dark abodes;
Where pining wander'd the rejected fair,
'Till harrass'd out, and worn away with care,
The sounding skeleton, of blood bereft,
Besides her bones and voice had nothing left.

Her bones are petrify'd, her voice is found
In vaults, where still it doubles ev'ry sound.
    Thus did the nymphs in vain caress the boy,
He still was lovely, but he still was coy;
When one fair virgin of the slighted train
Thus pray'd the Gods, provok'd by his disdain,
"Oh may he love like me, and love like me in vain!"
Rhamnusia pity'd the neglected fair,
And with just vengeance answer'd to her pray'r.
    There stands a fountain in a darksom wood,
Nor stain'd with falling leaves nor rising mud;
Untroubled by the breath of winds it rests,
Unsully'd by the touch of men or beasts;
High bow'rs of shady trees above it grow,
And rising grass and chearful greens below.
Pleas'd with the form and coolness of the place,
And over-heated by the morning chace,
Narcissus on the grassie verdure lyes:
But whilst within the chrystal fount he tries
To quench his heat, he feels new heats arise.
For as his own bright image he survey'd,
He fell in love with the fantastick shade;
And o'er the fair resemblance hung unmov'd,
Nor knew, fond youth! it was himself he lov'd.
The well-turn'd neck and shoulders he descries,
The spacious forehead, and the sparkling eyes;
The hands that *Bacchus* might not scorn to show,
And hair that round *Apollo's* head might flow;
With all the purple youthfulness of face,
That gently blushes in the wat'ry glass.
By his own flames consum'd the lover lyes,
And gives himself the wound by which he dies.
To the cold water oft he joins his lips,
Oft catching at the beauteous shade he dips
His arms, as often from himself he slips.

Nor knows he who it is his arms pursue
With eager clasps, but loves he knows not who.
    What could, fond youth, this helpless passion move?
What kindled in thee this unpity'd love?
Thy own warm blush within the water glows,
With thee the colour'd shadow comes and goes,
Its empty being on thy self relies;
Step thou aside, and the frail charmer dies.
    Still o'er the fountain's wat'ry gleam he stood,
Mindless of sleep, and negligent of food;
Still view'd his face, and languish'd as he view'd.
At length he rais'd his head, and thus began
To vent his griefs, and tell the woods his pain.
"You trees," says he, "and thou surrounding grove,
Who oft have been the kindly scenes of love,
Tell me, if e'er within your shades did lye
A youth so tortur'd, so perplex'd as I?
I, who before me see the charming fair,
Whilst there he stands, and yet he stands not there:
In such a maze of love my thoughts are lost:
And yet no bulwark'd town, nor distant coast,
Preserves the beauteous youth from being seen,
No mountains rise, nor oceans flow between.
A shallow water hinders my embrace;
And yet the lovely mimick wears a face
That kindly smiles, and when I bend to join
My lips to his, he fondly bends to mine.
Hear, gentle youth, and pity my complaint,
Come from thy well, thou fair inhabitant.
My charms an easy conquest have obtain'd
O'er other hearts, by thee alone disdain'd.
But why should I despair? I'm sure he burns
With equal flames, and languishes by turns.
When-e'er I stoop, he offers at a kiss,
And when my arms I stretch, he stretches his.

His eye with pleasure on my face he keeps,
He smiles my smiles, and when I weep he weeps.
When e'er I speak, his moving lips appear
To utter something, which I cannot hear.

  "Ah wretched me! I now begin too late
To find out all the long-perplex'd deceit;
It is my self I love, my self I see;
The gay delusion is a part of me.
I kindle up the fires by which I burn,
And my own beauties from the well return.
Whom should I court? how utter my complaint?
Enjoyment but produces my restraint,
And too much plenty makes me die for want.
How gladly would I from my self remove!
And at a distance set the thing I love.
My breast is warm'd with such unusual fire,
I wish him absent whom I most desire.
And now I faint with grief; my fate draws nigh;
In all the pride of blooming youth I die.
Death will the sorrows of my heart relieve.
Oh might the visionary youth survive,
I should with joy my latest breath resign!
But oh! I see his fate involv'd in mine."

  This said, the weeping youth again return'd
To the clear fountain, where again he burn'd;
His tears defac'd the surface of the well,
With circle after circle, as they fell:
And now the lovely face but half appears,
O'er-run with wrinkles, and deform'd with tears.
"Ah whither," cries Narcissus, "dost thou fly?
Let me still feed the flame by which I die;
Let me still see, tho' I'm no further blest."
Then rends his garment off, and beats his breast:
His naked bosom redden'd with the blow,
In such a blush as purple clusters show,

Ere yet the sun's autumnal heats refine
Their sprightly juice, and mellow it to wine.
The glowing beauties of his breast he spies,
And with a new redoubled passion dies.
As wax dissolves, as ice begins to run,
And trickle into drops before the sun;
So melts the youth, and languishes away,
His beauty withers, and his limbs decay;
And none of those attractive charms remain,
To which the slighted *Echo* su'd in vain.

　She saw him in his present misery,
Whom, spight of all her wrongs, she griev'd to see.
She answer'd sadly to the lover's moan,
Sigh'd back his sighs, and groan'd to ev'ry groan:
"Ah youth! belov'd in vain," *Narcissus* cries;
"Ah youth! belov'd in vain," the nymph replies.
"Farewel," says he; the parting sound scarce fell
From his faint lips, but she reply'd, "farewel."
Then on th' wholsome earth he gasping lyes,
'Till death shuts up those self-admiring eyes.
To the cold shades his flitting ghost retires,
And in the *Stygian* waves it self admires.

　For him the *Naiads* and the *Dryads* mourn,
Whom the sad *Echo* answers in her turn;
And now the sister-nymphs prepare his urn:
When, looking for his corps, they only found
A rising stalk, with yellow blossoms crown'd.

　This sad event gave blind *Tiresias* fame,
Through *Greece* establish'd in a prophet's name.

　Th' unhallow'd *Pentheus* only durst deride
The cheated people, and their eyeless guide.
To whom the prophet in his fury said,
Shaking the hoary honours of his head:
"'Twere well, presumptuous man, 'twere well for thee
If thou wert eyeless too, and blind, like me:

For the time comes, nay, 'tis already here,
When the young God's solemnities appear:
Which, if thou dost not with just rites adorn,
Thy impious carcass, into pieces torn,
Shall strew the woods, and hang on ev'ry thorn.
Then, then, remember what I now foretel,
And own the blind *Tiresias* saw too well."

    Still *Pentheus* scorns him, and derides his skill;
But time did all the prophet's threats fulfil.
For now through prostrate *Greece* young *Bacchus* rode,
Whilst howling matrons celebrate the God:
All ranks and sexes to his *Orgies* ran,
To mingle in the pomps, and fill the train.
When *Pentheus* thus his wicked rage express'd:
"What madness, *Thebans*, has your souls possess'd?
Can hollow timbrels, can a drunken shout,
And the lewd clamours of a beastly rout,
Thus quell your courage; can the weak alarm
Of women's yells those stubborn souls disarm,
Whom nor the sword nor trumpet e'er could fright,
Nor the loud din and horror of a fight?
And you, our sires, who left your old abodes,
And fix'd in foreign earth your country Gods;
Will you without a stroak your city yield,
And poorly quit an undisputed field?
But you, whose youth and vigour should inspire
Heroick warmth, and kindle martial fire,
Whom burnish'd arms and crested helmets grace,
Not flow'ry garlands and a painted face;
Remember him to whom you stand ally'd:
The serpent for his well of waters dy'd.
He fought the strong; do you his courage show,
And gain a conquest o'er a feeble foe.
If *Thebes* must fall, oh might the fates afford
A nobler doom from famine, fire, or sword.

Then might the *Thebans* perish with renown:
But now a beardless victor sacks the town;
Whom nor the prancing steed, nor pond'rous shield,
Nor the hack'd helmet, nor the dusty field,
But the soft joys of luxury and ease,
The purple vests, and flow'ry garlands please.
Stand then aside, I'll make the counterfeit
Renounce his god-head, and confess the cheat.
Acrisius from the *Grecian* walls repell'd
This boasted pow'r; why then should *Pentheus* yield?
Go quickly drag th' impostor boy to me;
I'll try the force of his divinity."
Thus did th' audacious wretch those rites profane;
His friends dissuade th' audacious wretch in vain:
In vain his grandsire urg'd him to give o'er
His impious threats; the wretch but raves the more.

   So have I seen a river gently glide,
In a smooth course, and inoffensive tide;
But if with dams its current we restrain,
It bears down all, and foams along the plain.

   But now his servants came besmear'd with blood,
Sent by their haughty prince to seize the God;
The God they found not in the frantick throng,
But dragg'd a zealous votary along.

   Him *Pentheus* view'd with fury in his look,
And scarce with-held his hands, whilst thus he spoke:
"Vile slave! whom speedy vengeance shall pursue,
And terrify thy base seditious crew:
Thy country and thy parentage reveal,
And, why thou joinest in these mad *Orgies*, tell."

   The captive views him with undaunted eyes,
And, arm'd with inward innocence, replies,

   "From high *Meonia's* rocky shores I came,
Of poor descent, *Acoetes* is my name:
My sire was meanly born; no oxen plow'd

His fruitful fields, nor in his pastures low'd.
His whole estate within the waters lay;
With lines and hooks he caught the finny prey,
His art was all his livelyhood; which he
Thus with his dying lips bequeath'd to me:
In streams, my boy, and rivers take thy chance;
There swims, said he, thy whole inheritance.
Long did I live on this poor legacy;
'Till tir'd with rocks, and my old native sky,
To arts of navigation I inclin'd;
Observ'd the turns and changes of the wind,
Learn'd the fit havens, and began to note
The stormy *Hyades*, the rainy *Goat*,
The bright *Taygete*, and the shining *Bears*,
With all the sailor's catalogue of stars.

    "Once, as by chance for *Delos* I design'd,
My vessel, driv'n by a strong gust of wind,
Moor'd in a *Chian* Creek; a-shore I went,
And all the following night in *Chios* spent.
When morning rose, I sent my mates to bring
Supplies of water from a neighb'ring spring,
Whilst I the motion of the winds explor'd;
Then summon'd in my crew, and went aboard.
Opheltes heard my summons, and with joy
Brought to the shore a soft and lovely boy,
With more than female sweetness in his look,
Whom straggling in the neighb'ring fields he took.
With fumes of wine the little captive glows,
And nods with sleep, and staggers as he goes.

    "I view'd him nicely, and began to trace
Each heav'nly feature, each immortal grace,
And saw divinity in all his face,
I know not who, said I, this God should be;
But that he is a God I plainly see:
And thou, who-e'er thou art, excuse the force

These men have us'd; and oh befriend our course!
Pray not for us, the nimble *Dictys* cry'd,
Dictys, that could the main-top mast bestride,
And down the ropes with active vigour slide.
To the same purpose old *Epopeus* spoke,
Who over-look'd the oars, and tim'd the stroke;
The same the pilot, and the same the rest;
Such impious avarice their souls possest.
Nay, Heav'n forbid that I should bear away
Within my vessel so divine a prey,
Said I; and stood to hinder their intent:
When *Lycabas*, a wretch for murder sent
From *Tuscany*, to suffer banishment,
With his clench'd fist had struck me over-board,
Had not my hands in falling grasp'd a cord.
  "His base confederates the fact approve;
When *Bacchus* (for 'twas he) begun to move,
Wak'd by the noise and clamours which they rais'd;
And shook his drowsie limbs, and round him gaz'd:
What means this noise? he cries; am I betray'd?
Ah, whither, whither must I be convey'd?
Fear not, said *Proreus*, child, but tell us where
You wish to land, and trust our friendly care.
To *Naxos* then direct your course, said he;
Naxos a hospitable port shall be
To each of you, a joyful home to me.
By ev'ry God, that rules the sea or sky,
The perjur'd villains promise to comply,
And bid me hasten to unmoor the ship.
With eager joy I launch into the deep;
And, heedless of the fraud, for *Naxos* stand.
They whisper oft, and beckon with the hand,
And give me signs, all anxious for their prey,
To tack about, and steer another way.
Then let some other to my post succeed,

Said I, I'm guiltless of so foul a deed.
What, says *Ethalion*, must the ship's whole crew
Follow your humour, and depend on you?
And strait himself he seated at the prore,
And tack'd about, and sought another shore.

　"The beauteous youth now found himself betray'd,
And from the deck the rising waves survey'd,
And seem'd to weep, and as he wept he said:
And do you thus my easy faith beguile?
Thus do you bear me to my native isle?
Will such a multitude of men employ
Their strength against a weak defenceless boy?

　"In vain did I the God-like youth deplore,
The more I begg'd, they thwarted me the more.
And now by all the Gods in Heav'n that hear
This solemn oath, by *Bacchus'* self, I swear,
The mighty miracle that did ensue,
Although it seems beyond belief, is true.
The vessel, fix'd and rooted in the flood,
Unmov'd by all the beating billows stood.
In vain the mariners would plow the main
With sails unfurl'd, and strike their oars in vain;
Around their oars a twining ivy cleaves,
And climbs the mast, and hides the cords in leaves:
The sails are cover'd with a chearful green,
And berries in the fruitful canvass seen.
Amidst the waves a sudden forest rears
Its verdant head, and a new Spring appears.

　"The God we now behold with open'd eyes;
A herd of spotted panthers round him lyes
In glaring forms; the grapy clusters spread
On his fair brows, and dangle on his head.
And whilst he frowns, and brandishes his spear,
My mates surpriz'd with madness or with fear,
Leap'd over board; first perjur'd *Madon* found

Rough scales and fins his stiff'ning sides surround;
Ah what, cries one, has thus transform'd thy look?
Strait his own mouth grew wider as he spoke;
And now himself he views with like surprize.
Still at his oar th' industrious *Libys* plies;
But, as he plies, each busy arm shrinks in,
And by degrees is fashion'd to a fin.
Another, as he catches at a cord,
Misses his arms, and, tumbling over-board,
With his broad fins and forky tail he laves
The rising surge, and flounces in the waves.
Thus all my crew transform'd around the ship,
Or dive below, or on the surface leap,
And spout the waves, and wanton in the deep.
Full nineteen sailors did the ship convey,
A shole of nineteen dolphins round her play.
I only in my proper shape appear,
Speechless with wonder, and half dead with fear,
'Till *Bacchus* kindly bid me fear no more.
With him I landed on the *Chian* shore,
And him shall ever gratefully adore."

"This forging slave," says *Pentheus*, "would prevail
O'er our just fury by a far-fetch'd tale:
Go, let him feel the whips, the swords, the fire,
And in the tortures of the rack expire."
Th' officious servants hurry him away,
And the poor captive in a dungeon lay.
But, whilst the whips and tortures are prepar'd,
The gates fly open, of themselves unbarr'd;
At liberty th' unfetter'd captive stands,
And flings the loosen'd shackles from his hands.

But *Pentheus*, grown more furious than before,
Resolv'd to send his messengers no more,
But went himself to the distracted throng,
Where high *Cithaeron* echo'd with their song.

And as the fiery war-horse paws the ground,
And snorts and trembles at the trumpet's sound;
Transported thus he heard the frantick rout,
And rav'd and madden'd at the distant shout.
　　A spacious circuit on the hill there stood.
Level and wide, and skirted round with wood;
Here the rash *Pentheus*, with unhallow'd eyes,
The howling dames and mystick *Orgies* spies.
His mother sternly view'd him where he stood,
And kindled into madness as she view'd:
Her leafy jav'lin at her son she cast,
And cries, "The boar that lays our country waste!
The boar, my sisters! Aim the fatal dart,
And strike the brindled monster to the heart."
　　Pentheus astonish'd heard the dismal sound,
And sees the yelling matrons gath'ring round;
He sees, and weeps at his approaching fate,
And begs for mercy, and repents too late.
"Help, help! my aunt *Autonoë*," he cry'd;
"Remember, how your own *Actaeon* dy'd."
Deaf to his cries, the frantick matron crops
One stretch'd-out arm, the other *Ino* lops.
In vain does *Pentheus* to his mother sue,
And the raw bleeding stumps presents to view:
His mother howl'd; and, heedless of his pray'r,
Her trembling hand she twisted in his hair,
"And this," she cry'd, "shall be *Agave's* share,"
When from the neck his struggling head she tore,
And in her hands the ghastly visage bore.
With pleasure all the hideous trunk survey;
Then pull'd and tore the mangled limbs away,
As starting in the pangs of death it lay,
Soon as the wood its leafy honours casts,
Blown off and scatter'd by autumnal blasts,
With such a sudden death lay *Pentheus* slain,

And in a thousand pieces strow'd the plain.
By so distinguishing a judgment aw'd,
The *Thebans* tremble, and confess the God.

The End of the Third Book.

BOOK THE FOURTH

Y ET still *Alcithöe* perverse remains,
     And *Bacchus* still, and all his rites, disdains.
     Too rash, and madly bold, she bids him prove
Himself a God, nor owns the son of *Jove*.
Her sisters too unanimous agree,
Faithful associates in impiety.

   Be this a solemn feast, the priest had said;
Be, with each mistress, unemploy'd each maid.
With skins of beasts your tender limbs enclose,
And with an ivy-crown adorn your brows,
The leafy *Thyrsus* high in triumph bear,
And give your locks to wanton in the air.

   These rites profan'd, the holy seer foreshow'd
A mourning people, and a vengeful God.

   Matrons and pious wives obedience show,
Distaffs, and wooll, half spun, away they throw:
Then incense burn, and, *Bacchus*, thee adore,
Or lov'st thou *Nysêus*, or *Lyaeus* more?
O! doubly got, O! doubly born, they sung,
Thou mighty *Bromius*, hail, from light'ning sprung!
Hail, *Thyon*, *Elelêus*! each name is thine:
Or, listen parent of the genial vine!
Iächus! Evan! loudly they repeat,
And not one *Grecian* attribute forget,
Which to thy praise, great Deity, belong,
Stil'd justly *Liber* in the *Roman* song.
Eternity of youth is thine! enjoy
Years roul'd on years, yet still a blooming boy.
In Heav'n thou shin'st with a superior grace;
Conceal thy horns, and 'tis a virgin's face.
Thou taught'st the tawny *Indian* to obey,
And *Ganges*, smoothly flowing, own'd thy sway.
Lycurgus, *Pentheus*, equally profane,
By thy just vengeance equally were slain.

By thee the *Tuscans*, who conspir'd to keep
Thee captive, plung'd, and cut with finns the deep.
With painted reins, all-glitt'ring from afar,
The spotted lynxes proudly draw thy car.
Around, the *Bacchae*, and the satyrs throng;
Behind, *Silenus*, drunk, lags slow along:
On his dull ass he nods from side to side,
Forbears to fall, yet half forgets to ride.
Still at thy near approach, applauses loud
Are heard, with yellings of the female crowd.
Timbrels, and boxen pipes, with mingled cries,
Swell up in sounds confus'd, and rend the skies.
Come, *Bacchus*, come propitious, all implore,
And act thy sacred orgies o'er and o'er.

   But *Mineus'* daughters, while these rites were pay'd,
At home, impertinently busie, stay'd.
Their wicked tasks they ply with various art,
And thro' the loom the sliding shuttle dart;
Or at the fire to comb the wooll they stand,
Or twirl the spindle with a dext'rous hand.
Guilty themselves, they force the guiltless in;
Their maids, who share the labour, share the sin.
At last one sister cries, who nimbly knew
To draw nice threads, and winde the finest clue,
While others idly rove, and Gods revere,
Their fancy'd Gods! they know not who, or where;
Let us, whom *Pallas* taught her better arts,
Still working, cheer with mirthful chat our hearts,
And to deceive the time, let me prevail
With each by turns to tell some antique tale.
She said: her sisters lik'd the humour well,
And smiling, bad her the first story tell.
But she a-while profoundly seem'd to muse,
Perplex'd amid variety to chuse:
And knew not, whether she should first relate

The poor *Dircetis*, and her wond'rous fate.
The *Palestines* believe it to a man,
And show the lake, in which her scales began.
Or if she rather should the daughter sing,
Who in the hoary verge of life took wing;
Who soar'd from Earth, and dwelt in tow'rs on high,
And now a dove she flits along the sky.
Or how lewd *Naïs*, when her lust was cloy'd,
To fishes turn'd the youths, she had enjoy'd,
By pow'rful verse, and herbs; effect most strange!
At last the changer shar'd herself the change.
Or how the tree, which once white berries bore,
Still crimson bears, since stain'd with crimson gore.
The tree was new; she likes it, and begins
To tell the tale, and as she tells, she spins.

　In *Babylon*, where first her queen, for state
Rais'd walls of brick magnificently great,
Liv'd *Pyramus*, and *Thisbe*, lovely pair!
He found no eastern youth his equal there,
And she beyond the fairest nymph was fair.
A closer neighbourhood was never known,
Tho' two the houses, yet the roof was one.
Acquaintance grew, th' acquaintance they improve
To friendship, friendship ripen'd into love:
Love had been crown'd, but impotently mad,
What parents could not hinder, they forbad.
For with fierce flames young *Pyramus* still burn'd,
And grateful *Thisbe* flames as fierce return'd.
Aloud in words their thoughts they dare not break,
But silent stand; and silent looks can speak.
The fire of love the more it is supprest,
The more it glows, and rages in the breast.

　When the division-wall was built, a chink
Was left, the cement unobserv'd to shrink.
So slight the cranny, that it still had been

For centuries unclos'd, because unseen.
But oh! what thing so small, so secret lies,
Which scapes, if form'd for love, a lover's eyes?
Ev'n in this narrow chink they quickly found
A friendly passage for a trackless sound.
Safely they told their sorrows, and their joys,
In whisper'd murmurs, and a dying noise.
By turns to catch each other's breath they strove,
And suck'd in all the balmy breeze of love.
Oft as on diff'rent sides they stood, they cry'd,
Malicious wall, thus lovers to divide!
Suppose, thou should'st a-while to us give place
To lock, and fasten in a close embrace:
But if too much to grant so sweet a bliss,
Indulge at least the pleasure of a kiss.
We scorn ingratitude: to thee, we know,
This safe conveyance of our minds we owe.

Thus they their vain petition did renew
'Till night, and then they softly sigh'd adieu.
But first they strove to kiss, and that was all;
Their kisses dy'd untasted on the wall.
Soon as the morn had o'er the stars prevail'd,
And warm'd by *Phoebus*, flow'rs their dews exhal'd,
The lovers to their well-known place return,
Alike they suffer, and alike they mourn.
At last their parents they resolve to cheat
(If to deceive in love be call'd deceit),
To steal by night from home, and thence unknown
To seek the fields, and quit th' unfaithful town.
But, to prevent their wand'ring in the dark,
They both agree to fix upon a mark;
A mark, that could not their designs expose:
The tomb of *Ninus* was the mark they chose.
There they might rest secure beneath the shade,
Which boughs, with snowy fruit encumber'd, made:

A wide-spread mulberry its rise had took
Just on the margin of a gurgling brook.
Impatient for the friendly dusk they stay;
And chide the slowness of departing day;
In western seas down sunk at last the light,
From western seas up-rose the shades of night.
The loving *Thisbe* ev'n prevents the hour,
With cautious silence she unlocks the door,
And veils her face, and marching thro' the gloom
Swiftly arrives at th' assignation-tomb.
For still the fearful sex can fearless prove;
Boldly they act, if spirited by love.
When lo! a lioness rush'd o'er the plain,
Grimly besmear'd with blood of oxen slain:
And what to the dire sight new horrors brought,
To slake her thirst the neighb'ring spring she sought.
Which, by the moon, when trembling *Thisbe* spies,
Wing'd with her fear, swift, as the wind, she flies;
And in a cave recovers from her fright,
But drop'd her veil, confounded in her flight.
When sated with repeated draughts, again
The queen of beasts scour'd back along the plain,
She found the veil, and mouthing it all o'er,
With bloody jaws the lifeless prey she tore.

　　The youth, who could not cheat his guards so soon,
Late came, and noted by the glimm'ring moon
Some savage feet, new printed on the ground,
His cheeks turn'd pale, his limbs no vigour found;
But when, advancing on, the veil he spied
Distain'd with blood, and ghastly torn, he cried,
One night shall death to two young lovers give,
But she deserv'd unnumber'd years to live!
'Tis I am guilty, I have thee betray'd,
Who came not early, as my charming maid.
Whatever slew thee, I the cause remain,

I nam'd, and fix'd the place where thou wast slain.
Ye lions from your neighb'ring dens repair,
Pity the wretch, this impious body tear!
But cowards thus for death can idly cry;
The brave still have it in their pow'r to die.
Then to th' appointed tree he hastes away,
The veil first gather'd, tho' all rent it lay:
The veil all rent yet still it self endears,
He kist, and kissing, wash'd it with his tears.
Tho' rich (he cry'd) with many a precious stain,
Still from my blood a deeper tincture gain.
Then in his breast his shining sword he drown'd,
And fell supine, extended on the ground.
As out again the blade he dying drew,
Out spun the blood, and streaming upwards flew.
So if a conduit-pipe e'er burst you saw,
Swift spring the gushing waters thro' the flaw:
Then spouting in a bow, they rise on high,
And a new fountain plays amid the sky.
The berries, stain'd with blood, began to show
A dark complexion, and forgot their snow;
While fatten'd with the flowing gore, the root
Was doom'd for ever to a purple fruit.
    Mean-time poor *Thisbe* fear'd, so long she stay'd,
Her lover might suspect a perjur'd maid.
Her fright scarce o'er, she strove the youth to find
With ardent eyes, which spoke an ardent mind.
Already in his arms, she hears him sigh
At her destruction, which was once so nigh.
The tomb, the tree, but not the fruit she knew,
The fruit she doubted for its alter'd hue.
Still as she doubts, her eyes a body found
Quiv'ring in death, and gasping on the ground.
She started back, the red her cheeks forsook,
And ev'ry nerve with thrilling horrors shook.

So trembles the smooth surface of the seas,
If brush'd o'er gently with a rising breeze.
But when her view her bleeding love confest,
She shriek'd, she tore her hair, she beat her breast.
She rais'd the body, and embrac'd it round,
And bath'd with tears unfeign'd the gaping wound.
Then her warm lips to the cold face apply'd,
And is it thus, ah! thus we meet, she cry'd!
My *Pyramus!* whence sprung thy cruel fate?
My *Pyramus!* — ah! speak, ere 'tis too late.
I, thy own *Thisbe*, but one word implore,
One word thy *Thisbe* never ask'd before.
At *Thisbe's* name, awak'd, he open'd wide
His dying eyes; with dying eyes he try'd
On her to dwell, but clos'd them slow, and dy'd.

　　The fatal cause was now at last explor'd,
Her veil she knew, and saw his sheathless sword:
From thy own hand thy ruin thou hast found,
She said, but love first taught that hand to wound,
Ev'n I for thee as bold a hand can show,
And love, which shall as true direct the blow.
I will against the woman's weakness strive,
And never thee, lamented youth, survive.
The world may say, I caus'd, alas! thy death,
But saw thee breathless, and resign'd my breath.
Fate, tho' it conquers, shall no triumph gain,
Fate, that divides us, still divides in vain.

　　Now, both our cruel parents, hear my pray'r;
My pray'r to offer for us both I dare;
Oh! see our ashes in one urn confin'd,
Whom love at first, and fate at last has join'd.
The bliss, you envy'd, is not our request;
Lovers, when dead, may sure together rest.
Thou, tree, where now one lifeless lump is laid,
Ere-long o'er two shalt cast a friendly shade.

Still let our loves from thee be understood,
Still witness in thy purple fruit our blood.
She spoke, and in her bosom plung'd the sword,
All warm and reeking from its slaughter'd lord.
The pray'r, which dying *Thisbe* had preferr'd,
Both Gods, and parents, with compassion heard.
The whiteness of the mulberry soon fled,
And rip'ning, sadden'd in a dusky red:
While both their parents their lost children mourn,
And mix their ashes in one golden urn.

Thus did the melancholy tale conclude,
And a short, silent interval ensu'd.
The next in birth unloos'd her artful tongue,
And drew attentive all the sister-throng.

The Sun, the source of light, by beauty's pow'r
Once am'rous grew; then hear the Sun's amour.
Venus, and *Mars*, with his far-piercing eyes
This God first spy'd; this God first all things spies.
Stung at the sight, and swift on mischief bent,
To haughty *Juno's* shapeless son he went:
The Goddess, and her God gallant betray'd,
And told the cuckold, where their pranks were play'd.
Poor *Vulcan* soon desir'd to hear no more,
He drop'd his hammer, and he shook all o'er:
Then courage takes, and full of vengeful ire
He heaves the bellows, and blows fierce the fire:
From liquid brass, tho' sure, yet subtile snares
He forms, and next a wond'rous net prepares,
Drawn with such curious art, so nicely sly,
Unseen the mashes cheat the searching eye.
Not half so thin their webs the spiders weave,
Which the most wary, buzzing prey deceive.
These chains, obedient to the touch, he spread
In secret foldings o'er the conscious bed:
The conscious bed again was quickly prest

By the fond pair, in lawless raptures blest.
Mars wonder'd at his *Cytherëa's* charms,
More fast than ever lock'd within her arms.
While *Vulcan* th' iv'ry doors unbarr'd with care,
Then call'd the Gods to view the sportive pair:
The Gods throng'd in, and saw in open day,
Where *Mars*, and beauty's queen, all naked, lay.
O! shameful sight, if shameful that we name,
Which Gods with envy view'd, and could not blame;
But, for the pleasure, wish'd to bear the shame.
Each Deity, with laughter tir'd, departs,
Yet all still laugh'd at *Vulcan* in their hearts.

Thro' Heav'n the news of this surprizal run,
But *Venus* did not thus forget the Sun.
He, who stol'n transports idly had betray'd,
By a betrayer was in kind repay'd.
What now avails, great God, thy piercing blaze,
That youth, and beauty, and those golden rays?
Thou, who can'st warm this universe alone,
Feel'st now a warmth more pow'rful than thy own:
And those bright eyes, which all things should survey,
Know not from fair *Leucothöe* to stray.
The lamp of light, for human good design'd,
Is to one virgin niggardly confin'd.
Sometimes too early rise thy eastern beams,
Sometimes too late they set in western streams:
'Tis then her beauty thy swift course delays,
And gives to winter skies long summer days.
Now in thy face thy love-sick mind appears,
And spreads thro' impious nations empty fears:
For when thy beamless head is wrapt in night,
Poor mortals tremble in despair of light.
'Tis not the moon, that o'er thee casts a veil,
'Tis love alone, which makes thy looks so pale.
Leucothöe is grown thy only care,

Not *Phäeton's* fair mother now is fair.
The youthful *Rhodos* moves no tender thought,
And beauteous *Porsa* is at last forgot.
Fond *Clytiè*, scorn'd, yet lov'd, and sought thy bed,
Ev'n then thy heart for other virgins bled.
Leucothöe has all thy soul possest,
And chas'd each rival passion from thy breast.
To this bright nymph *Eurynomè* gave birth
In the blest confines of the spicy Earth.
Excelling others, she herself beheld
By her own blooming daughter far excell'd.
The sire was *Orchamus*, whose vast command,
The sev'nth from *Belus*, rul'd the *Persian* Land.

   Deep in cool vales, beneath th' *Hesperian* sky,
For the Sun's fiery steeds the pastures lye.
Ambrosia there they eat, and thence they gain
New vigour, and their daily toils sustain.
While thus on heav'nly food the coursers fed,
And night, around, her gloomy empire spread,
The God assum'd the mother's shape and air,
And pass'd, unheeded, to his darling fair.
Close by a lamp, with maids encompass'd round,
The royal spinster, full employ'd, he found:
Then cry'd, A-while from work, my daughter, rest;
And, like a mother, scarce her lips he prest.
Servants retire! — nor secrets dare to hear,
Intrusted only to a daughter's ear.
They swift obey'd: not one, suspicious, thought
The secret, which their mistress would be taught.
Then he: since now no witnesses are near,
Behold! the God, who guides the various year!
The world's vast eye, of light the source serene,
Who all things sees, by whom are all things seen.
Believe me, nymph! (for I the truth have show'd)
Thy charms have pow'r to charm so great a God.

Confus'd, she heard him his soft passion tell,
And on the floor, untwirl'd, the spindle fell:
Still from the sweet confusion some new grace
Blush'd out by stealth, and languish'd in her face.
The lover, now inflam'd, himself put on,
And out at once the God, all-radiant, shone.
The virgin startled at his alter'd form,
Too weak to bear a God's impetuous storm:
No more against the dazling youth she strove,
But silent yielded, and indulg'd his love.

This *Clytié* knew, and knew she was undone,
Whose soul was fix'd, and doated on the Sun.
She rag'd to think on her neglected charms,
And *Phoebus*, panting in another's arms.
With envious madness fir'd, she flies in haste,
And tells the king, his daughter was unchaste.
The king, incens'd to hear his honour stain'd,
No more the father nor the man retain'd.
In vain she stretch'd her arms, and turn'd her eyes
To her lov'd God, th' enlightner of the skies.
In vain she own'd it was a crime, yet still
It was a crime not acted by her will.
The brutal sire stood deaf to ev'ry pray'r,
And deep in Earth entomb'd alive the fair.
What *Phoebus* could do, was by *Phoebus* done:
Full on her grave with pointed beams he shone:
To pointed beams the gaping Earth gave way;
Had the nymph eyes, her eyes had seen the day,
But lifeless now, yet lovely still, she lay.
Not more the God wept, when the world was fir'd,
And in the wreck his blooming boy expir'd.
The vital flame he strives to light again,
And warm the frozen blood in ev'ry vein:
But since resistless Fates deny'd that pow'r,
On the cold nymph he rain'd a nectar show'r.

Ah! undeserving thus (he said) to die,
Yet still in odours thou shalt reach the sky.
The body soon dissolv'd, and all around
Perfum'd with heav'nly fragrancies the ground,
A sacrifice for Gods up-rose from thence,
A sweet, delightful tree of frankincense.

Tho' guilty *Clytie* thus the sun betray'd,
By too much passion she was guilty made.
Excess of love begot excess of grief,
Grief fondly bad her hence to hope relief.
But angry *Phoebus* hears, unmov'd, her sighs,
And scornful from her loath'd embraces flies.
All day, all night, in trackless wilds, alone
She pin'd, and taught the list'ning rocks her moan.
On the bare earth she lies, her bosom bare,
Loose her attire, dishevel'd is her hair.
Nine times the morn unbarr'd the gates of light,
As oft were spread th' alternate shades of night,
So long no sustenance the mourner knew,
Unless she drunk her tears, or suck'd the dew.
She turn'd about, but rose not from the ground,
Turn'd to the Sun, still as he roul'd his round:
On his bright face hung her desiring eyes,
'Till fix'd to Earth, she strove in vain to rise.
Her looks their paleness in a flow'r retain'd,
But here, and there, some purple streaks they gain'd.
Still the lov'd object the fond leafs pursue,
Still move their root, the moving Sun to view,
And in the *Heliotrope* the nymph is true.

The sisters heard these wonders with surprise,
But part receiv'd them as romantick lies;
And pertly rally'd, that they could not see
In Pow'rs divine so vast an energy.
Part own'd, true Gods such miracles might do,
But own'd not *Bacchus*, one among the true.

At last a common, just request they make,
And beg *Alcithöe* her turn to take.
I will (she said) and please you, if I can.
Then shot her shuttle swift, and thus began.

   The fate of *Daphnis* is a fate too known,
Whom an enamour'd nymph transform'd to stone,
Because she fear'd another nymph might see
The lovely youth, and love as much as she:
So strange the madness is of jealousie!
Nor shall I tell, what changes *Scython* made,
And how he walk'd a man, or tripp'd a maid.
You too would peevish frown, and patience want
To hear, how *Celmis* grew an adamant.
He once was dear to *Jove*, and saw of old
Jove, when a child; but what he saw, he told.
Crocus, and *Smilax* may be turn'd to flow'rs,
And the *Curetes* spring from bounteous show'rs;
I pass a hundred legends stale, as these,
And with sweet novelty your taste will please.

   How *Salmacis*, with weak enfeebling streams
Softens the body, and unnerves the limbs,
And what the secret cause, shall here be shown;
The cause is secret, but th' effect is known.

   The *Naids* nurst an infant heretofore,
That *Cytherea* once to *Hermes* bore:
From both th' illustrious authors of his race
The child was nam'd; nor was it hard to trace
Both the bright parents thro' the infant's face.
When fifteen years in *Ida's* cool retreat
The boy had told, he left his native seat,
And sought fresh fountains in a foreign soil:
The pleasure lessen'd the attending toil,
With eager steps the *Lycian* fields he crost,
A river here he view'd so lovely bright,
It shew'd the bottom in a fairer light,

Nor kept a sand conceal'd from human sight.
The stream produc'd nor slimy ooze, nor weeds,
Nor miry rushes, nor the spiky reeds;
But dealt enriching moisture all around,
The fruitful banks with chearful verdure crown'd,
And kept the spring eternal on the ground.
A nymph presides, not practis'd in the chace,
Nor skilful at the bow, nor at the race;
Of all the blue-ey'd daughters of the main,
The only stranger to *Diana's* train:
Her sisters often, as 'tis said, wou'd cry,
"Fie *Salmacis*: what, always idle! fie.
Or take thy quiver, or thy arrows seize,
And mix the toils of hunting with thy ease."
Nor quiver she nor arrows e'er wou'd seize,
Nor mix the toils of hunting with her ease.
But oft would bathe her in the chrystal tide,
Oft with a comb her dewy locks divide;
Now in the limpid streams she views her face,
And drest her image in the floating glass:
On beds of leaves she now repos'd her limbs,
Now gather'd flow'rs that grew about her streams,
And then by chance was gathering, as he stood
To view the boy, and long'd for what she view'd.

Fain wou'd she meet the youth with hasty feet,
She fain wou'd meet him, but refus'd to meet
Before her looks were set with nicest care,
And well deserv'd to be reputed fair.
"Bright youth," she cries, "whom all thy features prove
A God, and, if a God, the God of love;
But if a mortal, blest thy nurse's breast,
Blest are thy parents, and thy sisters blest:
But oh how blest! how more than blest thy bride,
Ally'd in bliss, if any yet ally'd.
If so, let mine the stoln enjoyments be;

If not, behold a willing bride in me."
   The boy knew nought of love, and toucht with shame,
He strove, and blusht, but still the blush became:
In rising blushes still fresh beauties rose;
The sunny side of fruit such blushes shows,
And such the moon, when all her silver white
Turns in eclipses to a ruddy light.
The nymph still begs, if not a nobler bliss,
A cold salute at least, a sister's kiss:
And now prepares to take the lovely boy
Between her arms. He, innocently coy,
Replies, "Or leave me to my self alone,
You rude uncivil nymph, or I'll be gone."
"Fair stranger then," says she, "it shall be so";
And, for she fear'd his threats, she feign'd to go:
But hid within a covert's neighbouring green,
She kept him still in sight, herself unseen.
The boy now fancies all the danger o'er,
And innocently sports about the shore,
Playful and wanton to the stream he trips,
And dips his foot, and shivers as he dips.
The coolness pleas'd him, and with eager haste
His airy garments on the banks he cast;
His godlike features, and his heav'nly hue,
And all his beauties were expos'd to view.
His naked limbs the nymph with rapture spies,
While hotter passions in her bosom rise,
Flush in her cheeks, and sparkle in her eyes.
She longs, she burns to clasp him in her arms,
And looks, and sighs, and kindles at his charms.
   Now all undrest upon the banks he stood,
And clapt his sides, and leapt into the flood:
His lovely limbs the silver waves divide,
His limbs appear more lovely through the tide;
As lillies shut within a chrystal case,

Receive a glossy lustre from the glass.
He's mine, he's all my own, the *Naïd* cries,
And flings off all, and after him she flies.
And now she fastens on him as he swims,
And holds him close, and wraps about his limbs.
The more the boy resisted, and was coy,
The more she clipt, and kist the strugling boy.
So when the wrigling snake is snatcht on high
In *Eagle's* claws, and hisses in the sky,
Around the foe his twirling tail he flings,
And twists her legs, and wriths about her wings.

    The restless boy still obstinately strove
To free himself, and still refus'd her love.
Amidst his limbs she kept her limbs intwin'd,
"And why, coy youth," she cries, "why thus unkind!
Oh may the Gods thus keep us ever join'd!
Oh may we never, never part again!"

    So pray'd the nymph, nor did she pray in vain:
For now she finds him, as his limbs she prest,
Grow nearer still, and nearer to her breast;
'Till, piercing each the other's flesh, they run
Together, and incorporate in one:
Last in one face are both their faces join'd,
As when the stock and grafted twig combin'd
Shoot up the same, and wear a common rind:
Both bodies in a single body mix,
A single body with a double sex.

    The boy, thus lost in woman, now survey'd
The river's guilty stream, and thus he pray'd.
(He pray'd, but wonder'd at his softer tone,
Surpriz'd to hear a voice but half his own.)
You parent-Gods, whose heav'nly names I bear,
Hear your *Hermaphrodite*, and grant my pray'r;
Oh grant, that whomsoe'er these streams contain,
If man he enter'd, he may rise again

Supple, unsinew'd, and but half a man!
   The heav'nly parents answer'd from on high,
Their two-shap'd son, the double votary;
Then gave a secret virtue to the flood,
And ting'd its source to make his wishes good.
   But *Mineus'* daughters still their tasks pursue,
To wickedness most obstinately true:
At *Bacchus* still they laugh, when all around,
Unseen, the timbrels hoarse were heard to sound.
Saffron and myrrh their fragrant odours shed,
And now the present deity they dread.
Strange to relate! Here ivy first was seen,
Along the distaff crept the wond'rous green.
Then sudden-springing vines began to bloom,
And the soft tendrils curl'd around the loom:
While purple clusters, dangling from on high,
Ting'd the wrought purple with a second die.
   Now from the skies was shot a doubtful light,
The day declining to the bounds of night.
The fabrick's firm foundations shake all o'er,
False tigers rage, and figur'd lions roar.
Torches, aloft, seem blazing in the air,
And angry flashes of red light'nings glare.
To dark recesses, the dire sight to shun,
Swift the pale sisters in confusion run.
Their arms were lost in pinions, as they fled,
And subtle films each slender limb o'er-spread.
Their alter'd forms their senses soon reveal'd;
Their forms, how alter'd, darkness still conceal'd.
Close to the roof each, wond'ring, upwards springs,
Born on unknown, transparent, plumeless wings.
They strove for words; their little bodies found
No words, but murmur'd in a fainting sound.
In towns, not woods, the sooty bats delight,
And, never, 'till the dusk, begin their flight;

'Till *Vesper* rises with his ev'ning flame;
From whom the *Romans* have deriv'd their name.

The pow'r of *Bacchus* now o'er *Thebes* had flown:
With awful rev'rence soon the God they own.
Proud *Ino*, all around the wonder tells,
And on her nephew deity still dwells.
Of num'rous sisters, she alone yet knew
No grief, but grief, which she from sisters drew.

Imperial *Juno* saw her with disdain,
Vain in her offspring, in her consort vain,
Who rul'd the trembling *Thebans* with a nod,
But saw her vainest in her foster-God.
Could then (she cry'd) a bastard-boy have pow'r
To make a mother her own son devour?
Could he the *Tuscan* crew to fishes change,
And now three sisters damn to forms so strange?
Yet shall the wife of *Jove* find no relief?
Shall she, still unreveng'd, disclose her grief?
Have I the mighty freedom to complain?
Is that my pow'r? is that to ease my pain?
A foe has taught me vengeance; and who ought
To scorn that vengeance, which a foe has taught?
What sure destruction frantick rage can throw,
The gaping wounds of slaughter'd *Pentheus* show.
Why should not *Ino*, fir'd with madness, stray,
Like her mad sisters her own kindred slay?
Why, she not follow, where they lead the way?

Down a steep, yawning cave, where yews display'd
In arches meet, and lend a baleful shade,
Thro' silent labyrinths a passage lies
To mournful regions, and infernal skies.
Here *Styx* exhales its noisome clouds, and here,
The fun'ral rites once paid, all souls appear.
Stiff cold, and horror with a ghastly face
And staring eyes, infest the dreary place.

Ghosts, new-arriv'd, and strangers to these plains,
Know not the palace, where grim *Pluto* reigns.
They journey doubtful, nor the road can tell,
Which leads to the metropolis of Hell.
A thousand avenues those tow'rs command,
A thousand gates for ever open stand.
As all the rivers, disembogu'd, find room
For all their waters in old Ocean's womb:
So this vast city worlds of shades receives,
And space for millions still of worlds she leaves.
Th' unbody'd spectres freely rove, and show
Whate'er they lov'd on Earth, they love below.
The lawyers still, or right, or wrong, support,
The courtiers smoothly glide to *Pluto's* court.
Still airy heroes thoughts of glory fire,
Still the dead poet strings his deathless lyre,
And lovers still with fancy'd darts expire.

   The Queen of Heaven, to gratify her hate,
And sooth immortal wrath, forgets her state.
Down from the realms of day, to realms of night,
The Goddess swift precipitates her flight.
At Hell arriv'd, the noise Hell's porter heard,
Th' enormous dog his triple head up-rear'd:
Thrice from three grizly throats he howl'd profound,
Then suppliant couch'd, and stretch'd along the ground.
The trembling threshold, which *Saturnia* prest,
The weight of such divinity confest.

   Before a lofty, adamantine gate,
Which clos'd a tow'r of brass, the Furies sate:
Mis-shapen forms, tremendous to the sight,
Th' implacable foul daughters of the night.
A sounding whip each bloody sister shakes,
Or from her tresses combs the curling snakes.
But now great *Juno's* majesty was known;
Thro' the thick gloom, all heav'nly bright, she shone:

The hideous monsters their obedience show'd,
And rising from their seats, submissive bow'd.
   This is the place of woe, here groan the dead;
Huge *Tityus* o'er nine acres here is spread.
Fruitful for pain th' immortal liver breeds,
Still grows, and still th' insatiate vulture feeds.
Poor *Tantalus* to taste the water tries,
But from his lips the faithless water flies:
Then thinks the bending tree he can command,
The tree starts backwards, and eludes his hand.
The labour too of *Sisyphus* is vain,
Up the steep mount he heaves the stone with pain,
Down from the summet rouls the stone again.
The *Belides* their leaky vessels still
Are ever filling, and yet never fill:
Doom'd to this punishment for blood they shed,
For bridegrooms slaughter'd in the bridal bed.
Stretch'd on the rolling wheel *Ixion* lies;
Himself he follows, and himself he flies.
Ixion, tortur'd, *Juno* sternly ey'd,
Then turn'd, and toiling *Sisyphus* espy'd:
And why (she said) so wretched is the fate
Of him, whose brother proudly reigns in state?
Yet still my altars unador'd have been
By *Athamas*, and his presumptuous queen.
   What caus'd her hate, the Goddess thus confest,
What caus'd her journey now was more than guest.
That hate, relentless, its revenge did want,
And that revenge the Furies soon could grant:
They could the glory of proud *Thebes* efface,
And hide in ruin the *Cadmëan* race.
For this she largely promises, entreats,
And to intreaties adds imperial threats.
   Then fell *Tisiphonè* with rage was stung,
And from her mouth th' untwisted serpents flung.

To gain this trifling boon, there is no need
(She cry'd) in formal speeches to proceed.
Whatever thou command'st to do, is done;
Believe it finish'd, tho' not yet begun.
But from these melancholly seats repair
To happier mansions, and to purer air.
She spoke: the Goddess, darting upwards, flies,
And joyous re-ascends her native skies:
Nor enter'd there, till 'round her *Iris* threw
Ambrosial sweets, and pour'd celestial dew.

The faithful Fury, guiltless of delays,
With cruel haste the dire command obeys.
Girt in a bloody gown, a torch she shakes,
And round her neck twines speckled wreaths of snakes.
Fear, and dismay, and agonizing pain,
With frantick rage, compleat her loveless train.
To *Thebes* her flight she sped, and Hell forsook;
At her approach the *Theban* turrets shook:
The sun shrunk back, thick clouds the day o'er-cast,
And springing greens were wither'd as she past.

Now, dismal yellings heard, strange spectres seen,
Confound as much the monarch as the queen.
In vain to quit the palace they prepar'd,
Tisiphonè was there, and kept the ward.
She wide extended her unfriendly arms,
And all the Fury lavish'd all her harms.
Part of her tresses loudly hiss, and part
Spread poyson, as their forky tongues they dart.
Then from her middle locks two snakes she drew,
Whose merit from superior mischief grew:
Th' envenom'd ruin, thrown with spiteful care,
Clung to the bosoms of the hapless pair.
The hapless pair soon with wild thoughts were fir'd,
And madness, by a thousand ways inspir'd.
'Tis true, th' unwounded body still was sound,

But 'twas the soul which felt the deadly wound.
Nor did th' unsated monster here give o'er,
But dealt of plagues a fresh, unnumber'd store.
Each baneful juice too well she understood,
Foam, churn'd by *Cerberus*, and *Hydra's* blood.
Hot hemlock, and cold aconite she chose,
Delighted in variety of woes.
Whatever can untune th' harmonious soul,
And its mild, reas'ning faculties controul,
Give false ideas, raise desires profane,
And whirl in eddies the tumultuous brain,
Mix'd with curs'd art, she direfully around
Thro' all their nerves diffus'd the sad compound.
Then toss'd her torch in circles still the same,
Improv'd their rage, and added flame to flame.
The grinning Fury her own conquest spy'd,
And to her rueful shades return'd with pride,
And threw th' exhausted, useless snakes aside.

   Now *Athamas* cries out, his reason fled,
Here, fellow-hunters, let the toils be spread.
I saw a lioness, in quest of food,
With her two young, run roaring in this wood.
Again the fancy'd savages were seen,
As thro' his palace still he chac'd his queen;
Then tore *Learchus* from her breast: the child
Stretch'd little arms, and on its father smil'd:
A father now no more, who now begun
Around his head to whirl his giddy son,
And, quite insensible to Nature's call,
The helpless infant flung against the wall.
The same mad poyson in the mother wrought,
Young *Melicerta* in her arms she caught,
And with disorder'd tresses, howling, flies,
O! *Bacchus*, *Evôe*, *Bacchus*! loud she cries.
The name of *Bacchus Juno* laughd' to hear,

And said, Thy foster-God has cost thee dear.
   A rock there stood, whose side the beating waves
Had long consum'd, and hollow'd into caves.
The head shot forwards in a bending steep,
And cast a dreadful covert o'er the deep.
The wretched *Ino*, on destruction bent,
Climb'd up the cliff; such strength her fury lent:
Thence with her guiltless boy, who wept in vain,
At one bold spring she plung'd into the main.
   Her neice's fate touch'd *Cytherëa's* breast,
And in soft sounds she *Neptune* thus addrest:
Great God of waters, whose extended sway
Is next to his, whom Heav'n and Earth obey:
Let not the suit of *Venus* thee displease,
Pity the floaters on th' *Ionian* seas.
Encrease thy Subject-Gods, nor yet disdain
To add my kindred to that glorious train.
If from the sea I may such honours claim,
If 'tis desert, that from the sea I came,
As *Grecian* poets artfully have sung,
And in the name confest, from whence I sprung.
   Pleas'd *Neptune* nodded his assent, and free
Both soon became from frail mortality.
He gave them form, and majesty divine,
And bad them glide along the foamy brine.
For *Melicerta* is *Palaemon* known,
And *Ino* once, *Leucothöe* is grown.
   The *Theban* matrons their lov'd queen pursu'd,
And tracing to the rock, her footsteps view'd.
Too certain of her fate, they rend the skies
With piteous shrieks, and lamentable cries.
All beat their breasts, and *Juno* all upbraid,
Who still remember'd a deluded maid:
Who, still revengeful for one stol'n embrace,
Thus wreak'd her hate on the *Cadmean* race.

This *Juno* heard: And shall such elfs, she cry'd,
Dispute my justice, or my pow'r deride?
You too shall feel my wrath not idly spent;
A Goddess never for insults was meant.

　　She, who lov'd most, and who most lov'd had been,
Said, Not the waves shall part me from my queen.
She strove to plunge into the roaring flood;
Fix'd to the stone, a stone her self she stood.
This, on her breast would fain her blows repeat,
Her stiffen'd hands refus'd her breast to beat.
That, stretch'd her arms unto the seas; in vain
Her arms she labour'd to unstretch again.
To tear her comely locks another try'd,
Both comely locks, and fingers petryfi'd.
Part thus; but *Juno* with a softer mind
Part doom'd to mix among the feather'd kind.
Transform'd, the name of *Theban* birds they keep,
And skim the surface of that fatal deep.

　　Mean-time, the wretched *Cadmus* mourns, nor knows,
That they who mortal fell, immortal rose.
With a long series of new ills opprest,
He droops, and all the man forsakes his breast.
Strange prodigies confound his frighted eyes;
From the fair city, which he rais'd, he flies:
As if misfortune not pursu'd his race,
But only hung o'er that devoted place.
Resolv'd by sea to seek some distant land,
At last he safely gain'd th' *Illyrian* strand.
Chearless himself, his consort still he chears,
Hoary, and loaden'd both with woes and years.
Then to recount past sorrows they begin,
And trace them to the gloomy origin.
That serpent sure was hallow'd, *Cadmus* cry'd,
Which once my spear transfix'd with foolish pride;
When the big teeth, a seed before unknown,

By me along the wond'ring glebe were sown,
And sprouting armies by themselves o'erthrown.
If thence the wrath of Heav'n on me is bent,
May Heav'n conclude it with one sad event;
To an extended serpent change the man:
And while he spoke, the wish'd-for change began.
His skin with sea-green spots was vary'd 'round,
And on his belly prone he prest the ground.
He glitter'd soon with many a golden scale,
And his shrunk legs clos'd in a spiry tail.
Arms yet remain'd, remaining arms he spread
To his lov'd wife, and human tears yet shed.
Come, my *Harmonia*, come, thy face recline
Down to my face; still touch, what still is mine.
O! let these hands, while hands, be gently prest,
While yet the serpent has not all possest.
More he had spoke, but strove to speak in vain,
The forky tongue refus'd to tell his pain,
And learn'd in hissings only to complain.

Then shriek'd *Harmonia*, Stay, my *Cadmus*, stay,
Glide not in such a monstrous shape away!
Destruction, like impetuous waves, rouls on.
Where are thy feet, thy legs, thy shoulders gone?
Chang'd is thy visage, chang'd is all thy frame;
Cadmus is only *Cadmus* now in name.
Ye Gods, my *Cadmus* to himself restore,
Or me like him transform; I ask no more.

The husband-serpent show'd he still had thought,
With wonted fondness an embrace he sought;
Play'd 'round her neck in many a harmless twist,
And lick'd that bosom, which, a man, he kist.
The lookers-on (for lookers-on there were)
Shock'd at the sight, half-dy'd away with fear.
The transformation was again renew'd,
And, like the husband, chang'd the wife they view'd.

Both, serpents now, with fold involv'd in fold,
To the next covert amicably roul'd.
There curl'd they lie, or wave along the green,
Fearless see men, by men are fearless seen,
Still mild, and conscious what they once have been.
　Yet tho' this harsh, inglorious fate they found,
Each in the deathless grandson liv'd renown'd.
Thro' conquer'd *India Bacchus* nobly rode,
And *Greece* with temples hail'd the conqu'ring God.
In *Argos* only proud *Acrisius* reign'd,
Who all the consecrated rites profan'd.
Audacious wretch! thus *Bacchus* to deny,
And the great Thunderer's great son defie!
Nor him alone: thy daughter vainly strove,
Brave *Perseus* of celestial stem to prove,
And her self pregnant by a golden *Jove.*
Yet this was true, and truth in time prevails;
Acrisius now his unbelief bewails.
His former thought, an impious thought he found,
And both the heroe, and the God were own'd.
He saw, already one in Heav'n was plac'd,
And one with more than mortal triumphs grac'd,
The victor *Perseus* with the *Gorgon*-head,
O'er *Libyan* sands his airy journey sped.
The gory drops distill'd, as swift he flew,
And from each drop envenom'd serpents grew,
The mischiefs brooded on the barren plains,
And still th' unhappy fruitfulness remains.
　Thence *Perseus,* like a cloud, by storms was driv'n,
Thro' all th' expanse beneath the cope of Heaven.
The jarring winds unable to controul,
He saw the southern, and the northern pole:
And eastward thrice, and westward thrice was whirl'd,
And from the skies survey'd the nether world.
But when grey ev'ning show'd the verge of night,

He fear'd in darkness to pursue his flight.
He pois'd his pinions, and forgot to soar,
And sinking, clos'd them on th' *Hesperian* shore:
Then beg'd to rest, 'till *Lucifer* begun
To wake the morn, the morn to wake the sun.
　　Here *Atlas* reign'd, of more than human size,
And in his kingdom the world's limit lies.
Here *Titan* bids his weary'd coursers sleep,
And cools the burning axle in the deep.
The mighty monarch, uncontrol'd, alone,
His sceptre sways: no neighb'ring states are known.
A thousand flocks on shady mountains fed,
A thousand herds o'er grassy plains were spread.
Here wond'rous trees their shining stores unfold,
Their shining stores too wond'rous to be told,
Their leafs, their branches, and their apples, gold.
Then *Perseus* the gigantick prince addrest,
Humbly implor'd a hospitable rest.
If bold exploits thy admiration fire,
He said, I fancy, mine thou wilt admire.
Or if the glory of a race can move,
Not mean my glory, for I spring from *Jove.*
At this confession *Atlas* ghastly star'd,
Mindful of what an oracle declar'd,
That the dark womb of Time conceal'd a day,
Which should, disclos'd, the bloomy gold betray:
All should at once be ravish'd from his eyes,
And *Jove's* own progeny enjoy the prize.
For this, the fruit he loftily immur'd,
And a fierce dragon the strait pass secur'd.
For this, all strangers he forbad to land,
And drove them from th' inhospitable strand.
To *Perseus* then: Fly quickly, fly this coast,
Nor falsly dare thy acts and race to boast.
In vain the heroe for one night entreats,

Threat'ning he storms, and next adds force to threats.
By strength not *Perseus* could himself defend,
For who in strength with *Atlas* could contend?
But since short rest to me thou wilt not give,
A gift of endless rest from me receive,
He said, and backward turn'd, no more conceal'd
The present, and *Medusa's* head reveal'd.
Soon the high *Atlas* a high mountain stood,
His locks, and beard became a leafy wood.
His hands, and shoulders, into ridges went,
The summit-head still crown'd the steep ascent.
His bones a solid, rocky hardness gain'd:
He, thus immensely grown (as fate ordain'd),
The stars, the Heav'ns, and all the Gods sustain'd.

Now *Aeolus* had with strong chains confin'd,
And deep imprison'd e'vry blust'ring wind,
The rising *Phospher* with a purple light
Did sluggish mortals to new toils invite.
His feet again the valiant *Perseus* plumes,
And his keen sabre in his hand resumes:
Then nobly spurns the ground, and upwards springs,
And cuts the liquid air with sounding wings.
O'er various seas, and various lands he past,
'Till *Aethiopia's* shore appear'd at last.
Andromeda was there, doom'd to attone
By her own ruin follies not her own:
And if injustice in a God can be,
Such was the *Libyan* God's unjust decree.
Chain'd to a rock she stood; young *Perseus* stay'd
His rapid flight, to view the beauteous maid.
So sweet her frame, so exquisitely fine,
She seem'd a statue by a hand divine,
Had not the wind her waving tresses show'd,
And down her cheeks the melting sorrows flow'd.
Her faultless form the heroe's bosom fires;

The more he looks, the more he still admires.
Th' admirer almost had forgot to fly,
And swift descended, flutt'ring from on high.
O! Virgin, worthy no such chains to prove,
But pleasing chains in the soft folds of love;
Thy country, and thy name (he said) disclose,
And give a true rehearsal of thy woes.
    A quick reply her bashfulness refus'd,
To the free converse of a man unus'd.
Her rising blushes had concealment found
From her spread hands, but that her hands were bound.
She acted to her full extent of pow'r,
And bath'd her face with a fresh, silent show'r.
But by degrees in innocence grown bold,
Her name, her country, and her birth she told:
And how she suffer'd for her mother's pride,
Who with the *Nereids* once in beauty vy'd.
Part yet untold, the seas began to roar,
And mounting billows tumbled to the shore.
Above the waves a monster rais'd his head,
His body o'er the deep was widely spread:
Onward he flounc'd; aloud the virgin cries;
Each parent to her shrieks in shrieks replies:
But she had deepest cause to rend the skies.
Weeping, to her they cling; no sign appears
Of help, they only lend their helpless tears.
Too long you vent your sorrows, *Perseus* said,
Short is the hour, and swift the time of aid,
In me the son of thund'ring *Jove* behold,
Got in a kindly show'r of fruitful gold.
Medusa's snaky head is now my prey,
And thro' the clouds I boldly wing my way.
If such desert be worthy of esteem,
And, if your daughter I from death redeem,
Shall she be mine? Shall it not then be thought,

A bride, so lovely, was too cheaply bought?
For her my arms I willingly employ,
If I may beauties, which I save, enjoy.
The parents eagerly the terms embrace:
For who would slight such terms in such a case?
Nor her alone they promise, but beside,
The dowry of a kingdom with the bride.

    As well-rigg'd gallies, which slaves, sweating, row,
With their sharp beaks the whiten'd ocean plough;
So when the monster mov'd, still at his back
The furrow'd waters left a foamy track.
Now to the rock he was advanc'd so nigh,
Whirl'd from a sling a stone the space would fly.
Then bounding, upwards the brave *Perseus* sprung,
And in mid air on hov'ring pinions hung.
His shadow quickly floated on the main;
The monster could not his wild rage restrain,
But at the floating shadow leap'd in vain.
As when *Jove's* bird, a speckl'd serpent spies,
Which in the shine of *Phoebus* basking lies,
Unseen, he souses down, and bears away,
Truss'd from behind, the vainly-hissing prey.
To writh his neck the labour nought avails,
Too deep th' imperial talons pierce his scales.
Thus the wing'd heroe now descends, now soars,
And at his pleasure the vast monster gores.
Full in his back, swift stooping from above,
The crooked sabre to its hilt he drove.
The monster rag'd, impatient of the pain,
First bounded high, and then sunk low again.
Now, like a savage boar, when chaf'd with wounds,
And bay'd with opening mouths of hungry hounds,
He on the foe turns with collected might,
Who still eludes him with an airy flight;
And wheeling round, the scaly armour tries

Of his thick sides; his thinner tail now plies:
'Till from repeated strokes out gush'd a flood,
And the waves redden'd with the streaming blood.
At last the dropping wings, befoam'd all o'er,
With flaggy heaviness their master bore:
A rock he spy'd, whose humble head was low,
Bare at an ebb, but cover'd at a flow.
A ridgy hold, he, thither flying, gain'd,
And with one hand his bending weight sustain'd;
With th' other, vig'rous blows he dealt around,
And the home-thrusts the expiring monster own'd.
In deaf'ning shouts the glad applauses rise,
And peal on peal runs ratling thro' the skies.
The saviour-youth the royal pair confess,
And with heav'd hands their daughter's bridegroom bless.
The beauteous bride moves on, now loos'd from chains,
The cause, and sweet reward of all the heroe's pains,
   Mean-time, on shore triumphant *Perseus* stood,
And purg'd his hands, smear'd with the monster's blood:
Then in the windings of a sandy bed
Compos'd *Medusa's* execrable head.
But to prevent the roughness, leafs he threw,
And young, green twigs, which soft in waters grew,
There soft, and full of sap; but here, when lay'd,
Touch'd by the head, that softness soon decay'd.
The wonted flexibility quite gone,
The tender scyons harden'd into stone.
Fresh, juicy twigs, surpriz'd, the *Nereids* brought,
Fresh, juicy twigs the same contagion caught.
The nymphs the petrifying seeds still keep,
And propagate the wonder thro' the deep.
The pliant sprays of coral yet declare
Their stiff'ning Nature, when expos'd to air.
Those sprays, which did, like bending osiers, move,
Snatch'd from their element, obdurate prove,

And shrubs beneath the waves, grow stones above.
　　The great immortals grateful *Perseus* prais'd,
And to three Pow'rs three turfy altars rais'd.
To *Hermes* this; and that he did assign
To *Pallas*: the mid honours, *Jove*, were thine,
He hastes for *Pallas* a white cow to cull,
A calf for *Hermes*, but for *Jove* a bull.
Then seiz'd the prize of his victorious fight,
Andromeda, and claim'd the nuptial rite.
Andromeda alone he greatly sought,
The dowry kingdom was not worth his thought.
　　Pleas'd *Hymen* now his golden torch displays;
With rich oblations fragrant altars blaze,
Sweet wreaths of choicest flow'rs are hung on high,
And cloudless pleasure smiles in ev'ry eye.
The melting musick melting thoughts inspires,
And warbling songsters aid the warbling lyres.
The palace opens wide in pompous state,
And by his peers surrounded, *Cepheus* sate.
A feast was serv'd, fit for a king to give,
And fit for God-like heroes to receive.
The banquet ended, the gay, chearful bowl
Mov'd round, and brighten'd, and enlarg'd each soul.
Then *Perseus* ask'd, what customs there obtain'd,
And by what laws the people were restrain'd.
Which told; the teller a like freedom takes,
And to the warrior his petition makes,
To know, what arts had won *Medusa's* snakes.
　　The heroe with his just request complies,
Shows, how a vale beneath cold *Atlas* lies,
Where, with aspiring mountains fenc'd around,
He the two daughters of old *Phorcus* found.
Fate had one common eye to both assign'd,
Each saw by turns, and each by turns was blind.
But while one strove to lend her sister sight,

He stretch'd his hand, and stole their mutual light,
And left both eyeless, both involv'd in night.
Thro' devious wilds, and trackless woods he past,
And at the *Gorgon*-seats arriv'd at last:
But as he journey'd, pensive he survey'd,
What wasteful havock dire *Medusa* made.
Here, stood still breathing statues, men before;
There, rampant lions seem'd in stone to roar.
Nor did he, yet affrighted, quit the field,
But in the mirror of his polish'd shield
Reflected saw *Medusa* slumbers take,
And not one serpent by good chance awake.
Then backward an unerring blow he sped,
And from her body lop'd at once her head.
The gore prolifick prov'd; with sudden force
Sprung *Pegasus*, and wing'd his airy course.

The Heav'n-born warrior faithfully went on,
And told the num'rous dangers which he run.
What subject seas, what lands he had in view,
And nigh what stars th' advent'rous heroe flew.
At last he silent sate; the list'ning throng
Sigh'd at the pause of his delightful tongue.
Some beg'd to know, why this alone should wear,
Of all the sisters, such destructive hair.

Great *Perseus* then: With me you shall prevail,
Worth the relation, to relate a tale.
Medusa once had charms; to gain her love
A rival crowd of envious lovers strove.
They, who have seen her, own, they ne'er did trace
More moving features in a sweeter face.
Yet above all, her length of hair, they own,
In golden ringlets wav'd, and graceful shone.
Her *Neptune* saw, and with such beauties fir'd,
Resolv'd to compass, what his soul desir'd.
In chaste *Minerva's* fane, he, lustful, stay'd,

And seiz'd, and rifled the young, blushing maid.
The bashful Goddess turn'd her eyes away,
Nor durst such bold impurity survey;
But on the ravish'd virgin vengeance takes,
Her shining hair is chang'd to hissing snakes.
These in her *Aegis Pallas* joys to bear,
The hissing snakes her foes more sure ensnare,
Than they did lovers once, when shining hair.

The End of the Fourth Book.

BOOK THE FIFTH

WHILE *Perseus* entertain'd with this report
His father *Cepheus*, and the list'ning court,
Within the palace walls was heard aloud
The roaring noise of some unruly crowd;
Not like the songs which chearful friends prepare
For nuptial days, but sounds that threaten'd war;
And all the pleasures of this happy feast,
To tumult turn'd, in wild disorder ceas'd:
So, when the sea is calm, we often find
A storm rais'd sudden by some furious wind.

Chief in the riot *Phineus* first appear'd,
The rash ringleader of this boist'rous herd,
And brandishing his brazen-pointed lance,
Behold, he said, an injur'd man advance,
Stung with resentment for his ravish'd wife,
Nor shall thy wings, o *Perseus*, save thy life;
Nor *Jove* himself; tho' we've been often told
Who got thee in the form of tempting gold.
His lance was aim'd, when *Cepheus* ran, and said,
Hold, brother, hold; what brutal rage has made
Your frantick mind so black a crime conceive?
Are these the thanks that you to *Perseus* give?
This the reward that to his worth you pay,
Whose timely valour sav'd *Andromeda*?
Nor was it he, if you would reason right,
That forc'd her from you, but the jealous spight
Of envious *Nereids*, and *Jove's* high decree;
And that devouring monster of the sea,
That ready with his jaws wide gaping stood
To eat my child, the fairest of my blood.
You lost her then, when she seem'd past relief,
And wish'd perhaps her death, to ease your grief
With my afflictions: not content to view
Andromeda in chains, unhelp'd by you,

Her spouse, and uncle; will you grieve that he
Expos'd his life the dying maid to free?
And shall you claim his merit? Had you thought
Her charms so great, you shou'd have bravely sought
That blessing on the rocks, where fix'd she lay:
But now let *Perseus* bear his prize away,
By service gain'd, by promis'd faith possess'd;
To him I owe it, that my age is bless'd
Still with a child: Nor think that I prefer
Perseus to thee, but to the loss of her.

   Phineus on him, and *Perseus*, roul'd about
His eyes in silent rage, and seem'd to doubt
Which to destroy; 'till, resolute at length,
He threw his spear with the redoubled strength
His fury gave him, and at *Perseus* struck;
But missing *Perseus*, in his seat it stuck.
Who, springing nimbly up, return'd the dart,
And almost plung'd it in his rival's heart;
But he for safety to the altar ran,
Unfit protection for so vile a man;
Yet was the stroke not vain, as *Rhaetus* found,
Who in his brow receiv'd a mortal wound;
Headlong he tumbled, when his skull was broke,
From which his friends the fatal weapon took,
While he lay trembling, and his gushing blood
In crimson streams around the table flow'd.

   But this provok'd th' unruly rabble worse,
They flung their darts, and some in loud discourse
To death young *Perseus*, and the monarch doom;
But *Cepheus* left before the guilty room,
With grief appealing to the Gods above,
Who laws of hospitality approve,
Who faith protect, and succour injur'd right,
That he was guiltless of this barb'rous fight.

   Pallas her brother *Perseus* close attends,

And with her ample shield from harm defends,
Raising a sprightly courage in his heart:
But *Indian Athis* took the weaker part,
Born in the chrystal grottoes of the sea,
Limnatè's son, a fenny nymph, and she
Daughter of *Ganges*; graceful was his mein,
His person lovely, and his age sixteen.
His habit made his native beauty more;
A purple mantle fring'd with gold he wore;
His neck well-turn'd with golden chains was grac'd,
His hair with myrrh perfum'd, was nicely dress'd.
Tho' with just aim he cou'd the javelin throw,
Yet with more skill he drew the bending bow;
And now was drawing it with artful hand,
When *Perseus* snatching up a flaming brand,
Whirl'd sudden at his face the burning wood,
Crush'd his eyes in, and quench'd the fire with blood;
Thro' the soft skin the splinter'd bones appear,
And spoil'd the face that lately was so fair.
    When *Lycabas* his *Athis* thus beheld,
How was his heart with friendly horror fill'd!
A youth so noble, to his soul so dear,
To see his shapeless look, his dying groans to hear!
He snatch'd the bow the boy was us'd to bend,
And cry'd, With me, false traytor, dare contend;
Boast not a conquest o'er a child, but try
Thy strength with me, who all thy pow'rs defy;
Nor think so mean an act a victory.
While yet he spoke he flung the whizzing dart,
Which pierc'd the plaited robe, but miss'd his heart:
Perseus defy'd, upon him fiercely press'd
With sword, unsheath'd, and plung'd it in his breast;
His eyes o'erwhelm'd with night, he stumbling falls,
And with his latest breath on *Athis* calls;
Pleas'd that so near the lovely youth he lies,

He sinks his head upon his friend, and dies.
　　Next eager *Phorbas*, old *Methion's* son,
Came rushing forward with *Amphimedon*;
When the smooth pavement, slippery made with gore,
Trip'd up their feet, and flung 'em on the floor;
The sword of *Perseus*, who by chance was nigh,
Prevents their rise, and where they fall, they lye:
Full in his ribs *Amphimedon* he smote,
And then stuck fiery *Phorbas* in the throat.
Eurythus lifting up his ax, the blow
Was thus prevented by his nimble foe;
A golden cup he seizes, high embost,
And at his head the massy goblet tost:
It hits, and from his forehead bruis'd rebounds,
And blood, and brains he vomits from his wounds;
With his slain fellows on the floor he lies,
And death for ever shuts his swimming eyes.
Then *Polydaemon* fell, a Goddess-born;
Phlegias, and *Elycen* with locks unshorn
Next follow'd; next, the stroke of death he gave
To *Clytus*, *Abanis*, and *Lycetus* brave;
While o'er unnumber'd heaps of ghastly dead,
The *Argive* heroe's feet triumphant tread.
　　But *Phineus* stands aloof, and dreads to feel
His rival's force, and flies his pointed steel:
Yet threw a dart from far; by chance it lights
On *Idas*, who for neither party fights;
But wounded, sternly thus to *Phineus* said,
Since of a neuter thou a foe hast made,
This I return thee, drawing from his side
The dart; which, as he strove to fling, he dy'd.
Odites fell by *Clymenus's* sword,
The *Cephen* court had not a greater lord.
Hypseus his blade does in *Protenor* sheath,
But brave *Lyncides* soon reveng'd his death.

Here too was old *Emathion*, one that fear'd
The Gods, and in the cause of Heav'n appear'd,
Who only wishing the success of right,
And, by his age, exempted from the fight,
Both sides alike condemns: This impious war
Cease, cease, he cries; these bloody broils forbear.
This scarce the sage with high concern had said,
When *Chromis* at a blow struck off his head,
Which dropping, on the royal altar roul'd,
Still staring on the crowd with aspect bold;
And still it seem'd their horrid strife to blame,
In life and death, his pious zeal the same;
While clinging to the horns, the trunk expires,
The sever'd head consumes amidst the fires.

　　Then *Phineus*, who from far his javelin threw,
Broteas and *Ammon*, twins and brothers, slew;
For knotted gauntlets matchless in the field;
But gauntlets must to swords and javelins yield.
Ampycus next, with hallow'd fillets bound,
As *Ceres'* priest, and with a mitre crown'd,
His spear transfix'd, and struck him to the ground.

　　O *Iäpetides*, with pain I tell
How you, sweet lyrist, in the riot fell;
What worse than brutal rage his breast could fill,
Who did thy blood, o bard celestial! spill?
Kindly you press'd amid the princely throng,
To crown the feast, and give the nuptial song:
Discord abhorr'd the musick of thy lyre,
Whose notes did gentle peace so well inspire;
Thee, when fierce *Pettalus* far off espy'd,
Defenceless with thy harp, he scoffing cry'd,
Go; to the ghosts thy soothing lessons play;
We loath thy lyre, and scorn thy peaceful lay:
And, as again he fiercely bid him go,
He pierc'd his temples with a mortal blow.

His harp he held, tho' sinking on the ground,
Whose strings in death his trembling fingers found
By chance, and tun'd by chance a dying sound.
    With grief *Lycormas* saw him fall, from far,
And, wresting from the door a massy bar,
Full in his poll lays on a load of knocks,
Which stun him, and he falls like a devoted ox.
Another bar *Pelates* would have snach'd,
But *Corynthus* his motions slily watch'd;
He darts his weapon from a private stand,
And rivets to the post his veiny hand:
When strait a missive spear transfix'd his side,
By *Abas* thrown, and as he hung, he dy'd.
    Melaneus on the prince's side was slain;
And *Dorylas*, who own'd a fertile plain,
Of *Nasamonia's* fields the wealthy lord,
Whose crowded barns, could scarce contain their hoard.
A whizzing spear obliquely gave a blow,
Stuck in his groin, and pierc'd the nerves below;
His foe behld his eyes convulsive roul,
His ebbing veins, and his departing soul;
Then taunting said, Of all thy spacious plain,
This spot thy only property remains.
He left him thus; but had no sooner left,
Than *Perseus* in revenge his nostrils cleft;
From his friend's breast the murd'ring dart he drew,
And the same weapon at the murderer threw;
His head in halves the darted javelin cut,
And on each side the brain came issuing out.
    Fortune his friend, in deaths around he deals,
And this his lance, and that his faulchion feels:
Now *Clytius* dies; and by a diff'rent wound,
The twin, his brother *Clanis*, bites the ground.
In his rent jaw the bearded weapon sticks,
And the steel'd dart does *Clytius'* thigh transfix.

With these *Mendesian Celadon* he slew:
And *Astreus* next, whose mother was a Jew,
His sire uncertain: then by *Perseus* fell
Aethion, who cou'd things to come foretell;
But now he knows not whence the javelin flies
That wounds his breast, nor by whose arm he dies.
    The squire to *Phineus* next his valour try'd,
And fierce *Agyrtes* stain'd with paricide.
    As these are slain, fresh numbers still appear,
And wage with *Perseus* an unequal war;
To rob him of his right, the maid he won,
By honour, promise, and desert his own.
With him, the father of the beauteous bride,
The mother, and the frighted virgin side;
With shrieks, and doleful cries they rend the air:
Their shrieks confounded with the din of war,
With clashing arms, and groanings of the slain,
They grieve unpitied, and unheard complain.
The floor with ruddy streams *Bellona* stains,
And *Phineus* a new war with double rage maintains.
    Perseus begirt, from all around they pour
Their lances on him, a tempestuous show'r,
Aim'd all at him; a cloud of darts, and spears,
Or blind his eyes, or whistle round his ears.
Their numbers to resist, against the wall
He guards his back secure, and dares them all.
Here from the left *Molpeus* renews the fight,
And bold *Ethemon* presses on the right:
As when a hungry tyger near him hears
Two lowing herds, a-while he both forbears;
Nor can his hopes of this, or that renounce,
So strong he lusts to prey on both at once;
Thus *Perseus* now with that, or this is loth
To war distinct, but fain would fall on both.
And first *Chaonian Molpeus* felt his blow,

And fled, and never after fac'd his foe;
Then fierce *Ethemon*, as he turn'd his back,
Hurried with fury, aiming at his neck,
His brandish'd sword against the marble struck
With all his might; the brittle weapon broke,
And in his throat the point rebounding stuck.
Too slight the wound for life to issue thence,
And yet too great for battel, or defence;
His arms extended in this piteous state,
For mercy he wou'd sue, but sues too late;
Perseus has in his bosom plung'd the sword,
And, ere he speaks, the wound prevents the word.

The crowds encreasing, and his friends distress'd,
Himself by warring multitudes oppress'd:
Since thus unequally you fight, 'tis time,
He cry'd, to punish your presumptuous crime;
Beware, my friends; his friends were soon prepar'd,
Their sight averting, high the head he rear'd,
And *Gorgon* on his foes severely star'd.
Vain shift! says *Thescelus*, with aspect bold,
Thee, and thy bugbear monster, I behold
With scorn; he lifts his arm, but ere he threw
The dart, the heroe to a statue grew.
In the same posture still the marble stands,
And holds the warrior's weapons in its hands.
Amphyx, whom yet this wonder can't alarm,
Heaves at *Lyncides'* breast his impious arm;
But, while thus daringly he presses on,
His weapon and his arm are turn'd to stone.
Next *Nileus*, he who vainly said he ow'd
His origin to *Nile's* prolifick flood;
Who on his shield seven silver rivers bore,
His birth to witness by the arms he wore;
Full of his sev'n-fold father, thus express'd
His boast to *Perseus*, and his pride confess'd:

See whence we sprung; let this thy comfort be
In thy sure death, that thou didst die by me.
While yet he spoke, the dying accents hung
In sounds imperfect on his marble tongue;
Tho' chang'd to stone, his lips he seem'd to stretch,
And thro' th' insensate rock wou'd force a speech.

   This *Eryx* saw, but seeing wou'd not own;
The mischief by your selves, he cries, is done,
'Tis your cold courage turns your hearts to stone.
Come, follow me; fall on the stripling boy,
Kill him, and you his magick arms destroy.
Then rushing on, his arm to strike he rear'd,
And marbled o'er, his varied frame appear'd.

   These for affronting *Pallas* were chastis'd,
And justly met the death they had despis'd.
But brave *Aconteus*, *Perseus'* friend, by chance
Look'd back, and met the *Gorgon's* fatal glance:
A statue now become, he ghastly stares,
And still the foe to mortal combat dares.
Astyages the living likeness knew,
On the dead stone with vengeful fury flew;
But impotent his rage, the jarring blade
No print upon the solid marble made:
Again, as with redoubled might he struck,
Himself astonish'd in the quarry stuck.

   The vulgar deaths 'twere tedious to rehearse,
And fates below the dignity of verse;
Their safety in their flight two hundred found,
Two hundred, by *Medusa's* head were ston'd.
Fierce *Phineus* now repents the wrongful fight,
And views his varied friends, a dreadful sight;
He knows their faces, for their help he sues,
And thinks, not hearing him, that they refuse:
By name he begs their succour, one by one,
Then doubts their life, and feels the friendly stone.

Struck with remorse, and conscious of his pride,
Convict of sin, he turn'd his eyes aside;
With suppliant mien to *Perseus* thus he prays,
Hence with the head, as far as winds and seas
Can bear thee; hence, o quit the *Cephen* shore,
And never curse us with *Medusa* more,
That horrid head, which stiffens into stone
Those impious men who, daring death, look on.
I warr'd not with thee out of hate or strife,
My honest cause was to defend my wife,
First pledg'd to me; what crime cou'd I suppose,
To arm my friends, and vindicate my spouse?
But vain, too late I see, was our design;
Mine was the title, but the merit thine.
Contending made me guilty, I confess;
But penitence shou'd make that guilt the less:
'Twas thine to conquer by *Minerva's* pow'r;
Favour'd of Heav'n, thy mercy I implore;
For life I sue; the rest to thee I yield;
In pity, from my sight remove the shield.

     He suing said; nor durst revert his eyes
On the grim head: and *Perseus* thus replies:
Coward, what is in me to grant, I will,
Nor blood, unworthy of my valour, spill:
Fear not to perish by my vengeful sword,
From that secure; 'tis all the Fates afford.
Where I now see thee, thou shalt still be seen,
A lasting monument to please our queen;
There still shall thy betroth'd behold her spouse,
And find his image in her father's house.
This said; where *Phineus* turn'd to shun the shield,
Full in his face the staring head he held;
As here and there he strove to turn aside,
The wonder wrought, the man was petrify'd:
All marble was his frame, his humid eyes

Drop'd tears, which hung upon the stone like ice.
In suppliant posture, with uplifted hands,
And fearful look, the guilty statue stands.

　Hence *Perseus* to his native city hies,
Victorious, and rewarded with his prize.
Conquest, o'er *Praetus* the usurper, won,
He re-instates his grandsire in the throne.
Praetus, his brother dispossess'd by might,
His realm enjoy'd, and still detain'd his right:
But *Perseus* pull'd the haughty tyrant down,
And to the rightful king restor'd the throne.
Weak was th' usurper, as his cause was wrong;
Where *Gorgon's* head appears, what arms are strong?
When *Perseus* to his host the monster held,
They soon were statues, and their king expell'd.

　Thence, to *Seriphus* with the head he sails,
Whose prince his story treats as idle tales:
Lord of a little isle, he scorns to seem
Too credulous, but laughs at that, and him.
Yet did he not so much suspect the truth,
As out of pride, or envy, hate the youth.
The *Argive* prince, at his contempt enrag'd,
To force his faith by fatal proof engag'd.
Friends, shut your eyes, he cries; his shield he takes,
And to the king expos'd *Medusa's* snakes.
The monarch felt the pow'r he wou'd not own,
And stood convict of folly in the stone.

　Thus far *Minerva* was content to rove
With *Perseus*, offspring of her father *Jove*:
Now, hid in clouds, *Seriphus* she forsook;
And to the *Theban* tow'rs her journey took.
Cythnos and *Gyaros* lying to the right,
She pass'd unheeded in her eager flight;
And chusing first on *Helicon* to rest,
The virgin Muses in these words address'd:

Me, the strange tidings of a new-found spring,
Ye learned sisters, to this mountain bring.
If all be true that Fame's wide rumours tell,
'Twas *Pegasus* discover'd first your well;
Whose piercing hoof gave the soft earth a blow,
Which broke the surface where these waters flow.
I saw that horse by miracle obtain
Life, from the blood of dire *Medusa* slain;
And now, this equal prodigy to view,
From distant isles to fam'd *Boeotia* flew.

The Muse *Urania* said, Whatever cause
So great a Goddess to this mansion draws;
Our shades are happy with so bright a guest,
You, Queen, are welcome, and we Muses blest.
What Fame has publish'd of our spring is true,
Thanks for our spring to *Pegasus* are due.
Then, with becoming courtesy, she led
The curious stranger to their fountain's head;
Who long survey'd, with wonder, and delight,
Their sacred water, charming to the sight;
Their ancient groves, dark grottos, shady bow'rs,
And smiling plains adorn'd with various flow'rs.
O happy Muses! she with rapture cry'd,
Who, safe from cares, on this fair hill reside;
Blest in your seat, and free your selves to please
With joys of study, and with glorious ease.

Then one replies: O Goddess, fit to guide
Our humble works, and in our choir preside,
Who sure wou'd wisely to these fields repair,
To taste our pleasures, and our labours share,
Were not your virtue, and superior mind
To higher arts, and nobler deeds inclin'd;
Justly you praise our works, and pleasing seat,
Which all might envy in this soft retreat,
Were we secur'd from dangers, and from harms;

But maids are frighten'd with the least alarms,
And none are safe in this licentious time;
Still fierce *Pyreneus*, and his daring crime,
With lasting horror strikes my feeble sight,
Nor is my mind recover'd from the fright.
With *Thracian* arms this bold usurper gain'd
Daulis, and *Phocis*, where he proudly reign'd:
It happen'd once, as thro' his lands we went,
For the bright temple of *Parnassus* bent,
He met us there, and in his artful mind
Hiding the faithless action he design'd,
Confer'd on us (whom, oh! too well he knew)
All honours that to Goddesses are due.
Stop, stop, ye Muses, 'tis your friend who calls,
The tyrant said; behold the rain that falls
On ev'ry side, and that ill-boding sky,
Whose lowring face portends more storms are nigh.
Pray make my house your own, and void of fear,
While this bad weather lasts, take shelter here.
Gods have made meaner places their resort,
And, for a cottage, left their shining court.
   Oblig'd to stop, by the united force
Of pouring rains, and complaisant discourse,
His courteous invitation we obey,
And in his hall resolve a-while to stay.
Soon it clear'd up; the clouds began to fly,
The driving north refin'd the show'ry sky;
Then to pursue our journey we began:
But the false traitor to his portal ran,
Stopt our escape, the door securely barr'd,
And to our honour, violence prepar'd.
But we, transform'd to birds, avoid his snare,
On pinions rising in the yielding air.
   But he, by lust and indignation fir'd,
Up to his highest tow'r with speed retir'd,

And cries, In vain you from my arms withdrew,
The way you go your lover will pursue.
Then, in a flying posture wildly plac'd,
And daring from that height himself to cast,
The wretch fell headlong, and the ground bestrew'd
With broken bones, and stains of guilty blood.

    The Muse yet spoke; when they began to hear
A noise of wings that flutter'd in the air;
And strait a voice, from some high-spreading bough,
Seem'd to salute the company below.
The Goddess wonder'd, and inquir'd from whence
That tongue was heard, that spoke so plainly sense
(It seem'd to her a human voice to be,
But prov'd a bird's; for in a shady tree
Nine magpies perch'd lament their alter'd state,
And, what they hear, are skilful to repeat).

    The sister to the wondring Goddess said,
These, foil'd by us, by us were thus repaid.
These did *Evippè* of *Paeonia* bring
With nine hard labour-pangs to *Pella's* king.
The foolish virgins of their number proud,
And puff'd with praises of the senseless crowd,
Thro' all *Achaia*, and th' *Aemonian* plains,
Defy'd us thus, to match their artless strains;
No more, ye *Thespian* girls, your notes repeat,
Nor with false harmony the vulgar cheat;
In voice or skill, if you with us will vye,
As many we, in voice or skill will try.
Surrender you to us, if we excell,
Fam'd *Aganippè*, and *Medusa's* well.
The conquest yours, your prize from us shall be
The *Aemathian* plains to snowy *Paeonè*;
The nymphs our judges. To dispute the field,
We thought a shame; but greater shame to yield.
On seats of living stone the sisters sit,

And by the rivers swear to judge aright.
  Then rises one of the presumptuous throng,
Steps rudely forth, and first begins the song;
With vain address describes the giants' wars,
And to the Gods their fabled acts prefers.
She sings, from Earth's dark womb how *Typhon* rose,
And struck with mortal fear his heav'nly foes.
How the Gods fled to *Egypt's* slimy soil,
And hid their heads beneath the banks of *Nile*:
How *Typhon*, from the conquer'd skies, pursu'd
Their routed godheads to the sev'n-mouth'd flood;
Forc'd every God, his fury to escape,
Some beastly form to take, or earthly shape.
Jove (so she sung) was chang'd into a ram,
From whence the horns of *Libyan Ammon* came.
Bacchus a goat, *Apollo* was a crow,
Phaebè a cat; the wife of *Jove* a cow,
Whose hue was whiter than the falling snow.
Mercury to a nasty *Ibis* turn'd,
The change obscene, afraid of *Typhon*, mourn'd;
While *Venus* from a fish protection craves,
And once more plunges in her native waves.
  She sung, and to her harp her voice apply'd;
Then us again to match her they defy'd.
But our poor song, perhaps, for you to hear,
Nor leisure serves, nor is it worth your ear.
That causeless doubt remove, O Muse rehearse,
The Goddess cry'd, your ever-grateful verse.
Beneath a chequer'd shade she takes her seat,
And bids the sister her whole song repeat.
The sister thus: *Calliopè* we chose
For the performance. The sweet virgin rose,
With ivy crown'd she tunes her golden strings,
And to her harp this composition sings.

First *Ceres* taught the lab'ring hind to plow
The pregnant Earth, and quickning seed to sow.
She first for Man did wholsome food provide,
And with just laws the wicked world supply'd:
All good from her deriv'd, to her belong
The grateful tributes of the Muse's song.
Her more than worthy of our verse we deem,
Oh! were our verse more worthy of the theme.

Jove on the giant fair *Trinacria* hurl'd,
And with one bolt reveng'd his starry world.
Beneath her burning hills *Tiphaeus* lies,
And, strugling always, strives in vain to rise.
Down does *Pelorus* his right hand suppress
Tow'rd *Latium*, on the left *Pachynè* weighs.
His legs are under *Lilybaeum* spread,
And *Aetna* presses hard his horrid head.
On his broad back he there extended lies,
And vomits clouds of ashes to the skies.
Oft lab'ring with his load, at last he tires,
And spews out in revenge a flood of fires.
Mountains he struggles to o'erwhelm, and towns;
Earth's inmost bowels quake, and Nature groans.
His terrors reach the direful king of Hell;
He fears his throws will to the day reveal
The realms of night, and fright his trembling ghosts.

This to prevent, he quits the *Stygian* coasts,
In his black carr, by sooty horses drawn,
Fair *Sicily* he seeks, and dreads the dawn.
Around her plains he casts his eager eyes,
And ev'ry mountain to the bottom tries.
But when, in all the careful search, he saw
No cause of fear, no ill-suspected flaw;
Secure from harm, and wand'ring on at will,
Venus beheld him from her flow'ry hill:
When strait the dame her little *Cupid* prest

With secret rapture to her snowy breast,
And in these words the flutt'ring boy addrest.

O thou, my arms, my glory, and my pow'r,
My son, whom men, and deathless Gods adore;
Bend thy sure bow, whose arrows never miss'd,
No longer let Hell's king thy sway resist;
Take him, while stragling from his dark abodes
He coasts the kingdoms of superior Gods.
If sovereign *Jove*, if Gods who rule the waves,
And *Neptune*, who rules them, have been thy slaves;
Shall Hell be free? The tyrant strike, my son,
Enlarge thy mother's empire, and thy own.
Let not our Heav'n be made the mock of Hell,
But *Pluto* to confess thy pow'r compel.
Our rule is slighted in our native skies,
See *Pallas*, see *Diana* too defies
Thy darts, which *Ceres'* daughter wou'd despise.
She too our empire treats with aukward scorn;
Such insolence no longer's to be born.
Revenge our slighted reign, and with thy dart
Transfix the virgin's to the uncle's heart.

She said; and from his quiver strait he drew
A dart that surely wou'd the business do.
She guides his hand, she makes her touch the test,
And of a thousand arrows chose the best:
No feather better pois'd, a sharper head
None had, and sooner none, and surer sped.
He bends his bow, he draws it to his ear,
Thro' *Pluto's* heart it drives, and fixes there.

Near *Enna's* walls a spacious lake is spread,
Fam'd for the sweetly-singing swans it bred;
Pergusa is its name: and never more
Were heard, or sweeter on *Cäyster's* shore.
Woods crown the lake; and *Phoebus* ne'er invades
The tufted fences, or offends the shades:

Fresh fragrant breezes fan the verdant bow'rs,
And the moist ground smiles with enamel'd flow'rs
The chearful birds their airy carols sing,
And the whole year is one eternal spring.

  Here, while young *Proserpine*, among the maids,
Diverts herself in these delicious shades;
While like a child with busy speed and care
She gathers lillies here, and vi'lets there;
While first to fill her little lap she strives,
Hell's grizly monarch at the shade arrives;
Sees her thus sporting on the flow'ry green,
And loves the blooming maid, as soon as seen.
His urgent flame impatient of delay,
Swift as his thought he seiz'd the beauteous prey,
And bore her in his sooty carr away.
The frighted Goddess to her mother cries,
But all in vain, for now far off she flies;
Far she behind her leaves her virgin train;
To them too cries, and cries to them in vain,
And, while with passion she repeats her call,
The vi'lets from her lap, and lillies fall:
She misses 'em, poor heart! and makes new moan;
Her lillies, ah! are lost, her vi'lets gone.

  O'er hills, the ravisher, and vallies speeds,
By name encouraging his foamy steeds;
He rattles o'er their necks the rusty reins,
And ruffles with the stroke their shaggy manes.
O'er lakes he whirls his flying wheels, and comes
To the *Palici* breathing sulph'rous fumes.
And thence to where the *Bacchiads* of renown
Between unequal havens built their town;
Where *Arethusa*, round th' imprison'd sea,
Extends her crooked coast to *Cyanè*;
The nymph who gave the neighb'ring lake a name,
Of all *Sicilian* nymphs the first in fame,

She from the waves advanc'd her beauteous head,
The Goddess knew, and thus to *Pluto* said:
Farther thou shalt not with the virgin run;
Ceres unwilling, canst thou be her son?
The maid shou'd be by sweet perswasion won.
Force suits not with the softness of the fair;
For, if great things with small I may compare,
Me *Anapis* once lov'd; a milder course
He took, and won me by his words, not force.

  Then, stretcbing out her arms, she stopt his way;
But he, impatient of the shortest stay,
Throws to his dreadful steeds the slacken'd rein,
And strikes his iron sceptre thro' the main;
The depths profound thro' yielding waves he cleaves,
And to Hell's center a free passage leaves;
Down sinks his chariot, and his realms of night
The God soon reaches with a rapid flight.

  But still does *Cyanè* the rape bemoan,
And with the Goddess' wrongs laments her own;
For the stoln maid, and for her injur'd spring,
Time to her trouble no relief can bring.
In her sad heart a heavy load she bears,
'Till the dumb sorrow turns her all to tears.
Her mingling waters with that fountain pass,
Of which she late immortal Goddess was;
Her varied members to a fluid melt,
A pliant softness in her bones is felt;
Her wavy locks first drop away in dew,
And liquid next her slender fingers grew.
The body's change soon seizes its extreme,
Her legs dissolve, and feet flow off in stream.
Her arms, her back, her shoulders, and her side,
Her swelling breasts in little currents glide,
A silver liquor only now remains
Within the channel of her purple veins;

Nothing to fill love's grasp; her husband chaste
Bathes in that bosom he before embrac'd.

Thus, while thro' all the Earth, and all the main,
Her daughter mournful *Ceres* sought in vain;
Aurora, when with dewy looks she rose,
Nor burnish'd *Vesper* found her in repose,
At *Aetna's* flaming mouth two pitchy pines
To light her in her search at length she tines.
Restless, with these, thro' frosty night she goes,
Nor fears the cutting winds, nor heeds the snows;
And, when the morning-star the day renews,
From east to west her absent child pursues.

Thirsty at last by long fatigue she grows,
But meets no spring, no riv'let near her flows.
Then looking round, a lowly cottage spies,
Smoaking among the trees, and thither hies.
The Goddess knocking at the little door,
'Twas open'd by a woman old and poor,
Who, when she begg'd for water, gave her ale
Brew'd long, but well preserv'd from being stale.
The Goddess drank; a chuffy lad was by,
Who saw the liquor with a grutching eye,
And grinning cries, She's greedy more than dry.

Ceres, offended at his foul grimace,
Flung what she had not drunk into his face,
The sprinklings speckle where they hit the skin,
And a long tail does from his body spin;
His arms are turn'd to legs, and lest his size
Shou'd make him mischievous, and he might rise
Against mankind, diminutives his frame,
Less than a lizzard, but in shape the same.
Amaz'd the dame the wondrous sight beheld,
And weeps, and fain wou'd touch her quondam child.
Yet her approach th' affrighted vermin shuns,
And fast into the greatest crevice runs.

A name they gave him, which the spots exprest,
That rose like stars, and varied all his breast.
    What lands, what seas the Goddess wander'd o'er,
Were long to tell; for there remain'd no more.
Searching all round, her fruitless toil she mourns,
And with regret to *Sicily* returns.
At length, where *Cyanè* now flows, she came,
Who cou'd have told her, were she still the same
As when she saw her daughter sink to Hell;
But what she knows she wants a tongue to tell.
Yet this plain signal manifestly gave,
The virgin's girdle floating on a wave,
As late she dropt it from her slender waste,
When with her uncle thro' the deep she past.
Ceres the token by her grief confest,
And tore her golden hair, and beat her breast.
She knows not on what land her curse shou'd fall,
But, as ingrate, alike upbraids them all,
Unworthy of her gifts; *Trinacria* most,
Where the last steps she found of what she lost.
The plough for this the vengeful Goddess broke,
And with one death the ox, and owner struck.
In vain the fallow fields the peasant tills,
The seed, corrupted ere 'tis sown, she kills.
The fruitful soil, that once such harvests bore,
Now mocks the farmer's care, and teems no more.
And the rich grain which fills the furrow'd glade,
Rots in the seed, or shrivels in the blade;
Or too much sun burns up, or too much rain
Drowns, or black blights destroy the blasted plain;
Or greedy birds the new-sown seed devour,
Or darnel, thistles, and a crop impure
Of knotted grass along the acres stand,
And spread their thriving roots thro' all the land.
    Then from the waves soft *Arethusa* rears

Her head, and back she flings her dropping hairs.
O mother of the maid, whom thou so far
Hast sought, of whom thou canst no tidings hear;
O thou, she cry'd, who art to life a friend,
Cease here thy search, and let thy labour end.
Thy faithful *Sicily*'s a guiltless clime,
And shou'd not suffer for another's crime;
She neither knew, nor cou'd prevent the deed;
Nor think that for my country thus I plead;
My country's *Pisa*, I'm an alien here,
Yet these abodes to *Elis* I prefer,
No clime to me so sweet, no place so dear.
These springs I *Arethusa* now possess,
And this my seat, o gracious Goddess, bless:
This island why I love, and why I crost
Such spacious seas to reach *Ortygia's* coast,
To you I shall impart, when, void of care,
Your heart's at ease, and you're more fit to hear;
When on your brow no pressing sorrow sits,
For gay content alone such tales admits.
When thro' Earth's caverns I a-while have roul'd
My waves, I rise, and here again behold
The long-lost stars; and, as I late did glide
Near *Styx*, *Proserpina* there I espy'd.
Fear still with grief might in her face be seen;
She still her rape laments; yet, made a queen,
Beneath those gloomy shades her sceptre sways,
And ev'n th' infernal king her will obeys.

   This heard, the Goddess like a statue stood,
Stupid with grief; and in that musing mood
Continu'd long; new cares a-while supprest
The reigning pow'rs of her immortal breast.
At last to *Jove* her daughter's sire she flies,
And with her chariot cuts the chrystal skies;
She comes in clouds, and with dishevel'd hair,

Standing before his throne, prefers her pray'r.
   King of the Gods, defend my blood and thine,
And use it not the worse for being mine.
If I no more am gracious in thy sight,
Be just, o *Jove*, and do thy daughter right.
In vain I sought her the wide world around,
And, when I most despair'd to find her, found.
But how can I the fatal finding boast,
By which I know she is for ever lost?
Without her father's aid, what other Pow'r
Can to my arms the ravish'd maid restore?
Let him restore her, I'll the crime forgive;
My child, tho' ravish'd, I'd with joy receive.
Pity, your daughter with a thief shou'd wed,
Tho' mine, you think, deserves no better bed.
   Jove thus replies: It equally belongs
To both, to guard our common pledge from wrongs.
But if to things we proper names apply,
This hardly can be call'd an injury.
The theft is love; nor need we blush to own
The thief, if I can judge, to be our son.
Had you of his desert no other proof,
To be *Jove's* brother is methinks enough.
Nor was my throne by worth superior got,
Heav'n fell to me, as Hell to him, by lot:
If you are still resolv'd her loss to mourn,
And nothing less will serve than her return;
Upon these terms she may again be yours
(Th' irrevocable terms of fate, not ours),
Of *Stygian* food if she did never taste,
Hell's bounds may then, and only then, be past.
   The Goddess now, resolving to succeed,
Down to the gloomy shades descends with speed;
But adverse fate had otherwise decreed.
For, long before, her giddy thoughtless child

Had broke her fast, and all her projects spoil'd.
As in the garden's shady walk she stray'd,
A fair pomegranate charm'd the simple maid,
Hung in her way, and tempting her to taste,
She pluck'd the fruit, and took a short repast.
Seven times, a seed at once, she eat the food;
The fact *Ascalaphus* had only view'd;
Whom *Acheron* begot in *Stygian* shades
On *Orphnè*, fam'd among *Avernal* maids;
He saw what past, and by discov'ring all,
Detain'd the ravish'd nymph in cruel thrall.

But now a queen, she with resentment heard,
And chang'd the vile informer to a bird.
In *Phlegeton's* black stream her hand she dips,
Sprinkles his head, and wets his babling lips.
Soon on his face, bedropt with magick dew,
A change appear'd, and gawdy feathers grew.
A crooked beak the place of nose supplies,
Rounder his head, and larger are his eyes.
His arms and body waste, but are supply'd
With yellow pinions flagging on each side.
His nails grow crooked, and are turn'd to claws,
And lazily along his heavy wings he draws.
Ill-omen'd in his form, the unlucky fowl,
Abhorr'd by men, and call'd a screeching owl.

Justly this punishment was due to him,
And less had been too little for his crime;
But, o ye nymphs that from the flood descend,
What fault of yours the Gods cou'd so offend,
With wings and claws your beauteous forms to spoil,
Yet save your maiden face, and winning smile?
Were you not with her in *Pergusa's* bow'rs,
When *Proserpine* went forth to gather flow'rs?
Since *Pluto* in his carr the Goddess caught,
Have you not for her in each climate sought?

And when on land you long had search'd in vain,
You wish'd for wings to cross the pathless main;
That Earth and Sea might witness to your care:
The Gods were easy, and return'd your pray'r;
With golden wing o'er foamy waves you fled,
And to the sun your plumy glories spread.
But, lest the soft enchantment of your songs,
And the sweet musick of your flat'ring tongues
Shou'd quite be lost (as courteous fates ordain),
Your voice and virgin beauty still remain.

Jove some amends for Ceres lost to make,
Yet willing Pluto shou'd the joy partake,
Gives 'em of Proserpine an equal share,
Who, claim'd by both, with both divides the year.
The Goddess now in either empire sways,
Six moons in Hell, and six with Ceres stays.
Her peevish temper's chang'd; that sullen mind,
Which made ev'n Hell uneasy, now is kind,
Her voice refines, her mein more sweet appears,
Her forehead free from frowns, her eyes from tears,
As when, with golden light, the conqu'ring day
Thro' dusky exhalations clears a way.
Ceres her daughter's rape no longer mourn'd,
But back to Arethusa's spring return'd;
And sitting on the margin, bid her tell
From whence she came, and why a sacred well.

Still were the purling waters, and the maid
From the smooth surface rais'd her beauteous head,
Wipes off the drops that from her tresses ran,
And thus to tell Alpheus' loves began.

In Elis first I breath'd the living air,
The chase was all my pleasure, all my care.
None lov'd like me the forest to explore,
To pitch the toils, and drive the bristled boar.
Of fair, tho' masculine, I had the name,

But gladly wou'd to that have quitted claim:
It less my pride than indignation rais'd,
To hear the beauty I neglected, prais'd;
Such compliments I loath'd, such charms as these
I scorn'd, and thought it infamy to please.

   Once, I remember, in the summer's heat,
Tir'd with the chase, I sought a cool retreat;
And, walking on, a silent current found,
Which gently glided o'er the grav'ly ground.
The chrystal water was so smooth, so clear,
My eye distinguish'd ev'ry pebble there.
So soft its motion, that I scarce perceiv'd
The running stream, or what I saw believ'd.
The hoary willow, and the poplar, made
Along the shelving bank a grateful shade.
In the cool rivulet my feet I dipt,
Then waded to the knee, and then I stript;
My robe I careless on an osier threw,
That near the place commodiously grew;
Nor long upon the border naked stood,
But plung'd with speed into the silver flood.
My arms a thousand ways I mov'd, and try'd
To quicken, if I cou'd, the lazy tide;
Where, while I play'd my swimming gambols o'er,
I heard a murm'ring voice, and frighted sprung to shore.
Oh! whither, *Arethusa*, dost thou fly?
From the brook's bottom did *Alpheus* cry;
Again, I heard him, in a hollow tone,
Oh! whither, *Arethusa*, dost thou run?
Naked I flew, nor cou'd I stay to hide
My limbs, my robe was on the other side;
Alpheus follow'd fast, th' inflaming sight
Quicken'd his speed, and made his labour light;
He sees me ready for his eager arms,
And with a greedy glance devours my charms.

As trembling doves from pressing danger fly,
When the fierce hawk comes sousing from the sky;
And, as fierce hawks the trembling doves pursue,
From him I fled, and after me he flew.
First by *Orchomenus* I took my flight,
And soon had *Psophis* and *Cyllene* in sight;
Behind me then high *Maenalus* I lost,
And craggy *Erimanthus* scal'd with frost;
Elis was next; thus far the ground I trod
With nimble feet, before the distanc'd God.
But here I lagg'd, unable to sustain
The labour longer, and my flight maintain;
While he more strong, more patient of the toil,
And fir'd with hopes of beauty's speedy spoil,
Gain'd my lost ground, and by redoubled pace,
Now left between us but a narrow space.
Unweary'd I 'till now o'er hills, and plains,
O'er rocks, and rivers ran, and felt no pains:
The sun behind me, and the God I kept,
But, when I fastest shou'd have run, I stept.
Before my feet his shadow now appear'd;
As what I saw, or rather what I fear'd.
Yet there I could not be deceiv'd by fear,
Who felt his breath pant on my braided hair,
And heard his sounding tread, and knew him to be near.
Tir'd, and despairing, O celestial maid,
I'm caught, I cry'd, without thy heav'nly aid.
Help me, *Diana*, help a nymph forlorn,
Devoted to the woods, who long has worn
Thy livery, and long thy quiver born.
The Goddess heard; my pious pray'r prevail'd;
In muffling clouds my virgin head was veil'd,
The am'rous God, deluded of his hopes,
Searches the gloom, and thro' the darkness gropes;
Twice, where *Diana* did her servant hide

He came, and twice, O *Arethusa*! cry'd.
How shaken was my soul, how sunk my heart!
The terror seiz'd on ev'ry trembling part.
Thus when the wolf about the mountain prowls
For prey, the lambkin hears his horrid howls:
The tim'rous hare, the pack approaching nigh,
Thus hearkens to the hounds, and trembles at the cry;
Nor dares she stir, for fear her scented breath
Direct the dogs, and guide the threaten'd death.
Alpheus in the cloud no traces found
To mark my way, yet stays to guard the ground,
The God so near, a chilly sweat possest
My fainting limbs, at ev'ry pore exprest;
My strength distill'd in drops, my hair in dew,
My form was chang'd, and all my substance new.
Each motion was a stream, and my whole frame
Turn'd to a fount, which still preserves my name.
Resolv'd I shou'd not his embrace escape,
Again the God resumes his fluid shape;
To mix his streams with mine he fondly tries,
But still *Diana* his attempt denies.
She cleaves the ground; thro' caverns dark I run
A diff'rent current, while he keeps his own.
To dear *Ortygia* she conducts my way,
And here I first review the welcome day.

Here *Arethusa* stopt; then *Ceres* takes
Her golden carr, and yokes her fiery snakes;
With a just rein, along mid-heaven she flies
O'er Earth, and seas, and cuts the yielding skies.
She halts at *Athens*, dropping like a star,
And to *Triptolemus* resigns her carr.
Parent of seed, she gave him fruitful grain,
And bad him teach to till and plough the plain;
The seed to sow, as well in fallow fields,
As where the soil manur'd a richer harvest yields.

The youth o'er *Europe* and o'er *Asia* drives,
'Till at the court of *Lyncus* he arrives.
The tyrant *Scythia's* barb'rous empire sway'd;
And, when he saw *Triptolemus*, he said,
How cam'st thou, stranger, to our court, and why?
Thy country, and thy name? The youth did thus reply:
Triptolemus my name; my country's known
O'er all the world, *Minerva's* fav'rite town,
Athens, the first of cities in renown.
By land I neither walk'd, nor sail'd by sea,
But hither thro' the *Aether* made my way.
By me, the Goddess who the fields befriends,
These gifts, the greatest of all blessings, sends.
The grain she gives if in your soil you sow,
Thence wholsom food in golden crops shall grow.

Soon as the secret to the king was known,
He grudg'd the glory of the service done,
And wickedly resolv'd to make it all his own.
To hide his purpose, he invites his guest,
The friend of *Ceres*, to a royal feast,
And when sweet sleep his heavy eyes had seiz'd,
The tyrant with his steel attempts his breast.
Him strait a lynx's shape the Goddess gives,
And home the youth her sacred dragons drives.

The chosen Muse here ends her sacred lays;
The nymphs unanimous decree the bays,
And give the *Heliconian* Goddesses the praise.
Then, far from vain that we shou'd thus prevail,
But much provok'd to hear the vanquish'd rail,
Calliopè resumes: Too long we've born
Your daring taunts, and your affronting scorn;
Your challenge justly merited a curse,
And this unmanner'd railing makes it worse.
Since you refuse us calmly to enjoy
Our patience, next our passions we'll employ;

The dictates of a mind enrag'd pursue,
And, what our just resentment bids us, do.
    The railers laugh, our threats and wrath despise,
And clap their hands, and make a scolding noise:
But in the fact they're seiz'd; beneath their nails
Feathers they feel, and on their faces scales;
Their horny beaks at once each other scare,
Their arms are plum'd, and on their backs they bear
Py'd wings, and flutter in the fleeting air.
Chatt'ring, the scandal of the woods they fly,
And there continue still their clam'rous cry:
The same their eloquence, as maids, or birds,
Now only noise, and nothing then but words.

The End of the Fifth Book.

BOOK THE SIXTH

PALLAS, attending to the Muse's song,
Approv'd the just resentment of their wrong;
And thus reflects: While tamely I commend
Those who their injur'd deities defend,
My own divinity affronted stands,
And calls aloud for justice at my hands;
Then takes the hint, asham'd to lag behind,
And on *Arachnè* bends her vengeful mind;
One at the loom so excellently skill'd,
That to the Goddess she refus'd to yield.

    Low was her birth, and small her native town,
She from her art alone obtain'd renown.
Idmon, her father, made it his employ,
To give the spungy fleece a purple dye:
Of vulgar strain her mother, lately dead,
With her own rank had been content to wed;
Yet she their daughter, tho' her time was spent
In a small hamlet, and of mean descent,
Thro' the great towns of *Lydia* gain'd a name,
And fill'd the neighb'ring countries with her fame.

    Oft, to admire the niceness of her skill,
The *Nymphs* would quit their fountain, shade, or hill:
Thither, from green *Tymolus*, they repair,
And leave the vineyards, their peculiar care;
Thither, from fam'd *Pactolus'* golden stream,
Drawn by her art, the curious *Naiads* came.
Nor would the work, when finish'd, please so much,
As, while she wrought, to view each graceful touch;
Whether the shapeless wool in balls she wound,
Or with quick motion turn'd the spindle round,
Or with her pencil drew the neat design,
Pallas her mistress shone in every line.
This the proud maid with scornful air denies,
And ev'n the Goddess at her work defies;

Disowns her heav'nly mistress ev'ry hour,
Nor asks her aid, nor deprecates her pow'r.
Let us, she cries, but to a tryal come,
And, if she conquers, let her fix my doom.

The Goddess then a beldame's form put on,
With silver hairs her hoary temples shone;
Prop'd by a staff, she hobbles in her walk,
And tott'ring thus begins her old wives' talk.

Young maid attend, nor stubbornly despise
The admonitions of the old, and wise;
For age, tho' scorn'd, a ripe experience bears,
That golden fruit, unknown to blooming years:
Still may remotest fame your labours crown,
And mortals your superior genius own;
But to the Goddess yield, and humbly meek
A pardon for your bold presumption seek;
The Goddess will forgive. At this the maid,
With passion fir'd, her gliding shuttle stay'd;
And, darting vengeance with an angry look,
To *Pallas* in disguise thus fiercely spoke.

Thou doating thing, whose idle babling tongue
But too well shews the plague of living long;
Hence, and reprove, with this your sage advice,
Your giddy daughter, or your aukward neice;
Know, I despise your counsel, and am still
A woman, ever wedded to my will;
And, if your skilful Goddess better knows,
Let her accept the tryal I propose.

She does, impatient *Pallas* strait replies,
And, cloath'd with heavenly light, sprung from her odd
The *Nymphs*, and virgins of the plain adore   [disguise.
The awful Goddess, and confess her pow'r;
The maid alone stood unappall'd; yet show'd
A transient blush, that for a moment glow'd,
Then disappear'd; as purple streaks adorn

The opening beauties of the rosy morn;
Till *Phoebus* rising prevalently bright,
Allays the tincture with his silver light.
Yet she persists, and obstinately great,
In hopes of conquest hurries on her fate.
The Goddess now the challenge waves no more,
Nor, kindly good, advises as before.
Strait to their posts appointed both repair,
And fix their threaded looms with equal care:
Around the solid beam the web is ty'd,
While hollow canes the parting warp divide;
Thro' which with nimble flight the shuttles play,
And for the woof prepare a ready way;
The woof and warp unite, press'd by the toothy slay.

Thus both, their mantles button'd to their breast,
Their skilful fingers ply with willing haste,
And work with pleasure; while they chear the eye
With glowing purple of the *Tyrian* dye:
Or, justly intermixing shades with light,
Their colourings insensibly unite.
As when a show'r transpierc'd with sunny rays,
Its mighty arch along the heav'n displays;
From whence a thousand diff'rent colours rise,
Whose fine transition cheats the clearest eyes;
So like the intermingled shading seems,
And only differs in the last extreams.
Then threads of gold both artfully dispose,
And, as each part in just proportion rose,
Some antique fable in their work disclose.

Pallas in figures wrought the heav'nly Pow'rs,
And *Mars's* hill among th' *Athenian* tow'rs.
On lofty thrones twice six celestials sate,
Jove in the midst, and held their warm debate;
The subject weighty, and well-known to fame,
From whom the city shou'd receive its name.

Each God by proper features was exprest,
Jove with majestick mein excell'd the rest.
His three-fork'd mace the dewy sea-God shook,
And, looking sternly, smote the ragged rock;
When from the stone leapt forth a spritely steed,
And *Neptune* claims the city for the deed.

   Herself she blazons, with a glitt'ring spear,
And crested helm that veil'd her braided hair,
With shield, and scaly breast-plate, implements of war.
Struck with her pointed launce, the teeming Earth
Seem'd to produce a new surprizing birth;
When, from the glebe, the pledge of conquest sprung,
A tree pale-green with fairest olives hung.

   And then, to let her giddy rival learn
What just rewards such boldness was to earn,
Four tryals at each corner had their part,
Design'd in miniature, and touch'd with art.
Haemus in one, and *Rodopè* of *Thrace*,
Transform'd to mountains, fill'd the foremost place;
Who claim'd the titles of the Gods above,
And vainly us'd the epithets of *Jove*.
Another shew'd, where the *Pigmaean* dame,
Profaning *Juno's* venerable name,
Turn'd to an airy crane, descends from far,
And with her *Pigmy* subjects wages war.
In a third part, the rage of Heav'n's great queen,
Display'd on proud *Antigonè*, was seen:
Who with presumptuous boldness dar'd to vye,
For beauty with the empress of the sky.
Ah! what avails her ancient princely race,
Her sire a king, and *Troy* her native place:
Now, to a noisy stork transform'd, she flies,
And with her whiten'd pinions cleaves the skies.
And in the last remaining part was drawn
Poor *Cinyras* that seem'd to weep in stone;

Clasping the temple steps, he sadly mourn'd
His lovely daughters, now to marble turn'd.
With her own tree the finish'd piece is crown'd,
And wreaths of peaceful olive all the work surround.

　　Arachnè drew the fam'd intrigues of *Jove*,
Chang'd to a bull to gratify his love;
How thro' the briny tide all foaming hoar,
Lovely *Europa* on his back he bore.
The sea seem'd waving, and the trembling maid
Shrunk up her tender feet, as if afraid;
And, looking back on the forsaken strand,
To her companions wafts her distant hand.
Next she design'd *Asteria's* fabled rape,
When *Jove* assum'd a soaring eagle's shape:
And shew'd how *Leda* lay supinely press'd,
Whilst the soft snowy swan sate hov'ring o'er her breast,
How in a satyr's form the God beguil'd,
When fair *Antiopè* with twins he fill'd.
Then, like *Amphytrion*, but a real *Jove*,
In fair *Alcmena's* arms he cool'd his love.
In fluid gold to *Danae's* heart he came,
Aegina felt him in a lambent flame.
He took *Mnemosynè* in shepherd's make,
And for *Dëois* was a speckled snake.

　　She made thee, *Neptune*, like a wanton steer,
Pacing the meads for love of *Arnè* dear;
Next like a stream, thy burning flame to slake,
And like a ram, for fair *Bisaltis'* sake.
Then *Ceres* in a steed your vigour try'd,
Nor cou'd the mare the yellow Goddess hide.
Next, to a fowl transform'd, you won by force
The snake-hair'd mother of the winged horse;
And, in a dolphin's fishy form, subdu'd
Melantho sweet beneath the oozy flood.

　　All these the maid with lively features drew,

And open'd proper landskips to the view.
There *Phoebus*, roving like a country swain,
Attunes his jolly pipe along the plain;
For lovely *Isse's* sake in shepherd's weeds,
O'er pastures green his bleating flock he feeds,
There *Bacchus*, imag'd like the clust'ring grape,
Melting bedrops *Erigonè's* fair lap;
And there old *Saturn*, stung with youthful heat,
Form'd like a stallion, rushes to the feat.
Fresh flow'rs, which twists of ivy intertwine,
Mingling a running foliage, close the neat design.
    This the bright Goddess passionately mov'd,
With envy saw, yet inwardly approv'd.
The scene of heav'nly guilt with haste she tore,
Nor longer the affront with patience bore;
A boxen shuttle in her hand she took,
And more than once *Arachnè's* forehead struck.
Th' unhappy maid, impatient of the wrong,
Down from a beam her injur'd person hung;
When *Pallas*, pitying her wretched state,
At once prevented, and pronounc'd her fate:
Live; but depend, vile wretch, the Goddess cry'd,
Doom'd in suspence for ever to be ty'd;
That all your race, to utmost date of time,
May feel the vengeance, and detest the crime.
    Then, going off, she sprinkled her with juice,
Which leaves of baneful aconite produce.
Touch'd with the pois'nous drug, her flowing hair
Fell to the ground, and left her temples bare;
Her usual features vanish'd from their place,
Her body lessen'd all, but most her face.
Her slender fingers, hanging on each side
With many joynts, the use of legs supply'd:
A spider's bag the rest, from which she gives
A thread, and still by constant weaving lives.

Swift thro' the *Phrygian* towns the rumour flies,
And the strange news each female tongue employs:
Niobè, who before she married knew
The famous nymph, now found the story true;
Yet, unreclaim'd by poor *Arachnè's* fate,
Vainly above the Gods assum'd a state.
Her husband's fame, their family's descent,
Their pow'r, and rich dominion's wide extent,
Might well have justify'd a decent pride;
But not on these alone the dame rely'd.
Her lovely progeny, that far excell'd,
The mother's heart with vain ambition swell'd:
The happiest mother not unjustly styl'd,
Had no conceited thoughts her tow'ring fancy fill'd.

For once a prophetess with zeal inspir'd,
Their slow neglect to warm devotion fir'd;
Thro' ev'ry street of *Thebes* who ran possess'd,
And thus in accents wild her charge express'd:
Haste, haste, ye *Theban* matrons, and adore,
With hallow'd rites, *Latona's* mighty pow'r;
And, to the heav'nly twins that from her spring,
With laurel crown'd, your smoking incense bring.
Strait the great summons ev'ry dame obey'd,
And due submission to the Goddess paid:
Graceful, with laurel chaplets dress'd, they came,
And offer'd incense in the sacred flame.

Mean-while, surrounded with a courtly guard,
The royal *Niobè* in state appear'd;
Attir'd in robes embroider'd o'er with gold,
And mad with rage, yet lovely to behold:
Her comely tresses, trembling as she stood,
Down her fine neck with easy motion flow'd;
Then, darting round a proud disdainful look,
In haughty tone her hasty passion broke,
And thus began: What madness this, to court

A Goddess, founded meerly on report?
Dare ye a poor pretended Pow'r invoke,
While yet no altars to my godhead smoke?
Mine, whose immediate lineage stands confess'd
From *Tantalus*, the only mortal guest
That e'er the Gods admitted to their feast.
A sister of the *Pleiads* gave me birth;
And *Atlas*, mightiest mountain upon Earth,
Who bears the globe of all the stars above,
My grandsire was, and *Atlas* sprung from *Jove*.
The *Theban* towns my majesty adore,
And neighb'ring *Phrygia* trembles at my pow'r:
Rais'd by my husband's lute, with turrets crown'd,
Our lofty city stands secur'd around.
Within my court, where-e'er I turn my eyes,
Unbounded treasures to my prospect rise:
With these my face I modestly may name,
As not unworthy of so high a claim;
Seven are my daughters, of a form divine,
With seven fair sons, an indefective line.
Go, fools! consider this; and ask the cause
From which my pride its strong presumption draws;
Consider this; and then prefer to me
Caeus the *Titan's* vagrant progeny;
To whom, in travel, the whole spacious Earth
No room afforded for her spurious birth.
Not the least part in Earth, in Heav'n, or seas,
Would grant your out-law'd Goddess any ease:
'Till pitying hers, from his own wand'ring case,
Delos, the floating island, gave a place.
There she a mother was, of two at most;
Only the seventh part of what I boast.
My joys all are beyond suspicion fix'd;
With no pollutions of misfortune mix'd;
Safe on the *Basis* of my pow'r I stand,

Above the reach of *Fortune's* fickle hand.
Lessen she may my inexhausted store,
And much destroy, yet still must leave me more.
Suppose it possible that some may dye
Of this my num'rous lovely progeny;
Still with *Latona* I might safely vye.
Who, by her scanty breed, scarce fit to name,
But just escapes the childless woman's shame.
Go then, with speed your laurel'd heads uncrown,
And leave the silly farce you have begun.

    The tim'rous throng their sacred rites forbore,
And from their heads the verdant laurel tore;
Their haughty queen they with regret obey'd,
And still in gentle murmurs softly pray'd.

    High, on the top of *Cynthus'* shady mount,
With grief the Goddess saw the base affront;
And, the abuse revolving in her breast,
The mother her twin-offspring thus addrest.

    Lo I, my children, who with comfort knew
Your God-like birth, and thence my glory drew;
And thence have claim'd precedency of place
From all but *Juno* of the heav'nly race,
Must now despair, and languish in disgrace.
My godhead question'd, and all rites divine,
Unless you succour, banish'd from my shrine.
Nay more, the imp of *Tantalus* has flung
Reflections with her vile paternal tongue;
Has dar'd prefer her mortal breed to mine,
And call'd me childless; which, just fate, may she repine!

    When to urge more the Goddess was prepar'd,
Phoebus in haste replies, Too much we've heard,
And ev'ry moment's lost, while vengeance is defer'd.
Diana spoke the same. Then both enshroud
Their heav'nly bodies in a sable cloud;
And to the *Theban* tow'rs descending light,

Thro' the soft yielding air direct their flight.
  Without the wall there lies a champian ground
With even surface, far extending round,
Beaten and level'd, while it daily feels
The trampling horse, and chariot's grinding wheels.
Part of proud *Niobè's* young rival breed,
Practising there to ride the manag'd steed,
Their bridles boss'd with gold, were mounted high
On stately furniture of *Tyrian* dye.
Of these, *Ismenos*, who by birth had been
The first fair issue of the fruitful queen,
Just as he drew the rein to guide his horse,
Around the compass of the circling course,
Sigh'd deeply, and the pangs of smart express'd,
While the shaft stuck, engor'd within his breast:
And, the reins dropping from his dying hand,
He sunk quite down, and tumbled on the sand.
Sipylus next the rattling quiver heard,
And with full speed for his escape prepar'd;
As when the pilot from the black'ning skies
A gath'ring storm of wintry rain descries,
His sails unfurl'd, and crowded all with wind,
He strives to leave the threat'ning cloud behind:
So fled the youth; but an unerring dart
O'ertook him, quick discharg'd, and sped with art;
Fix'd in his neck behind, it trembling stood,
And at his throat display'd the point besmear'd with blood.
Prone, as his posture was, he tumbled o'er,
And bath'd his courser's mane with steaming gore.
Next at young *Phaedimus* they took their aim,
And *Tantalus*, who bore his grandsire's name:
These, when their other exercise was done,
To try the wrestler's oily sport begun;
And, straining ev'ry nerve, their skill express'd
In closest grapple, joining breast to breast:

When from the bending bow an arrow sent,
Joyn'd as they were, thro' both their bodies went:
Both groan'd, and writhing both their limbs with pain,
They fell together bleeding on the plain;
Then both their languid eye-balls faintly roul,
And thus together breathe away their soul.
With grief *Alphenor* saw their doleful plight,
And smote his breast, and sicken'd at the sight;
Then to their succour ran with eager haste,
And, fondly griev'd, their stiff'ning limbs embrac'd;
But in the action falls: a thrilling dart,
By *Phoebus* guided, pierc'd him to the heart.
This, as they drew it forth, his midriff tore,
Its barbed point the fleshy fragments bore,
And let the soul gush out in streams of purple gore.
But *Damasichthon*, by a double wound,
Beardless, and young, lay gasping on the ground.
Fix'd in his sinewy ham, the steely point
Stuck thro' his knee, and pierc'd the nervous joint:
And, as he stoop'd to tug the painful dart,
Another struck him in a vital part;
Shot thro' his wezon, by the wing it hung.
The life-blood forc'd it out, and darting upward sprung,
Ilioneus, the last, with terror stands,
Lifting in pray'r his unavailing hands;
And, ignorant from whom his griefs arise,
Spare me, o all ye heav'nly Pow'rs, he cries:
Phoebus was touch'd too late, the sounding bow
Had sent the shaft, and struck the fatal blow;
Which yet but gently gor'd his tender side,
So by a slight and easy wound he dy'd.

   Swift to the mother's ears the rumour came,
And doleful sighs the heavy news proclaim;
With anger and surprize inflam'd by turns,
In furious rage her haughty stomach burns:

First she disputes th' effects of heav'nly pow'r,
Then at their daring boldness wonders more;
For poor *Amphion* with sore grief distrest,
Hoping to sooth his cares by endless rest,
Had sheath'd a dagger in his wretched breast.
And she, who toss'd her high disdainful head,
When thro' the streets in solemn pomp she led
The throng that from *Latona's* altar fled,
Assuming state beyond the proudest queen;
Was now the miserablest object seen.
Prostrate among the clay-cold dead she fell,
And kiss'd an undistinguish'd last farewel.
Then her pale arms advancing to the skies,
Cruel *Latona!* triumph now, she cries.
My grieving soul in bitter anguish drench,
And with my woes your thirsty passion quench;
Feast your black malice at a price thus dear,
While the sore pangs of sev'n such deaths I bear.
Triumph, too cruel rival, and display
Your conqu'ring standard; for you've won the day.
Yet I'll excel; for yet, tho' sev'n are slain,
Superior still in number I remain.
Scarce had she spoke; the bow-string's twanging sound
Was heard, and dealt fresh terrors all around;
Which all, but *Niobè* alone, confound.
Stunn'd, and obdurate by her load of grief,
Insensible she sits, nor hopes relief.
  Before the fun'ral biers, all weeping sad,
Her daughters stood, in vests of sable clad,
When one, surpriz'd, and stung with sudden smart,
In vain attempts to draw the sticking dart:
But to grim death her blooming youth resigns,
And o'er her brother's corpse her dying head reclines.
This, to asswage her mother's anguish tries,
And, silenc'd in the pious action, dies;

Shot by a secret arrow, wing'd with death,
Her fault'ring lips but only gasp'd for breath.
One, on her dying sister, breathes her last;
Vainly in flight another's hopes are plac'd:
This hiding, from her fate a shelter seeks;
That trembling stands, and fills the air with shrieks.
And all in vain; for now all six had found
Their way to death, each by a diff'rent wound.
The last, with eager care the mother veil'd,
Behind her spreading mantle close conceal'd,
And with her body guarded, as a shield.
Only for this, this youngest, I implore,
Grant me this one request, I ask no more;
O grant me this! she passionately cries:
But while she speaks, the destin'd virgin dies.

    Widow'd, and childless, lamentable state!
A doleful sight, among the dead she sate;
Harden'd with woes, a statue of despair,
To ev'ry breath of wind unmov'd her hair;
Her cheek still red'ning, but its colour dead,
Faded her eyes, and set within her head.
No more her pliant tongue its motion keeps,
But stands congeal'd within her frozen lips.
Stagnate, and dull, within her purple veins,
Its current stop'd, the lifeless blood remains.
Her feet their usual offices refuse,
Her arms, and neck their graceful gestures lose:
Action, and life from ev'ry part are gone,
And ev'n her entrails turn to solid stone;
Yet still she weeps, and whirl'd by stormy winds,
Born thro' the air, her native country finds;
There fix'd, she stands upon a bleaky hill,
There yet her marble cheeks eternal tears distil.

    Then all, reclaim'd by this example, show'd
A due regard for each peculiar God:

Both men, and women their devoirs express'd,
And great *Latona's* awful pow'r confess'd.
Then, tracing instances of older time,
To suit the nature of the present crime,
Thus one begins his tale. — Where *Lycia* yields
A golden harvest from its fertile fields,
Some churlish peasants, in the days of yore,
Provok'd the Goddess to exert her pow'r.
The thing indeed the meanness of the place
Has made obscure, surprizing as it was;
But I my self once happen'd to behold
This famous lake of which the story's told.
My father then, worn out by length of days,
Nor able to sustain the tedious ways,
Me with a guide had sent the plains to roam,
And drive his well-fed stragling heifers home.
Here, as we saunter'd thro' the verdant meads,
We spy'd a lake o'er-grown with trembling reeds,
Whose wavy tops an op'ning scene disclose,
From which an antique smoaky altar rose.
I, as my susperstitious guide had done,
Stop'd short, and bless'd my self, and then went on;
Yet I enquir'd to whom the altar stood,
Faunus, the *Naids*, or some native God?
No silvan deity, my friend replies,
Enshrin'd within this hallow'd altar lies.
For this, o youth, to that fam'd Goddess stands,
Whom, at th' imperial *Juno's* rough commands,
Of ev'ry quarter of the Earth bereav'd,
Delos, the floating isle, at length receiv'd.
Who there, in spite of enemies, brought forth,
Beneath an olive's shade, her great twin-birth.

Hence too she fled the furious stepdame's pow'r,
And in her arms a double godhead bore;
And now the borders of fair *Lycia* gain'd,

Just when the summer solstice parch'd the land.
With thirst the Goddess languishing, no more
Her empty'd breast would yield its milky store;
When, from below, the smiling valley show'd
A silver lake that in its bottom flow'd:
A sort of clowns were reaping, near the bank,
The bending osier, and the bullrush dank;
The cresse, and water-lilly, fragrant weed,
Whose juicy stalk the liquid fountains feed.
The Goddess came, and kneeling on the brink,
Stoop'd at the fresh repast, prepar'd to drink.
Then thus, being hinder'd by the rabble race,
In accents mild expostulates the case.
Water I only ask, and sure 'tis hard
From *Nature's* common rights to be debar'd:
This, as the genial sun, and vital air,
Should flow alike to ev'ry creature's share.
Yet still I ask, and as a favour crave,
That which, a publick bounty, Nature gave.
Nor do I seek my weary limbs to drench;
Only, with one cool draught, my thirst I'd quench.
Now from my throat the usual moisture dries,
And ev'n my voice in broken accents dies:
One draught as dear as life I should esteem,
And water, now I thirst, would nectar seem.
Oh! let my little babes your pity move,
And melt your hearts to charitable love;
They (as by chance they did) extend to you
Their little hands, and my request pursue.

    Whom would these soft perswasions not subdue,
Tho' the most rustick, and unmanner'd crew?
Yet they the Goddess's request refuse,
And with rude words reproachfully abuse:
Nay more, with spiteful feet the villains trod
O'er the soft bottom of the marshy flood,

And blacken'd all the lake with clouds of rising mud.
   Her thirst by indignation was suppress'd;
Bent on revenge, the Goddess stood confess'd.
Her suppliant hands uplifting to the skies,
For a redress, to Heav'n she now applies.
And, May you live, she passionately cry'd,
Doom'd in that pool for ever to abide.
   The Goddess has her wish; for now they chuse
To plunge, and dive among the watry ooze;
Sometimes they shew their head above the brim,
And on the glassy surface spread to swim;
Often upon the bank their station take,
Then spring, and leap into the cooly lake.
Still, void of shame, they lead a clam'rous life,
And, croaking, still scold on in endless strife;
Compell'd to live beneath the liquid stream,
Where still they quarrel, and attempt to skream.
Now, from their bloated throat, their voice puts on
Imperfect murmurs in a hoarser tone;
Their noisy jaws, with bawling now grown wide,
An ugly sight! extend on either side:
Their motly back, streak'd with a list of green,
Joyn'd to their head, without a neck is seen;
And, with a belly broad and white, they look
Meer frogs, and still frequent the muddy brook.
   Scarce had the man this famous story told,
Of vengeance on the *Lycians* shown of old,
When strait another pictures to their view
The *Satyr's* fate, whom angry *Phoebus* slew;
Who, rais'd with high conceit, and puff'd with pride,
At his own pipe the skilful God defy'd.
Why do you tear me from my self, he cries?
Ah cruel! must my skin be made the prize?
This for a silly pipe? he roaring said,
Mean-while the skin from off his limbs was flay'd.

All bare, and raw, one large continu'd wound,
With streams of blood his body bath'd the ground.
The blueish veins their trembling pulse disclos'd,
The stringy nerves lay naked, and expos'd;
His guts appear'd, distinctly each express'd,
With ev'ry shining fibre of his breast.

   The *Fauns*, and *Silvans*, with the *Nymphs* that rove
Among the *Satyrs* in the shady grove;
Olympus, known of old, and ev'ry swain
That fed, or flock, or herd upon the plain,
Bewail'd the loss; and with their tears that flow'd,
A kindly moisture on the earth bestow'd;
That soon, conjoyn'd, and in a body rang'd,
Sprung from the ground, to limpid water chang'd;
Which, down thro' *Phrygia's* rocks, a mighty stream,
Comes tumbling to the sea, and *Marsya* is its name.

   From these relations strait the people turn
To present truths, and lost *Amphion* mourn:
The mother most was blam'd, yet some relate
That *Pelops* pity'd, and bewail'd her fate,
And stript his cloaths, and laid his shoulder bare,
And made the iv'ry miracle appear.
This shoulder, from the first, was form'd of flesh,
As lively as the other, and as fresh;
But, when the youth was by his father slain,
The Gods restor'd his mangled limbs again;
Only that place which joins the neck and arm,
The rest untouch'd, was found to suffer harm:
The loss of which an iv'ry piece sustain'd;
And thus the youth his limbs, and life regain'd.

   To *Thebes* the neighb'ring princes all repair,
And with condolance the misfortune share.
Each bord'ring state in solemn form address'd,
And each betimes a friendly grief express'd.
Argos, with *Sparta's*, and *Mycenae's* towns,

And *Calydon*, yet free from fierce *Diana's* frowns.
Corinth for finest brass well fam'd of old,
Orthomenos for men of courage bold:
Cleönae lying in the lowly dale,
And rich *Messenè* with its fertile vale:
Pylos, for *Nestor's* City after fam'd,
And *Tröezen*, not as yet from *Pittheus* nam'd.
And those fair cities, which are hem'd around
By double seas within the *Isthmian* ground;
And those, which farther from the sea-coast stand,
Lodg'd in the bosom of the spacious land.

Who can believe it? *Athens* was the last:
Tho' for politeness fam'd for ages past.
For a strait siege, which then their walls enclos'd,
Such acts of kind humanity oppos'd:
And thick with ships, from foreign nations bound,
Sea-ward their city lay invested round.

These, with auxiliar forces led from far,
Tereus of *Thrace*, brave, and inur'd to war,
Had quite defeated, and obtain'd a name,
The warrior's due, among the sons of *Fame*.
This, with his wealth, and pow'r, and ancient line,
From *Mars* deriv'd, *Pandions's* thoughts incline
His daughter *Procnè* with the prince to joyn.

Nor *Hymen*, nor the *Graces* here preside,
Nor *Juno* to befriend the blooming bride;
But *Fiends* with fun'ral brands the process led,
And *Furies* waited at the *Genial* bed:
And all night long the scrieching owl aloof,
With baleful notes, sate brooding o'er the roof.
With such ill *Omens* was the match begun,
That made them parents of a hopeful son.
Now *Thrace* congratulates their seeming joy,
And they, in thankful rites, their minds employ.
If the fair queen's espousals pleas'd before,

Itys, the new-born prince, now pleases more;
And each bright day, the birth, and bridal feast,
Were kept with hallow'd pomp above the rest.
So far true happiness may lye conceal'd,
When, by false lights, we fancy 'tis reveal'd!

Now, since their nuptials, had the golden sun
Five courses round his ample zodiac run;
When gentle *Procnè* thus her lord address'd,
And spoke the secret wishes of her breast:
If I, she said, have ever favour found,
Let my petition with success be crown'd:
Let me at *Athens* my dear sister see,
Or let her come to *Thrace*, and visit me.
And, lest my father should her absence mourn,
Promise that she shall make a quick return.
With thanks I'd own the obligation due
Only, o *Tereus*, to the Gods, and you.

Now, ply'd with oar, and sail at his command,
The nimble gallies reach'd th' *Athenian* land,
And anchor'd in the fam'd *Piraean* bay,
While *Tereus* to the palace takes his way;
The king salutes, and ceremonies past,
Begins the fatal embassy at last;
The occasion of his voyage he declares,
And, with his own, his wife's request prefers:
Asks leave that, only for a little space,
Their lovely sister might embark for *Thrace*.

Thus while he spoke, appear'd the royal maid,
Bright *Philomela*, splendidly array'd;
But most attractive in her charming face,
And comely person, turn'd with ev'ry grace:
Like those fair *Nymphs*, that are describ'd to rove
Across the glades, and op'nings of the grove;
Only that these are dress'd for silvan sports,
And less become the finery of courts.

 Tereus beheld the virgin, and admir'd,
And with the coals of burning lust was fir'd:
Like crackling stubble, or the summer hay,
When forked lightnings o'er the meadows play.
Such charms in any breast might kindle love,
But him the heats of inbred lewdness move;
To which, tho' *Thrace* is naturally prone,
Yet his is still superior, and his own.
Strait her attendants he designs to buy,
And with large bribes her governess would try:
Herself with ample gifts resolves to bend,
And his whole kingdom in th' attempt expend:
Or, snatch'd away by force of arms, to bear,
And justify the rape with open war.
The boundless passion boils within his breast,
And his projecting soul admits no rest.

 And now, impatient of the least delay,
By pleading *Procnè's* cause, he speeds his way:
The eloquence of love his tongue inspires,
And, in his wife's, he speaks his own desires;
Hence all his importunities arise,
And tears unmanly trickle from his eyes.

 Ye Gods! what thick involving darkness blinds
The stupid faculties of mortal minds!
Tereus the credit of good-nature gains
From these his crimes; so well the villain feigns.
And, unsuspecting of his base designs,
In the request fair *Philomela* joyns;
Her snowy arms her aged sire embrace,
And clasp his neck with an endearing grace:
Only to see her sister she entreats,
A seeming blessing, which a curse compleats.
Tereus surveys her with a luscious eye,
And in his mind forestalls the blissful joy:
Her circling arms a scene of lust inspire,

And ev'ry kiss foments the raging fire.
Fondly he wishes for the father's place,
To feel, and to return the warm embrace;
Since not the nearest ties of filial blood
Would damp his flame, and force him to be good.

At length, for both their sakes, the king agrees;
And *Philomela*, on her bended knees,
Thanks him for what her fancy calls success,
When cruel fate intends her nothing less.

Now *Phoebus*, hastning to ambrosial rest,
His fiery steeds drove sloping down the west:
The sculptur'd gold with sparkling wines was fill'd,
And, with rich meats, each chearful table smil'd.
Plenty, and mirth the royal banquet close,
Then all retire to sleep, and sweet repose.
But the lewd monarch, tho' withdrawn apart,
Still feels love's poison rankling in his heart:
Her face divine is stamp'd within his breast,
Fancy imagines, and improves the rest:
And thus, kept waking by intense desire,
He nourishes his own prevailing fire.

Next day the good old king for *Tereus* sends,
And to his charge the virgin recommends;
His hand with tears th' indulgent father press'd,
Then spoke, and thus with tenderness address'd.

Since the kind instances of pious love,
Do all pretence of obstacle remove;
Since *Procnè's*, and her own, with your request,
O'er-rule the fears of a paternal breast;
With you, dear son, my daughter I entrust,
And by the Gods adjure you to be just;
By truth, and ev'ry consanguineal tye,
To watch, and guard her with a father's eye.
And, since the least delay will tedious prove,
In keeping from my sight the child I love,

With speed return her, kindly to asswage
The tedious troubles of my lingring age.
And you, my *Philomel*, let it suffice,
To know your sister's banish'd from my eyes;
If any sense of duty sways your mind,
Let me from you the shortest absence find.
He wept; then kiss'd his child; and while he speaks,
The tears fall gently down his aged cheeks.
Next, as a pledge of fealty, he demands,
And, with a solemn charge, conjoyns their hands;
Then to his daughter, and his grandson sends,
And by their mouth a blessing recommends;
While, in a voice with dire forebodings broke,
Sobbing, and faint, the last farewel was spoke.

　　Now *Philomela*, scarce receiv'd on board,
And in the royal gilded bark secur'd,
Beheld the dashes of the bending oar,
The ruffled sea, and the receding shore;
When strait (his joy impatient of disguise)
We've gain'd our point, the rough *Barbarian* cries;
Now I possess the dear, the blissful hour,
And ev'ry wish subjected to my pow'r.
Transports of lust his vicious thoughts employ,
And he forbears, with pain, th' expected joy.
His gloting eyes incessantly survey'd
The virgin beauties of the lovely maid:
As when the bold rapacious bird of *Jove*,
With crooked talons stooping from above,
Has snatcht, and carry'd to his lofty nest
A captive hare, with cruel gripes opprest;
Secure, with fix'd, and unrelenting eyes,
He sits, and views the helpless, trembling prize.

　　Their vessels now had made th' intended land,
And all with joy descend upon the strand;
When the false tyrant seiz'd the princely maid,

And to a lodge in distant woods convey'd;
Pale, sinking, and distress'd with jealous fears,
And asking for her sister all in tears.
The letcher, for enjoyment fully bent,
No longer now conceal'd his base intent;
But with rude haste the bloomy girl deflow'r'd,
Tender, defenceless, and with ease o'erpower'd.
Her piercing accents to her sire complain,
And to her absent sister, but in vain:
In vain she importunes, with doleful cries,
Each unattentive godhead of the skies.
She pants and trembles, like the bleating prey,
From some close-hunted wolf just snatch'd away;
That still, with fearful horror, looks around,
And on its flank regards the bleeding wound.
Or, as the tim'rous dove, the danger o'er,
Beholds her shining plumes besmear'd with gore,
And, tho' deliver'd from the faulcon's claw,
Yet shivers, and retains a secret awe.
　　But when her mind a calm reflection shar'd,
And all her scatter'd spirits were repair'd:
Torn, and disorder'd while her tresses hung,
Her livid hands, like one that mourn'd, she wrung;
Then thus, with grief o'erwhelm'd her languid eyes,
Savage, inhumane, cruel wretch! she cries;
Whom not a parent's strict commands could move,
Tho' charg'd, and utter'd with the tears of love;
Nor virgin innocence, nor all that's due
To the strong contract of the nuptial vow:
Virtue, by this, in wild confusion's laid,
And I compell'd to wrong my sister's bed;
Whilst you, regardless of your marriage oath,
With stains of incest have defil'd us both.
Tho' I deserv'd some punishment to find,
This was, ye Gods! too cruel, and unkind.

Yet, villain, to compleat your horrid guilt,
Stab here, and let my tainted blood be spilt.
Oh happy! had it come, before I knew
The curs'd embrace of vile perfidious you;
Then my pale ghost, pure from incestuous love,
Had wander'd spotless thro' th' *Elysian* grove.
But, if the Gods above have pow'r to know,
And judge those actions that are done below;
Unless the dreaded thunders of the sky,
Like me, subdu'd, and violated lye;
Still my revenge shall take its proper time,
And suit the baseness of your hellish crime.
My self, abandon'd, and devoid of shame,
Thro' the wide world your actions will proclaim;
Or tho' I'm prison'd in this lonely den,
Obscur'd, and bury'd from the sight of men,
My mournful voice the pitying rocks shall move,
And my complainings eccho thro' the grove.
Hear me, o Heav'n! and, if a God be there,
Let him regard me, and accept my pray'r.
   Struck with these words, the tyrant's guilty breast
With fear, and anger, was, by turns, possest;
Now, with remorse his conscience deeply stung,
He drew the faulchion that beside her hung,
And first her tender arms behind her bound,
Then drag'd her by the hair along the ground.
The princess willingly her throat reclin'd,
And view'd the steel with a contented mind;
But soon her tongue the girding pinchers strain,
With anguish, soon she feels the piercing pain:
Oh father! father! she would fain have spoke,
But the sharp torture her intention broke;
In vain she tries, for now the blade has cut
Her tongue sheer off, close to the trembling root.
The mangled part still quiver'd on the ground,

Murmuring with a faint imperfect sound:
And, as a serpent writhes his wounded train,
Uneasy, panting, and possess'd with pain;
The piece, while life remain'd, still trembled fast,
And to its mistress pointed to the last.

   Yet, after this so damn'd, and black a deed,
Fame (which I scarce can credit) has agreed,
That on her rifled charms, still void of shame,
He frequently indulg'd his lustful flame,
At last he ventures to his *Procnè's* sight,
Loaded with guilt, and cloy'd with long delight;
There, with feign'd grief, and false, dissembled sighs,
Begins a formal narrative of lies;
Her sister's death he artfully declares,
Then weeps, and raises credit from his tears.
Her vest, with flow'rs of gold embroider'd o'er,
With grief distress'd, the mournful matron tore,
And a beseeming suit of gloomy sable wore.
With cost, an honorary tomb she rais'd,
And thus th' imaginary ghost appeas'd.
Deluded queen! the fate of her you love,
Nor grief, nor pity, but revenge should move.

   Thro' the twelve signs had pass'd the circling sun,
And round the compass of the *Zodiac* run;
What must unhappy *Philomela* do,
For ever subject to her keeper's view?
Huge walls of massy stone the lodge surround,
From her own mouth no way of speaking's found.
But all our wants by wit may be supply'd,
And art makes up, what fortune has deny'd:
With skill exact a *Phrygian* web she strung,
Fix'd to a loom that in her chamher hung,
Where in-wrought letters, upon white display'd,
In purple notes, her wretched case betray'd:
The piece, when finish'd, secretly she gave

Into the charge of one poor menial slave;
And then, with gestures, made him understand,
It must be safe convey'd to *Procnè's* hand.
The slave, with speed, the queen's apartment sought,
And render'd up his charge, unknowing what he brought
But when the cyphers, figur'd in each fold,
Her sister's melancholy story told
(Strange that she could!) with silence, she survey'd
The tragick piece, and without weeping read:
In such tumultuous haste her passions sprung,
They choak'd her voice, and quite disarm'd her tongue.
No room for female tears; the *Furies* rise,
Darting vindictive glances from her eyes;
And, stung with rage, she bounds from place to place,
While stern revenge sits low'ring in her face.

Now the triennial celebration came,
Observ'd to *Bacchus* by each *Thracian* dame;
When, in the privacies of night retir'd,
They act his rites, with sacred rapture fir'd:
By night, the tinkling cymbals ring around,
While the shrill notes from *Rhodopè* resound;
By night, the queen, disguis'd, forsakes the court,
To mingle in the festival resort.
Leaves of the curling vine her temples shade,
And, with a circling wreath, adorn her head:
Adown her back the stag's rough spoils appear,
Light on her shoulder leans a cornel spear.

Thus, in the fury of the God conceal'd,
Procnè her own mad headstrong passion veil'd;
Now, with her gang, to the thick wood she flies,
And with religious yellings fills the skies;
The fatal lodge, as 'twere by chance, she seeks,
And, thro' the bolted doors, an entrance breaks;
From thence, her sister snatching by the hand,
Mask'd like the ranting *Bacchanalian* band,

Within the limits of the court she drew,
Shading, with ivy green, her outward hue.
But *Philomela*, conscious of the place,
Felt new reviving pangs of her disgrace;
A shiv'ring cold prevail'd in ev'ry part,
And the chill'd blood ran trembling to her heart.

   Soon as the queen a fit retirement found,
Stript of the garlands that her temples crown'd,
She strait unveil'd her blushing sister's face,
And fondly clasp'd her with a close embrace:
But, in confusion lost, th' unhappy maid,
With shame dejected, hung her drooping head,
As guilty of a crime that stain'd her sister's bed.
That speech, that should her injur'd virtue clear,
And make her spotless innocence appear,
Is now no more; only her hands, and eyes
Appeal, in signals, to the conscious skies.
In *Procnè's* breast the rising passions boil,
And burst in anger with a mad recoil;
Her sister's ill-tim'd grief, with scorn, she blames,
Then, in these furious words her rage proclaims.

   Tears, unavailing, but defer our time,
The stabbing sword must expiate the crime;
Or worse, if wit, on bloody vengeance bent,
A weapon more tormenting can invent.
O sister! I've prepar'd my stubborn heart,
To act some hellish, and unheard-of part;
Either the palace to surround with fire,
And see the villain in the flames expire;
Or, with a knife, dig out his cursed eyes,
Or, his false tongue with racking engines seize;
Or, cut away the part that injur'd you,
And, thro' a thousand wounds, his guilty soul pursue.
Tortures enough my passion has design'd,
But the variety distracts my mind.

A-while, thus wav'ring, stood the furious dame,
When *Itys* fondling to his mother came;
From him the cruel fatal hint she took,
She view'd him with a stern remorseless look:
Ah! but too like thy wicked sire, she said,
Forming the direful purpose in her head.
At this a sullen grief her voice supprest,
While silent passions struggle in her breast.

Now, at her lap arriv'd, the flatt'ring boy
Salutes his parent with a smiling joy:
About her neck his little arms are thrown,
And he accosts her in a pratling tone.
Then her tempestuous anger was allay'd,
And in its full career her vengeance stay'd;
While tender thoughts, in spite of passion, rise,
And melting tears disarm her threat'ning eyes.
But when she found the mother's easy heart,
Too fondly swerving from th' intended part;
Her injur'd sister's face again she view'd:
And, as by turns surveying both she stood,
While this fond boy (she said) can thus express
The moving accents of his fond address;
Why stands my sister of her tongue bereft,
Forlorn, and sad, in speechless silence left?
O *Procnè*, see the fortune of your house!
Such is your fate, when match'd to such a spouse!
Conjugal duty, if observ'd to him,
Would change from virtue, and become a crime;
For all respect to *Tereus* must debase
The noble blood of great *Pandion's* race.

Strait at these words, with big resentment fill'd,
Furious her look, she flew, and seiz'd her child;
Like a fell tigress of the savage kind,
That drags the tender suckling of the hind
Thro' *India's* gloomy groves, where *Ganges* laves

The shady scene, and rouls his streamy waves.
   Now to a close apartment they were come,
Far off retir'd within the spacious dome;
When *Procnè*, on revengeful mischief bent,
Home to his heart a piercing ponyard sent.
Itys, with rueful cries, but all too late,
Holds out his hands, and deprecates his fate;
Still at his mother's neck he fondly aims,
And strives to melt her with endearing names;
Yet still the cruel mother perseveres,
Nor with concern his bitter anguish hears.
This might suffice; but *Philomela* too
Across his throat a shining curtlass drew.
Then both, with knives, dissect each quiv'ring part,
And carve the butcher'd limbs with cruel art;
Which, whelm'd in boiling cauldrons o'er the fire,
Or turn'd on spits, in steamy smoak aspire:
While the long entries, with their slipp'ry floor,
Run down in purple streams of clotted gore.
   Ask'd by his wife to this inhuman feast,
Tereus unknowingly is made a guest:
Whilst she her plot the better to disguise,
Styles it some unknown mystick sacrifice;
And such the nature of the hallow'd rite,
The wife her husband only could invite,
The slaves must all withdraw, and be debarr'd the sight.
Tereus, upon a throne of antique state,
Loftily rais'd, before the banquet sate;
And glutton like, luxuriously pleas'd,
With his own flesh his hungry maw appeas'd.
Nay, such a blindness o'er his senses falls,
That he for *Itys* to the table calls.
When *Procnè*, now impatient to disclose
The joy that from her full revenge arose,
Cries out, in transports of a cruel mind,

Within your self your *Itys* you may find.
Still, at this puzzling answer, with surprise,
Around the room he sends his curious eyes;
And, as he still inquir'd, and call'd aloud,
Fierce *Philomela*, all besmear'd with blood,
Her hands with murder stain'd, her spreading hair
Hanging dishevel'd with a ghastly air,
Stept forth, and flung full in the tyrant's face
The head of *Itys*, goary as it was:
Nor ever long'd so much to use her tongue,
And with a just reproach to vindicate her wrong.

The *Thracian* monarch from the table flings,
While with his cries the vaulted parlour rings;
His imprecations eccho down to Hell,
And rouze the snaky *Furies* from their *Stygian* cell.
One while he labours to disgorge his breast,
And free his stomach from the cursed feast;
Then, weeping o'er his lamentable doom,
He styles himself his son's sepulchral tomb.
Now, with drawn sabre, and impetuous speed,
In close pursuit he drives *Pandion's* breed;
Whose nimble feet spring with so swift a force
Across the fields, they seem to wing their course.
And now, on real wings themselves they raise,
And steer their airy flight by diff'rent ways;
One to the woodland's shady covert hies,
Around the smoaky roof the other flies;
Whose feathers yet the marks of murder stain,
Where stampt upon her breast, the crimson spots remai
Tereus, through grief, and haste to be reveng'd,
Shares the like fate, and to a bird is chang'd:
Fix'd on his head, the crested plumes appear,
Long is his beak, and sharpen'd like a spear;
Thus arm'd, his looks his inward mind display,
And, to a lapwing turn'd, he fans his way.

Exceeding trouble, for his children's fate,
Shorten'd *Pandion's* days, and chang'd his date;
Down to the shades below, with sorrow spent,
An earlier, unexpected ghost he went.

Erechtheus next th' *Athenian* sceptre sway'd,
Whose rule the state with joynt consent obey'd;
So mix'd his justice with his valour flow'd,
His reign one scene of princely goodness shew'd.
Four hopeful youths, as many females bright,
Sprung from his loyns, and sooth'd him with delight.

Two of these sisters, of a lovelier air,
Excell'd the rest, tho' all the rest were fair.
Procris, to *Cephalus* in wedlock ty'd,
Bless'd the young silvan with a blooming bride:
For *Orithyia Boreas* suffer'd pain,
For the coy maid sued long, but sued in vain;
Tereus his neighbour, and his *Thracian* blood,
Against the match a main objection stood;
Which made his vows, and all his suppliant love,
Empty as air and ineffectual prove.

But when he found his soothing flatt'ries fail,
Nor saw his soft addresses cou'd avail;
Blust'ring with ire, he quickly has recourse
To rougher arts, and his own native force.
'Tis well, he said; such usage is my due,
When thus disguis'd by foreign ways I sue;
When my stern airs, and fierceness I disclaim,
And sigh for love, ridiculously tame;
When soft addresses foolishly I try,
Nor my own stronger remedies apply.
By force and violence I chiefly live,
By them the lowring stormy tempests drive;
In foaming billows raise the hoary deep,
Writhe knotted oaks, and sandy desarts sweep;
Congeal the falling flakes of fleecy snow,

And bruise, with ratling hail, the plains below.
I, and my brother-winds, when joyn'd above,
Thro' the waste champian of the skies we rove,
With such a boist'rous full career engage,
That Heav'n's whole concave thunders at our rage.
While, struck from nitrous clouds, fierce lightnings play,
Dart thro' the storm, and gild the gloomy day.
Or when, in subterraneous caverns pent,
My breath, against the hollow Earth, is bent,
The quaking world above, and ghosts below,
My mighty pow'r, by dear experience, know,
Tremble with fear, and dread the fatal blow.
This is the only cure to be apply'd,
Thus to *Erechtheus* I should be ally'd;
And thus the scornful virgin should be woo'd,
Not by intreaty, but by force subdu'd.

   Boreas, in passion, spoke these huffing things,
And, as he spoke, he shook his dreadful wings;
At which, afar the shiv'ring sea was fan'd,
And the wide surface of the distant land:
His dusty mantle o'er the hills he drew,
And swept the lowly vallies, as he flew;
Then, with his yellow wings, embrac'd the maid,
And, wrapt in dusky clouds, far off convey'd.
The sparkling blaze of Love's prevailing fire
Shone brighter as he flew, and flam'd the higher.
And now the God, possess'd of his delight,
To northern *Thrace* pursu'd his airy flight,
Where the young ravish'd nymph became his bride,
And soon the luscious sweets of wedlock try'd.

   Two lovely twins, th' effect of this embrace,
Crown their soft labours, and their nuptials grace;
Who, like their mother, beautiful, and fair,
Their father's strength, and feather'd pinions share:
Yet these, at first, were wanting, as 'tis said,

And after, as they grew, their shoulders spread.
Zethes and *Calaïs*, the pretty twins,
Remain'd unfledg'd, while smooth their beardless chins;
But when, in time, the budding silver down
Shaded their face, and on their cheeks was grown,
Two sprouting wings upon their shoulders sprung,
Like those in birds, that veil the callow young.
Then as their age advanc'd, and they began
From greener youth to ripen into man,
With *Jason's Argonauts* they cross'd the seas,
Embark'd in quest of the fam'd golden fleece;
There, with the rest, the first frail vessel try'd,
And boldly ventur'd on the swelling tide.

The End of the Sixth Book.

BOOK THE SEVENTH

THE *Argonauts* now stemm'd the foaming tide,
     And to *Arcadia's* shore their course apply'd;
     Where sightless *Phineus* spent his age in grief,
But *Boreas'* sons engage in his relief;
And those unwelcome guests, the odious race
Of *Harpyes*, from the monarch's table chase.
With *Jason* then they greater toils sustain,
And *Phasis'* slimy banks at last they gain,
Here boldly they demand the golden prize
Of *Scythia's* king, who sternly thus replies:
That mighty labours they must first o'ercome,
Or sail their *Argo* thence unfreighted home.
     Meanwhile *Medea*, seiz'd with fierce desire,
By reason strives to quench the raging fire;
But strives in vain! — Some God (she said) withstands,
And reason's baffl'd council countermands.
What unseen Pow'r does this disorder move?
'Tis love, — at least 'tis like, what men call love.
Else wherefore shou'd the king's commands appear
To me too hard? — But so indeed they are.
Why shou'd I for a stranger fear, lest he
Shou'd perish, whom I did but lately see?
His death, or safety, what are they to me?
Wretch, from thy virgin-breast this flame expel,
And soon — Oh cou'd I, all wou'd then be well!
But love, resistless love, my soul invades;
Discretion this, affection that perswades.
I see the right, and I approve it too,
Condemn the wrong — and yet the wrong pursue.
Why, royal maid, shou'dst thou desire to wed
A wanderer, and court a foreign bed?
Thy native land, tho' barb'rous, can present
A bridegroom worth a royal bride's content:
And whether this advent'rer lives, or dies,

In Fate, and Fortune's fickle pleasure lies.
Yet may be live! for to the Pow'rs above,
A virgin, led by no impulse of love,
So just a suit may, for the guiltless, move.
Whom wou'd not *Jason's* valour, youth and blood
Invite? or cou'd these merits be withstood,
At least his charming person must encline
The hardest heart — I'm sure 'tis so with mine!
Yet, if I help him not, the flaming breath
Of bulls, and earth-born foes, must be his death.
Or, should he through these dangers force his way,
At last he must be made the dragon's prey.
If no remorse for such distress I feel,
I am a tigress, and my breast is steel.
Why do I scruple then to see him slain,
And with the tragick scene my eyes prophane?
My magick's art employ, not to asswage
The *Salvages*, but to enflame their rage?
His earth-born foes to fiercer fury move,
And accessary to his murder prove?
The Gods forbid — But pray'rs are idle breath,
When action only can prevent his death.
Shall I betray my father, and the state,
To intercept a rambling hero's fate;
Who may sail off next hour, and sav'd from harms
By my assistance, bless another's arms?
Whilst I, not only of my hopes bereft,
But to unpity'd punishment am left.
If he is false, let the ingrateful bleed!
But no such symptom in his looks I read.
Nature wou'd ne'er have lavish'd so much grace
Upon his person, if his soul were base.
Besides, he first shall plight his faith, and swear
By all the Gods; what therefore can'st thou fear?
Medea haste, from danger set him free,

Jason shall thy eternal debtor be.
And thou, his queen, with sov'raign state enstall'd,
By *Graecian* dames the *Kind Preserver* call'd.
Hence idle dreams, by love-sick fancy bred!
Wilt thou, *Medea*, by vain wishes led,
To sister, brother, father bid adieu?
Forsake thy country's Gods, and country too?
My father's harsh, my brother but a child,
My sister rivals me, my country's wild;
And for its Gods, the greatest of 'em all
Inspires my breast, and I obey his call.
That great endearments I forsake, is true,
But greater far the hopes that I pursue:
The pride of having sav'd the youths of *Greece*
(Each life more precious than our golden fleece);
A nobler soil by me shall be possest,
I shall see towns with arts and manners blest;
And, what I prize above the world beside,
Enjoy my *Jason* — and when once his bride,
Be more than mortal, and to Gods ally'd.
They talk of hazards I must first sustain,
Of floating islands justling in the main;
Our tender barque expos'd to dreadful shocks
Of fierce *Charybdis'* gulf, and *Scylla's* rocks,
Where breaking waves in whirling eddies rowl,
And rav'nous dogs that in deep caverns howl:
Amidst these terrors, while I lye possest
Of him I love, and lean on *Jason's* breast,
In tempests unconcern'd I will appear,
Or, only for my husband's safety fear.
Didst thou say husband? — canst thou so deceive
Thy self, fond maid, and thy own cheat believe?
In vain thou striv'st to varnish o'er thy shame,
And grace thy guilt with wedlock's sacred name.
Pull off the coz'ning masque, and oh! in time

Discover and avoid the fatal crime.
She ceas'd — the Graces now, with kind surprize,
And virtue's lovely train, before her eyes
Present themselves, and vanquish'd *Cupid* flies.

　　She then retires to *Hecate's* shrine, that stood
Far in the covert of a shady wood:
She finds the fury of her flames asswag'd,
But, seeing *Jason* there, again they rag'd.
Blushes, and paleness did by turns invade
Her tender cheeks, and secret grief betray'd.
As fire, that sleeping under ashes lyes,
Fresh-blown, and rous'd, does up in blazes rise,
So flam'd the virgin's breast —
New kindled by her lover's sparkling eyes.
For chance, that day, had with uncommon grace
Adorn'd the lovely youth, and through his face
Display'd an air so pleasing as might charm
A Goddess, and a Vestal's bosom warm.
Her ravish'd eyes survey him o'er and o'er,
As some gay wonder never seen before;
Transported to the skies she seems to be,
And thinks she gazes on a deity.
But when he spoke, and prest her trembling hand,
And did with tender words her aid demand,
With vows, and oaths to make her soon his bride,
She wept a flood of tears, and thus reply'd:
I see my error, yet to ruin move,
Nor owe my fate to ignorance, but love:
Your life I'll guard, and only crave of you
To swear once more — and to your oath be true.
He swears by *Hecate* he would all fulfil,
And by her grandfather's prophetick skill,
By ev'ry thing that doubting love cou'd press,
His present danger, and desir'd success.
She credits him, and kindly does produce

Enchanted herbs, and teaches him their use:
Their mystick names, and virtues he admires,
And with his booty joyfully retires.
Impatient for the wonders of the day,
Aurora drives the loyt'ring stars away.
Now *Mars's* mount the pressing people fill,
The crowd below, the nobles crown the hill;
The king himself high-thron'd above the rest,
With iv'ry scepter, and in purple drest.

Forthwith the brass-hoof'd bulls are set at large,
Whose furious nostrils sulph'rous flame discharge:
The blasted herbage by their breath expires;
As forges rumble with excessive fires,
And furnaces with fiercer fury glow,
When water on the panting mass ye throw;
With such a noise, from their convulsive breast,
Thro' bellowing throats, the struggling vapour prest.

Yet *Jason* marches up without concern,
While on th' advent'rous youth the monsters turn
Their glaring eyes, and, eager to engage,
Brandish their steel-tipt horns in threatning rage:
With brazen hoofs they beat the ground, and choak
The ambient air with clouds of dust and smoak:
Each gazing *Graecian* for his champion shakes,
While bold advances he securely makes
Thro' sindging blasts; such wonders magick art
Can work, when love conspires, and plays his part.
The passive savages like statues stand,
While he their dew-laps stroaks with soothing hand;
To unknown yokes their brawny necks they yield,
And, like tame oxen, plow the wond'ring field.
The *Colchians* stare; the *Graecians* shout, and raise
Their champion's courage with inspiring praise.

Embolden'd now, on fresh attempts he goes,
With serpent's teeth the fertile furrows sows;

The glebe, fermenting with inchanted juice,
Makes the snake's teeth a human crop produce.
For as an infant, pris'ner to the womb,
Contented sleeps, 'till to perfection come,
Then does the cell's obscure confinement scorn,
He tosses, throbs, and presses to be born;
So from the lab'ring Earth no single birth,
But a whole troop of lusty youths rush forth;
And, what's more strange, with martial fury warm'd,
And for encounter all compleatly arm'd;
In rank and file, as they were sow'd, they stand,
Impatient for the signal of command.
No foe but the *Aemonian* youth appears;
At him they level their steel-pointed spears;
His frighted friends, who triumph'd just before,
With peals of sighs his desp'rate case deplore:
And where such hardy warriors are afraid,
What must the tender, and enamour'd maid?
Her spirits sink, the blood her cheek forsook;
She fears, who for his safety undertook:
She knew the vertue of the spells she gave,
She knew the force, and knew her lover brave;
But what's a single champion to an host?
Yet scorning thus to see him tamely lost,
Her strong reserve of secret arts she brings,
And last, her never-failing song she sings.
Wonders ensue; among his gazing foes
The massy fragment of a rock he throws;
This charm in civil war engag'd 'em all;
By mutual wounds those Earth-born brothers fall.

   The *Greeks*, transported with the strange success,
Leap from their seats the conqu'ror to caress;
Commend, and kiss, and clasp him in their arms:
So would the kind contriver of the charms;
But her, who felt the tenderest concern,

Honour condemns in secret flames to burn;
Committed to a double guard of fame,
Aw'd by a virgin's, and a princess' name.
But thoughts are free, and fancy unconfin'd,
She kisses, courts, and hugs him in her mind;
To fav'ring Pow'rs her silent thanks she gives,
By whose indulgence her lov'd hero lives.

    One labour more remains, and, tho' the last,
In danger far surmounting all the past;
That enterprize by Fates in store was kept,
To make the dragon sleep that never slept,
Whose crest shoots dreadful lustre; from his jaws
A tripple tire of forked stings he draws,
With fangs, and wings of a prodigious size:
Such was the guardian of the golden prize.
Yet him, besprinkled with *Lethaean* dew,
The fair inchantress into slumber threw;
And then, to fix him, thrice she did repeat
The rhyme, that makes the raging winds retreat,
In stormy seas can halcyon seasons make,
Turn rapid streams into a standing lake;
While the soft guest his drowzy eye-lids seals,
Th' ungarded golden fleece the stranger steals;
Proud to possess the purchase of his toil,
Proud of his royal bride, the richer spoil;
To sea both prize, and patroness he bore,
And lands triumphant on his native shore.

    Aemonian matrons, who their absence mourn'd,
Rejoyce to see their prosp'rous sons return'd:
Rich curling fumes of incense feast the skies,
An hecatomb of voted victims dies,
With gilded horns, and garlands on their head,
And all the pomp of death, to th' altar led.
Congratulating bowls go briskly round,
Triumphant shouts in louder musick drown'd.

Amidst these revels, why that cloud of care
On *Jason's* brow? (to whom the largest share
Of mirth was due) — His father was not there.
Aeson was absent, once the young, and brave,
Now crush'd with years, and bending to the grave.
At last withdrawn, and by the crowd unseen,
Pressing her hand (with starting sighs between),
He supplicates his kind, and skilful queen.

O patroness! preserver of my life!
(Dear when my mistress, and much dearer wife)
Your favours to so vast a sum amount,
'Tis past the pow'r of numbers to recount;
Or cou'd they be to computation brought,
The history would a romance be thought:
And yet, unless you add one favour more,
Greater than all that you conferr'd before,
But not too hard for love and magick skill,
Your past are thrown away, and *Jason's* wretched still.
The morning of my life is just begun,
But my declining father's race is run;
From my large stock retrench the long arrears,
And add 'em to expiring *Aeson's* years.

Thus spake the gen'rous youth, and wept the rest.
Mov'd with the piety of his request,
To his ag'd sire such filial duty shown,
So diff'rent from her treatment of her own,
But still endeav'ring her remorse to hide,
She check'd her rising sighs, and thus reply'd.

How cou'd the thought of such inhuman wrong
Escape (said she) from pious *Jason's* tongue?
Does the whole world another *Jason* bear,
Whose life *Medea* can to yours prefer?
Or cou'd I with so dire a change dispence,
Hecate will never join in that offence:
Unjust is the request you make, and I

In kindness your petition shall deny;
Yet she that grants not what you do implore,
Shall yet essay to give her *Jason* more;
Find means t' encrease the stock of *Aeson's* years,
Without retrenchment of your life's arrears;
Provided that the triple Goddess join
A strong confed'rate in my bold design.

Thus was her enterprize resolv'd; but still
Three tedious nights are wanting to fulfil
The circling crescents of th' encreasing moon;
Then, in the height of her nocturnal noon,
Medea steals from court; her ankles bare,
Her garments closely girt, but loose her hair;
Thus sally'd, like a solitary sprite,
She traverses the terrors of the night.

Men, beasts, and birds in soft repose lay charm'd,
No boistrous wind the mountain-woods alarm'd;
Nor did those walks of love, the myrtle-trees,
Of am'rous *Zephir* hear the whisp'ring breeze;
All elements chain'd in unactive rest,
No sense but what the twinkling stars exprest;
To them (that only wak'd) she rears her arm,
And thus commences her mysterious charms.

She turn'd her thrice about, as oft she threw
On her pale tresses the nocturnal dew;
Then yelling thrice a most enormous sound,
Her bare knee bended on the flinty ground.
O night (said she) thou confident and guide
Of secrets, such as darkness ought to hide;
Ye stars and moon, that, when the sun retires,
Support his empire with succeeding fires;
And thou, great *Hecate*, friend to my design;
Songs, mutt'ring spells, your magick forces join;
And thou, o Earth, the magazine that yields
The midnight sorcerer drugs; skies, mountains, fields;

Ye wat'ry Pow'rs of fountain, stream, and lake;
Ye sylvan Gods, and Gods of night, awake,
And gen'rously your parts in my adventure take.
  Oft by your aid swift currents I have led
Thro' wand'ring banks, back to their fountain head;
Transform'd the prospect of the briny deep,
Made sleeping billows rave, and raving billows sleep;
Made clouds, or sunshine; tempests rise, or fall;
And stubborn lawless winds obey my call:
With mutter'd words disarm'd the viper's jaw;
Up by the roots vast oaks, and rocks cou'd draw,
Make forests dance, and trembling mountains come,
Like malefactors, to receive their doom;
Earth groan, and frighted ghosts forsake their tomb.
Thee, *Cynthia*, my resistless rhymes drew down,
When tinkling cymbals strove my voice to drown;
Nor stronger *Titan* could their force sustain,
In full career compell'd to stop his wain:
Nor could *Aurora's* virgin blush avail,
With pois'nous herbs I turn'd her roses pale;
The fury of the fiery bulls I broke,
Their stubborn necks submitting to my yoke;
And when the sons of Earth with fury burn'd,
Their hostile rage upon themselves I turn'd;
The brothers made with mutual wounds to bleed,
And by their fatal strife my lover freed;
And, while the dragon slept, to distant *Greece*,
Thro' cheated guards, convey'd the golden fleece.
But now to bolder action I proceed,
Of such prevailing juices now have need,
That wither'd years back to their bloom can bring,
And in dead winter raise a second spring.
And you'll perform't —
You will; for lo! the stars, with sparkling fires,
Presage as bright success to my desires:

And now another happy omen see!
A chariot drawn by dragons waits for me.
    With these last words he leaps into the wain,
Stroaks the snakes' necks, and shakes the golden rein;
That signal giv'n, they mount her to the skies,
And now beneath her fruitful *Tempè* lies,
Whose stories she ransacks, then to *Crete* she flies;
There *Ossa*, *Pelion*, *Othrys*, *Pindus*, all
To the fair ravisher, a booty fall;
The tribute of their verdure she collects,
Nor proud *Olympus'* height his plants protects.
Some by the roots she plucks; the tender tops
Of others with her culling sickle crops.
Nor could the plunder of the hills suffice,
Down to the humble vales, and meads she flies;
Apidanus, *Amphrysus*, the next rape
Sustain, nor could *Enipeus'* bank escape;
Thro' *Beebè's* marsh, and thro' the border rang'd
Whose pasture *Glaucus* to a Triton chang'd.
    Now the ninth day, and ninth successive night,
Had wonder'd at the restless rover's flight;
Mean-while her dragons, fed with no repast,
But her exhaling simples od'rous blast,
Their tarnish'd scales, and wrinkled skins had cast.
At last return'd before her palace gate,
Quitting her chariot, on the ground she sate;
The sky her only canopy of state.
All conversation with her sex she fled,
Shun'd the caresses of the nuptial bed:
Two altars next of grassy turf she rears,
This *Hecate's* name, that *Youth's* inscription bears;
With forest-boughs, and vervain these she crown'd;
Then delves a double trench in lower ground,
And sticks a black-fleec'd ram, that ready stood,
And drench'd the ditches with devoted blood:

New wine she pours, and milk from th' udder warm,
With mystick murmurs to compleat the charm,
And subterranean deities alarm.
To the stern king of ghosts she next apply'd,
And gentle *Proserpine*, his ravish'd bride,
That for old *Aeson* with the laws of Fate
They would dispense, and lengthen his short date;
Thus with repeated pray'rs she long assails
Th' infernal tyrant, and at last prevails;
Then calls to have decrepit *Aeson* brought,
And stupifies him with a sleeping draught;
On Earth his body, like a corpse, extends,
Then charges *Jason* and his waiting friends
To quit the place, that no unhallow'd eye
Into her art's forbidden secrets pry.
This done, th' inchantress, with her locks unbound,
About her altars trips a frantick round;
Piece-meal the consecrated wood she splits,
And dips the splinters in the bloody pits,
Then hurles 'em on the piles; the sleeping sire
She lustrates thrice, with sulphur, water, fire.

    In a large cauldron now the med'cine boils,
Compounded of her late-collected spoils,
Blending into the mesh the various pow'rs
Of wonder-working juices, roots, and flow'rs;
With gems i' th' eastern ocean's cell refin'd,
And such as ebbing tides had left behind;
To them the midnight's pearly dew she flings,
A scretch-owl's carcase, and ill boding wings;
Nor could the wizard wolf's warm entrails scape
(That wolf who counterfeits a human shape).
Then, from the bottom of her conj'ring bag,
Snakes' skins, and liver of a long-liv'd stag;
Last a crow's head to such an age arriv'd,
That he had now nine centuries surviv'd;

These, and with these a thousand more that grew
In sundry soils, into her pot she threw;
Then with a wither'd olive-bough she rakes
The bubling broth; the bough fresh verdure takes;
Green leaves at first the perish'd plant surround,
Which the next minute with ripe fruit were crown'd.
The foaming juices now the brink o'er-swell;
The barren heath, where-e'er the liquor fell,
Sprang out with vernal grass, and all the pride
Of blooming *May* — When this *Medea* spy'd,
She cuts her patient's throat; th' exhausted blood
Recruiting with her new enchanted flood;
While at his mouth, and thro' his op'ning wound,
A double inlet her infusion found;
His feeble frame resumes a youthful air,
A glossy brown his hoary beard and hair.
The meager paleness from his aspect fled,
And in its room sprang up a florid red;
Thro' all his limbs a youthful vigour flies,
His empty'd art'ries swell with fresh supplies:
Gazing spectators scarce believe their eyes.
But *Aeson* is the most surpriz'd to find
A happy change in body and in mind;
In sense and constitution the same man,
As when his fortieth active year began.

   Bacchus, who from the clouds this wonder view'd,
Medea's method instantly pursu'd,
And his indulgent nurse's youth renew'd.

   Thus far obliging love employ'd her art,
But now revenge must act a tragick part;
   Medea feigns a mortal quarrel bred
Betwixt her, and the partner of her bed;
On this pretence to *Pelias'* court she flies,
Who languishing with age and sickness lies:
His guiltless daughters, with inveigling wiles,

And well dissembled friendship, she beguiles:
The strange achievements of her art she tells,
With *Aeson*'s cure, and long on that she dwells,
'Till them to firm perswasion she has won,
The same for their old father may be done:
For him they court her to employ her skill,
And put upon the cure what price she will.
At first she's mute, and with a grave pretence
Of difficulty, holds 'em in suspense;
Then promises, and bids 'em, from the fold
Chuse out a ram, the most infirm and old;
That so by fact their doubts may be remov'd,
And first on him the operation prov'd.
     A wreath-horn'd ram is brought, so far o'er-grown
With years, his age was to that age unknown;
Of sense too dull the piercing point to feel,
And scarce sufficient blood to stain the steel.
His carcass she into a cauldron threw,
With drugs whose vital qualities she knew;
His limbs grow less, he casts his horns, and years,
And tender bleatings strike their wond'ring ears.
Then instantly leaps forth a frisking lamb,
That seeks (too young to graze) a suckling dam.
The sisters, thus confirm'd with the success,
Her promise with renew'd entreaty press;
To countenance the cheat, three nights and days
Before experiment th' inchantress stays;
Then into limpid water, from the springs,
Weeds, and ingredients of no force she flings;
With antique ceremonies for pretence
And rambling rhymes without a word of sense.
     Mean-while the king with all his guards lay bound
In magick sleep, scarce that of death so sound;
The daughters now are by the sorc'ress led
Into his chamber, and surround his bed.

Your father's health's concern'd, and can ye stay?
Unnat'ral nymphs, why this unkind delay?
Unsheath your swords, dismiss his lifeless blood,
And I'll recruit it with a vital flood:
Your father's life and health is in your hand,
And can ye thus like idle gazers stand?
Unless you are of common sense bereft,
If yet one spark of piety is left,
Dispatch a father's cure, and disengage
The monarch from his toilsome load of age:
Come — drench your weapons in his putrid gore;
'Tis charity to wound, when wounding will restore.

    Thus urg'd, the poor deluded maids proceed,
Betray'd by zeal, to an inhumane deed,
And, in compassion, make a father bleed.
Yes, she who had the kindest, tend'rest heart,
Is foremost to perform the bloody part.

    Yet, tho' to act the butchery betray'd,
They could not bear to see the wounds they made;
With looks averted, backward they advance,
Then strike, and stab, and leave the blows to chance.

    Waking in consternation, he essays
(Weltring in blood) his feeble arms to raise:
Environ'd with so many swords — From whence
This barb'rous usage? what is my offence?
What fatal fury, what infernal charm,
'Gainst a kind father does his daughters arm?

    Hearing his voice, as thunder-struck they stopt,
Their resolution, and their weapons dropt:
Medea then the mortal blow bestows,
And that perform'd, the tragick scene to close,
His corpse into the boiling cauldron throws.

    Then, dreading the revenge that must ensue,
High mounted on her dragon-coach she flew;
And in her stately progress thro' the skies,

Beneath her shady *Pelion* first she spies,
With *Othrys*, that above the clouds did rise;
With skilful *Chiron's* cave, and neighb'ring ground,
For old *Cerambus'* strange escape renown'd,
By nymphs deliver'd, when the world was drown'd;
Who him with unexpected wings supply'd,
When delug'd hills a safe retreat deny'd.
Aeolian Pitanè on her left hand
She saw, and there the statu'd dragon stand;
With *Ida's* grove, where *Bacchus*, to disguise
His son's bold theft, and to secure the prize,
Made the stoln steer a stag to represent;
Cocytus' father's sandy monument;
And fields that held the murder'd sire's remains,
Where howling *Moera* frights the startled plains.
Euryphilus' high town, with tow'rs defac'd
By *Hercules*, and matrons more disgrac'd
With sprouting horns, in signal punishment,
From *Juno*, or resenting *Venus* sent.
Then *Rhodes*, which *Phoebus* did so dearly prize,
And *Jove* no less severely did chastize;
For he the wizard native's pois'ning sight,
That us'd the farmer's hopeful crops to blight,
In rage o'erwhelm'd with everlasting night.
Cartheia's ancient walls come next in view,
Where once the sire almost a statue grew
With wonder, which a strange event did move,
His daughter turn'd into a turtle-dove.
Then *Hyrie's* lake, and *Tempè's* field o'er-ran,
Fam'd for the boy who there became a swan;
For there enamour'd *Phyllius*, like a slave,
Perform'd what tasks his paramour would crave.
For presents he had mountain-vultures caught,
And from the desart a tame lion brought;
Then a wild bull commanded to subdue,

The conquer'd savage by the horns he drew;
But, mock'd so oft, the treatment he disdains,
And from the craving boy this prize detains.
Then thus in choler the resenting lad:
Won't you deliver him? — You'll wish you had:
Nor sooner said, but, in a peevish mood,
Leapt from the precipice on which he stood:
The standers-by were struck with fresh surprize,
Instead of falling, to behold him rise
A snowy swan, and soaring to the skies.

But dearly the rash prank his mother cost,
Who ignorantly gave her son for lost;
For his misfortune wept, 'till she became
A lake, and stil renown'd with *Hyrie's* name.

Thence to *Latona's* isle, where once were seen,
Transform'd to birds, a monarch, and his queen.
Far off she saw how old *Cephisus* mourn'd
His son, into a seele by *Phoebus* turn'd;
And where, astonish'd at a stranger sight,
Eumelus gaz'd on his wing'd daughter's flight.

Aetolian Pleuron she did next survey,
Where sons a mother's murder did essay,
But sudden plumes the matron bore away.
On her right hand, *Cyllenè*, a fair soil,
Fair, 'till *Menephron* there the beauteous hill
Attempted with foul incest to defile.

Her harness'd dragons now direct she drives
For *Corinth*, and at *Corinth* she arrives;
Where, if what old tradition tells, be true,
In former ages men from mushrooms grew.

But here *Medea* finds her bed supply'd,
During her absence, by another bride;
And hopeless to recover her lost game,
She sets both bride and palace in a flame.
Nor could a rival's death her wrath asswage,

Nor stopt at *Creon's* family her rage,
She murders her own infants, in despight
To faithless *Jason*, and in *Jason's* sight;
Yet e'er his sword could reach her, up she springs,
Securely mounted on her dragon's wings.

From hence to *Athens* she directs her flight,
Where *Phineus*, so renown'd for doing right;
Where *Periphas*, and *Polyphemon's* neece,
Soaring with sudden plumes amaz'd the towns of *Greece*

Here *Aegeus* so engaging she addrest,
That first he treats her like a royal guest;
Then takes the sorc'ress for his wedded wife;
The only blemish of his prudent life.

Mean-while his son, from actions of renown,
Arrives at court, but to his sire unknown.
Medea, to dispatch a dang'rous heir
(She knew him), did a pois'nous draught prepare;
Drawn from a drug, was long reserv'd in store
For desp'rate uses, from the *Scythian* shore;
That from the *Echydnaean* monster's jaws
Deriv'd its origin, and this the cause.

Thro' a dark cave a craggy passage lies,
To ours, ascending from the nether skies;
Thro' which, by strength of hand, *Alcides* drew
Chain'd *Cerberus*, who lagg'd, and restive grew,
With his blear'd eyes our brighter day to view.
Thrice he repeated his enormous yell,
With which he scares the ghosts, and startles Hell;
At last outragious (tho' compell'd to yield)
He sheds his foam in fury on the field;
Which, with its own, and rankness of the ground,
Produc'd a weed, by sorcerers renown'd,
The strongest constitution to confound;
Call'd *Aconite*, because it can unlock
All bars, and force its passage thro' a rock.

The pious father, by her wheedles won,
Presents this deadly potion to his son;
Who, with the same assurance takes the cup,
And to the monarch's health had drank it up,
But in the very instant he apply'd
The goblet to his lips, old *Aegeus* spy'd
The iv'ry hilted sword that grac'd his side.
That certain signal of his son he knew,
And snatcht the bowl away; the sword he drew,
Resolv'd, for such a son's endanger'd life,
To sacrifice the most perfidious wife.
Revenge is swift, but her more active charms
A whirlwind rais'd, that snatch'd her from his arms.
While conjur'd clouds their baffled sense surprize,
She vanishes from their deluded eyes,
And thro' the hurricane triumphant flies.

The gen'rous king, altho' o'er-joy'd to find
His son was safe, yet bearing still in mind
The mischief by his treach'rous queen design'd;
The horrour of the deed, and then how near
The danger drew, he stands congeal'd with fear.
But soon that fear into devotion turns,
With grateful incense ev'ry altar burns;
Proud victims, and unconscious of their fate,
Stalk to the temple, there to die in state.
In *Athens* never had a day been found
For mirth, like that grand festival, renown'd.
Promiscuously the peers, and people dine,
Promiscuously their thankful voices join,
In songs of wit, sublim'd by spritely wine.
To list'ning spheres their joint applause they raise,
And thus resound their matchless *Theseus'* praise.

Great *Theseus!* Thee the *Marathonian* plain
Admires, and wears with pride the noble stain
Of the dire monster's blood, by valiant *Theseus* slain.

That now *Cromyon's* swains in safety sow,
And reap their fertile field, to thee they owe.
By thee th' infested *Epidaurian* coast
Was clear'd, and now can a free commerce boast.
The traveller his journey can pursue,
With pleasure the late dreadful valley view,
And cry, Here *Theseus* the grand robber slew.
Cephysus' flood cries to his rescu'd shore,
The merciless *Procrustes* is no more.
In peace, *Eleusis*, *Ceres'* rites renew,
Since *Theseus'* sword the fierce *Cercyon* slew.
By him the tort'rer *Sinis* was destroy'd,
Of strength (but strength to barb'rous use employ'd)
That tops of tallest pines to Earth could bend,
And thus in pieces wretched captives rend.
Inhuman *Scyron* now has breath'd his last,
And now *Alcatho's* roads securely past;
By *Theseus* slain, and thrown into the deep:
But Earth nor Sea his scatter'd bones wou'd keep,
Which, after floating long, a rock became,
Still infamous with *Scyron's* hated name.
When Fame to count thy acts and years proceeds,
Thy years appear but cyphers to thy deeds.
For thee, brave youth, as for our common-wealth,
We pray; and drink, in yours, the publick health.
Your praise the senate, and plebeians sing,
With your lov'd name the court, and cottage ring.
You make our shepherds and our sailors glad,
And not a house in this vast city's sad.

But mortal bliss will never come sincere,
Pleasure may lead, but grief brings up the rear;
While for his sons' arrival, rev'ling joy
Aegeus, and all his subjects does employ;
While they for only costly feasts prepare,
His neighb'ring monarch, *Minos*, threatens war:

Weak in land-forces, nor by sea more strong,
But pow'rful in a deep resented wrong
For a son's murder, arm'd with pious rage;
Yet prudently before he would engage,
To raise auxiliaries resolv'd to sail,
And with the pow'rful princes to prevail.

First *Anaphè*, then proud *Astypalaea* gains,
By presents that, and this by threats obtains:
Low *Myconè*, *Cymolus*, chalky soil,
Tall *Cythnos*, *Scyros*, flat *Seriphos'* isle;
Paros, with marble cliffs afar display'd;
Impregnable *Sithonia*; yet betray'd
To a weak foe by a gold-admiring maid,
Who, chang'd into a daw of sable hue,
Still hoards up gold, and hides it from the view.

But as these islands chearfully combine,
Others refuse t' embark in his design.
Now leftward with an easy sail he bore,
And prosp'rous passage to *Oenopia's* shore;
Oenopia once, but now *Aegina* call'd,
And with his royal mother's name install'd
By *Aeacus*, under whose reign did spring
The *Myrmidons*, and now their reigning king.

Down to the port, amidst the rabble, run
The princes of the blood; with *Telamon*,
Peleus the next, and *Phocus* the third son:
Then *Aeacus*, altho' opprest with years,
To ask the cause of their approach appears.

That question does the *Gnossian's* grief renew,
And sighs from his afflicted bosom drew;
Yet after a short solemn respite made,
The ruler of the hundred cities said:

Assist our arms, rais'd for a murder'd son,
In this religious war no risque you'll run:
Revenge the dead — for who refuse to give

Rest to their urns, unworthy are to live.

What you request, thus *Aeacus* replies,
Not I, but truth and common faith denies;
Athens and we have long been sworn allies:
Our leagues are fix'd, confed'rate are our pow'rs,
And who declare themselves their foes, are ours.

Minos rejoins, Your league shall dearly cost
(Yet, mindful how much safer 'twas to boast,
Than there to waste his forces, and his fame,
Before in field with his grand foe he came),
Parts without blows — nor long had left the shore,
E're into port another navy bore,
With *Cephalus*, and all his jolly crew;
Th' *Aeacides* their old acquaintance knew:
The princes bid him welcome, and in state
Conduct the heroe to their palace gate;
Who entr'ring, seem'd the charming mein to wear,
As when in youth he paid his visit there.
In his right hand an olive-branch he holds,
And, salutation past, the chief unfolds
His embassy from the *Athenian* state,
Their mutual friendship, leagues of ancient date;
Their common danger, ev'ry thing cou'd wake
Concern, and his address successful make:
Strength'ning his plea with all the charms of sense,
And those, with all the charms of eloquence.

Then thus the king: Like suitors do you stand
For that assistance which you may command?
Athenians, all our listed forces use
(They're such as no bold service will refuse);
And when y' ave drawn them off, the Gods be prais'd,
Fresh legions can within our isle be rais'd:
So stock'd with people, that we can prepare
Both for domestick, and for distant war,
Ours, or our friends' insulters to chastize.

Long may ye flourish thus, the prince replies.
Strange transport seiz'd me as I pass'd along,
To meet so many troops, and all so young,
As if your army did of twins consist;
Yet amongst them my late acquaintance miss'd:
Ev'n all that to your palace did resort,
When first you entertain'd me at your court;
And cannot guess the cause from whence cou'd spring
So vast a change — Then thus the sighing king:
   Illustrious guest, to my strange tale attend,
Of sad beginning, but a joyful end:
The whole to a vast history wou'd swell,
I shall but half, and that confus'dly, tell.
That race whom so deserv'dly you admir'd,
Are all into their silent tombs retir'd:
They fell; and falling, how they shook my state,
Thought may conceive, but words can ne'er relate.
   A dreadful plague from angry *Juno* came,
To scourge the land, that bore her rival's name;
Before her fatal anger was reveal'd,
And teeming malice lay as yet conceal'd,
All remedies we try, all med'cines use,
Which Nature cou'd supply, or art produce;
Th' unconquer'd foe derides the vain design,
And art, and Nature foil'd, declare the cause divine.
   At first we only felt th' oppressive weight
Of gloomy clouds, then teeming with our fate,
And lab'ring to discarge unactive heat:
But ere four moons alternate changes knew,
With deadly blasts the fatal *South-wind* blew,
Infected all the air, and poison'd as it flew.
Our fountains too a dire infection yield,
For crowds of vipers creep along the field,
And with polluted gore, and baneful steams,
Taint all the lakes, and venom all the streams.

The young disease with milder force began,
And rag'd on birds, and beasts, excusing Man.
The lab'ring oxen fall before the plow,
Th' unhappy plow-men stare, and wonder how:
The tabid sheep, with sickly bleatings, pines;
Its wool decreasing, as its strength declines:
The warlike steed, by inward foes compell'd,
Neglects his honours, and deserts the field;
Unnerv'd, and languid, seeks a base retreat,
And at the manger groans, but wish'd a nobler fate:
The stags forget their speed, the boars their rage,
Nor can the bears the stronger herds engage:
A gen'ral faintness does invade 'em all,
And in the woods, and fields, promiscuously they fall.
The air receives the stench, and (strange to say)
The rav'nous birds and beasts avoid the prey:
Th' offensive bodies rot upon the ground,
And spread the dire contagion all around.

But now the plague, grown to a larger size,
Riots on Man, and scorns a meaner prize.
Intestine heats begin the civil war,
And flushings first the latent flame declare,
And breath inspir'd, which seem'd like fiery air.
Their black dry tongues are swell'd, and scarce can move,
And short thick sighs from panting lung are drove.
They gape for air, with flatt'ring hopes t' abate
Their raging flames, but that augments their heat.
No bed, no cov'ring can the wretches bear,
But on the ground, expos'd to open air,
They lye, and hope to find a pleasing coolness there.
The suff'ring Earth, with that oppression curst,
Returns the heat which they imparted first.

In vain physicians would bestow their aid,
Vain all their art, and useless all their trade;
And they, ev'n they, who fleeting life recall,

Feel the same Pow'rs, and undistinguish'd fall.
If any proves so daring to attend
His sick companion, or his darling friend,
Th' officious wretch sucks in contagious breath,
And with his friend does sympathize in death.

And now the care and hopes of life are past,
They please their fancies, and indulge their taste;
At brooks and streams, regardless of their shame,
Each sex, promiscuous, strives to quench their flame;
Nor do they strive in vain to quench it there,
For thirst, and life at once extinguish'd are.
Thus in the brooks the dying bodies sink,
But heedless still the rash survivors drink.

So much uneasy down the wretches hate,
They fly their beds, to struggle with their fate;
But if decaying strength forbids to rise,
The victim crawls and rouls, 'till on the ground he lies.
Each shuns his bed, as each wou'd shun his tomb,
And thinks th' infection only lodg'd at home.

Here one, with fainting steps, does slowly creep
O'er heaps of dead, and strait augments the heap;
Another, while his strength and tongue prevail'd,
Bewails his friend, and falls himself bewail'd:
This with imploring looks surveys the skies,
The last dear office of his closing eyes,
But finds the Heav'ns implacable, and dies.

What now, ah! what employ'd my troubled mind?
But only hopes my subjects' fate to find.
What place soe'er my weeping eyes survey,
There in lamented heaps the vulgar lay;
As acorns scatter when the winds prevail,
Or mellow fruit from shaken branches fall.

You see that dome which rears its front so high:
'Tis sacred to the monarch of the sky:
How many there, with unregarded tears,

And fruitless vows, sent up successless pray'rs?
There fathers for expiring sons implor'd,
And there the wife bewail'd her gasping lord;
With pious off'rings they'd appease the skies,
But they, ere yet th' attoning vapours rise,
Before the altars fall, themselves a sacrifice:
They fall, while yet their hands the gums contain,
The gums surviving, but their off'rers slain.

The destin'd ox, with holy garlands crown'd,
Prevents the blow, and feels th' expected wound:
When I my self invok'd the Pow'rs divine,
To drive the fatal pest from me and mine;
When now the priest with hands uplifted stood,
Prepar'd to strike, and shed the sacred blood,
The Gods themselves the mortal stroke bestow,
The victim falls, but they impart the blow:
Scarce was the knife with the pale purple stain'd,
And no presages cou'd be then obtain'd,
From putrid entrails, where th' infection reign'd.

Death stalk'd around with such resistless sway,
The temples of the Gods his force obey,
And suppliants feel his stroke, while yet they pray.
Go now, said he, your deities implore
For fruitless aid, for I defie their pow'r.
Then with a curst malicious joy survey'd
The very altars, stain'd with trophies of the dead.

The rest grown mad, and frantick with despair,
Urge their own fate, and so prevent the fear.
Strange madness that, when Death pursu'd so fast,
T' anticipate the blow with impious haste.

No decent honours to their urns are paid,
Nor cou'd the graves receive the num'rous dead;
For, or they lay unbury'd on the ground,
Or unadorn'd a needy fun'ral found:
All rev'rence past, the fainting wretches fight

For fun'ral piles which were another's right.
    Unmourn'd they fall: for, who surviv'd to mourn?
And sires, and mothers unlamented burn:
Parents, and sons sustain an equal fate,
And wand'ring ghosts their kindred shadows meet.
The dead a larger space of ground require,
Nor are the trees sufficient for the fire.
    Despairing under grief's oppressive weight,
And sunk by these tempestuous blasts of Fate,
O *Jove*, said I, if common fame says true,
If e'er *Aegina* gave those joys to you,
If e'er you lay enclos'd in her embrace,
Fond of her charms, and eager to possess;
O father, if you do not yet disclaim
Paternal care, nor yet disown the name;
Grant my petitions, and with speed restore
My subjects num'rous as they were before,
Or make me partner of the fate they bore.
I spoke, and glorious lightning shone around,
And ratling thunder gave a prosp'rous sound;
So let it be, and may these omens prove
A pledge, said I, of your returning love.
    By chance a rev'rend oak was near the place,
Sacred to *Jove*, and of *Dodona's* race,
Where frugal ants laid up their winter meat,
Whose little bodies bear a mighty weight:
We saw them march along, and hide their store,
And much admir'd their number, and their pow'r;
Admir'd at first, but after envy'd more.
Full of amazement, thus to *Jove* I pray'd,
O grant, since thus my subjects are decay'd,
As many subjects to supply the dead.
I pray'd, and strange convulsions mov'd the oak,
Which murmur'd, tho' by ambient winds unshook:
My trembling hands, and stiff-erected hair,

Exprest all tokens of uncommon fear;
Yet both the earth and sacred oak I kist,
And scarce cou'd hope, yet still I hop'd the best;
For wretches, whatsoe'er the Fates divine,
Expound all omens to their own design.

But now 'twas night, when ev'n distraction wears
A pleasing look, and dreams beguile our cares,
Lo! the same oak appears before my eyes,
Nor alter'd in his shape, nor former size;
As many ants the num'rous branches bear,
The same their labour, and their frugal care;
The branches too a like commotion sound,
And shook th' industrious creatures on the ground,
Who, by degrees (what's scarce to be believ'd)
A nobler form, and larger bulk receiv'd,
And on the earth walk'd an unusual pace,
With manly strides, and an erected face;
Their num'rous legs, and former colour lost,
The insects cou'd a human figure boast.

I wake, and waking find my cares again,
And to the unperforming Gods complain,
And call their promise, and pretences, vain.
Yet in my court I heard the murm'ring voice
Of strangers, and a mixt uncommon noise:
But I suspected all was still a dream,
'Till *Telamon* to my apartment came,
Op'ning the door with an impetuous haste,
O come, said he, and see your faith and hopes surpast:
I follow, and, confus'd with wonder, view
Those shapes which my presaging slumbers drew:
I saw, and own'd, and call'd them subjects; they
Confest my pow'r, submissive to my sway.
To *Jove*, restorer of my race decay'd,
My vows were first with due oblations paid,
I then divide with an impartial hand

My empty city, and my ruin'd land,
To give the new-born youth an equal share,
And call them *Myrmidons*, from what they were.
You saw their persons, and they still retain
The thrift of ants, tho' now transform'd to men.
A frugal people, and inur'd to sweat,
Lab'ring to gain, and keeping what they get.
These, equal both in strength and years, shall join
Their willing aid, and follow your design,
With the first southern gale that shall present
To fill your sails, and favour your intent.

   With such discourse they entertain the day;
The ev'ning past in banquets, sport, and play:
Then, having crown'd the night with sweet repose,
Aurora (with the wind at east) arose.
Now *Pallas'* sons to *Cephalus* resort,
And *Cephalus* with *Pallas'* sons to court,
To the king's levee; him sleep's silken chain,
And pleasing dreams, beyond his hour detain;
But then the princes of the blood, in state,
Expect, and meet 'em at the palace gate.

   To th' inmost courts the *Grecian* youths were led,
And plac'd by *Phocus* on a *Tyrian* bed;
Who, soon observing *Cephalus* to hold
A dart of unknown wood, but arm'd with gold:
None better loves (said he) the huntsman's sport,
Or does more often to the woods resort;
Yet I that jav'lin's stem with wonder view,
Too brown for box, too smooth a grain for yew.
I cannot guess the tree; but never art
Did form, or eyes behold so fair a dart!
The guest then interrupts him — 'Twou'd produce
Still greater wonder, if you knew its use.
It never fails to strike the game, and then
Comes bloody back into your hand again.

Then *Phocus* each particular desires,
And th' author of the wond'rous gift enquires.
To which the owner thus, with weeping eyes,
And sorrow for his wife's sad fate, replies,
This weapon here (o prince!) can you believe
This dart the cause for which so much I grieve;
And shall continue to grieve on, 'till Fate
Afford such wretched life no longer date.
Would I this fatal gift had ne'er enjoy'd,
This fatal gift my tender wife destroy'd:
Procris her name, ally'd in charms and blood
To fair *Orythia* courted by a God.
Her father seal'd my hopes with rites divine,
But firmer love before had made her mine.
Men call'd me blest, and blest I was indeed.
The second month our nuptials did succeed;
When (as upon *Hymettus'* dewy head,
For mountain stags my net betimes I spread)
Aurora spy'd, and ravish'd me away,
With rev'rence to the Goddess, I must say,
Against my will, for *Procris* had my heart,
Nor wou'd her image from my thoughts depart.
At last, in rage she cry'd, Ingrateful boy
Go to your *Procris*, take your fatal joy;
And so dismiss'd me: musing, as I went,
What those expressions of the Goddess meant,
A thousand jealous fears possess me now,
Lest *Procris* had prophan'd her nuptial vow:
Her youth and charms did to my fancy paint
A lewd adultress, but her life a saint.
Yet I was absent long, the Goddess too
Taught me how far a woman cou'd be true.
Aurora's treatment much suspicion bred;
Besides, who truly love, ev'n shadows dread.
I strait impatient for the tryal grew,

What courtship back'd with richest gifts cou'd do.
Aurora's envy aided my design,
And lent me features far unlike to mine.
In this disguise to my own house I came,
But all was chaste, no conscious sign of blame:
With thousand arts I scarce admittance found,
And then beheld her weeping on the ground
For her lost husband; hardly I retain'd
My purpose, scarce the wish'd embrace refrain'd.
How charming was her grief! Then, *Phocus*, guess
What killing beauties waited on her dress.
Her constant answer, when my suit I prest,
Forbear, my lord's dear image guards this breast;
Where-e'er he is, whatever cause detains,
Who-e'er has his, my heart unmov'd remains.
What greater proofs of truth than these cou'd be?
Yet I persist, and urge my destiny.
At length, she found, when my own form return'd,
Her jealous lover there, whose loss she mourn'd.
Enrag'd with my suspicion, swift as wind,
She fled at once from me and all mankind;
And so became, her purpose to retain,
A nymph, and huntress in *Diana's* train:
Forsaken thus, I found my flames encrease,
I own'd my folly, and I su'd for peace.
It was a fault, but not of guilt, to move
Such punishment, a fault of too much love.
Thus I retriev'd her to my longing arms,
And many happy days possess'd her charms.
But with herself she kindly did confer,
What gifts the Goddess had bestow'd on her;
The fleetest grey-hound, with this lovely dart,
And I of both have wonders to impart.
Near *Thebes* a savage beast, of race unknown,
Laid waste the field, and bore the vineyards down;

The swains fled from him, and with one consent
Our *Grecian* youth to chase the monster went;
More swift than light'ning he the toils surpast,
And in his course spears, men, and trees o'er-cast.
We slipt our dogs, and last my *Lelaps* too,
When none of all the mortal race wou'd do:
He long before was struggling from my hands,
And, e're we cou'd unloose him, broke his bands.
That minute where he was, we cou'd not find,
And only saw the dust he left behind.
I climb'd a neighb'ring hill to view the chase,
While in the plain they held an equal race;
The savage now seems caught, and now by force
To quit himself, nor holds the same strait course;
But running counter, from the foe withdraws,
And with short turning cheats his gaping jaws:
Which he retrieves, and still so closely prest,
You'd fear at ev'ry stretch he were possess'd;
Yet for the gripe his fangs in vain prepare;
The game shoots from him, and he chops the air.
To cast my jav'lin then I took my stand;
But as the thongs were fitting to my hand,
While to the valley I o'er-look'd the wood,
Before my eyes two marble statues stood;
That, as pursu'd appearing at full stretch,
This barking after, and at point to catch:
Some God their course did with this wonder grace,
That neither might be conquer'd in the chase.
A sudden silence here his tongue supprest,
He here stops short, and fain wou'd wave the rest.

The eager prince then urg'd him to impart,
The Fortune that attended on the dart.
First then (said he) past joys let me relate,
For bliss was the foundation of my fate.
No language can those happy hours express,

Did from our nuptials me, and *Procris* bless:
The kindest pair! What more cou'd Heav'n confer?
For she was all to me, and I to her.
Had *Jove* made love, great *Jove* had been despis'd;
And I my *Procris* more than *Venus* priz'd:
Thus while no other joy we did aspire,
We grew at last one soul, and one desire.
Forth to the woods I went at break of day
(The constant practice of my youth) for prey:
Nor yet for servant, horse, or dog did call,
I found this single dart to serve for all.
With slaughter tir'd, I sought the cooler shade,
And winds that from the mountains pierc'd the glade:
Come, gentle air (so was I wont to say)
Come, gentle air, sweet *Aura* come away.
This always was the burden of my song,
Come 'swage my flames, sweet *Aura* come along.
Thou always art most welcome to my breast;
I faint; approach, thou dearest, kindest guest!
These blandishments, and more than these, I said
(By Fate to unsuspected ruin led),
Thou art my joy, for thy dear sake I love
Each desart hill, and solitary grove;
When (faint with labour) I refreshment need,
For cordials on thy fragrant breath I feed.
At last a wand'ring swain in hearing came,
And cheated with the sound of *Aura's* name,
He thought I had some assignation made;
And to my *Procris'* ear the news convey'd.
Great love is soonest with suspicion fir'd:
She swoon'd, and with the tale almost expir'd.
Ah! wretched heart! (she cry'd) ah! faithless man.
And then to curse th' imagin'd nymph began:
Yet oft she doubts, oft hopes she is deceiv'd,
And chides herself, that ever she believ'd

Her lord to such injustice cou'd proceed,
'Till she her self were witness of the deed.
Next morn I to the woods again repair,
And, weary with the chase, invoke the air:
Approach, dear *Aura*, and my bosom chear:
At which a mournful sound did strike my ear;
Yet I proceeded, 'till the thicket by,
With rustling noise and motion, drew my eye:
I thought some beast of prey was shelter'd there,
And to the covert threw my certain spear;
From whence a tender sigh my soul did wound,
Ah me! it cry'd, and did like *Procris* sound.
Procris was there, too well the voice I knew,
And to the place with headlong horror flew;
Where I beheld her gasping on the ground,
In vain attempting from the deadly wound
To draw the dart, her love's dear fatal gift!
My guilty arms had scarce the strength to lift
The beauteous load; my silks, and hair I tore
(If possible) to stanch the pressing gore;
For pity beg'd her keep her flitting breath,
And not to leave me guilty of her death.
While I intreat she fainted fast away,
And these few words had only strength to say:
By all the sacred bonds of plighted love,
By all your rev'rence to the Pow'rs above,
By all the truth for which you held me dear,
And last by love, the cause through which I bleed,
Let *Aura* never to my bed succeed.
I then perceiv'd the error of our fate,
And told it her, but found and told too late!
I felt her lower to my bosom fall,
And while her eyes had any sight at all,
On mine she fix'd them; in her pangs still prest
My hand, and sigh'd her soul into my breast;

Yet, being undeceiv'd, resign'd her breath
Methought more chearfully, and smil'd in death.
    With such concern the weeping heroe told
This tale, that none who heard him cou'd with-hold
From melting into sympathizing tears,
'Till *Aeacus* with his two sons appears;
Whom he commits, with their new-levy'd bands,
To Fortune's, and so brave a gen'ral's hands.

The End of the Seventh Book.

BOOK THE EIGHTH

Now shone the morning star in bright array,
To vanquish night, and usher in the day:
The wind veers southward, and moist clouds arise,
That blot with shades the blue meridian skies.
Cephalus feels with joy the kindly gales,
His new allies unfurl the swelling sails;
Steady their course, they cleave the yielding main,
And, with a wish, th' intended harbour gain.

Mean-while King *Minos*, on the *Attick* strand,
Displays his martial skill, and wastes the land.
His army lies encampt upon the plains,
Before *Alcathoë's* walls, where *Nisus* reigns;
On whose grey head a lock of purple hue,
The strength, and fortune of his kingdom, grew.

Six moons were gone, and past, when still from far
Victoria hover'd o'er the doubtful war.
So long, to both inclin'd, th' impartial maid
Between 'em both her equal wings display'd.
High on the walls, by *Phoebus* vocal made,
A turret of the palace rais'd its head;
And where the God his tuneful harp resign'd,
The sound within the stones still lay enshrin'd:
Hither the daughter of the purple king
Ascended oft, to hear its musick ring;
And, striking with a pebble, wou'd release
Th' enchanted notes, in times of happy peace.
But now, from thence, the curious maid beheld
Rough feats of arms, and combats of the field:
And, since the siege was long, had learnt the name
Of ev'ry chief, his character, and fame;
Their arms, their horse, and quiver she descry'd,
Nor cou'd the dress of war the warriour hide.

Europa's son she knew above the rest,
And more, than well became a virgin breast:

In vain the crested morion veils his face,
She thinks it adds a more peculiar grace:
His ample shield, embost with burnish'd gold,
Still makes the bearer lovelier to behold:
When the tough jav'lin, with a whirl, he sends,
His strength and skill the sighing maid commends;
Or, when he strains to draw the circling bow,
And his fine limbs a manly posture show,
Compar'd with *Phoebus*, he performs so well,
Let her be judge, and *Minos* shall excell.

But when the helm put off, display'd to sight,
And set his features in an open light;
When, vaulting to his seat, his steed he prest,
Caparison'd in gold, and richly drest;
Himself in scarlet sumptuously array'd,
New passions rise, and fire the frantick maid.
O happy spear! she cries, that feels his touch;
Nay, ev'n the reins he holds are blest too much.
Oh! were it lawful, she cou'd wing her way
Thro' the stern hostile troops without dismay;
Or throw her body to the distant ground,
And in the *Cretans* happy camp be found.
Wou'd *Minos* but desire it! she'd expose
Her native country to her country's foes;
Unbar the gates, the town with flames infest,
Or any thing that *Minos* shou'd request.

And as she sate, and pleas'd her longing sight,
Viewing the king's pavilion veil'd with white,
Shou'd joy, or grief, she said, possess my breast,
To see my country by a war opprest?
I'm in suspense! For, tho' 'tis grief to know
I love a man that is declar'd my foe;
Yet, in my own despite, I must approve
That lucky war, which brought the man I love.
Yet, were I tender'd as a pledge of peace,

The cruelties of war might quickly cease.
Oh! with what joy I'd wear the chains he gave!
A patient hostage, and a willing slave.
Thou lovely object! if the nymph that bare
Thy charming person, were but half so fair;
Well might a God her virgin bloom desire,
And with a rape indulge his amorous fire.
Oh! had I wings to glide along the air,
To his dear tent I'd fly, and settle there:
There tell my quality, confess my flame,
And grant him any dowry that he'd name.
All, all I'd give; only my native land,
My dearest country, shou'd excepted stand,
For, perish love, and all expected joys,
E're, with so base a thought, my soul complies.
Yet, oft the vanquish'd some advantage find,
When conquer'd by a noble, gen'rous mind.
Brave *Minos* justly has the war begun,
Fir'd with resentment for his murder'd son:
The righteous Gods a righteous cause regard,
And will, with victory, his arms reward:
We must be conquer'd; and the captive's fate
Will surely seize us, tho' it seize us late.
Why then shou'd love be idle, and neglect
What *Mars*, by arms and perils, will effect?
Oh! Prince, I dye, with anxious fear opprest,
Lest some rash hand shou'd wound my charmer's breast:
For, if they saw, no barb'rous mind cou'd dare
Against that lovely form to raise a spear.
    But I'm resolv'd, and fix'd in this decree,
My father's country shall my dowry be.
Thus I prevent the loss of life and blood,
And, in effect, the action must be good.
Vain resolution! for, at ev'ry gate
The trusty centinels, successive, wait:

The keys my father keeps; ah! there's my grief;
'Tis he obstructs all hopes of my relief.
Gods! that this hated light I'd never seen!
Or, all my life, without a father been!
But Gods we all may be; for those that dare,
Are Gods, and Fortune's chiefest favours share.
The ruling Pow'rs a lazy pray'r detest,
The bold adventurer succeeds the best.
What other maid, inspir'd with such a flame,
But wou'd take courage, and abandon shame?
But wou'd, tho' ruin shou'd ensue, remove
Whate'er oppos'd, and clear the way to love?
This, shall another's feeble passion dare?
While I sit tame, and languish in despair:
No; for tho' fire and sword before me lay,
Impatient love thro' both shou'd force its way.
Yet I have no such enemies to fear,
My sole obstruction is my father's hair;
His purple lock my sanguine hope destroys,
And clouds the prospect of my rising joys.

    Whilst thus she spoke, amid the thick'ning air
Night supervenes, the greatest nurse of care:
And, as the Goddess spreads her sable wings,
The virgin's fears decay, and courage springs.
The hour was come, when Man's o'er-labour'd breast
Surceas'd its care, by downy sleep possest:
All things now hush'd, *Scylla* with silent tread
Urg'd her approach to *Nisus'* royal bed:
There, of the fatal lock (accursed theft!)
She her unwitting father's head bereft.
In safe possession of her impious prey,
Out at a postern gate she takes her way.
Embolden'd, by the merit of the deed,
She traverses the adverse camp with speed,
'Till *Minos'* tent she reach'd: the righteous king

She thus bespoke, who shiver'd at the thing.
    Behold th' effect of love's resistless sway!
I, *Nisus'* royal seed, to thee betray
My country, and my Gods. For this strange task,
Minos, no other boon but thee I ask.
This purple lock, a pledge of love, receive;
No worthless present, since in it I give
My father's head. — Mov'd at a crime so new,
And with abhorrence fill'd, back *Minos* drew,
Nor touch'd th' unhallow'd gift; but thus exclaim'd
(With mien indignant, and with eyes inflam'd),
Perdition seize thee, thou, thy kind's disgrace!
May thy devoted carcass find no place
In earth, or air, or sea, by all out-cast!
Shall *Minos,* with so foul a monster, blast
His *Cretan* world, where cradled *Jove* was nurst?
Forbid it Heav'n! — away, thou most accurst!
    And now *Alcathoë,* its lord exchang'd,
Was under *Minos'* domination rang'd.
While the most equal king his care applies
To curb the conquer'd, and new laws devise,
The fleet, by his command, with hoisted sails,
And ready oars, invites the murm'ring gales.
At length the *Cretan* hero anchor weigh'd,
Repaying, with neglect, th' abandon'd maid.
Deaf to her cries, he furrows up the main:
In vain she prays, sollicits him in vain.
    And now she furious grows in wild despair,
She wrings her hands, and throws aloft her hair.
Where run'st thou? (thus she vents her deep distress)
Why shun'st thou her that crown'd thee with success?
Her, whose fond love to thee cou'd sacrifice
Her country, and her parent, sacred ties!
Can nor my love, nor proffer'd presents find
A passage to thy heart, and make thee kind?

Can nothing move thy pity? O ingrate,
Can'st thou behold my lost, forlorn estate,
And not be soften'd? Can'st thou throw off one
Who has no refuge left but thee alone?
Where shall I seek for comfort? whither fly?
My native country does in ashes lye:
Or were't not so, my treason bars me there,
And bids me wander. Shall I next repair
To a wrong'd father, by my guilt undone? —
Me all Mankind deservedly will shun.
I, out of all the world, my self have thrown,
To purchase an access to *Crete* alone;
Which, since refus'd, ungen'rous man, give o'er
To boast thy race; *Europa* never bore
A thing so savage. Thee some tygress bred,
On the bleak *Syrt's* inhospitable bed;
Or where *Charybdis* pours its rapid tide
Tempestuous. Thou art not to *Jove* ally'd;
Nor did the king of Gods thy mother meet
Beneath a bull's forg'd shape, and bear to *Crete*.
That fable of thy glorious birth is feign'd;
Some wild outrageous bull thy dam sustain'd.
O father *Nisus*, now my death behold;
Exult, o city, by my baseness sold:
Minos, obdurate, has aveng'd ye all;
But 'twere more just by those I wrong'd to fall:
For why shou'dst thou, who only didst subdue
By my offending, my offence pursue?
Well art thou matcht to one whose am'rous flame
Too fiercely rag'd, for human-kind to tame;
One who, within a wooden heifer thrust,
Courted a low'ring bull's mistaken lust;
And, from whose monster-teeming womb, the Earth
Receiv'd, what much it mourn'd, a bi-form birth.
But what avails my plaints? the whistling wind,

Which bears him far away, leaves them behind.
Well weigh'd *Pasiphaë*, when she prefer'd
A bull to thee, more brutish than the herd.
But ah! Time presses, and the labour'd oars
To distance drive the fleet, and lose the less'ning shores.
Think not, ungrateful man, the liquid way
And threat'ning billows shall inforce my stay.
I'll follow thee in spite: My arms I'll throw
Around thy oars, or grasp thy crooked prow,
And drag thro' drenching seas. Her eager tongue
Had hardly clos'd the speech, when forth she sprung
And prov'd the deep. *Cupid* with added force
Recruits each nerve, and aids her wat'ry course.
Soon she the ship attains, unwelcome guest;
And, as with close embrace its sides she prest,
A hawk from upper air came pouring down
('Twas *Nisus* cleft the sky with wings new grown).
At *Scylla's* head his horny bill he aims;
She, fearful of the blow, the ship disclaims,
Quitting her hold: and yet she fell not far,
But wond'ring, finds her self sustain'd in air.
Chang'd to a lark, she mottled pinions shook,
And, from the ravish'd lock, the name of *Ciris* took.

Now *Minos*, landed on the *Cretan* shore,
Performs his vows to *Jove's* protecting pow'r;
A hundred bullocks of the largest breed,
With flowrets crown'd, before his altar bleed:
While trophies of the vanquish'd, brought from far
Adorn the palace with the spoils of war.

Mean-while the monster of a human-beast,
His family's reproach, and stain, increas'd.
His double kind the rumour swiftly spread,
And evidenc'd the mother's beastly deed.
When *Minos*, willing to conceal the shame
That sprung from the reports of tatling Fame,

Resolves a dark inclosure to provide,
And, far from sight, the two-form'd creature hide.
    Great *Daedalus* of *Athens* was the man
That made the draught, and form'd the wondrous plan;
Where rooms within themselves encircled lye,
With various windings, to deceive the eye.
As soft *Maeander's* wanton current plays,
When thro' the *Phrygian* fields it loosely strays;
Backward and forward rouls the dimpl'd tide,
Seeming, at once, two different ways to glide:
While circling streams their former banks survey,
And waters past succeeding waters see:
Now floating to the sea with downward course,
Now pointing upward to its ancient source,
Such was the work, so intricate the place,
That scarce the workman all its turns cou'd trace;
And *Daedalus* was puzzled how to find
The secret ways of what himself design'd.
    These private walls the *Minotaur* include,
Who twice was glutted with *Athenian* blood:
But the third tribute more successful prov'd,
Slew the foul monster, and the plague remov'd.
When *Theseus*, aided by the virgin's art,
Had trac'd the guiding thread thro' ev'ry part,
He took the gentle maid, that set him free,
And, bound for *Dias*, cut the briny sea.
There, quickly cloy'd, ungrateful, and unkind,
Left his fair consort in the isle behind,
Whom *Bacchus* saw, and straining in his arms
Her rifled bloom, and violated charms,
Resolves, for this, the dear engaging dame
Shou'd shine for ever in the rolls of Fame;
And bids her crown among the stars be plac'd,
With an eternal constellation grac'd.
The golden circlet mounts; and, as it flies,

Its diamonds twinkle in the distant skies;
There, in their pristin form, the gemmy rays
Between *Alcides*, and the dragon blaze.

In tedious exile now too long detain'd,
Daedalus languish'd for his native land:
The sea foreclos'd his flight; yet thus he said:
Tho' Earth and water in subjection laid,
O cruel *Minos*, thy dominion be,
We'll go thro' air; for sure the air is free.
Then to new arts his cunning thought applies,
And to improve the work of Nature tries.
A row of quils in gradual order plac'd,
Rise by degrees in length from first to last;
As on a cliff th' ascending thicket grows,
Or, different reeds the rural pipe compose.
Along the middle runs a twine of flax,
The bottom stems are joyn'd by pliant wax.
Thus, well compact, a hollow bending brings
The fine composure into real wings.

His boy, young *Icarus*, that near him stood,
Unthinking of his fate, with smiles pursu'd
The floating feathers, which the moving air
Bore loosely from the ground, and wasted here and there.
Or with the wax impertinently play'd,
And with his childish tricks the great design delay'd.

The final master-stroke at last impos'd,
And now, the neat machine compleatly clos'd;
Fitting his pinions on, a flight he tries,
And hung self-ballanc'd in the beaten skies.
Then thus instructs his child: My boy, take care
To wing your course along the middle air;
If low, the surges wet your flagging plumes;
If high, the sun the melting wax consumes:
Steer between both: nor to the northern skies,
Nor south *Orion* turn your giddy eyes;

But follow me: let me before you lay
Rules for the flight, and mark the pathless way.
Then teaching, with a fond concern, his son,
He took the untry'd wings, and fix'd 'em on;
But fix'd with trembling hands; and as he speaks,
The tears roul gently down his aged cheeks.
Then kiss'd, and in his arms embrac'd him fast,
But knew not this embrace must be the last.
And mounting upward, as he wings his flight,
Back on his charge he turns his aking sight;
As parent birds, when first their callow care
Leave the high nest to tempt the liquid air.
Then chears him on, and oft, with fatal art,
Reminds the stripling to perform his part.

These, as the angler at the silent brook,
Or mountain-shepherd leaning on his crook,
Or gaping plowman, from the vale descries,
They stare, and view 'em with religious eyes,
And strait conclude 'em Gods; since none, but they,
Thro' their own azure skies cou'd find a way.

Now *Delos*, *Paros* on the left are seen,
And *Samos*, favour'd by *Jove's* haughty queen;
Upon the right, the isle *Lebynthos* nam'd,
And fair *Calymnè* for its honey fam'd.
When now the boy, whose childish thoughts aspire
To loftier aims, and make him ramble high'r,
Grown wild, and wanton, more embolden'd flies
Far from his guide, and soars among the skies.
The soft'ning wax, that felt a nearer sun,
Dissolv'd apace, and soon began to run.
The youth in vain his melting pinions shakes,
His feathers gone, no longer air he takes:
Oh! Father, father, as he strove to cry,
Down to the sea he tumbled from on high,
And found his Fate; yet still subsists by fame,

Among those waters that retain his name.
   The father, now no more a father, cries,
Ho *Icarus!* where are you? as he flies;
Where shall I seek my boy? he cries again,
And saw his feathers scatter'd on the main.
Then curs'd his art; and fun'ral rites confer'd,
Naming the country from the youth interr'd.
   A partridge, from a neighb'ring stump, beheld
The sire his monumental marble build;
Who, with peculiar call, and flutt'ring wing,
Chirpt joyful, and malicious seem'd to sing:
The only bird of all its kind, and late
Transform'd in pity to a feather'd state:
From whence, o *Daedalus*, thy guilt we date.
   His sister's son, when now twelve years were past,
Was, with his uncle, as a scholar plac'd;
The unsuspecting mother saw his parts,
And genius fitted for the finest arts.
This soon appear'd; for when the spiny bone
In fishes' backs was by the stripling known,
A rare invention thence he learnt to draw,
Fil'd teeth in ir'n, and made the grating saw.
He was the first, that from a knob of brass
Made two strait arms with widening stretch to pass;
That, while one stood upon the center's place,
The other round it drew a circling space.
Daedalus envy'd this, and from the top
Of fair *Minerva's* temple let him drop;
Feigning, that, as he lean'd upon the tow'r,
Careless he stoop'd too much, and tumbled o'er.
   The Goddess, who th' ingenious still befriends,
On this occasion her asssistance lends;
His arms with feathers, as he fell, she veils,
And in the air a new made bird he sails.
The quickness of his genius, once so fleet,

Still in his wings remains, and in his feet:
Still, tho' transform'd, his ancient name he keeps,
And with low flight the new-shorn stubble sweeps,
Declines the lofty trees, and thinks it best
To brood in hedge-rows o'er its humble nest;
And, in remembrance of the former ill,
Avoids the heights, and precipices still.

At length, fatigu'd with long laborious flights,
On fair *Sicilia's* plains the artist lights;
Where *Cocalus* the king, that gave him aid,
Was, for his kindness, with esteem repaid.
Athens no more her doleful tribute sent,
That hardship gallant *Theseus* did prevent;
Their temples hung with garlands, they adore
Each friendly God, but most *Minerva's* pow'r:
To her, to *Jove*, to all, their altars smoak,
They each with victims, and perfumes invoke.

Now talking Fame, thro' every *Grecian* town,
Had spread, immortal *Theseus*, thy renown.
From him the neighb'ring nations in distress,
In suppliant terms implore a kind redress.

From him the *Caledonians* sought relief;
Though valiant *Meleagros* was their chief.
The cause, a boar, who ravag'd far and near:
Of *Cynthia's* wrath, th' avenging minister.
For *Oeneus* with autumnal plenty bless'd,
By gifts to Heav'n his gratitude express'd:
Cull'd sheafs, to *Ceres*; to *Lyaeus*, wine;
To *Pan*, and *Pales*, offer'd sheep and kine;
And fat of olives, to *Minerva's* shrine.
Beginning from the rural Gods, his hand
Was lib'ral to the Pow'rs of high command:
Each deity in ev'ry kind was bless'd,
'Till at *Diana's* fane th' invidious honour ceas'd.

Wrath touches ev'n the Gods; the Queen of Night,

Fir'd with disdain, and jealous of her right,
Unhonour'd though I am, at least, said she,
Not unreveng'd that impious act shall be.
Swift as the word, she sped the boar away,
With charge on those devoted fields to prey.
No larger bulls th' *Aegyptian* pastures feed,
And none so large *Sicilian* meadows breed:
His eye-balls glare with fire suffus'd with blood;
His neck shoots up a thick-set thorny wood;
His bristled back a trench impal'd appears,
And stands erected, like a field of spears;
Froth fills his chaps, he sends a grunting sound,
And part he churns, and part befoams the ground,
For tusks with *Indian* elephants he strove,
And *Jove's* own thunder from his mouth he drove.
He burns the leaves; the scorching blast invades
The tender corn, and shrivels up the blades:
Or suff'ring not their yellow beards to rear,
He tramples down the spikes, and intercepts the year:
In vain the barns expect their promis'd load,
Nor barns at home, nor recks are heap'd abroad:
In vain the hinds the threshing-floor prepare,
And exercise their flail in empty air.
With olives ever-green the ground is strow'd,
And grapes ungather'd shed their gen'rous blood.
Amid the fold he rages, nor the sheep
Their shepherds, nor the grooms their bulls can keep.
    From fields to walls the frighted rabble run,
Nor think themselves secure within the town:
'Till *Meleagros*, and his chosen crew,
Contemn the danger, and the praise pursue.
Fair *Leda's* twins (in time to stars decreed)
One fought on foot, one curb'd the fiery steed;
Then issu'd forth fam'd *Jason* after these,
Who mann'd the foremost ship that sail'd the seas;

Then *Theseus* join'd with bold *Perithous* came;
A single concord in a double name:
The *Thestian* sons, *Idas* who swiftly ran,
And *Ceneus*, once a woman, now a man.
Lynceus, with eagle's eyes, and lion's heart;
Leucippus, with his never-erring dart;
Acastus, *Phileus*, *Phoenix*, *Telamon*,
Echion, *Lelix*, and *Eurytion*,
Achilles' father, and great *Phocus'* son;
Dryas the fierce, and *Hippasus* the strong;
With twice old *Iolas*, and *Nestor* then but young.
Laertes active, and *Ancaeus* bold;
Mopsus the sage, who future things foretold;
And t' other seer, yet by his wife unsold.
A thousand others of immortal fame;
Among the rest, fair *Atalanta* came,
Grace of the woods: a diamond buckle bound
Her vest behind, that else had flow'd upon the ground
And shew'd her buskin'd legs; her head was bare,
But for her native ornament of hair;
Which in a simple knot was ty'd above,
Sweet negligence! unheeded bait of love!
Her sounding quiver, on her shoulder ty'd,
One hand a dart, and one a bow supply'd.
Such was her face, as in a nymph display'd
A fair fierce boy, or in a boy betray'd
The blushing beauties of a modest maid.
The *Caledonian* chief at once the dame
Beheld, at once his heart receiv'd the flame,
With Heav'ns averse. O happy youth, he cry'd;
For whom thy fates reserve so fair a bride!
He sigh'd, and had no leisure more to say;
His honour call'd his eyes another way,
And forc'd him to pursue the now-neglected prey.

    There stood a forest on a mountain's brow,

Which over-look'd the shaded plains below.
No sounding ax presum'd those trees to bite;
Coeval with the world, a venerable sight.
The heroes there arriv'd, some spread around
The toils; some search the footsteps on the ground:
Some from the chains the faithful dogs unbound.
Of action eager, and intent in thought,
The chiefs their honourable danger sought:
A valley stood below; the common drain
Of waters from above, and falling rain:
The bottom was a moist, and marshy ground,
Whose edges were with bending oziers crown'd:
The knotty bulrush next in order stood,
And all within of reeds a trembling wood.

From hence the boar was rous'd, and sprung amain,
Like lightning sudden, on the warrior train;
Beats down the trees before him, shakes the ground.
The forest echoes to the crackling sound;
Shout the fierce youth, and clamours ring around.
All stood with their protended spears prepar'd,
With broad steel heads the brandish'd weapons glar'd.
The beast impetuous with his tusks aside
Deals glancing wounds; the fearful dogs divide:
All spend their mouths aloof, but none abide.
Echion threw the first, but miss'd his mark,
And stuck his boar-spear on a maple's bark.
Then *Jason*; and his javelin seem'd to take,
But fail'd with over-force, and whiz'd above his back.
Mopsus was next; but e'er he threw, address'd
To *Phoebus*, thus: O patron, help thy priest:
If I adore, and ever have ador'd
Thy pow'r divine, thy present aid afford;
That I may reach the beast. The God allow'd
His pray'r, and smiling, gave him what he cou'd:
He reach'd the savage, but no blood he drew:

Dian unarm'd the javelin, as it flew.
This chaf'd the boar, his nostrils flames expire,
And his red eye-balls roul with living fire.
Whirl'd from a sling, or from an engine thrown,
Amid the foes, so flies a mighty stone,
As flew the beast: the left wing put to flight,
The chiefs o'er-born, he rushes on the right.
Eupalamos and *Pelagon* he laid
In dust, and next to death, but for their fellows' aid.
Onesimus far'd worse, prepar'd to fly,
The fatal fang drove deep within his thigh,
And cut the nerves: the nerves no more sustain
The bulk; the bulk unprop'd, falls headlong on the plain.

Nestor had fail'd the fall of *Troy* to see,
But leaning on his lance, he vaulted on a tree;
Then gath'ring up his feet, look'd down with fear,
And thought his monstrous foe was still too near.
Against a stump his tusk the monster grinds,
And in the sharpen'd edge new vigour finds;
Then, trusting to his arms, young *Othrys* found,
And ranch'd his hips with one continu'd wound.

Now *Leda's* twins, the future stars, appear;
White were their habits, white their horses were:
Conspicuous both, and both in act to throw,
Their trembling lances brandish'd at the foe:
Nor had they miss'd; but he to thickets fled,
Conceal'd from aiming spears, not pervious to the steed.
But *Telamon* rush'd in, and happ'd to meet
A rising root, that held his fastned feet;
So down he fell, whom, sprawling on the ground,
His brother from the wooden gyves unbound.

Mean-time the virgin-huntress was not slow
T' expel the shaft from her contracted bow:
Beneath his ear the fastned arrow stood,
And from the wound appear'd the trickling blood.

She blush'd for joy: but *Meleagros* rais'd
His voice with loud applause, and the fair archer prais'd.
He was the first to see, and first to show
His friends the marks of the successful blow.
Nor shall thy valour want the praises due,
He said; a virtuous envy seiz'd the crew.
They shout; the shouting animates their hearts,
And all at once employ their thronging darts:
But out of order thrown, in air they joyn,
And multitude makes frustrate the design.
With both his hands the proud *Ancaeus* takes,
And flourishes his double-biting ax:
Then, forward to his fate, he took a stride
Before the rest, and to his fellows cry'd,
Give place, and mark the diff'rence, if you can,
Between a woman warrior, and a man,
The boar is doom'd; nor though *Diana* lend
Her aid, *Diana* can her beast defend.
Thus boasted he; then stretch'd, on tiptoe stood,
Secure to make his empty promise good.
But the more wary beast prevents the blow,
And upward rips the groin of his audacious foe.
Ancaeus falls; his bowels from the wound
Rush out, and clotted blood distains the ground.

   Perithous, no small portion of the war,
Press'd on, and shook his lance: to whom from far
Thus *Theseus* cry'd; O stay, my better part,
My more than mistress; of my heart, the heart.
The strong may fight aloof; *Ancaeus* try'd
His force too near, and by presuming dy'd:
He said, and while he spake his javelin threw,
Hissing in air th' unerring weapon flew;
But on an arm of oak, that stood betwixt
The marks-man and the mark, his lance he fixt.

   Once more bold *Jason* threw, but fail'd to wound

The boar, and slew an undeserving hound,
And thro' the dog the dart was nail'd to ground.
  Two spears from *Meleager's* hand were sent,
With equal force, but various in th' event:
The first was fix'd in earth, the second stood
On the boar's bristled back, and deeply drank his blood.
Now while the tortur'd savage turns around,
And flings about his foam, impatient of the wound,
The wound's great author close at hand provokes
His rage, and plies him with redoubled strokes;
Wheels, as he wheels; and with his pointed dart
Explores the nearest passage to his heart.
Quick, and more quick he spins in giddy gires,
Then falls, and in much foam his soul expires.
This act with shouts heav'n-high the friendly band
Applaud, and strain in theirs the victor's hand.
Then all approach the slain with vast surprize,
Admire on what a breadth of earth he lies,
And scarce secure, reach out their spears afar,
And blood their points, to prove their partnership of war.
  But he, the conqu'ring chief, his foot impress'd
On the strong neck of that destructive beast;
And gazing on the nymph with ardent eyes,
Accept, said he, fair *Nonacrine*, my prize,
And, though inferior, suffer me to join
My labours, and my part of praise, with thine:
At this presents her with the tusky head
And chine, with rising bristles roughly spread.
Glad she receiv'd the gift; and seem'd to take
With double pleasure, for the giver's sake.
The rest were seiz'd with sullen discontent,
And a deaf murmur through the squadron went:
All envy'd; but the *Thestyan* brethren show'd
The least respect, and thus they vent their spleen aloud:
Lay down those honour'd spoils, nor think to share,

Weak woman as thou art, the prize of war:
Ours is the title, thine a foreign claim,
Since *Meleagrus* from our lineage came.
Trust not thy beauty; but restore the prize,
Which he, besotted on that face, and eyes,
Would rend from us: at this, enflam'd with spite,
From her they snatch the gift, from him the giver's right.

But soon th' impatient prince his fauchion drew,
And cry'd, Ye robbers of another's due,
Now learn the diff'rence, at your proper cost,
Betwixt true valour, and an empty boast.
At this advanc'd, and sudden as the word,
In proud *Plexippus'* bosom plung'd the sword:
Toxeus amaz'd, and with amazement slow,
Or to revenge, or ward the coming blow,
Stood doubting; and while doubting thus he stood,
Receiv'd the steel bath'd in his brother's blood.

Pleas'd with the first, unknown the second news;
Althaea to the temples pays their dues
For her son's conquest; when at length appear
Her grisly brethren stretch'd upon the bier:
Pale at the sudden sight, she chang'd her cheer,
And with her cheer her robes; but hearing tell
The cause, the manner, and by whom they fell,
'Twas grief no more, or grief and rage were one
Within her soul; at last 'twas rage alone;
Which burning upwards in succession, dries
The tears, that stood consid'ring in her eyes.

There lay a log unlighted on the hearth,
When she was lab'ring in the throws of birth
For th' unborn chief; the fatal sisters came,
And rais'd it up, and toss'd it on the flame:
Then on the rock a scanty measure place
Of vital flax, and turn'd the wheel apace;
And turning sung, To this red brand and thee,

O new born babe, we give an equal destiny;
So vanish'd out of view. The frighted dame
Sprung hasty from her bed, and quench'd the flame:
The log, in secret lock'd, she kept with care,
And that, while thus preserv'd, preserv'd her heir.
This brand she now produc'd; and first she strows
The hearth with heaps of chips, and after blows;
Thrice heav'd her hand, and heav'd, she thrice repress'd:
The sister and the mother long contest,
Two doubtful titles, in one tender breast:
And now her eyes, and cheeks with fury glow,
Now pale her cheeks, her eyes with pity flow:
Now low'ring looks presage approaching storms,
And now prevailing love her face reforms:
Resolv'd, she doubts again; the tears she dry'd
With burning rage, are by new tears supply'd;
And as a ship, which winds and waves assail,
Now with the current drives, now with the gale,
Both opposite, and neither long prevail:
She feels a double force, by turns obeys
Th' imperious tempest, and th' impetuous seas:
So fares *Althaea's* mind, she first relents
With pity, of that pity then repents:
Sister, and mother long the scales divide,
But the beam nodded on the sister's side.
Sometimes she softly sigh'd, then roar'd aloud;
But sighs were stifled in the cries of blood.

   The pious, impious wretch at length decreed,
To please her brothers' ghost, her son should bleed:
And when the fun'ral flames began to rise,
Receive, she said, a sister's sacrifice;
A mother's bowels burn: high in her hand,
Thus while she spoke, she held the fatal brand;
Then thrice before the kindled pile she bow'd,
And the three Furies thrice invok'd aloud:

Come, come, revenging sisters, come, and view
A sister paying her dead brothers due:
A crime I punish, and a crime commit;
But blood for blood, and death for death is fit:
Great crimes must be with greater crimes repaid,
And second fun'rals on the former laid.
Let the whole houshold in one ruin fall,
And may *Diana's* curse o'ertake us all.
Shall Fate to happy *Oenus* still allow
One son, while *Thestius* stands depriv'd of two?
Better three lost, than one unpunish'd go.
Take then, dear ghosts (while yet admitted new
In Hell you wait my duty), take your due:
A costly off'ring on your tomb is laid,
When with my blood the price of yours is paid.

   Ah! whither am I hurry'd? Ah! forgive,
Ye shades, and let your sister's issue live;
A mother cannot give him death; tho' he
Deserves it, he deserves it not from me.

   Then shall th' unpunish'd wretch insult the slain,
Triumphant live, nor only live, but reign?
While you, thin shades, the sport of winds, are tost
O'er dreary plains, or tread the burning coast.
I cannot, cannot bear; 'tis past, 'tis done;
Perish this impious, this detested son:
Perish his sire, and perish I withal;
And let the house's heir, and the hop'd kingdom fall.

   Where is the mother fled, her pious love,
And where the pains with which ten months I strove!
Ah! had'st thou dy'd, my son, in infant years,
Thy little herse had been bedew'd with tears.

   Thou liv'st by me; to me thy breath resign;
Mine is the merit, the demerit thine.
Thy life by double title I require;
Once giv'n at birth, and once preserv'd from fire:

One murder pay, or add one murder more,
And me to them who fell by thee restore.

I would, but cannot: my son's image stands
Before my sight; and now their angry hands
My brothers hold, and vengeance these exact;
This pleads compassion, and repents the fact.

He pleads in vain, and I pronounce his doom:
My brothers, though unjustly, shall o'ercome.
But having paid their injur'd ghosts their due,
My son requires my death, and mine shall his pursue.

At this, for the last time, she lifts her hand,
Averts her eyes, and, half unwilling, drops the brand.
The brand, amid the flaming fewel thrown,
Or drew, or seem'd to draw, a dying groan;
The fires themselves but faintly lick'd their prey,
Then loath'd their impious food, and would have shrunk

Just then the heroe cast a doleful cry,   [away.
And in those absent flames began to fry:
The blind contagion rag'd within his veins;
But he with manly patience bore his pains:
He fear'd not Fate, but only griev'd to die
Without an honest wound, and by a death so dry.
Happy *Ancaeus*, thrice aloud he cry'd,
With what becoming fate in arms he dy'd!
Then call'd his brothers, sisters, sire around,
And, her to whom his nuptial vows were bound,
Perhaps his mother; a long sigh she drew,
And his voice failing, took his last adieu.
For as the flames augment, and as they stay
At their full height, then languish to decay,
They rise and sink by fits; at last they soar
In one bright blaze, and then descend no more:
Just so his inward heats, at height, impair,
'Till the last burning breath shoots out the soul in air.

Now lofty *Calidon* in ruins lies;

All ages, all degrees unsluice their eyes,
And Heav'n, and Earth resound with murmurs, groans, and
Matrons and maidens beat their breasts, and tear   [cries.
Their habits, and root up their scatter'd hair:
The wretched father, father now no more,
With sorrow sunk, lies prostrate on the floor,
Deforms his hoary locks with dust obscene,
And curses age, and loaths a life prolong'd with pain.
By steel her stubborn soul his mother freed,
And punish'd on her self her impious deed.

　　Had I a hundred tongues, a wit so large
As could their hundred offices discharge;
Had *Phoebus* all his *Helicon* bestow'd
In all the streams, inspiring all the God;
Those tongues, that wit, those streams, that God in vain
Would offer to describe his sisters' pain:
They beat their breasts with many a bruizing blow,
'Till they turn livid, and corrupt the snow.
The corps they cherish, while the corps remains,
And exercise, and rub with fruitless pains;
And when to fun'ral flames 'tis born away,
They kiss the bed on which the body lay:
And when those fun'ral flames no longer burn
(The dust compos'd within a pious urn),
Ev'n in that urn their brother they confess,
And hug it in their arms, and to their bosoms press.

　　His tomb is rais'd; then, stretch'd along the ground,
Those living monuments his tomb surround:
Ev'n to his name, inscrib'd, their tears they pay,
'Till tears, and kisses wear his name away.

　　But *Cynthia* now had all her fury spent,
Not with less ruin than a race content:
Excepting *Gorgè*, perish'd all the seed,
And her whom Heav'n for *Hercules* decreed.
Satiate at last, no longer she pursu'd

The weeping sisters; but with wings endu'd,
And horny beaks, and sent to flit in air;
Who yearly round the tomb in feather'd flocks repair.
    Theseus mean-while acquitting well his share
In the bold chace confed'rate like a war,
To *Athens'* lofty tow'rs his march ordain'd,
By *Pallas* lov'd, and where *Erectheus* reign'd.
But *Acheloüs* stop'd him on the way,
By rains a deluge, and constrain'd his stay.
    O fam'd for glorious deeds, and great by blood,
Rest here, says he, nor trust the rapid flood;
It solid oaks has from its margin tore,
And rocky fragments down its current bore,
The murmur hoarse, and terrible the roar.
Oft have I seen herds with their shelt'ring fold
Forc'd from the banks, and in the torrent roul'd;
Nor strength the bulky steer from ruin freed,
Nor matchless swiftness sav'd the racing steed.
In cataracts when the dissolving snow
Falls from the hills, and floods the plains below;
Toss'd by the eddies with a giddy round,
Strong youths are in the sucking whirlpools drown'd.
'Tis best with me in safety to abide,
'Till usual bounds restrain the ebbing tide,
And the low waters in their channel glide.
    Theseus perswaded, in compliance bow'd:
So kind an offer, and advice so good,
O *Acheloüs*, cannot be refus'd;
I'll use them both, said he; and both he us'd.
    The grot he enter'd, pumice built the hall,
And tophi made the rustick of the wall;
The floor, soft moss, an humid carpet spread,
And various shells the chequer'd roof inlaid.
'Twas now the hour when the declining sun
Two thirds had of his daily journey run;

At the spread table *Theseus* took his place,
Next his companions in the daring chace;
Perithous here, there elder *Lelex* lay,
His locks betraying age with sprinkled grey.
Acharnia's river-God dispos'd the rest,
Grac'd with the equal honour of the feast,
Elate with joy, and proud of such a guest.
The nymphs were waiters, and with naked feet
In order serv'd the courses of the meat.
The banquet done, delicious wine they brought,
Of one transparent gem the cup was wrought.

   Then the great heroe of this gallant train,
Surveying far the prospect of the main:
What is that land, says he, the waves embrace?
(And with his finger pointed at the place);
Is it one parted isle which stands alone?
How nam'd? and yet methinks it seems not one.
To whom the watry God made this reply;
'Tis not one isle, but five; distinct they lye;
'Tis distance which deceives the cheated eye.
But that *Diana's* act may seem less strange,
These once proud *Naiads* were, before their change.
'Twas on a day more solemn than the rest,
Ten bullocks slain, a sacrificial feast:
The rural Gods of all the region near
They bid to dance, and taste the hallow'd cheer.
Me they forgot: affronted with the slight,
My rage, and stream swell'd to the greatest height;
And with the torrent of my flooding store,
Large woods from woods, and fields from fields I tore.
The guilty nymphs, oh! then, remembring me,
I, with their country, wash'd into the sea;
And joining waters with the social main,
Rent the gross land, and split the firm champagne.
Since, the *Echinades*, remote from shore

Are view'd as many isles, as nymphs before.
　　But yonder far, lo, yonder does appear
An isle, a part to me for ever dear.
From that (it sailors *Perimele* name)
I doating, forc'd by rape a virgin's fame.
Hippodamas's passion grew so strong,
Gall'd with th' abuse, and fretted at the wrong,
He cast his pregnant daughter from a rock;
I spread my waves beneath, and broke the shock;
And as her swimming weight my stream convey'd,
I su'd for help divine, and thus I pray'd:
O pow'rful thou, whose trident does command
The realm of waters, which surround the land;
We sacred rivers, wheresoe'er begun,
End in thy lot, and to thy empire run.
With favour hear, and help with present aid;
Her whom I bear 'twas guilty I betray'd.
Yet if her father had been just, or mild,
He would have been less impious to his child;
In her, have pity'd force in the abuse;
In me, admitted love for my excuse.
O let relief for her hard case be found,
Her, whom paternal rage expell'd from ground,
Her, whom paternal rage relentless drown'd.
Grant her some place, or change her to a place,
Which I may ever clasp with my embrace.
　　His nodding head the sea's great ruler bent,
And all his waters shook with his assent.
The nymph still swam, tho' with the fright distrest,
I felt her heart leap trembling in her breast;
But hardning soon, whilst I her pulse explore,
A crusting Earth cas'd her stiff body o'er;
And as accretions of new-cleaving soil
Inlarg'd the mass, the nymph became an isle.

Thus *Acheloüs* ends: his audience hear
With admiration, and admiring, fear
The Pow'rs of Heav'n; except *Ixion's* Son,
Who laugh'd at all the Gods, believ'd in none:
He shook his impious head, and thus replies.
These legends are no more than pious lies:
You attribute too much to heav'nly sway,
To think they give us forms, and take away.

The rest of better minds, their sense declar'd
Against this doctrine, and with horror heard.
Then *Lelex* rose, an old experienc'd man,
And thus with sober gravity began;
Heav'n's pow'r is infinite: Earth, Air, and Sea,
The manufacture mass, the making Pow'r obey:
By proof to clear your doubt; in *Phrygian* ground
Two neighb'ring trees, with walls encompass'd round,
Stand on a mod'rate rise, with wonder shown,
One a hard oak, a softer linden one:
I saw the place, and them, by *Pittheus* sent
To *Phrygian* realms, my grandsire's government.
Not far from thence is seen a lake, the haunt
Of coots, and of the fishing cormorant:
Here *Jove* with *Hermes* came; but in disguise
Of mortal men conceal'd their deities;
One laid aside his thunder, one his rod;
And many toilsome steps together trod:
For harbour at a thousand doors they knock'd,
Not one of all the thousand but was lock'd.
At last an hospitable house they found,
A homely shed; the roof, not far from ground,
Was thatch'd with reeds, and straw, together bound.
There *Baucis* and *Philemon* liv'd, and there
Had liv'd long marry'd, and a happy pair:
Now old in love, though little was their store,
Inur'd to want, their poverty they bore,

Nor aim'd at wealth, professing to be poor.
For master, or for servant here to call,
Was all alike, where only two were all.
Command was none, where equal love was paid,
Or rather both commanded, both obey'd.

From lofty roofs the Gods repuls'd before,
Now stooping, enter'd through the little door:
The man (their hearty welcome first express'd)
A common settle drew for either guest,
Inviting each his weary limbs to rest.
But ere they sate, officious *Baucis* lays
Two cushions stuff'd with straw, the seat to raise;
Coarse, but the best she had; then rakes the load
Of ashes from the hearth, and spreads abroad
The living coals; and, lest they should expire,
With leaves, and bark she feeds her infant fire:
It smoaks; and then with trembling breath she blows,
'Till in a chearful blaze the flames arose.
With brush-wood, and with chips she strengthens these,
And adds at last the boughs of rotten trees.
The fire thus form'd, she sets the kettle on
(Like burnish'd gold the little seether shone),
Next took the coleworts which her husband got
From his own ground (a small well-water'd spot);
She stripp'd the stalks of all their leaves; the best
She cull'd, and them with handy care she drest.
High o'er the hearth a chine of bacon hung;
Good old *Philemon* seiz'd it with a prong,
And from the sooty rafter drew it down,
Then cut a slice, but scarce enough for one;
Yet a large portion of a little store,
Which for their sakes alone he wish'd were more.
This in the pot he plung'd without delay,
To tame the flesh, and drain the salt away.
The time beween, before the fire they sat,

And shorten'd the delay by pleasing chat.
  A beam there was, on which a beechen pail
Hung by the handle, on a driven nail:
This fill'd with water, gently warm'd, they set
Before their guests; in this they bath'd their feet,
And after with clean towels dry'd their sweat.
This done, the host produc'd the genial bed,
Sallow the feet, the borders, and the sted,
Which with no costly coverlet they spread,
But coarse old garments; yet such robes as these
They laid alone, at feasts, on holidays.
The good old housewife, tucking up her gown,
The table sets; th' invited Gods lie down.
The trivet-table of a foot was lame,
A blot which prudent *Baucis* overcame,
Who thrusts beneath the limping leg a sherd,
So was the mended board exactly rear'd:
Then rubb'd it o'er with newly gather'd mint,
A wholsom herb, that breath'd a grateful scent.
Pallas began the feast, where first was seen
The party-colour'd olive, black, and green:
Autumnal cornels next in order serv'd,
In lees of wine well pickled, and preserv'd.
A garden-sallad was the third supply,
Of endive, radishes, and succory:
Then curds, and cream, the flow'r of country fare,
And new-laid eggs, which *Baucis*' busie care
Turn'd by a gentle fire, and roasted rare.
All these in earthen ware were serv'd to board;
And next in place, an earthen pitcher stor'd,
With liquor of the best the cottage could afford.
This was the table's ornament and pride,
With figures wrought: like pages at his side
Stood beechen bowls; and these were shining clean,
Varnish'd with wax without, and lin'd within.

By this the boiling kettle had prepar'd,
And to the table sent the smoking lard;
On which with eager appetite they dine,
A sav'ry bit, that serv'd to relish wine:
The wine itself was suiting to the rest,
Still working in the must, and lately press'd.
The second course succeeds like that before,
Plums, apples, nuts, and of their wintry store
Dry figs, and grapes, and wrinkled dates were set
In canisters, t' enlarge the little treat:
All these a milk-white honey-comb surround,
Which in the midst the country-banquet crown'd:
But the kind hosts their entertainment grace
With hearty welcome, and an open face:
In all they did, you might discern with ease,
A willing mind, and a desire to please.

   Mean-time the beechen bowls went round, and still,
Though often empty'd, were observ'd to fill;
Fill'd without hands, and of their own accord
Ran without feet, and danc'd about the board.
Devotion seiz'd the pair, to see the feast
With wine, and of no common grape, increas'd;
And up they held their hands, and fell to pray'r,
Excusing, as they could, their country fare.

   One goose they had ('twas all they could allow),
A wakeful centry, and on duty now,
Whom to the Gods for sacrifice they vow:
Her with malicious zeal the couple view'd;
She ran for life, and limping they pursu'd:
Full well the fowl perceiv'd their bad intent,
And would not make her master's compliment;
But persecuted, to the Pow'rs she flies,
And close between the legs of *Jove* she lies:
He with a gracious ear the suppliant heard,
And sav'd her life; then what he has declar'd,

And own'd the God. The neighbourhood, said he,
Shall justly perish for impiety:
You stand alone exempted; but obey
With speed, and follow where we lead the way:
Leave these accurs'd; and to the mountain's height
Ascend; nor once look backward in your flight.

They haste, and what their tardy feet deny'd,
The trusty staff (their better leg) supply'd.
An arrow's flight they wanted to the top,
And there secure, but spent with travel, stop;
Then turn their now no more forbidden eyes;
Lost in a lake the floated level lies:
A watry desart covers all the plains,
Their cot alone, as in an isle, remains.
Wondring, with weeping eyes, while they deplore
Their neighbours' fate, and country now no more,
Their little shed, scarce large enough for two,
Seems, from the ground increas'd, in height and bulk to
A stately temple shoots within the skies,   [grow.
The crotches of their cot in columns rise:
The pavement polish'd marble they behold,
The gates with sculpture grac'd, the spires and tiles of gold.

Then thus the sire of Gods, with looks serene,
Speak thy desire, thou only just of men;
And thou, o woman, only worthy found
To be with such a man in marriage bound.

A-while they whisper; then, to *Jove* address'd,
Philemon thus prefers their joint request:
We crave to serve before your sacred shrine,
And offer at your altars rites divine:
And since not any action of our life
Has been polluted with domestick strife;
We beg one hour of death, that neither she
With widow's tears may live to bury me,
Nor weeping I, with wither'd arms may bear

My breathless *Baucis* to the sepulcher.
   The Godheads sign their suit. They run their race
In the same tenour all th' appointed space:
Then, when their hour was come, while they relate
These past adventures at the temple gate,
Old *Baucis* is by old *Philemon* seen
Sprouting with sudden leaves of spritely green:
Old *Baucis* look'd where old *Philemon* stood,
And saw his lengthen'd arms a sprouting wood:
New roots their fasten'd feet begin to bind,
Their bodies stiffen in a rising rind:
Then, ere the bark above their shoulders grew,
They give, and take at once their last adieu.
At once, Farewell, o faithful spouse, they said;
At once th' incroaching rinds their closing lips invade.
Ev'n yet, an ancient *Tyanaean* shows
A spreading oak, that near a linden grows;
The neighbourhood confirm the prodigy,
Grave men, not vain of tongue, or like to lie.
I saw my self the garlands on their boughs,
And tablets hung for gifts of granted vows;
And off'ring fresher up, with pious pray'r,
The good, said I, are God's peculiar care,
And such as honour Heav'n, shall heav'nly honour share.
   He ceas'd in his relation to proceed,
Whilst all admir'd the author, and the deed;
But *Theseus* most, inquisitive to know
From Gods what wondrous alterations grow.
Whom thus the *Calydonian* stream address'd,
Rais'd high to speak, the couch his elbow press'd.
Some, when transform'd, fix in the lasting change;
Some with more right, thro' various figures range.
Proteus, thus large thy privilege was found,
Thou inmate of the seas, which Earth surround.
Sometimes a blooming youth you grac'd the shore;

Oft a fierce lion, or a furious boar:
With glist'ring spires now seem'd an hissing snake,
The bold would tremble in his hands to take:
With horns assum'd a bull; sometimes you prov'd
A tree by roots, a stone by weight unmov'd:
Sometimes two wav'ring contraries became,
Flow'd down in water, or aspir'd in flame.

In various shapes thus to deceive the eyes,
Without a settled stint of her disguise,
Rash *Erisichthon's* daughter had the pow'r,
And brought it to *Autolicus* in dow'r.
Her atheist sire the slighted Gods defy'd,
And ritual honours to their shrines deny'd.
As fame reports, his hand an ax sustain'd,
Which *Ceres'* consecrated grove prophan'd;
Which durst the venerable gloom invade,
And violate with light the awful shade.
An ancient oak in the dark center stood,
The covert's glory, and itself a wood:
Garlands embrac'd its shaft, and from the boughs
Hung tablets, monuments of prosp'rous vows.
In the cool dusk its unpierc'd verdure spread,
The *Dryads* oft their hallow'd dances led;
And oft, when round their gaging arms they cast,
Full fifteen ells it measu'rd in the waste:
Its height all under standards did surpass,
As they aspir'd above the humbler grass.

These motives, which would gentler minds restrain,
Could not make *Triope's* bold son abstain;
He sternly charg'd his slaves with strict decree,
To fell with gashing steel the sacred tree.
But whilst they, lingring, his commands delay'd,
He snatch'd an Ax, and thus blaspheming said:
Was this no oak, nor *Ceres'* favourite care,
But *Ceres'* self, this arm, unaw'd, shou'd dare

Its leafy honours in the dust to spread,
And level with the earth its airy head.
He spoke, and as he poiz'd a slanting stroak,
Sighs heav'd, and tremblings shook the frighted oak;
Its leaves look'd sickly, pale its acorns grew,
And its long branches sweat a chilly dew.
But when his impious hand a wound bestow'd,
Blood from the mangled bark in currents flow'd.
When a devoted bull of mighty size,
A sinning nation's grand atonement, dies;
With such a plenty from the spouting veins,
A crimson stream the turfy altars stains.

   The wonder all amaz'd; yet one more bold,
The fact dissuading, strove his ax to hold.
But the *Thessalian*, obstinately bent,
Too proud to change, too harden'd to repent,
On his kind monitor, his eyes, which burn'd
With rage, and with his eyes his weapon turn'd;
Take the reward, says he, of pious dread:
Then with a blow lopp'd off his parted head.
No longer check'd, the wretch his crime pursu'd,
Doubled his strokes, and sacrilege renew'd;
When from the groaning trunk a voice was heard,
A *Dryad* I, by *Ceres*' love preferr'd,
Within the circle of this clasping rind
Coëval grew, and now in ruin join'd;
But instant vengeance shall thy sin pursue,
And death is chear'd with this prophetick view.

   At last the oak with cords enforc'd to bow,
Strain'd from the top, and sap'd with wounds below,
The humbler wood, partaker of its fate,
Crush'd with its fall, and shiver'd with its weight.

   The grove destroy'd, the sister *Dryads* moan,
Griev'd at its loss, and frighted at their own.
Strait, suppliants for revenge to *Ceres* go,

In sable weeds, expressive of their woe.
   The beauteous Goddess with a graceful air
Bow'd in consent, and nodded to their pray'r.
The awful motion shook the fruitful ground,
And wav'd the fields with golden harvests crown'd.
Soon she contriv'd in her projecting mind
A plague severe, and piteous in its kind
(If plagues for crimes of such presumptuous height
Could pity in the softest breast create).
With pinching want, and hunger's keenest smart,
To tear his vitals, and corrode his heart.
But since her near approach by Fate's deny'd
To famine, and broad climes their pow'rs divide,
A nymph, the mountain's ranger, she address'd,
And thus resolv'd, her high commands express'd.
   Where frozen *Scythia's* utmost bound is plac'd,
A desart lies, a melancholy waste:
In yellow crops there Nature never smil'd,
No fruitful tree to shade the barren wild.
There sluggish cold its icy station makes,
There paleness, frights, and aguish trembling shakes,
Of pining famine this the fated seat,
To whom my orders in these words repeat:
Bid her this miscreant with her sharpest pains
Chastise, and sheath herself into his veins;
Be unsubdu'd by plenty's baffled store,
Reject my empire, and defeat my pow'r.
And lest the distance, and the tedious way,
Should with the toil, and long fatigue dismay,
Ascend my chariot, and convey'd on high,
Guide the rein'd dragons thro' the parting sky.
   The nymph, accepting of the granted carr,
Sprung to the seat, and posted thro' the air;
Nor stop'd 'till she to a bleak mountain came
Of wondrous height, and *Caucasus* its name.

There in a stony field the fiend she found,
Herbs gnawing, and roots scratching from the ground.
Her elfelock hair in matted tresses grew,
Sunk were her eyes, and pale her ghastly hue,
Wan were her lips, and foul with clammy glew.
Her throat was furr'd, her guts appear'd within
With snaky crawlings thro' her parchment skin.
Her jutting hips seem'd starting from their place,
And for a belly was a belly's space,
Her dugs hung dangling from her craggy spine,
Loose to her breast, and fasten'd to her chine.
Her joints protuberant by leanness grown,
Consumption sunk the flesh, and rais'd the bone.
Her knees large orbits bunch'd to monstrous size,
And ancles to undue proportion rise.

   This plague the nymph, not daring to draw near,
At distance hail'd, and greeted from afar.
And tho' she told her charge without delay,
Tho' her arrival late, and short her stay,
She felt keen famine, or she seem'd to feel,
Invade her blood, and on her vitals steal.
She turn'd, from the infection to remove,
And back to *Thessaly* the serpents drove.

   The fiend obey'd the Goddess' command
(Tho' their effects in opposition stand),
She cut her way, supported by the wind,
And reach'd the mansion by the nymph assign'd.

   'Twas night, when entring *Erisichthon's* room,
Dissolv'd in sleep, and thoughtless of his doom,
She clasp'd his limbs, by impious labour tir'd,
With battish wings, but her whole self inspir'd;
Breath'd on his throat and chest a tainting blast,
And in his veins infus'd an endless fast.

   The task dispatch'd, away the Fury flies
From plenteous regions, and from rip'ning skies;

To her old barren north she wings her speed,
And cottages distress'd with pinching need.

    Still slumbers *Erisichthon's* senses drown,
And sooth his fancy with their softest down.
He dreams of viands delicate to eat,
And revels on imaginary meat,
Chaws with his working mouth, but chaws in vain,
And tires his grinding teeth with fruitless pain;
Deludes his throat with visionary fare,
Feasts on the wind, and banquets on the air.

    The morning came, the night, and slumbers past,
But still the furious pangs of hunger last;
The cank'rous rage still gnaws with griping pains,
Stings in his throat, and in his bowels reigns.

    Strait he requires, impatient in demand,
Provisions from the air, the seas, the land.
But tho' the land, air, seas, provisions grant,
Starves at full tables, and complains of want.
What to a people might in dole be paid,
Or victual cities for a long blockade,
Could not one wolfish appetite asswage;
For glutting nourishment increas'd its rage.
As rivers pour'd from ev'ry distant shore,
The sea insatiate drinks, and thirsts for more;
Or as the fire, which all materials burns,
And wasted forests into ashes turns,
Grows more voracious, as the more it preys,
Recruits dilate the flame, and spread the blaze:
So impious *Erisichthon's* hunger raves,
Receives refreshments, and refreshments craves.
Food raises a desire for food, and meat
Is but a new provocative to eat.
He grows more empty, as the more supply'd,
And endless cramming but extends the void.

Now riches hoarded by paternal care
Were sunk, the glutton swallowing up the heir.
Yet the devouring flame no stores abate,
Nor less his hunger grew with his estate.
One daughter left, as left his keen desire,
A daughter worthy of a better sire:
Her too he sold, spent Nature to sustain;
She scorn'd a lord with generous disdain,
And flying, spread her hand upon the main.
Then pray'd: Grant, thou, I bondage may escape,
And with my liberty reward thy rape;
Repay my virgin treasure with thy aid
('Twas *Neptune* who deflower'd the beauteous maid).
    The God was mov'd, at what the fair had su'd,
When she so lately by her master view'd
In her known figure, on a sudden took
A fisher's habit, and a manly look.
To whom her owner hasted to enquire;
O thou, said he, whose baits hide treach'rous wire;
Whose art can manage, and experienc'd skill
The taper angle, and the bobbing quill,
So may the sea be ruffled with no storm,
But smooth with calms, as you the truth inform;
So your deceit may no shy fishes feel,
'Till struck, and fasten'd on the bearded steel.
Did not you standing view upon the strand,
A wand'ring maid? I'm sure I saw her stand;
Her hair disorder'd, and her homely dress
Betray'd her want, and witness'd her distress.
    Me heedless, she reply'd, whoe'er you are,
Excuse, attentive to another care.
I settled on the deep my steady eye;
Fix'd on my float, and bent on my employ.
And that you may not doubt what I impart,
So may the ocean's God assist my art,

If on the beach since I my sport pursu'd,
Or man, or woman but my self I view'd.
Back o'er the sands, deluded, he withdrew,
Whilst she for her old form put off her new.

Her sire her shifting pow'r to change perceiv'd;
And various chapmen by her sale deceiv'd.
A fowl with spangled plumes, a brinded steer,
Sometimes a crested mare, or antler'd deer:
Sold for a price, she parted, to maintain
Her starving parent with dishonest gain.

At last all means, as all provisions, fail'd;
For the disease by remedies prevail'd;
His muscles with a furious bite he tore,
Gorg'd his own tatter'd flesh, and gulph'd his gore.
Wounds were his feast, his life to life a prey,
Supporting Nature by its own decay.

But foreign stories why shou'd I relate?
I too my self can to new forms translate,
Tho' the variety's not unconfin'd,
But fix'd, in number, and restrain'd in kind:
For often I this present shape retain,
Oft curl a snake the volumes of my train.
Sometimes my strength into my horns transfer'd,
A bull I march, the captain of the herd.
But whilst I once those goring weapons wore,
Vast wresting force one from my forehead tore.
Lo, my maim'd brows the injury still own;
He ceas'd; his words concluding with a groan.

The End of the Eighth Book.

BOOK THE NINTH

Theseus requests the God to tell his woes,
 Whence his maim'd brow, and whence his groans arose
 Whence thus the *Calydonian* stream reply'd,
With twining reeds his careless tresses ty'd:
Ungrateful is the tale; for who can bear,
When conquer'd, to rehearse the shameful war?
Yet I'll the melancholy story trace;
So great a conqu'ror softens the disgrace:
Nor was it still so mean the prize to yield,
As great, and glorious to dispute the field.

 Perhaps you've heard of *Deïanira's* name,
For all the country spoke her beauty's fame.
Long was the nymph by num'rous suitors woo'd,
Each with address his envy'd hopes pursu'd:
I joyn'd the loving band; to gain the fair,
Reveal'd my passion to her father's ear.
Their vain pretensions all the rest resign,
Alcides only strove to equal mine;
He boasts his birth from *Jove*, recounts his spoils,
His step-dame's hate subdu'd, and finish'd toils.

 Can mortals then (said I), with Gods compare?
Behold a God; mine is the watry care:
Through your wide realms I take my mazy way,
Branch into streams, and o'er the region stray:
No foreign guest your daughter's charms adores,
But one who rises in your native shores.
Let not his punishment your pity move;
Is *Juno's* hate an argument for love?
Though you your life from fair *Alcmena* drew,
Jove's a feign'd father, or by fraud a true.
Chuse then; confess thy mother's honour lost,
Or thy descent from *Jove* no longer boast.

 While thus I spoke, he look'd with stern disdain,
Nor could the sallies of his wrath restrain,
Which thus break forth. This arm decides our right;

Vanquish in words, be mine the prize in fight.
    Bold he rush'd on. My honour to maintain,
I fling my verdant garments on the plain,
My arms stretch forth, my pliant limbs prepare,
And with bent hands expect the furious war.
O'er my sleek skin now gather'd dust he throws,
And yellow sand his mighty muscles strows.
Oft he my neck, and nimble legs assails,
He seems to grasp me, but as often fails.
Each part he now invades with eager hand;
Safe in my bulk, immoveable I stand.
So when loud storms break high, and foam and roar
Against some mole that stretches from the shore;
The firm foundation lasting tempests braves,
Defies the warring winds, and driving waves.
    A-while we breathe, then forward rush amain,
Renew the combat, and our ground maintain;
Foot strove with foot, I prone extend my breast,
Hands war with hands, and forehead forehead prest.
Thus have I seen two furious bulls engage,
Inflam'd with equal love, and equal rage;
Each claims the fairest heifer of the grove,
And conquest only can decide their love:
The trembling herds survey the fight from far,
'Till victory decides th' important war.
Three times in vain he strove my joints to wrest,
To force my hold, and throw me from his breast;
The fourth he broke my gripe, that clasp'd him round,
Then with new force he stretch'd me on the ground;
Close to my back the mighty burthen clung,
As if a mountain o'er my limbs were flung.
Believe my tale; nor do I, boastful, aim
By feign'd narration to extol my fame.
No sooner from his grasp I freedom get,
Unlock my arms, that flow'd with trickling sweat,

But quick he seized me, and renew'd the strife,
As my exhausted bosom pants for life:
My neck he gripes, my knee to earth he strains;
I fall, and bite the sand with shame, and pains.

   O'er-match'd in strength, to wiles, and arts I take,
And slip his hold, in form of speckled snake;
Who, when I wreath'd in spires my body round,
Or show'd my forky tongue with hissing sound,
Smiles at my threats: Such foes my cradle knew,
He cries, dire snakes my infant hand o'erthrew;
A dragon's form might other conquests gain,
To war with me you take that shape in vain.
Art thou proportion'd to the *Hydra's* length,
Who by his wounds receiv'd augmented strength?
He rais'd a hundred hissing heads in air;
When one I lopt, up-sprung a dreadful pair.
By his wounds fertile, and with slaughter strong,
Singly I quell'd him, and stretch'd dead along.
What canst thou do, a form precarious, prone,
To rouse my rage with terrors not thy own?
He said; and round my neck his hands he cast,
And with his straining fingers wrung me fast;
My throat he tortur'd, close as pincers clasp,
In vain I strove to loose the forceful grasp.

   Thus vanquish'd too, a third form still remains,
Chang'd to a bull, my lowing fills the plains.
Strait on the left his nervous arms were thrown
Upon my brindled neck, and tugg'd it down;
Then deep he struck my horn into the sand,
And fell'd my bulk among the dusty land.
Nor yet his fury cool'd; 'twixt rage and scorn,
From my maim'd front he tore the stubborn horn:
This, heap'd with flow'rs, and fruits, the *Naiads* bear,
Sacred to plenty, and the bounteous year.

   He spoke; when lo, a beauteous nymph appears,

Girt like *Diana's* train, with flowing hairs;
The horn she brings in which all Autumn's stor'd,
And ruddy apples for the second board.

Now morn begins to dawn, the sun's bright fire
Gilds the high mountains, and the youths retire;
Nor stay'd they, 'till the troubled stream subsides,
And in its bounds with peaceful current glides.
But *Acheloüs* in his oozy bed
Deep hides his brow deform'd, and rustick head:
No real wound the victor's triumph show'd,
But his lost honours griev'd the watry God;
Yet ev'n that loss the willow's leaves o'erspread,
And verdant reeds, in garlands, bind his head.

This virgin too, thy love, O *Nessus*, found,
To her alone you owe the fatal wound.
As the strong son of *Jove* his bride conveys,
Where his paternal lands their bulwarks raise;
Where from her slopy urn, *Evenus* pours
Her rapid current, swell'd by wintry show'rs,
He came. The frequent eddies whirl'd the tide,
And the deep rolling waves all pass deny'd.
As for himself, he stood unmov'd by fears,
For now his bridal charge employ'd his cares,
The strong-limb'd *Nessus* thus officious cry'd
(For he the shallows of the stream had try'd),
Swim thou, *Alcides*, all thy strength prepare,
On yonder bank I'll lodge thy nuptial care.

Th' *Aonian* chief to *Nessus* trusts his wife,
All pale, and trembling for her heroe's life:
Cloath'd as he stood in the fierce lion's hide,
The laden quiver o'er his shoulder ty'd
(For cross the stream his bow and club were cast),
Swift he plung'd in: These billows shall be past,
He said, nor sought where smoother waters glide,
But stem'd the rapid dangers of the tide.

The bank he reach'd; again the bow he bears;
When, hark! his bride's known voice alarms his ears.
Nessus, to thee I call (aloud he cries)
Vain is thy trust in flight, be timely wise:
Thou monster double-shap'd, my right set free;
If thou no rev'rence owe my fame and me,
Yet kindred should thy lawless lust deny;
Think not, perfidious wretch, from me to fly,
Tho' wing'd with horse's speed; wounds shall pursue;
Swift as his words the fatal arrow flew:
The centaur's back admits the feather'd wood,
And thro' his breast the barbed weapon stood;
Which when, in anguish, thro' the flesh he tore,
From both the wounds gush'd forth the spumy gore
Mix'd with *Lernaean* venom; this he took,
Nor dire revenge his dying breast forsook.
His garment, in the reeking purple dy'd,
To rouse love's passion, he presents the bride.

    Now a long interval of time succeeds,
When the great son of *Jove's* immortal deeds,
And step-dame's hate, had fill'd Earth's utmost round;
He from *Oechalia*, with new lawrels crown'd,
In triumph was return'd. He rites prepares,
And to the King of Gods directs his pray'rs;
When Fame (who falshood cloaths in truth's disguise,
And swells her little bulk with growing lies)
Thy tender ear, o *Deïanira*, mov'd,
That *Hercules* the fair *Iole* lov'd.
Her love believes the tale; the truth she fears
Of his new passion, and gives way to tears.
The flowing tears diffus'd her wretched grief,
Why seek I thus, from streaming eyes, relief?
She cries; indulge not thus these fruitless cares,
The harlot will but triumph in thy tears:
Let something be resolv'd, while yet there's time;

My bed not conscious of a rival's crime.
In silence shall I mourn, or loud complain?
Shall I seek *Calydon*, or here remain?
What tho', ally'd to *Meleager's* fame,
I boast the honours of a sister's name?
My wrongs, perhaps, now urge me to pursue
Some desp'rate deed, by which the world shall view
How far revenge, and woman's rage can rise,
When weltring in her blood the harlot dies.

    Thus various passions rul'd by turns her breast,
She now resolves to send the fatal vest,
Dy'd with *Lernaean* gore, whose pow'r might move
His soul anew, and rouse declining love.
Nor knew she what her sudden rage bestows,
When she to *Lychas* trusts her future woes;
With soft endearments she the boy commands,
To bear the garment to her husband's hands.

    Th' unwitting hero takes the gift in haste,
And o'er his shoulders *Lerna's* poison cast,
As first the fire with frankincense he strows,
And utters to the Gods his holy vows;
And on the marble altar's polish'd frame
Pours forth the grapy stream; the rising flame
Sudden dissolves the subtle pois'nous juice,
Which taints his blood, and all his nerves bedews.
With wonted fortitude he bore the smart,
And not a groan confess'd his burning heart.
At length his patience was subdu'd by pain,
He rends the sacred altar from the plain;
Oete's wide forests echo with his cries:
Now to rip off the deathful robe he tries.
Where-e'er he plucks the vest, the skin he tears,
The mangled muscles, and huge bones he bares
(A ghastful sight!), or raging with his pain,
To rend the sticking plague he tugs in vain.

As the red iron hisses in the flood,
So boils the venom in his curdling blood.
Now with the greedy flame his entrails glow,
And livid sweats down all his body flow;
The cracking nerves burnt up are burst in twain,
The lurking venom melts his swimming brain.

Then, lifting both his hands aloft, he cries,
Glut thy revenge, dread Empress of the skies;
Sate with my death the rancour of thy heart,
Look down with pleasure, and enjoy my smart.
Or, if e'er pity mov'd a hostile breast
(For here I stand thy enemy profest),
Take hence this hateful life, with tortures torn,
Inur'd to trouble, and to labours born.
Death is the gift most welcome to my woe,
And such a gift a stepdame may bestow.
Was it for this *Busiris* was subdu'd,
Whose barb'rous temples reek'd with strangers' blood?
Press'd in these arms his fate *Antaeus* found,
Nor gain'd recruited vigour from the ground.
Did I not triple-form'd *Geryon* fell?
Or did I fear the triple dog of Hell?
Did not these hands the bull's arm'd forehead hold?
Are not our mighty toils in *Elis* told?
Do not *Stymphalian* lakes proclaim thy fame?
And fair *Parthenian* woods resound thy name?
Who seiz'd the golden belt of *Thermodon*?
And who the dragon-guarded apples won?
Could the fierce centaur's strength my force withstand,
Or the fell boar that spoil'd th' *Arcadian* land?
Did not these arms the *Hydra's* rage subdue,
Who from his wounds to double fury grew?
What if the *Thracian* horses, fat with gore,
Who human bodies in their mangers tore,
I saw, and with their barb'rous lord o'erthrew?

What if these hands *Nemaea's* lion slew?
Did not this neck the heav'nly globe sustain?
The female partner of the Thunderer's reign
Fatigu'd, at length suspends her harsh commands,
Yet no fatigue hath slack'd these valiant hands.
But now new plagues pursue me, neither force,
Nor arms, nor darts can stop their raging course.
Devouring flame thro' my rack'd entrails strays,
And on my lungs and shrivel'd muscles preys.
Yet still *Eurystheus* breathes the vital air.
What mortal now shall seek the Gods with pray'r?
     The hero said; and with the torture stung,
Furious o'er *Oete's* lofty hills he sprung.
Stuck with the shaft, thus scours the tyger round,
And seeks the flying author of his wound.
Now might you see him trembling, now he vents
His anguish'd soul in groans, and loud laments;
He strives to tear the clinging vest in vain,
And with up-rooted forests strows the plain;
Now kindling into rage, his hands he rears,
And to his kindred Gods directs his pray'rs.
When *Lychas*, lo, he spies; who trembling flew,
And in a hollow rock conceal'd from view,
Had shun'd his wrath. Now grief renew'd his pain,
His madness chaf'd, and thus he raves again.
     Lychas, to thee alone my fate I owe,
Who bore the gift, the cause of all my woe.
The youth all pale, with shiv'ring fear was stung,
And vain excuses falter'd on his tongue.
Alcides snatch'd him, as with suppliant face
He strove to clasp his knees, and beg for grace:
He toss'd him o'er his head with airy course,
And hurl'd with more than with an engine's force;
Far o'er th' *Eubaean* main aloof he flies,
And hardens by degrees amid the skies.

So showry drops, when chilly tempests blow,
Thicken at first, then whiten into snow,
In balls congeal'd the rolling fleeces bound,
In solid hail result upon the ground.
Thus, whirl'd with nervous force thro' distant air,
The purple tide forsook his veins, with fear;
All moisture left his limbs. Transform'd to stone,
In ancient days the craggy flint was known;
Still in the *Eubaean* waves his front he rears,
Still the small rock in human form appears,
And still the name of hapless *Lychas* bears.

But now the hero of immortal birth
Fells *Oete's* forests on the groaning Earth;
A pile he builds; to *Philoctetes'* care
He leaves his deathful instruments of war;
To him commits those arrows, which again
Shall see the bulwarks of the *Trojan* reign.
The son of *Paean* lights the lofty pyre,
High round the structure climbs the greedy fire;
Plac'd on the top, thy nervous shoulders spread
With the *Nemaean* spoils, thy careless head
Rais'd on a knotty club, with look divine,
Here thou, dread hero, of celestial line,
Wert stretch'd at ease; as when a chearful guest,
Wine crown'd thy bowls, and flow'rs thy temples drest.

Now on all sides the potent flames aspire,
And crackle round those limbs that mock the fire
A sudden terror seiz'd th' immortal host,
Who thought the world's profess'd defender lost.
This when the Thund'rer saw, with smiles he cries,
'Tis from your fears, ye Gods, my pleasures rise;
Joy swells my breast, that my all-ruling hand
O'er such a grateful people boasts command,
That you my suff'ring progeny would aid;
Tho' to his deeds this just respect be paid,

Me you've oblig'd. Be all your fears forborn,
Th' *Oetean* fires do thou, great hero, scorn.
Who vanquish'd all things, shall subdue the flame.
That part alone of gross maternal frame
Fire shall devour; while what from me he drew
Shall live immortal, and its force subdue;
That, when he's dead, I'll raise to realms above;
May all the Pow'rs the righteous act approve.
If any God dissent, and judge too great
The sacred honours of the heav'nly seat,
Ev'n he shall own his deeds deserve the sky,
Ev'n he reluctant, shall at length comply.
Th' assembled Pow'rs assent. No frown 'till now
Had mark'd with passion vengeful *Juno's* brow,
Mean-while whate'er was in the pow'r of flame
Was all consum'd; his body's nervous frame
No more was known, of human form bereft,
Th' eternal part of *Jove* alone was left.
As an old serpent casts his scaly vest,
Wreathes in the sun, in youthful glory drest;
So when *Alcides* mortal mold resign'd,
His better part enlarg'd, and grew refin'd;
August his visage shone; almighty *Jove*
In his swift carr his honour'd offspring drove;
High o'er the hollow clouds the coursers fly,
And lodge the hero in the starry sky.

   Atlas perceiv'd the load of Heav'n's new guest.
Revenge still rancour'd in *Eurystheus'* breast
Against *Alcides'* race. *Alcmena* goes
To Iole, to vent maternal woes;
Here she pours forth her grief, recounts the spoils
Her son had bravely reap'd in glorious toils.
This *Iole*, by *Hercules'* commands,
Hyllus had lov'd, and joyn'd in nuptial bands.
Her swelling womb the teeming birth confess'd,

To whom *Alcmena* thus her speech address'd.

    O, may the Gods protect thee, in that hour,
When, 'midst thy throws, thou call'st th' *Ilithyan* Pow'r!
May no delays prolong thy racking pain,
As when I su'd for *Juno's* aid in vain.

    When now *Alcides'* mighty birth drew nigh,
And the tenth sign roll'd forward on the sky,
My womb extends with such a mighty load,
As *Jove* the parent of the burthen show'd.
I could no more th' encreasing smart sustain,
My horror kindles to recount the pain;
Cold chills my limbs while I the tale pursue,
And now methinks I feel my pangs anew.
Seven days and nights amidst incessant throws,
Fatigu'd with ills I lay, nor knew repose;
When lifting high my hands, in shrieks I pray'd,
Implor'd the Gods, and call'd *Lucina's* aid.
She came, but prejudic'd, to give my Fate
A sacrifice to vengeful *Juno's* hate.
She hears the groaning anguish of my fits,
And on the altar at my door she sits.
O'er her left knee her crossing leg she cast,
Then knits her fingers close, and wrings them fast:
This stay'd the birth; in mutt'ring verse she pray'd,
The mutt'ring verse th' unfinish'd birth delay'd.
Now with fierce struggles, raging with my pain,
At *Jove's* ingratitude I rave in vain.
How did I wish for death! such groans I sent,
As might have made the flinty heart relent.

    Now the *Cadmeian* matrons round me press,
Offer their vows, and seek to bring redress;
Among the *Theban* dames *Galanthis* stands,
Strong limb'd, red hair'd, and just to my commands:
She first perceiv'd that all these racking woes
From the persisting hate of *Juno* rose.

As here and there she pass'd, by chance she sees
The seated Goddess; on her close-press'd knees
Her fast-knit hands she leans; with chearful voice
Galanthis cries, Whoe'er thou art, rejoyce,
Congratulate the dame, she lies at rest,
At length the Gods *Alcmena's* womb have blest.
Swift from her seat the startled Goddess springs,
No more conceal'd, her hands abroad she flings;
The charm unloos'd, the birth my pangs reliev'd;
Galanthis' laughter vex'd the Pow'r deceiv'd.
Fame says, the Goddess dragg'd the laughing maid
Fast by the hair; in vain her force essay'd
Her grov'ling body from the ground to rear;
Chang'd to fore-feet her shrinking arms appear:
Her hairy back her former hue retains,
The form alone is lost; her strength remains;
Who, since the lye did from her mouth proceed,
Shall from her pregnant mouth bring forth her breed;
Nor shall she quit her long-frequented home,
But haunt those houses where she lov'd to roam.
    She said, and for her lost *Galanthis* sighs;
When the fair consort of her son replies;
Since you a servant's ravish'd form bemoan,
And kindly sigh for sorrows not your own,
Let me (if tears and grief permit) relate
A nearer woe, a sister's stranger fate.
    No nymph of all *Oechaloa* could compare
For beauteous form with *Dryopè* the fair;
Her tender mother's only hope and pride
(My self the offspring of a second bride),
This nymph, compress'd by him who rules the day,
Whom *Delphi*, and the *Delian* isle obey,
Andraemon lov'd; and blest in all those charms
That pleas'd a God, succeeded to her arms.
    A lake there was, with shelving banks around,

Whose verdant summit fragrant myrtles crown'd.
Those shades, unknowing of the fates, she sought;
And to the *Naiads* flow'ry garlands brought;
Her smiling babe (a pleasing charge) she prest
Between her arms, and nourish'd at her breast.
Not distant far a watry lotos grows;
The Spring was new, and all the verdant boughs,
Acorn'd with blossoms, promis'd fruits that vye
In glowing colours with the *Tyrian* dye.
Of these she cropt, to please her infant son,
And I my self the same rash act had done,
But, lo! I saw (as near her side I stood)
The violated blossoms drop with blood;
Upon the tree I cast a frightful look,
The trembling tree with sudden horror shook.
Lotis the nymph (if rural tales be true)
As from *Priapus'* lawless lust she flew,
Forsook her form; and fixing here became
A flow'ry plant, which still preserves her name.

   This change unknown, astonish'd at the sight,
My trembling sister strove to urge her flight;
Yet first the pardon of the *Nymphs* implor'd,
And those offended *Sylvan* pow'rs ador'd:
But when she backward would have fled, she found
Her stiff'ning feet were rooted to the ground:
In vain to free her fasten'd feet she strove,
And as she struggles only moves above;
She feels th' incroaching bark around her grow,
By slow degrees, and cover all below:
Surpriz'd at this, her trembling hand she heaves
To rend her hair; her hand is fill'd with leaves;
Where late was hair, the shooting leaves are seen
To rise, and shade her with a sudden green.
The Child *Amphisus*, to her bosom prest,
Perceiv'd a colder and a harder breast,

And found the springs, that n'er 'till then deny'd
Their milky moisture, on a sudden dry'd.
I saw, unhappy, what I now relate,
And stood the helpless witness of thy fate;
Embrac'd thy boughs, the rising bark delay'd,
There wish'd to grow, and mingle shade with shade.

Behold *Andraemon*, and th' unhappy sire
Appear, and for their *Dryopè* enquire;
A springing tree for *Dryopè* they find,
And print warm kisses on the panting rind;
Prostrate, with tears their kindred plant bedew,
And close embrac'd, as to the roots they grew;
The face was all that now remain'd of thee;
No more a woman, nor yet quite a tree:
Thy branches hung with humid pearls appear,
From ev'ry leaf distills a trickling tear;
And strait a voice, while yet a voice remains,
Thus thro' the trembling boughs in sighs complains.

If to the wretched any faith be giv'n,
I swear by all th' unpitying Pow'rs of Heav'n,
No wilful crime this heavy vengeance bred,
In mutual innocence our lives we led.
If this be false, let these new greens decay,
Let sounding axes lop my limbs away,
And crackling flames on all my honours prey.
Now from my branching arms this infant bear,
Let some kind nurse supply a mother's care;
Yet to his mother let him oft be led,
Sport in her shades, and in her shades be fed;
Teach him, when first his infant voice shall frame
Imperfect words, and lisp his mother's name,
To hail this tree, and say with weeping eyes,
Within this plant my hapless parent lies;
And when in youth he seeks the shady woods,
Oh, let him fly the chrystal lakes and floods,

Nor touch the fatal flow'rs; but warn'd by me,
Believe a Goddess shrin'd in ev'ry tree.
My sire, my sister, and my spouse farewel!
If in your breasts or love, or pity, dwell,
Protect your plant, nor let my branches feel
The browzing cattle, or the piercing steel.
Farewel! and since I cannot bend to join
My lips to yours, advance at least to mine.
My son, thy mother's parting kiss receive,
While yet thy mother has a kiss to give.
I can no more; the creeping rind invades
My closing lips, and hides my head in shades:
Remove your hands; the bark shall soon suffice,
Without their aid, to seal these dying eyes.
She ceas'd at once to speak, and ceas'd to be;
And all the nymph was lost within the tree:
Yet latent life thro' her new branches reign'd,
And long the plant a human heat retain'd.

While *Iolè* the fatal change declares,
Alcmena's pitying hand oft wip'd her tears.
Grief too stream'd down her cheeks; soon sorrow flies,
And rising joy the trickling moisture dries,
Lo *Iolaus* stands before their eyes.
A youth he stood; and the soft down began
O'er his smooth chin to spread, and promise man.
Hebe submitted to her husband's pray'rs,
Instill'd new vigour, and restor'd his years.

Now from her lips a solemn oath had past,
That *Iolaus* this gift alone shou'd taste,
Had not just *Themis* thus maturely said
(Which check'd her vow, and aw'd the blooming maid).

Thebes is embroil'd in war. *Capaneus* stands
Invincible, but by the Thund'rer's hands.
Ambition shall the guilty brothers fire,
Both rush to mutual wounds, and both expire.

The reeling Earth shall ope her gloomy womb,
Where the yet breathing bard shall find his tomb.
The son shall bath his hands in parents' blood,
And in one act be both unjust, and good.
Of home, and sense depriv'd, where-e'er he flies,
The Furies, and his mother's ghost he spies.
His wife the fatal bracelet shall implore,
And *Phegeus* stain his sword in kindred gore.
Callirhöe shall then with suppliant pray'r
Prevail on *Jupiter's* relenting ear.
Jove shall with youth her infant sons inspire,
And bid their bosoms glow with manly fire.

When *Themis* thus with prescient voice had spoke,
Among the Gods a various murmur broke;
Dissention rose in each immortal breast,
That one should grant, what was deny'd the rest.
Aurora for her aged spouse complains,
And *Ceres* grieves for *Jason's* freezing veins;
Vulcan would *Erichthonius'* years renew,
Her future race the care of *Venus* drew,
She would *Anchises'* blooming age restore;
A diff'rent care employ'd each heav'nly Pow'r:
Thus various int'rests did their jars encrease,
'Till *Jove* arose; he spoke, their tumults cease.

Is any rev'rence to our presence giv'n,
Then why this discord 'mong the Pow'rs of Heav'n?
Who can the settled will of Fate subdue?
'Twas by the Fates that *Iolaus* knew
A second youth. The Fates' determin'd doom
Shall give *Callirhöe's* race a youthful bloom.
Arms, nor ambition can this pow'r obtain;
Quell your desires; ev'n me the Fates restrain.
Could I their will controul, no rolling years
Had *Aeacus* bent down with silver hairs;
Then *Rhadamanthus* still had youth possess'd,

And *Minos* with eternal bloom been bless'd.
Jove's words the synod mov'd; the Pow'rs give o'er,
And urge in vain unjust complaint no more.
Since *Rhadamanthus'* veins now slowly flow'd,
And *Aeacus*, and *Minos* bore the load;
Minos, who in the flow'r of youth, and fame,
Made mighty nations tremble at his name,
Infirm with age, the proud *Miletus* fears,
Vain of his birth, and in the strength of years,
And now regarding all his realms as lost,
He durst not force him from his native coast.
But you by choice, *Miletus*, fled his reign,
And thy swift vessel plow'd th' *Aegean* main;
On *Asiatick* shores a town you frame,
Which still is honour'd with the founder's name.
Here you *Cyanëe* knew, the beauteous maid,
As on her father's winding banks she stray'd:
Caunus and *Byblis* hence their lineage trace,
The double offspring of your warm embrace.

Let the sad fate of wretched *Byblis* prove
A dismal warning to unlawful love;
One birth gave being to the hapless pair,
But more was *Caunus* than a sister's care;
Unknown she lov'd, for yet the gentle fire
Rose not in flames, nor kindled to desire;
'Twas thought no sin to wonder at his charms,
Hang on his neck, and languish in his arms;
Thus wing'd with joy, fled the soft hours away,
And all the fatal guilt on harmless Nature lay.

But love (too soon from piety declin'd)
Insensibly deprav'd her yielding mind.
Dress'd she appears, with nicest art adorn'd,
And ev'ry youth, but her lov'd brother, scorn'd;
For him alone she labour'd to be fair,
And curst all charms that might with hers compare.

'Twas she, and only she, must *Caunus* please,
Sick at her heart, yet knew not her disease:
She call'd him lord, for brother was a name
Too cold, and dull for her aspiring flame;
And when he spoke, if sister he reply'd,
For *Byblis* change that frozen word, she cry'd.
Yet waking still she watch'd her strugling breast,
And love's approaches were in vain address'd,
'Till gentle sleep an easy conquest made,
And in her soft embrace the conqueror was laid.
But oh too soon the pleasing vision fled,
And left her blushing on the conscious bed:
Ah me! (she cry'd) how monstrous do I seem?
Why these wild thoughts? and this incestuous dream?
Envy herself ('tis true) must own his charms,
But what is beauty in a sister's arms?
Oh were I not that despicable she,
How bless'd, how pleas'd, how happy shou'd I be!
But unregarded now must bear my pain,
And but in dreams, my wishes can obtain.

   O sea-born Goddess! with thy wanton boy!
Was ever such a charming scene of joy?
Such perfect bliss! such ravishing delight!
Ne'er hid before in the kind shades of night.
How pleas'd my heart! in what sweet raptures tost!
Ev'n life it self in the soft combat lost,
While breathless he on my heav'd bosom lay,
And snatch'd the treasures of my soul away.

   If the bare fancy so affects my mind,
How shou'd I rave if to the substance join'd?
Oh, gentle *Caunus*! quit thy hated line,
Or let thy parents be no longer mine!
Oh that in common all things were enjoy'd,
But those alone who have our hopes destroy'd.
Were I a princess, thou an humble swain,

The proudest kings shou'd rival thee in vain.
It cannot be, alas! the dreadful ill
Is fix'd by Fate, and he's my brother still.
Hear me, ye Gods! I must have friends in Heav'n,
For *Jove* himself was to a sister giv'n:
But what are their prerogatives above,
To the short liberties of human love?
Fantastick thoughts! down, down, forbidden fires,
Or instant death extinguish my desires.
Strict virtue, then, with thy malicious leave,
Without a crime I may a kiss receive:
But say shou'd I in spight of laws comply,
Yet cruel *Caunus* might himself deny,
No pity take of an afflicted maid
(For love's sweet game must be by couples play'd).
Yet why shou'd youth, and charms like mine, despair?
Such fears ne'er startled the *Aeolian* pair;
No ties of blood could their full hopes destroy,
They broke thro' all, for the prevailing joy;
And who can tell but *Caunus* too may be
Rack'd and tormented in his breast for me?
Like me, to the extreamest anguish drove,
Like me, just waking from a dream of love?
But stay! Oh whither wou'd my fury run!
What arguments I urge to be undone!
Away fond *Byblis*, quench these guilty flames;
Caunus thy love but as brother claims;
Yet had he first been touch'd with love of me,
The charming youth cou'd I despairing see?
Oppress'd with grief, and dying by disdain?
Ah no! too sure I shou'd have eas'd his pain!
Since then, if *Caunus* ask'd me, it were done;
Asking my self, what dangers can I run?
But canst thou ask? and see that right betray'd,
From *Pyrrha* down to thy whole sex convey'd?

That self-denying gift we all enjoy,
Of wishing to be won, yet seeming to be coy.
Well then, for once, let a fond mistress woo;
The force of love no custom can subdue;
This frantick passion he by words shall know,
Soft as the melting heart from whence they flow.
The pencil then in her fair hand she held,
By fear discourag'd, but by love compell'd;
She writes, then blots, writes on, and blots again,
Likes it as fit, then razes it as vain:
Shame, and assurance in her face appear,
And a faint hope just yielding to despair;
Sister was wrote, and blotted as a word
Which she, and *Caunus* too (she hop'd) abhorr'd;
But now resolv'd to be no more controul'd
By scrup'lous virtue, thus her grief she told.

Thy lover (gentle *Caunus*) wishes thee
That health, which thou alone canst give to me.
O charming youth! the gift I ask bestow,
Ere thou the name of the fond writer know;
To thee without a name I would be known,
Since knowing that, my frailty I must own.
Yet why shou'd I my wretched name conceal?
When thousand instances my flames reveal:
Wan looks, and weeping eyes have spoke my pain,
And sighs discharg'd from my heav'd heart in vain;
Had I not wish'd my passion might be seen,
What cou'd such fondness and embraces mean?
Such kisses too! (Oh heedless lovely boy)
Without a crime no sister cou'd enjoy:
Yet (tho' extreamest rage has rack'd my soul,
And raging fires in my parch'd bosom roul)
Be witness, Gods! how piously I strove,
To rid my thoughts of this enchanting love.
But who cou'd scape so fierce, and sure a dart,

Aim'd at a tender, and defenceless heart?
Alas! what maid cou'd suffer, I have born,
Ere the dire secret from my breast was torn;
To thee a helpless vanquish'd wretch I come,
'Tis you alone can save, or give my doom;
My life, or death this moment you may chuse.
Yet think, oh think, no hated stranger sues,
No foe; but one, alas! too near ally'd,
And wishing still much nearer to be ty'd.
The forms of decency let age debate,
And virtue's rules by their cold morals state;
Their ebbing joys give leisure to enquire,
And blame those noble flights our youth inspire:
Where Nature kindly summons let us go,
Our sprightly years no bounds in love shou'd know,
Shou'd feel no check of guilt, and fear no ill;
Lovers, and Gods act all things at their will:
We gain one blessing from our hated kin,
Since our paternal freedom hides the sin;
Uncensur'd in each other's arms we lye,
Think then how easie to compleat our joy.
Oh, pardon and oblige a blushing maid,
Whose rage the pride of her vain sex betray'd;
Nor let my tomb thus mournfully complain,
Here *Byblis* lies, by her lov'd *Caunus* slain.
   Forc'd here to end, she with a falling tear
Temper'd the pliant wax, which did the signet bear:
The curious cypher was impress'd by art,
But love had stamp'd one deeper in her heart;
Her page, a youth of confidence, and skill,
(Secret as night) stood waiting on her will;
Sighing (she cry'd): Bear this, thou faithful boy,
To my sweet partner in eternal joy:
Here a long pause her secret guilt confess'd,
And when at length she would have spoke the rest,

Half the dear name lay bury'd in her breast.
    Thus as he listned to her vain command,
Down fell the letter from her trembling hand.
The omen shock'd her soul. Yet go, she cry'd;
Can a request from *Byblis* be deny'd?
    To the *Maeandrian* youth this message's born,
The half-read lines by his fierce rage were torn;
Hence, hence, he cry'd, thou pandar to her lust,
Bear hence the triumph of thy impious trust:
Thy instant death will but divulge her shame,
Or thy life's blood shou'd quench the guilty flame.
Frighted, from threatning *Caunus* he withdrew,
And with the dreadful news to his lost mistress flew.
The sad repulse so struck the wounded fair,
Her sense was bury'd in her wild despair;
Pale was her visage, as the ghastly dead;
And her scar'd soul from the sweet mansion fled;
Yet with her life renew'd, her love returns,
And faintly thus her cruel fate she mourns:
'Tis just, ye Gods! was my false reason blind?
To write a secret of this tender kind?
With female craft I shou'd at first have strove,
By dubious hints to sound his distant love;
And try'd those useful, tho' dissembled, arts,
Which women practise on disdainful hearts:
I shou'd have watch'd whence the black storm might rise;
Ere I had trusted the unfaithful skies.
Now on the rouling billows I am tost,
And with extended sails, on the blind shelves am lost.
Did not indulgent Heav'n my doom foretell,
When from my hand the fatal letter fell?
What madness seiz'd my soul? and urg'd me on
To take the only course to be undone?
I cou'd my self have told the moving tale
With such alluring grace as must prevail;

Then had his eyes beheld my blushing fears,
My rising sighs, and my descending tears;
Round his dear neck these arms I then had spread,
And, if rejected, at his feet been dead:
If singly these had not his thoughts inclin'd,
Yet all united would have shock'd his mind.
Perhaps, my careless page might be in fault,
And in a luckless hour the fatal message brought;
Business, and worldly thoughts might fill his breast,
Sometimes ev'n love itself may be an irksome guest:
He cou'd not else have treated me with scorn,
For *Caunus* was not of a tygress born;
Nor steel, nor adamant has fenc'd his heart;
Like mine, 'tis naked to the burning dart.

Away false fears! he must, he shall be mine;
In death alone I will my claim resign;
'Tis vain to wish my written crime unknown,
And for my guilt much vainer to atone.
Repuls'd and baffled, fiercer still she burns,
And *Caunus* with disdain her impious love returns.
He saw no end of her injurious flame,
And fled his country to avoid the shame.
Forsaken *Byblis*, who had hopes no more;
Burst out in rage, and her loose robes she tore;
With her fair hands she smote her tender breast,
And to the wond'ring world her love confess'd;
O'er hills and dales, o'er rocks and streams she flew,
But still in vain did her wild lust pursue:
Wearied at length, on the cold earth she fell,
And now in tears alone could her sad story tell.
Relenting Gods in pity fix'd her there,
And to a fountain turn'd the weeping fair.

The fame of this, perhaps, thro' *Crete* had flown:
But *Crete* had newer wonders of her own,
In *Iphis* chang'd; for, near the *Gnossian* bounds

(As loud report the miracle resounds),
At *Phaestus* dwelt a man of honest blood,
But meanly born, and not so rich as good;
Esteem'd, and lov'd by all the neighbourhood;
Who to his wife, before the time assign'd
For child-birth came, thus bluntly spoke his mind.
If Heav'n, said *Lygdus*, will vouchsafe to hear,
I have but two petitions to prefer;
Short pains for thee, for me a son and heir.
Girls cost as many throes in bringing forth;
Beside, when born, the titts are little worth;
Weak puling things, unable to sustain
Their share of labour, and their bread to gain.
If, therefore, thou a creature shalt produce,
Of so great charges, and so little use
(Bear witness, Heav'n, with what reluctancy),
Her hapless innocence I doom to die.
He said, and common tears the common grief display,
Of him who bad, and her who must obey.

　　Yet *Telethusa* still persists, to find
Fit arguments to move a father's mind;
T' extend his wishes to a larger scope,
And in one vessel not confine his hope.
Lygdus continues hard: her time drew near,
And she her heavy load could scarcely bear;
When slumbring, in the latter shades of night,
Before th' approaches of returning light,
She saw, or thought she saw, before her bed,
A glorious train, and *Isis* at their head:
Her moony horns were on her forehead plac'd,
And yellow shelves her shining temples grac'd:
A mitre, for a crown, she wore on high;
The dog, and dappl'd bull were waiting by;
Osyris, sought along the banks of *Nile*;
The silent God: the sacred crocodile;

And, last, a long procession moving on,
With timbrels, that assist the lab'ring moon.
Her slumbers seem'd dispell'd, and, broad awake,
She heard a voice, that thus distinctly spake.
My votary, thy babe from death defend,
Nor fear to save whate'er the Gods will send.
Delude with art thy husband's dire decree:
When danger calls, repose thy trust on me:
And know thou hast not serv'd a thankless deity.
This promise made, with night the Goddess fled;
With joy the woman wakes, and leaves her bed;
Devoutly lifts her spotless hands on high,
And prays the Pow'rs their gift to ratifie.

Now grinding pains proceed to bearing throes,
'Till its own weight the burden did disclose.
'Twas of the beauteous kind, and brought to light
With secrecy, to shun the father's sight.
Th' indulgent mother did her care employ,
And past it on her husband for a boy.
The nurse was conscious of the fact alone;
The father paid his vows as for a son;
And call'd him *Iphis*, by a common name,
Which either sex with equal right may claim.
Iphis his grandsire was; the wife was pleas'd,
Of half the fraud by Fortune's favour eas'd:
The doubtful name was us'd without deceit,
And truth was cover'd with a pious cheat.
The habit shew'd a boy, the beauteous face
With manly fierceness mingled female grace.

Now thirteen years of age were swiftly run,
When the fond father thought the time drew on
Of settling in the world his only son.
Ianthe was his choice; so wondrous fair,
Her form alone with *Iphis* cou'd compare;
A neighbour's daughter of his own degree,

And not more bless'd with Fortune's goods than he.
    They soon espous'd; for they with ease were join'd,
Who were before contracted in the mind.
Their age the same, their inclinations too;
And bred together, in one school they grew.
Thus, fatally dispos'd to mutual fires,
They felt, before they knew, the same desires.
Equal their flame, unequal was their care;
One lov'd with hope, one languish'd in despair.
The maid accus'd the lingring day alone:
For whom she thought a man, she thought her own.
But *Iphis* bends beneath a greater grief;
As fiercely burns, but hopes for no relief.
Ev'n her despair adds fuel to her fire;
A maid with madness does a maid desire.
And, scarce refraining tears, Alas, said she,
What issue of my love remains for me!
How wild a passion works within my breast,
With what prodigious flames am I possest!
Could I the care of Providence deserve,
Heav'n must destroy me, if it would preserve.
And that's my fate, or sure it would have sent
Some usual evil for my punishment:
Not this unkindly curse; to rage, and burn,
Where Nature shews no prospect of return.
Nor cows for cows consume with fruitless fire;
Nor mares, when hot, their fellow-mares desire:
The father of the fold supplies his ewes;
The stag through secret woods his hind pursues;
And birds for mates the males of their own species chuse.
Her females Nature guards from female flame,
And joins two sexes to preserve the game:
Wou'd I were nothing, or not what I am!
Crete, fam'd for monsters, wanted of her store,
'Till my new love produc'd one monster more.

The daughter of the sun a bull desir'd,
And yet ev'n then a male a female fir'd:
Her passion was extravagantly new,
But mine is much the madder of the two.
To things impossible she was not bent,
But found the means to compass her intent.
To cheat his eyes she took a different shape;
Yet still she gain'd a lover, and a leap.
Shou'd all the wit of all the world conspire,
Shou'd *Daedalus* assist my wild desire,
What art can make me able to enjoy,
Or what can change *Ianthe* to a boy?
Extinguish then thy passion, hopeless maid,
And recollect thy reason for thy aid.
Know what thou art, and love as maidens ought,
And drive these golden wishes from thy thought.
Thou canst not hope thy fond desires to gain;
Where hope is wanting, wishes are in vain.

    And yet no guards against our joys conspire;
No jealous husband hinders our desire;
My parents are propitious to my wish,
And she herself consenting to the bliss.
All things concur to prosper our design;
All things to prosper any love but mine.
And yet I never can enjoy the fair;
'Tis past the pow'r of Heav'n to grant my pray'r.
Heav'n has been kind, as far as Heav'n can be;
Our parents with our own desires agree;
But Nature, stronger than the Gods above,
Refuses her assistance to my love;
She sets the bar that causes all my pain;
One gift refus'd, makes all their bounty vain.
And now the happy day is just at hand,
To bind our hearts in *Hymen's* holy band:
Our hearts, but not our bodies: thus accurs'd,

In midst of water I complain of thirst.
Why com'st thou, *Juno*, to these barren rites,
To bless a bed defrauded of delights?
But why shou'd *Hymen* lift his torch on high,
To see two brides in cold embraces lye?

    Thus love-sick *Iphis* her vain passion mourns;
With equal ardour fair *Ianthe* burns,
Invoking *Hymen's* name, and *Juno's* pow'r,
To speed the work, and haste the happy hour.

    She hopes, while *Telethusa* fears the day,
And strives to interpose some new delay:
Now feigns a sickness, now is in a fright
For this bad omen, or that boding sight.
But having done whate'er she could devise,
And empty'd all her magazine of lies,
The time approach'd; the next ensuing day
The fatal secret must to light betray.
Then *Telethusa* had recourse to pray'r,
She, and her daughter with dishevel'd hair;
Trembling with fear, great *Isis* they ador'd,
Embrac'd her altar, and her aid implor'd.

    Fair queen, who dost on fruitful *Egypt* smile,
Who sway'st the sceptre of the *Pharian* isle,
And sev'n-fold falls of disemboguing *Nile*,
Relieve, in this our last distress, she said,
A suppliant mother, and a mournful maid.
Thou, Goddess, thou wert present to my sight;
Reveal'd I saw thee by thy own fair light:
I saw thee in my dream, as now I see,
With all thy marks of awful majesty:
The glorious train that compass'd thee around;
And heard the hollow timbrels holy sound.
Thy words I noted, which I still retain;
Let not thy sacred oracles be vain.
That *Iphis* lives, that I myself am free

From shame, and punishment, I owe to thee.
On thy protection all our hopes depend.
Thy counsel sav'd us, let thy pow'r defend.

   Her tears pursu'd her words; and while she spoke,
The Goddess nodded, and her altar shook:
The temple doors, as with a blast of wind,
Were heard to clap; the lunar horns that bind
The brows of *Isis* cast a blaze around;
The trembling timbrel made a murm'ring sound.

   Some hopes these happy omens did impart;
Forth went the mother with a beating heart:
Not much in fear, nor fully satisfy'd;
But *Iphis* follow'd with a larger stride:
The whiteness of her skin forsook her face;
Her looks embolden'd with an awful grace;
Her features, and her strength together grew,
And her long hair to curling locks withdrew.
Her sparkling eyes with manly vigour shone,
Big was her voice, audacious was her tone.
The latent parts, at length reveal'd, began
To shoot, and spread, and burnish into man.
The maid becomes a youth; no more delay
Your vows, but look, and confidently pay.
Their gifts the parents to the temple bear:
The votive tables this inscription wear;
Iphis the man, has to the Goddess paid
The vows, that *Iphis* offer'd when a maid.

   Now when the star of day had shewn his face,
Venus and *Juno* with their presence grace
The nuptial rites, and *Hymen* from above
Descending to compleat their happy love;
The Gods of marriage lend their mutual aid;
And the warm youth enjoys the lovely maid.

The End of the Ninth Book.

BOOK THE TENTH

THENCE, in his saffron robe, for distant *Thrace*,
    Hymen departs, thro' air's unmeasur'd space;
    By *Orpheus* call'd, the nuptial Pow'r attends,
But with ill-omen'd augury descends;
Nor chearful look'd the God, nor prosp'rous spoke,
Nor blaz'd his torch, but wept in hissing smoke.
In vain they whirl it round, in vain they shake,
No rapid motion can its flames awake.

    With dread these inauspicious signs were view'd,
And soon a more disastrous end ensu'd;
For as the bride, amid the *Naïad* train,
Ran joyful, sporting o'er the flow'ry plain,
A venom'd viper bit her as she pass'd;
Instant she fell, and sudden breath'd her last.

    When long his loss the *Thracian* had deplor'd,
Not by superior Pow'rs to be restor'd;
Inflam'd by love, and urg'd by deep despair,
He leaves the realms of light, and upper air;
Daring to tread the dark *Tenarian* road,
And tempt the shades in their obscure abode;
Thro' gliding spectres of th' interr'd to go,
And phantom people of the world below:
Persephonè he seeks, and him who reigns
O'er ghosts, and Hell's uncomfortable plains.
Arriv'd, he, tuning to his voice his strings,
Thus to the king and queen of shadows sings.

    Ye Pow'rs, who under Earth your realms extend,
To whom all mortals must one day descend;
If here 'tis granted sacred truth to tell:
I come not curious to explore your Hell;
Nor come to boast (by vain ambition fir'd)
How *Cerberus* at my approach retir'd.
My wife alone I seek; for her lov'd sake
These terrors I support, this journey take.

She, luckless wandring, or by fate mis-led,
Chanc'd on a lurking viper's crest to tread;
The vengeful beast, enflam'd with fury, starts,
And thro' her heel his deathful venom darts.
Thus was she snatch'd untimely to her tomb;
Her growing years cut short, and springing bloom.
Long I my loss endeavour'd to sustain,
And strongly strove, but strove, alas, in vain:
At length I yielded, won by mighty love;
Well known is that omnipotence above!
But here, I doubt, his unfelt influence fails;
And yet a hope within my heart prevails.
That here, ev'n here, he has been known of old;
At least if truth be by tradition told;
If fame of former rapes belief may find,
You both by love, and love alone, were join'd.
Now, by the horrors which these realms surround;
By the vast chaos of these depths profound;
By the sad silence which eternal reigns
O'er all the waste of these wide-stretching plains;
Let me again *Eurydice* receive,
Let Fate her quick-spun thread of life re-weave.
All our possessions are but loans from you,
And soon, or late, you must be paid your due;
Hither we haste to human-kind's last seat,
Your endless empire, and our sure retreat.
She too, when ripen'd years she shall attain,
Must, of avoidless right, be yours again:
I but the transient use of that require,
Which soon, too soon, I must resign entire.
But if the destinies refuse my vow,
And no remission of her doom allow;
Know, I'm determin'd to return no more;
So both retain, or both to life restore.

   Thus, while the bard melodiously complains,

And to his lyre accords his vocal strains,
The very bloodless shades attention keep,
And silent, seem compassionate to weep;
Ev'n *Tantalus* his flood unthirsty views,
Nor flies the stream, nor he the stream pursues;
Ixion's wond'ring wheel its whirl suspends,
And the voracious vulture, charm'd, attends;
No more the *Belides* their toil bemoan,
And *Sisiphus* reclin'd, sits list'ning on his stone.

Then first ('tis said) by sacred verse subdu'd,
The Furies felt their cheeks with tears bedew'd:
Nor could the rigid king, or queen of Hell,
Th' impulse of pity in their hearts repell.

Now, from a troop of shades that last arriv'd,
Eurydicè was call'd, and stood reviv'd:
Slow she advanc'd, and halting seem to feel
The fatal wound, yet painful in her heel.
Thus he obtains the suit so much desir'd,
On strict observance of the terms requir'd:
For if, before he reach the realms of air,
He backward cast his eyes to view the fair,
The forfeit grant, that instant, void is made,
And she for ever left a lifeless shade.

Now thro' the noiseless throng their way they bend,
And both with pain the rugged road ascend;
Dark was the path, and difficult, and steep,
And thick with vapours from the smoaky deep.
They well-nigh now had pass'd the bounds of night,
And just approach'd the margin of the light,
When he, mistrusting lest her steps might stray,
And gladsome of the glympse of dawning day,
His longing eyes, impatient, backward cast
To catch a lover's look, but look'd his last;
For, instant dying, she again descends,
While he to empty air his arms extends.

Again she dy'd, nor yet her lord reprov'd;
What could she say, but that too well he lov'd?
One last farewell she spoke, which scarce he heard;
So soon she drop'd, so sudden disappear'd.

    All stunn'd he stood, when thus his wife he view'd
By second Fate, and double death subdu'd:
Not more amzement by that wretch was shown,
Whom *Cerberus* beholding, turn'd to stone;
Nor *Olenus* cou'd more astonish'd look,
When on himself *Lethaea's* fault he took,
His beauteous wife, who too secure had dar'd
Her face to vye with Goddesses compar'd:
Once join'd by love, they stand united still,
Turn'd to contiguous rocks on *Ida's* hill.

    Now to repass the *Styx* in vain he tries,
Charon averse, his pressing suit denies.
Sev'n days entire, along th' infernal shores,
Disconsolate, the bard *Eurydicè* deplores;
Defil'd with filth his robe, with tears his cheeks,
No sustenance but grief, and cares, he seeks:
Of rigid Fate incessant he complains,
And Hell's inexorable Gods arraigns.
This ended, to high *Rhodopè* he hastes,
And *Haemus'* mountain, bleak with northern blasts.

    And now his yearly race the circling sun
Had thrice compleat thro' wat'ry *Pisces* run,
Since *Orpheus* fled the face of womankind,
And all soft union with the sex declin'd.
Whether his ill success this change had bred,
Or binding vows made to his former bed;
Whate'er the cause, in vain the nymphs contest,
With rival eyes to warm his frozen breast:
For ev'ry nymph with love his lays inspir'd,
But ev'ry nymph repuls'd, with grief retir'd.

    A hill there was, and on that hill a mead,

With verdure thick, but destitute of shade.
Where, now, the Muse's son no sooner sings,
No sooner strikes his sweet resounding strings,
But distant groves the flying sounds receive,
And list'ning trees their rooted stations leave;
Themselves transplanting, all around they grow,
And various shades their various kinds bestow.
Here, tall *Chaönian* oaks their branches spread,
While weeping poplars there erect their head.
The foodful *Esculus* here shoots his leaves,
That turf soft lime-tree, this, fat beach receives;
Here, brittle hazels, lawrels here advance,
And there tough ash to form the heroe's lance;
Here silver firs with knotless trunks ascend,
There, scarlet oaks beneath their acorns bend.
That spot admits the hospitable plane,
On this, the maple grows with clouded grain;
Here, watry willows are with *Lotus* seen;
There, tamarisk, and box for ever green.
With double hue here mirtles grace the ground,
And laurestines, with purple berries crown'd.
With pliant feet, now, ivies this way wind,
Vines yonder rise, and elms with vines entwin'd.
Wild *Ornus* now, the pitch-tree next takes root,
And *Arbutus* adorn'd with blushing fruit.
Then easy-bending palms, the victor's prize,
And pines erect with bristly tops arise.
For *Rhea* grateful still the pine remains,
For *Atys* still some favour she retains;
He once in human shape her breast had warm'd,
And now is cherish'd, to a tree transform'd.

   Amid the throng of this promiscuous wood,
With pointed top, the taper cypress stood;
A tree, which once a youth, and heav'nly fair,
Was of that deity the darling care,

Whose hand adapts, with equal skill, the strings
To bows with which he kills, and harps to which he sings.
    For heretofore, a mighty stag was bred,
Which on the fertile fields of *Caea* fed;
In shape and size he all his kind excell'd,
And to *Carthaean* nymphs was sacred held.
His beamy head, with branches high display'd,
Afforded to itself an ample shade;
His horns were gilt, and his smooth neck was grac'd
With silver collars thick with gems enchas'd:
A silver boss upon his forehead hung,
And brazen pendants in his ear-rings rung.
Frequenting houses, he familiar grew,
And learnt by custom, Nature to subdue;
'Till by degrees, of fear, and wildness, broke,
Ev'n stranger hands his proffer'd neck might stroak.
    Much was the beast by *Caea's* youth caress'd,
But thou, sweet *Cyparissus*, lov'dst him best:
By thee, to pastures fresh, he oft was led,
By thee oft water'd at the fountain's head:
His horns with garlands, now, by thee were ty'd,
And, now, thou on his back wou'dst wanton ride;
Now here, now there wou'dst bound along the plains,
Ruling his tender mouth with purple reins.
    'Twas when the summer sun, at noon of day,
Thro' glowing *Cancer* shot his burning ray,
'Twas then, the fav'rite stag, in cool retreat,
Had sought a shelter from the scorching heat;
Along the grass his weary limbs he laid,
Inhaling freshness from the breezy shade:
When *Cyparissus* with his pointed dart,
Unknowing, pierc'd him to the panting heart.
But when the youth, surpriz'd, his error found,
And saw him dying of the cruel wound,
Himself he would have slain thro' desp'rate grief:

What said not *Phoebus*, that might yield relief!
To cease his mourning, he the boy desir'd,
Or mourn no more than such a loss requir'd.
But he, incessant griev'd: at length address'd
To the superior Pow'rs a last request;
Praying, in expiation of his crime,
Thenceforth to mourn to all succeeding time.

And now, of blood exhausted he appears,
Drain'd by a torrent of continual tears;
The fleshy colour in his body fades,
And a green tincture all his limbs invades;
From his fair head, where curling locks late hung,
A horrid bush with bristled branches sprung,
Which stiffning by degrees, its stem extends,
'Till to the starry skies the spire ascends.

Apollo sad look'd on, and sighing, cry'd,
Then, be for ever, what thy pray'r imply'd:
Bemoan'd by me, in others grief excite;
And still preside at ev'ry fun'ral rite.

Thus the sweet artist in a wondrous shade
Of verdant trees, which harmony had made,
Encircled sate, with his own triumphs crown'd,
Of listning birds, and savages around.
Again the trembling strings he dext'rous tries,
Again from discord makes soft musick rise.
Then tunes his voice: O Muse, from whom I sprung,
Jove be my theme, and thou inspire my song.
To *Jove* my grateful voice I oft have rais'd,
Oft his almighty pow'r with pleasure prais'd.
I sung the giants in a solemn strain,
Blasted, and thunder-struck on *Phlegra's* plain.
Now be my lyre in softer accents mov'd,
To sing of blooming boys by Gods belov'd;
And to relate what virgins, void of shame,
Have suffer'd vengeance for a lawless flame.

The King of Gods once felt the burning joy,
And sigh'd for lovely *Ganimede* of *Troy*:
Long was he puzzled to assume a shape
Most fit, and expeditious for the rape;
A bird's was proper, yet he scorns to wear
Any but that which might his thunder bear.
Down with his masquerading wings he flies,
And bears the little *Trojan* to the skies;
Where now, in robes of heav'nly purple drest,
He serves the nectar at th' Almighty's feast,
To slighted *Juno* an unwelcome guest.

 Phoebus for thee too, *Hyacinth*, design'd
A place among the Gods, had Fate been kind:
Yet this he gave; as oft as wintry rains
Are past, and vernal breezes sooth the plains,
From the green turf a purple flow'r you rise,
And with your fragrant breath perfume the skies.

 You when alive were *Phoebus'* darling boy;
In you he plac'd his Heav'n, and fix'd his joy:
Their God the *Delphic* priests consult in vain;
Eurotas now he loves, and *Sparta's* plain:
His hands the use of bow and harp forget,
And hold the dogs, or bear the corded net;
O'er hanging cliffs swift he pursues the game;
Each hour his pleasure, each augments his flame.

 The mid-day sun now shone with equal light
Between the past, and the succeeding night;
They strip, then, smooth'd with suppling oyl, essay
To pitch the rounded quoit, their wonted play:
A well-pois'd disk first hasty *Phoebus* threw,
It cleft the air, and whistled as it flew;
It reach'd the mark, a most surprizing length;
Which spoke an equal share of art, and strength.
Scarce was it fall'n, when with too eager hand
Young *Hyacinth* ran to snatch it from the sand;

But the curst orb, which met a stony soil,
Flew in his face with violent recoil.
Both faint, both pale, and breathless now appear,
The boy with pain, the am'rous God with fear.
He ran, and rais'd him bleeding from the ground,
Chafes his cold limbs, and wipes the fatal wound:
Then herbs of noblest juice in vain applies;
The wound is mortal, and his skill defies.

　　As in a water'd garden's blooming walk,
When some rude hand has bruis'd its tender stalk,
A fading lilly droops its languid head,
And bends to earth, its life, and beauty fled:
So *Hyacinth*, with head reclin'd, decays,
And, sickning, now no more his charms displays.

　　O thou art gone, my boy, *Apollo* cry'd,
Defrauded of thy youth in all its pride!
Thou, once my joy, art all my sorrow now;
And to my guilty hand my grief I owe.
Yet from my self I might the fault remove,
Unless to sport, and play, a fault should prove,
Unless it too were call'd a fault to love.
Oh cou'd I for thee, or but with thee, dye!
But cruel Fates to me that pow'r deny.
Yet on my tongue thou shalt for ever dwell;
Thy name my lyre shall sound, my verse shall tell;
And to a flow'r transform'd, unheard-of yet,
Stamp'd on thy leaves my cries thou shalt repeat.
The time shall come, prophetick I foreknow,
When, joyn'd to thee, a mighty chief shall grow,
And with my plaints his name thy leaf shall show.

　　While *Phoebus* thus the laws of Fate reveal'd,
Behold, the blood which stain'd the verdant field,
Is blood no longer; but a flow'r full blown,
Far brighter than the *Tyrian* scarlet shone.
A lilly's form it took; its purple hue

Was all that made a diff'rence to the view,
Nor stop'd he here; the God upon its leaves
The sad expression of his sorrow weaves;
And to this hour the mournful purple wears
Ai, Ai, inscrib'd in funeral characters.
Nor are the *Spartans*, who so much are fam'd
For virtue, of their *Hyacinth* asham'd;
But still with pompous woe, and solemn state,
The *Hyacinthian* feasts they yearly celebrate

   Enquire of *Amathus*, whose wealthy ground
With veins of every metal does abound,
If she to her *Propoetides* wou'd show,
The honour *Sparta* does to him allow?
Nor more, she'd say, such wretches wou'd we grace,
Than those whose crooked horns deform'd their face,
From thence *Cerastae* call'd, an impious race:
Before whose gates a rev'rend altar stood,
To *Jove* inscrib'd, the hospitable God:
This had some stranger seen with gore besmear'd,
The blood of lambs, and bulls it had appear'd:
Their slaughter'd guests it was; nor flock nor herd.

   Venus these barb'rous sacrifices view'd
With just abhorrence, and with wrath pursu'd:
At first, to punish such nefarious crimes,
Their towns she meant to leave, her once-lov'd climes:
But why, said she, for their offence shou'd I
My dear delightful plains, and cities fly?
No, let the impious people, who have sinn'd,
A punishment in death, or exile, find:
If death, or exile too severe be thought,
Let them in some vile shape bemoan their fault.
While next her mind a proper form employs,
Admonish'd by their horns, she fix'd her choice.
Their former crest remains upon their heads,
And their strong limbs an ox's shape invades.

The blasphemous *Propoetides* deny'd
Worship of *Venus*, and her pow'r defy'd:
But soon that pow'r they felt, the first that sold
Their lewd embraces to the world for gold.
Unknowing how to blush, and shameless grown,
A small transition changes them to stone.
  Pygmalion loathing their lascivious life,
Abhorr'd all womankind, but most a wife:
So single chose to live, and shunn'd to wed,
Well pleas'd to want a consort of his bed.
Yet fearing idleness, the nurse of ill,
In sculpture exercis'd his happy skill;
And carv'd in iv'ry such a maid, so fair,
As Nature could not with his art compare,
Were she to work; but in her own defence
Must take her pattern here, and copy hence.
Pleas'd with his idol, he commends, admires,
Adores; and last, the thing ador'd, desires.
A very virgin in her face was seen,
And had she mov'd, a living maid had been:
One wou'd have thought she cou'd have stirr'd, but strove
With modesty, and was asham'd to move.
Art hid with art, so well perform'd the cheat,
It caught the carver with his own deceit:
He knows 'tis madness, yet he must adore,
And still the more he knows it, loves the more:
The flesh, or what so seems, he touches oft,
Which feels so smooth, that he believes it soft.
Fir'd with this thought, at once he strain'd the breast,
And on the lips a burning kiss impress'd.
'Tis true, the harden'd breast resists the gripe,
And the cold lips return a kiss unripe:
But when, retiring back, he look'd again,
To think it iv'ry, was a thought too mean:
So wou'd believe she kiss'd, and courting more,

Again embrac'd her naked body o'er;
And straining hard the statue, was afraid
His hands had made a dint, and hurt his maid:
Explor'd her limb by limb, and fear'd to find
So rude a gripe had left a livid mark behind:
With flatt'ry now he seeks her mind to move,
And now with gifts (the pow'rful bribes of love),
He furnishes her closet first; and fills
The crowded shelves with rarities of shells;
Adds orient pearls, which from the conchs he drew,
And all the sparkling stones of various hue:
And parrots, imitating human tongue,
And singing-birds in silver cages hung:
And ev'ry fragrant flow'r, and od'rous green,
Were sorted well, with lumps of amber laid between:
Rich fashionable robes her person deck,
Pendants her ears, and pearls adorn her neck:
Her taper'd fingers too with rings are grac'd,
And an embroider'd zone surrounds her slender waste.
Thus like a queen array'd, so richly dress'd,
Beauteous she shew'd, but naked shew'd the best.
Then, from the floor, he rais'd a royal bed,
With cov'rings of *Sydonian* purple spread:
The solemn rites perform'd, he calls her bride,
With blandishments invites her to his side;
And as she were with vital sense possess'd,
Her head did on a plumy pillow rest.

The feast of *Venus* came, a solemn day,
To which the *Cypriots* due devotion pay;
With gilded horns the milk-white heifers led,
Slaughter'd before the sacred altars, bled.

Pygmalion off'ring, first approach'd the shrine,
And then with pray'rs implor'd the Pow'rs divine:
Almighty Gods, if all we mortals want,
If all we can require, be yours to grant;

Make this fair statue mine, he wou'd have said,
But chang'd his words for shame; and only pray'd,
Give me the likeness of my iv'ry maid.

The golden Goddess, present at the pray'r,
Well knew he meant th' inanimated fair,
And gave the sign of granting his desire;
For thrice in chearful flames ascends the fire.
The youth, returning to his mistress, hies,
And impudent in hope, with ardent eyes,
And beating breast, by the dear statue lies.
He kisses her white lips, renews the bliss,
And looks, and thinks they redden at the kiss;
He thought them warm before: nor longer stays,
But next his hand on her hard bosom lays:
Hard as it was, beginning to relent,
It seem'd, the breast beneath his fingers bent;
He felt again, his fingers made a print;
'Twas flesh, but flesh so firm, it rose against the dint:
The pleasing task he fails not to renew;
Soft, and more soft at ev'ry touch it grew;
Like pliant wax, when chasing hands reduce
The former mass to form, and frame for use.
He would believe, but yet is still in pain,
And tries his argument of sense again,
Presses the pulse, and feels the leaping vein.
Convinc'd, o'erjoy'd, his studied thanks, and praise,
To her, who made the miracle, he pays:
Then lips to lips he join'd; now freed from fear,
He found the savour of the kiss sincere:
At this the waken'd image op'd her eyes,
And view'd at once the light, and lover with surprize.
The Goddess, present at the match she made,
So bless'd the bed, such fruitfulness convey'd,
That ere ten months had sharpen'd either horn,
To crown their bliss, a lovely boy was born;

Paphos his name, who grown to manhood, wall'd
The city *Paphos*, from the founder call'd.
   Nor him alone produc'd the fruitful queen;
But *Cinyras*, who like his sire had been
A happy prince, had he not been a sire.
Daughters, and fathers, from my song retire;
I sing of horror; and could I prevail,
You shou'd not hear, or not believe my tale.
Yet if the pleasure of my song be such,
That you will hear, and credit me too much,
Attentive listen to the last event,
And, with the sin, believe the punishment:
Since Nature cou'd behold so dire a crime,
I gratulate at least my native clime,
That such a land, which such a monster bore,
So far is distant from our *Thracian* shore.
Let *Araby* extol her happy coast,
Her cinamon, and sweet *Amomum* boast,
Her fragrant flow'rs, her trees with precious tears,
Her second harvests, and her double years;
How can the land be call'd so bless'd, that *Myrrha* bears?
Nor all her od'rous tears can cleanse her crime;
Her plant alone deforms the happy clime:
Cupid denies to have inflam'd thy heart,
Disowns thy love, and vindicates his dart:
Some Fury gave thee those infernal pains,
And shot her venom'd vipers in thy veins.
To hate thy sire, had merited a curse;
But such an impious love deserv'd a worse.
The neighb'ring monarchs, by thy beauty led,
Contend in crowds, ambitious of thy bed:
The world is at thy choice; except but one,
Except but him, thou canst not chuse, alone.
She knew it too, the miserable maid,
Ere impious love her better thoughts betray'd,

And thus within her secret soul she said:
Ah *Myrrha*! whither wou'd thy wishes tend?
Ye Gods, ye sacred laws, my soul defend
From such a crime as all mankind detest,
And never lodg'd before in human breast!
But is it sin? Or makes my mind alone
Th' imagin'd sin? For Nature makes it none.
What tyrant then these envious laws began,
Made not for any other beast, but Man!
The father-bull his daughter may bestride,
The horse may make his mother-mare a bride;
What piety forbids the lusty ram,
Or more salacious goat, to rut their dam?
The hen is free to wed the chick she bore,
And make a husband, whom she hatch'd before.
All creatures else are of a happier kind,
Whom nor ill-natur'd laws from pleasure bind,
Nor thoughts of sin disturb their peace of mind.
But Man a slave of his own making lives;
The fool denies himself what Nature gives:
Too-busie senates, with an over-care,
To make us better than our kind can bear,
Have dash'd a spice of envy in the laws,
And straining up too high, have spoil'd the cause.
Yet some wise nations break their cruel chains,
And own no laws, but those which love ordains;
Where happy daughters with their sires are join'd,
And piety is doubly paid in kind.
O that I had been born in such a clime,
Not here, where 'tis the country makes the crime!
But whither wou'd my impious fancy stray?
Hence hopes, and ye forbidden thoughts away!
His worth deserves to kindle my desires,
But with the love, that daughters bear to sires.
Then had not *Cinyras* my father been,

What hinder'd *Myrrha's* hopes to be his queen?
But the perverseness of my fate is such,
That he's not mine, because he's mine too much:
Our kindred-blood debars a better tie;
He might be nearer, were he not so nigh.
Eyes, and their objects, never must unite;
Some distance is requir'd to help the sight:
Fain wou'd I travel to some foreign shore,
Never to see my native country more,
So might I to my self my self restore;
So might my mind these impious thoughts remove,
And ceasing to behold, might cease to love.
But stay I must, to feed my famish'd sight,
To talk, to kiss, and more, if more I might:
More, impious maid! What more canst thou design?
To make a monstrous mixture in thy line,
And break all statutes human and divine!
Can'st thou be call'd (to save thy wretched life)
Thy mother's rival, and thy father's wife?
Confound so many sacred names in one,
Thy brother's mother! Sister to thy son!
And fear'st thou not to see th' infernal bands,
Their heads with snakes, with torches arm'd their hands
Full at thy face th' avenging brands to bear,
And shake the serpents from their hissing hair;
But thou in time th' increasing ill controul,
Nor first debauch the body by the soul;
Secure the sacred quiet of thy mind,
And keep the sanctions Nature has design'd.
Suppose I shou'd attempt, th' attempt were vain,
No thoughts like mine, his sinless soul profane;
Observant of the right: and o that he
Cou'd cure my madness, or be mad like me!
Thus she: but *Cinyras*, who daily sees
A crowd of noble suitors at his knees,

Among so many, knew not whom to chuse,
Irresolute to grant, or to refuse.
But having told their names, enquir'd of her
Who pleas'd her best, and whom she would prefer.
The blushing maid stood silent with surprize,
And on her father fix'd her ardent eyes,
And looking sigh'd, and as she sigh'd, began
Round tears to shed, that scalded as they ran.
The tender sire, who saw her blush, and cry,
Ascrib'd it all to maiden modesty,
And dry'd the falling drops, and yet more kind,
He stroak'd her cheeks, and holy kisses join'd.
She felt a secret venom fire her blood,
And found more pleasure, than a daughter shou'd;
And, ask'd again what lover of the crew
She lik'd the best, she answer'd, One like you.
Mistaking what she meant, her pious will
He prais'd, and bid her so continue still:
The word of pious heard, she blush'd with shame
Of secret guilt, and cou'd not bear the name.

  'Twas now the mid of night, when slumbers close
Our eyes, and sooth our cares with soft repose;
But no repose cou'd wretched *Myrrha* find,
Her body rouling, as she roul'd her mind:
Mad with desire, she ruminates her sin,
And wishes all her wishes o'er again:
Now she despairs, and now resolves to try;
Wou'd not, and wou'd again, she knows not why;
Stops, and returns; makes, and retracts the vow;
Fain wou'd begin, but understands not how.
As when a pine is hew'd upon the plains,
And the last mortal stroke alone remains,
Lab'ring in pangs of death, and threatning all,
This way, and that she nods, consid'ring where to fall:
So *Myrrha's* mind, impell'd on either side,

Takes ev'ry bent, but cannot long abide;
Irresolute on which she shou'd relie,
At last, unfix'd in all, is only fix'd to die.
On that sad thought she rests, resolv'd on death,
She rises, and prepares to choak her breath:
Then while about the beam her zone she ties,
Dear *Cinyras* farewell, she softly cries;
For thee I die, and only wish to be
Not hated, when thou know'st die I for thee:
Pardon the crime, in pity to the cause:
This said, about her neck the noose she draws.
The nurse, who lay without, her faithful guard,
Though not the words, the murmurs over-heard;
And sighs, and hollow sounds: surpriz'd with fright,
She starts, and leaves her bed, and springs a light;
Unlocks the door, and entring out of breath,
The dying saw, and instruments of death;
She shrieks, she cuts the zone with trembling haste,
And in her arms her fainting charge embrac'd:
Next (for she now had leisure for her tears),
She weeping ask'd, in these her blooming years,
What unforeseen misfortune caus'd her care,
To loath her life, and languish in despair!
The maid, with down-cast eyes, and mute with grief
For death unfinish'd, and ill-tim'd relief,
Stood sullen to her suit: the beldame press'd
The more to know, and bar'd her wither'd breast,
Adjur'd her by the kindly food she drew
From those dry founts, her secret ill to shew.
Sad *Myrrha* sigh'd, and turn'd her eyes aside:
The nurse still urg'd, and wou'd not be deny'd:
Nor only promis'd secresie, but pray'd
She might have leave to give her offer'd aid.
Good-will, she said, my want of strength supplies,
And diligence shall give what age denies:

If strong desires thy mind to fury move,
With charms and med'cines I can cure thy love:
If envious eyes their hurtful rays have cast,
More pow'rful verse shall free thee from the blast:
If Heav'n offended sends thee this disease,
Offended Heav'n with pray'rs we can appease.
What then remains, that can these cares procure?
Thy house is flourishing, thy fortune sure:
Thy careful mother yet in health survives,
And, to thy comfort, thy kind father lives.
The virgin started at her father's name,
And sigh'd profoundly, conscious of the shame
Nor yet the nurse her impious love divin'd,
But yet surmis'd that love disturb'd her mind:
Thus thinking, she pursu'd her point, and laid,
And lull'd within her lap the mourning maid;
Then softly sooth'd her thus; I guess your grief:
You love, my child; your love shall find relief.
My long-experienc'd age shall be your guide;
Rely on that, and lay distrust aside.
No breath of air shall on the secret blow,
Nor shall (what most you fear) your father know.
Struck once again, as with a thunder-clap,
The guilty virgin bounded from her lap,
And threw her body prostrate on the bed.
And, to conceal her blushes, hid her head;
There silent lay, and warn'd her with her hand
To go: but she receiv'd not the command;
Remaining still importunate to know:
Then *Myrrha* thus: Or ask no more, or go;
I pr'ythee go, or staying spare my shame;
What thou would'st hear, is impious ev'n to name.
At this, on high the beldame holds her hands,
And trembling both with age, and terror stands;
Adjures, and falling at her feet intreats,

Sooths her with blandishments, and frights with threats,
To tell the crime intended, or disclose
What part of it she knew, if she no farther knows.
And last, if conscious to her counsel made,
Confirms anew the promise of her aid.
Now *Myrrha* rais'd her head; but soon oppress'd
With shame, reclin'd it on her nurse's breast;
Bath'd it with tears, and strove to have confess'd:
Twice she began, and stopp'd; again she try'd;
The falt'ring tongue its office still deny'd.
At last her veil before her face she spread,
And drew a long preluding sigh, and said,
O happy mother, in thy marriage-bed!
Then groan'd, and ceas'd. The good old woman shook,
Stiff were her eyes, and ghastly was her look:
Her hoary hair upright with horror stood,
Made (to her grief) more knowing than she wou'd.
Much she reproach'd, and many things she said,
To cure the madness of th' unhappy maid,
In vain: for *Myrrha* stood convict of ill;
Her reason vanquish'd, but unchang'd her will:
Perverse of mind, unable to reply;
She stood resolv'd, or to possess, or die.
At length the fondness of a nurse prevail'd
Against her better sense, and virtue fail'd:
Enjoy, my child, since such is thy desire,
Thy love, she said; she durst not say, thy sire:
Live, though unhappy, live on any terms;
Then with a second oath her faith confirms.

  The solemn feast of *Ceres* now was near,
When long white linnen stoles the matrons wear;
Rank'd in procession walk the pious train,
Off'ring first-fruits, and spikes of yellow grain:
For nine long nights the nuptial-bed they shun,
And sanctifying harvest, lie alone.

Mix'd with the crowd, the queen forsook her lord,
And *Ceres'* pow'r with secret rites ador'd:
The royal couch, now vacant for a time,
The crafty crone, officious in her crime,
The first occasion took: the king she found
Easie with wine, and deep in pleasures drown'd,
Prepar'd for love: the beldame blew the flame,
Confess'd the passion, but conceal'd the name.
Her form she prais'd; the monarch ask'd her years;
And she reply'd, The same thy *Myrrha* bears.
Wine, and commended beauty fir'd his thought;
Impatient, he commands her to be brought.
Pleas'd with her charge perform'd, she hies her home,
And gratulates the nymph, the task was overcome.
Myrrha was joy'd the welcome news to hear;
But clog'd with guilt, the joy was unsincere:
So various, so discordant is the mind,
That in our will a diff'rent will we find.
Ill she presag'd, and yet pursu'd her lust;
For guilty pleasures give a double gust.
    'Twas depth of night: *Arctophylax* had driv'n
His lazy wain half round the northern Heav'n,
When *Myrrha* hasten'd to the crime desir'd:
The moon beheld her first, and first retir'd:
The stars amaz'd, ran backward from the sight,
And (shrunk within their sockets) lost their light.
Icarius first withdraws his holy flame:
The virgin sign, in Heav'n the second name,
Slides down the belt, and from her station flies,
And night with sable clouds involves the skies.
Bold *Myrrha* still pursues her black intent;
She stumbled thrice (an omen of th' event);
Thrice shriek'd the fun'ral owl, yet on she went,
Secure of shame, because secure of sight;
Ev'n bashful sins are impudent by night.

Link'd hand in hand, th' accomplice, and the dame,
Their way exploring, to the chamber came:
The door was ope; they blindly grope their way,
Where dark in bed th' expecting monarch lay.
Thus far her courage held, but here forsakes;
Her faint knees knock at ev'ry step she makes.
The nearer to her crime, the more within
She feels remorse, and horror of her sin;
Repents too late her criminal desire,
And wishes, that unknown she could retire.
Her lingring thus, the nurse (who fear'd delay
The fatal secret might at length betray)
Pull'd forward, to compleat the work begun,
And said to *Cinyras*, Receive thy own.
Thus saying, she deliver'd kind to kind,
Accurs'd, and their devoted bodies join'd.
The sire, unknowing of the crime, admits
His bowels, and prophanes the hallow'd sheets;
He found she trembled, but believ'd she strove
With maiden modesty against her love,
And sought with flatt'ring words vain fancies to remove.
Perhaps he said, My daughter, cease thy fears
(Because the title suited with her years);
And, Father, she might whisper him again,
That names might not be wanting to the sin.
   Full of her sire, she left th' incestuous bed,
And carry'd in her womb the crime she bred.
Another, and another night she came;
For frequent sin had left no sense of shame:
'Till *Cinyras* desir'd to see her face,
Whose body he had held in close embrace,
And brought a taper; the revealer, light,
Expos'd both crime, and criminal to sight.
Grief, rage, amazement, could no speech afford,
But from the sheath he drew th' avenging sword:

The guilty fled: the benefit of night,
That favour'd first the sin, secur'd the flight.
Long wand'ring thro' the spacious fields, she bent
Her voyage to th' *Arabian* continent;
Then pass'd the region which *Panchaea* join'd,
And flying, left the palmy plains behind.
Nine times the moon had mew'd her horns; at length
With travel weary, unsupply'd with strength,
And with the burden of her womb oppress'd,
Sabaean fields afford her needful rest:
There, loathing life, and yet of death afraid,
In anguish of her spirit, thus she pray'd:
Ye Pow'rs, if any so propitious are
T' accept my penitence, and hear my pray'r;
Your judgments, I confess, are justly sent;
Great sins deserve as great a punishment:
Yet since my life the living will profane,
And since my death the happy dead will stain,
A middle state your mercy may bestow,
Betwixt the realms above, and those below:
Some other form to wretched *Myrrha* give,
Nor let her wholly die, nor wholly live.

The pray'rs of penitents are never vain;
At least she did her last request obtain:
For while she spoke, the ground began to rise,
And gather'd round her feet, her legs, and thighs;
Her toes in roots descend, and spreading wide,
A firm foundation for the trunk provide:
Her solid bones convert to solid wood,
To pith her marrow, and to sap her blood:
Her arms are boughs, her fingers change their kind,
Her tender skin is harden'd into rind.
And now the rising tree her womb invests,
Now shooting upwards still, invades her breasts,
And shades the neck; when weary with delay,

She sunk her head within, and met it half the way.
And tho' with outward shape she lost her sense,
With bitter tears she wept her last offence;
And still she weeps, nor sheds her tears in vain;
For still the precious drops her name retain.
Mean-time the mis-begotten infant grows,
And ripe for birth, distends with deadly throes
The swelling rind, with unavailing strife,
To leave the wooden womb, and pushes into life.
The mother-tree, as if oppress'd with pain,
Writhes here, and there, to break the bark, in vain;
And, like a lab'ring woman, wou'd have pray'd,
But wants a voice to call *Lucina's* aid:
The bending bole sends out a hollow sound,
And trickling tears fall thicker on the ground.
The mild *Lucina* came uncall'd, and stood
Beside the struggling boughs, and heard the groaning wood;
Then reach'd her midwife-hand to speed the throes,
And spoke the pow'rful spells, that babes to birth disclose.
The bark divides, the living load to free,
And safe delivers the convulsive tree.
The ready nymphs receive the crying child,
And wash him in the tears the parent plant distill'd.
They swath'd him with their scarfs; beneath him spread
The ground with herbs; with roses rais'd his head.
The lovely babe was born with ev'ry grace,
Ev'n envy must have prais'd so fair a face:
Such was his form, as painters when they show
Their utmost art, on naked loves bestow:
And that their arms no diff'rence might betray,
Give him a bow, or his from *Cupid* take away.
Time glides along with undiscover'd haste,
The future but a length behind the past;
So swift are years. The babe, whom just before
His grandsire got, and whom his sister bore;

The drop, the thing, which late the tree inclos'd,
And late the yawning bark to life expos'd;
A babe, a boy, a beauteous youth appears,
And lovelier than himself at riper years.
Now to the queen of love he gave desires,
And, with her pains, reveng'd his mother's fires.

   For *Cytherëa's* lips while *Cupid* prest,
He with a heedless arrow raz'd her breast,
The Goddess felt it, and with fury stung,
The wanton mischief from her bosom flung:
Yet thought at first the danger slight, but found
The dart too faithful, and too deep the wound.
Fir'd with a mortal beauty, she disdains
To haunt th' *Idalian* mount, or *Phrygian* plains.
She seeks not *Cnidos*, nor her *Paphian* shrines,
Nor *Amathus*, that teems with brazen mines:
Ev'n Heav'n itself with all its sweets unsought,
Adonis far a sweeter Heav'n is thought.
On him she hangs, and fonds with ev'ry art,
And never, never knows from him to part.
She, whose soft limbs had only been display'd
On rosie beds beneath the myrtle shade,
Whose pleasing care was to improve each grace,
And add more charms to an unrival'd face,
Now buskin'd, like the virgin huntress, goes
Thro' woods, and pathless wilds, and mountain-snows
With her own tuneful voice she joys to cheer
The panting hounds, that chace the flying deer.
She runs the labyrinth of fearful hares,
But fearless beasts, and dang'rous prey forbears,
Hunts not the grinning wolf, or foamy boar,
And trembles at the lion's hungry roar.
Thee too, *Adonis*, with a lover's care
She warns, if warn'd thou wou'dst avoid the snare,
To furious animals advance not nigh,

Fly those that follow, follow those that fly;
'Tis chance alone must the survivors save,
Whene'er brave spirits will attempt the brave.
O! lovely youth! in harmless sports delight;
Provoke not beasts, which, arm'd by Nature, fight.
For me, if not thy self, vouchsafe to fear;
Let not thy thirst of glory cost me dear.
Boars know not how to spare a blooming age;
No sparkling eyes can sooth the lion's rage.
Not all thy charms a savage breast can move,
Which have so deeply touch'd the queen of love.
When bristled boars from beaten thickets spring,
In grinded tusks a thunderbolt they bring.
The daring hunters lions rouz'd devour,
Vast is their fury, and as vast their pow'r:
Curst be their tawny race! If thou would'st hear
What kindled thus my hate, then lend an ear:
The wond'rous tale I will to thee unfold,
How the fell monsters rose from crimes of old.
But by long toils I faint: see! wide-display'd,
A grateful poplar courts us with a shade.
The grassy turf, beneath, so verdant shows,
We may secure delightfully repose.
With her *Adonis* here be *Venus* blest;
And swift at once the grass and him she prest.
Then sweetly smiling, with a raptur'd mind,
On his lov'd bosom she her head reclin'd,
And thus began; but mindful still of bliss,
Seal'd the soft accents with a softer kiss.

Perhaps thou may'st have heard a virgin's name,
Who still in swiftness swiftest youths o'ercame.
Wondrous! that female weakness should outdo
A manly strength; the wonder yet is true.
'Twas doubtful, if her triumphs in the field
Did to her form's triumphant glories yield;

Whether her face could with more ease decoy
A crowd of lovers, or her feet destroy.
For once *Apollo* she implor'd to show
If courteous Fates a consort would allow:
A consort brings thy ruin, he reply'd;
O! learn to want the pleasures of a bride!
Nor shalt thou want them to thy wretched cost,
And *Atalanta* living shall be lost.
With such a rueful Fate th' affrighted maid
Sought green recesses in the wood-land glade.
Nor sighing suiters her resolves could move,
She bad them show their speed, to show their love.
He only, who could conquer in the race,
Might hope the conquer'd virgin to embrace;
While he, whose tardy feet had lagg'd behind,
Was doom'd the sad reward of death to find.
Tho' great the prize, yet rigid the decree,
But blind with beauty, who can rigour see?
Ev'n on these laws the fair they rashly sought,
And danger in excess of love forgot.

　　There sat *Hippomenes*, prepar'd to blame
In lovers such extravagance of flame.
And must, he said, the blessing of a wife
Be dearly purchas'd by a risk of life?
But when he saw the wonders of her face,
And her limbs naked, springing to the race,
Her limbs, as exquisitely turn'd, as mine,
Or if a woman thou, might vie with thine,
With lifted hands, he cry'd, forgive the tongue
Which durst, ye youths, your well-tim'd courage wrong.
I knew not that the nymph, for whom you strove,
Deserv'd th' unbounded transports of your love.
He saw, admir'd, and thus her spotless frame
He prais'd, and praising, kindled his own flame.
A rival now to all the youths who run,

Envious, he fears they should not be undone.
But why (reflects he) idly thus is shown
The fate of others, yet untry'd my own?
The coward must not on love's aid depend;
The God was ever to the bold a friend.
Mean-time the virgin flies, or seems to fly,
Swift as a *Scythian* arrow cleaves the sky:
Still more and more the youth her charms admires.
The race itself t' exalt her charms conspires.
The golden pinions, which her feet adorn,
In wanton flutt'rings by the winds are born.
Down from her head, the long, fair tresses flow,
And sport with lovely negligence below.
The waving ribbands, which her buskins tie,
Her snowy skin with waving purple die;
As crimson veils in palaces display'd,
To the white marble lend a blushing shade.
Nor long he gaz'd, yet while he gaz'd, she gain'd
The goal, and the victorious wreath obtain'd.
The vanquish'd sigh, and, as the law decreed,
Pay the dire forfeit, and prepare to bleed.

   Then rose *Hippomenes*, not yet afraid,
And fix'd his eyes full on the beauteous maid.
Where is (he cry'd) the mighty conquest won,
To distance those, who want the nerves to run?
Here prove superior strength, nor shall it be
Thy loss of glory, if excell'd by me.
High my descent, near *Neptune* I aspire,
For *Neptune* was grand-parent to my sire.
From that great God the fourth my self I trace,
Nor sink my virtues yet beneath my race.
Thou from *Hippomenes*, o'ercome, may'st claim
An envy'd triumph, and a deathless fame.

   While thus the youth the virgin pow'r defies,
Silent she views him still with softer eyes.

Thoughts in her breast a doubtful strife begin,
If 'tis not happier now to lose, than win.
What God, a foe to beauty, would destroy
The promis'd ripeness of this blooming boy?
With his life's danger does he seek my bed?
Scarce am I half so greatly worth, she said.
Nor has his beauty mov'd my breast to love,
And yet, I own, such beauty well might move:
'Tis not his charms, 'tis pity would engage
My soul to spare the greenness of his age.
What, that heroick conrage fires his breast,
And shines thro' brave disdain of Fate confest?
What, that his patronage by close degrees
Springs from th' imperial ruler of the seas?
Then add the love, which bids him undertake
The race, and dare to perish for my sake.
Of bloody nuptials, heedless youth, beware!
Fly, timely fly from a too barb'rous fair.
At pleasure chuse; thy love will be repaid
By a less foolish, and more beauteous maid.
But why this tenderness, before unknown?
Why beats, and pants my breast for him alone?
His eyes have seen his num'rous rivals yield;
Let him too share the rigour of the field,
Since, by their fates untaught, his own he courts,
And thus with ruin insolently sports.
Yet for what crime shall he his death receive?
Is it a crime with me to wish to live?
Shall his kind passion his destruction prove?
Is this the fatal recompence of love?
So fair a youth, destroy'd, would conquest shame,
Aud nymphs eternally detest my fame.
Still why should nymphs my guiltless fame upbraid?
Did I the fond adventurer persuade?
Alas! I wish thou would'st the course decline,

Or that my swiftness was excell'd by thine.
See! what a virgin's bloom adorns the boy!
Why wilt thou run, and why thy self destroy?
Hippomenes! O that I ne'er had been
By those bright eyes unfortunately seen!
Ah! tempt not thus a swift, untimely Fate;
Thy life is worthy of the longest date.
Were I less wretched, did the galling chain
Of rigid Gods not my free choice restrain,
By thee alone I could with joy be led
To taste the raptures of a nuptial bed.

    Thus she disclos'd the woman's secret heart,
Young, innocent, and new to *Cupid's* dart.
Her thoughts, her words, her actions wildly rove,
With love she burns, yet knows not that 'tis love.

    Her royal sire now with the murm'ring crowd
Demands the race impatiently aloud.
Hippomenes then with true fervour pray'd,
My bold attempt let *Venus* kindly aid.
By her sweet pow'r I felt this am'rous fire,
Still may she succour, whom she did inspire.
A soft, unenvious wind, with speedy care,
Wafted to Heav'n the lover's tender pray'r.
Pity, I own, soon gain'd the wish'd consent,
And all th' assistance he implor'd I lent.
The *Cyprian* lands, tho' rich, in richness yield
To that, surnam'd the *Tamasenian* field.
That field of old was added to my shrine,
And its choice products consecrated mine.
A tree there stands, full glorious to behold,
Gold are the leafs, the crackling branches gold.
It chanc'd, three apples in my hand I bore,
Which newly from the tree I sportive tore;
Seen by the youth alone, to him I brought
The fruit, and when, and how to use it, taught.

The signal sounding by the king's command,
Both start at once, and sweep th' imprinted sand.
So swiftly mov'd their feet, they might with ease,
Scarce moisten'd, skim along the glassy seas;
Or with a wondrous levity be born
O'er yellow harvests of unbending corn.
Now fav'ring peals resound from ev'ry part,
Spirit the youth, and fire his fainting heart.
Hippomenes! (they cry'd) thy life preserve,
Intensely labour, and stretch ev'ry nerve.
Base fear alone can baffle thy design,
Shoot boldly onward, and the goal is thine.
'Tis doubtful whether shouts, like these, convey'd
More pleasures to the youth, or to the maid.
When a long distance oft she could have gain'd,
She check'd her swiftness, and her feet restrain'd:
She sigh'd, and dwelt, and languish'd on his face,
Then with unwilling speed pursu'd the race.
O'er-spent with heat, his breath he faintly drew,
Parch'd was his mouth, nor yet the goal in view,
And the first apple on the plain he threw.
The nymph stop'd sudden at th' unusual sight,
Struck with the fruit so beautifully bright.
Aside she starts, the wonder to behold,
And eager stoops to catch the rouling gold.
Th' observant youth past by, and scour'd along,
While peals of joy rung from th' applauding throng.
Unkindly she corrects the short delay,
And to redeem the time fleets swift away,
Swift, as the lightning, or the northern wind,
And far she leaves the panting youth behind.
Again he strives the flying nymph to hold
With the temptation of the second gold:
The bright temptation fruitlessly was tost,
So soon, alas! she won the distance lost.

Now but a little interval of space
Remain'd for the decision of the race.
Fair author of the precious gift, he said,
Be thou, o Goddess, author of my aid!
Then of the shining fruit the last he drew,
And with his full-collected vigour threw:
The virgin still the longer to detain,
Threw not directly, but a-cross the plain.
She seem'd a-while perplex'd in dubious thought,
If the far-distant apple should be sought:
I lur'd her backward mind to seize the bait,
And to the massie gold gave double weight.
My favour to my votary was show'd,
Her speed I lessen'd, and encreas'd her load.
But lest, tho' long, the rapid race be run,
Before my longer, tedious tale is done,
The youth the goal, and so the virgin won.

Might I, *Adonis*, now not hope to see
His grateful thanks pour'd out for victory?
His pious incense on my altars laid?
But he nor grateful thanks, nor incense paid.
Enrag'd I vow'd, that with the youth the fair,
For his contempt, should my keen vengeance share;
That future lovers might my pow'r revere,
And, from their sad examples, learn to fear.
The silent fanes, the sanctify'd abodes,
Of *Cybelè*, great mother of the Gods,
Rais'd by *Echion* in a lonely wood,
And full of brown, religious horror stood.
By a long painful journey faint, they chose!
Their weary limbs here secret to repose.
But soon my pow'r inflam'd the lustful boy,
Careless of rest he sought untimely joy.
A hallow'd gloomy cave, with moss o'er-grown,
The temple join'd, of native pumice-stone,

Where antique images by priests were kept.
And wooden deities securely slept.
Thither the rash *Hippomenes* retires,
And gives a loose to all his wild desires,
And the chaste cell pollutes with wanton fires.
The sacred statues trembled with surprize,
The tow'ry Goddess, blushing, veil'd her eyes;
And the lewd pair to *Stygian* sounds had sent,
But unrevengeful seem'd that punishment,
A heavier doom such black prophaneness draws,
Their taper figures turn to crooked paws.
No more their necks the smoothness can retain,
Now cover'd sudden with a yellow mane.
Arms change to legs: each finds the hard'ning breast
Of rage unknown, and wond'rous strength possest.
Their alter'd looks with fury grim appear,
And on the ground their brushing tails they hear.
They haunt the woods: their voices, which before
Were musically sweet, now hoarsly roar.
Hence lions, dreadful to the lab'ring swains,
Are tam'd by *Cybelè*, and curb'd with reins,
And humbly draw her car along the plains.
But thou, *Adonis*, my delightful care,
Of these, and beasts, as fierce as these, beware!
The savage, which not shuns thee, timely shun,
For by rash prowess should'st thou be undone,
A double ruin is contain'd in one.
Thus cautious *Venus* school'd her fav'rite boy;
But youthful heat all cautions will destroy.
His sprightly soul beyond grave counsels flies,
While with yok'd swans the Goddess cuts the skies.
His faithful hounds, led by the tainted wind,
Lodg'd in thick coverts chanc'd a boar to find.
The callow hero show'd a manly heart,
And pierc'd the savage with a side-long dart.

The flying savage, wounded, turn'd again,
Wrench'd out the gory dart, and foam'd with pain.
The trembling boy by flight his safety sought,
And now recall'd the lore, which *Venus* taught;
But now too late to fly the boar he strove,
Who in the groin his tusks impetuous drove,
On the discolour'd grass *Adonis* lay,
The monster trampling o'er his beauteous prey.

   Fair *Cytherëa*, *Cyprus* scarce in view,
Heard from afar his groans, and own'd them true,
And turn'd her snowy swans, and backward flew.
But as she saw him gasp his latest breath,
And quiv'ring agonize in pangs of death,
Down with swift flight she plung'd, nor rage forbore,
At once her garments, and her hair she tore.
With cruel blows she beat her guiltless breast,
The Fates upbraided, and her love confest.
Nor shall they yet (she cry'd) the whole devour
With uncontroul'd, inexorable pow'r:
For thee, lost youth, my tears, and restless pain
Shall in immortal monuments remain,
With solemn pomp in annual rites return'd,
Be thou for ever, my *Adonis*, mourn'd,
Could *Pluto's* queen with jealous fury storm,
And *Menthé* to a fragrant herb transform?
Yet dares not *Venus* with a change surprise,
And in a flow'r bid her fall'n heroe rise?
Then on the blood sweet nectar she bestows,
The scented blood in little bubbles rose:
Little as rainy drops, which flutt'ring fly,
Born by the winds, along a low'ring sky.
Short time ensu'd, 'till where the blood was shed,
A flow'r began to rear its purple head:
Such, as on *Punick* apples is reveal'd,
Or in the filmy rind but half conceal'd.

Still here the Fate of lovely forms we see,
So sudden fades the sweet *Anemonie*.
The feeble stems, to stormy blasts a prey,
Their sickly beauties droop, and pine away.
The winds forbid the flow'rs to flourish long,
Which owe to winds their names in *Grecian* song.

The End of the Tenth Book.

BOOK THE ELEVENTH

HERE, while the *Thracian* bard's enchanting strain
Sooths beasts, and woods, and all the listn'ing plain,
The female *Bacchanals*, devoutly mad,
In shaggy skins, like savage creatures, clad,
Warbling in air perceiv'd his lovely lay,
And from a rising ground beheld him play.
When one, the wildest, with dishevel'd hair,
That loosely stream'd, and ruffled in the air;
Soon as her frantick eye the lyrist spy'd,
See, see! the hater of our sex, she cry'd.
Then at his face her missive javelin sent,
Which whiz'd along, and brusht him as it went;
But the soft wreathes of ivy twisted round,
Prevent a deep impression of the wound.
Another, for a weapon, hurls a stone,
Which, by the sound subdu'd as soon as thrown,
Falls at his feet, and with a seeming sense
Implores his pardon for its late offence.
  But now their frantick rage unbounded grows,
Turns all to madness, and no measure knows:
Yet this the charms of musick might subdue,
But that, with all its charms, is conquer'd too;
In louder strains their hideous yellings rise,
And squeaking horn-pipes eccho thro' the skies,
Which, in hoarse consort with the drum, confound
The moving lyre, and ev'ry gentle sound:
Then 'twas the deafen'd stones flew on with speed,
And saw, unsooth'd, their tuneful poet bleed.
The birds, the beasts, and all the savage crew
Which the sweet lyrist to attention drew,
Now, by the female mob's more furious rage,
Are driv'n, and forc'd to quit the shady stage.
Next their fierce hands the bard himself assail,
Nor can his song against their wrath prevail:

They flock, like birds, when in a clustring flight,
By day they chase the boding fowl of night.
So crowded amphitheatres survey
The stag, to greedy dogs a future prey.
Their steely javelins, which soft curls entwine
Of budding tendrils from the leafy vine,
For sacred rites of mild religion made,
Are flung promiscuous at the poet's head.
Those clods of earth or flints discharge, and these
Hurl prickly branches sliver'd from the trees.
And, lest their passion shou'd be unsupply'd,
The rabble crew, by chance, at distance spy'd
Where oxen, straining at the heavy yoke,
The fallow'd field with slow advances broke;
Nigh which the brawny peasants dug the soil,
Procuring food with long laborious toil.
These, when they saw the ranting throng draw near,
Quitted their tools, and fled, possest with fear.
Long spades, and rakes of mighty size were found,
Carelesly left upon the broken ground.
With these the furious lunaticks engage,
And first the lab'ring oxen feel their rage;
Then to the poet they return with speed,
Whose fate was, past prevention, now decreed:
In vain he lifts his suppliant hands, in vain
He tries, before, his never-failing strain.
And, from those sacred lips, whose thrilling sound
Fierce tygers, and insensate rocks cou'd wound,
Ah Gods! how moving was the mournful sight!
To see the fleeting soul now take its flight.
Thee the soft warblers of the feather'd kind
Bewail'd; for thee thy savage audience pin'd;
Those rocks and woods that oft thy strain had led,
Mourn for their charmer, and lament him dead;
And drooping trees their leafy glories shed.

Naïds and *Dryads* with dishevel'd hair
Promiscuous weep, and scarfs of sable wear;
Nor cou'd the river-Gods conceal their moan,
But with new floods of tears augment their own.
His mangled limbs lay scatter'd all around,
His head, and harp a better fortune found;
In *Hebrus'* streams they gently roul'd along,
And sooth'd the waters with a mournful song.
Soft deadly notes the lifeless tongue inspire,
A doleful tune sounds from the floating lyre;
The hollows banks in solemn consort mourn,
And the sad strain in ecchoing groans return.
Now with the current to the sea they glide,
Born by the billows of the briny tide;
And driv'n where waves round rocky *Lesbos* roar,
They strand, and lodge upon *Methymna's* shore.

But here, when landed on the foreign soil,
A venom'd snake, the product of the isle
Attempts the head, and sacred locks embru'd
With clotted gore, and still fresh-dropping blood.
Phoebus, at last, his kind protection gives,
And from the fact the greedy monster drives:
Whose marbled jaws his impious crime atone,
Still grinning ghastly, tho' transform'd to stone.

His ghost flies downward to the *Stygian* shore,
And knows the places it had seen before:
Among the shadows of the pious train
He finds *Eurydicè*, and loves again;
With pleasure views the beauteous phantom's charms,
And clasps her in his unsubstantial arms.
There side by side they unmolested walk,
Or pass their blissful hours in pleasing talk;
Aft or before the bard securely goes,
And, without danger, can review his spouse.

Bacchus, resolving to revenge the wrong,
Of *Orpheus* murder'd, on the madding throng,
Decreed that each accomplice dame should stand
Fix'd by the roots along the conscious land.
Their wicked feet, that late so nimbly ran
To wreak their malice on the guiltless man,
Sudden with twisted ligatures were bound,
Like trees, deep planted in the turfy ground.
And, as the fowler with his subtle gins,
His feather'd captives by the feet entwines,
That flutt'ring pant, and struggle to get loose,
Yet only closer draw the fatal noose;
So these were caught; and, as they strove in vain
To quit the place, they but encreas'd their pain.
They flounce and toil, yet find themselves controul'd;
The root, tho' pliant, toughly keeps its hold.
In vain their toes and feet they look to find,
For ev'n their shapely legs are cloath'd with rind.
One smites her thighs with a lamenting stroke,
And finds the flesh transform'd to solid oak;
Another, with surprize, and grief distrest,
Lays on above, but beats a wooden breast.
A rugged bark their softer neck invades,
Their branching arms shoot up delightful shades;
At once they seem, and are, a real grove,
With mossy trunks below, and verdant leaves above.

Nor this suffic'd; the God's disgust remains,
And he resolves to quit their hated plains;
The vineyards of *Tymole* ingross his care,
And, with a better choir, he fixes there;
Where the smooth streams of clear *Pactolus* roll'd,
Then undistinguish'd for its sands of gold.
The satyrs with the nymphs, his usual throng,
Come to salute their God, and jovial danc'd along.
Silenus only miss'd; for while he reel'd,

Feeble with age, and wine, about the field,
The hoary drunkard had forgot his way,
And to the *Phrygian* clowns became a prey;
Who to king *Midas* drag the captive God,
While on his totty pate the wreaths of ivy nod.
    Midas from *Orpheus* had been taught his lore,
And knew the rites of *Bacchus* long before.
He, when he saw his venerable guest,
In honour of the God ordain'd a feast.
Ten days in course, with each continu'd night,
Were spent in genial mirth, and brisk delight:
Then on th' eleventh, when with brighter ray
Phosphor had chac'd the fading stars away,
The king thro' *Lydia's* fields young *Bacchus* sought,
And to the God his foster-father brought.
Pleas'd with the welcome sight, he bids him soon
But name his wish, and swears to grant the boon.
A glorious offer! yet but ill bestow'd
On him whose choice so little judgment show'd.
Give me, says he (nor thought he ask'd too much),
That with my body whatsoe'er I touch,
Chang'd from the nature which it held of old,
May be converted into yellow gold.
He had his wish; but yet the God repin'd,
To think the fool no better wish could find.
    But the brave king departed from the place,
With smiles of gladness sparkling in his face:
Nor could contain, but, as he took his way,
Impatient longs to make the first essay.
Down from a lowly branch a twig he drew,
The twig strait glitter'd with a golden hue:
He takes a stone, the stone was turn'd to gold;
A clod he touches, and the crumbling mold
Acknowledg'd soon the great transforming pow'r,
In weight and substance like a mass of ore.

He pluck'd the corn, and strait his grasp appears
Fill'd with a bending tuft of golden ears.
An apple next he takes, and seems to hold
The bright *Hesperian* vegetable gold.
His hand he careless on a pillar lays.
With shining gold the fluted pillars blaze:
And while he washes, as the servants pour,
His touch converts the stream to *Danae's* show'r.

  To see these miracles so finely wrought,
Fires with transporting joy his giddy thought.
The ready slaves prepare a sumptuous board,
Spread with rich dainties for their happy lord;
Whose pow'rful hands the bread no sooner hold,
But its whole substance is transform'd to gold:
Up to his mouth he lifts the sav'ry meat,
Which turns to gold as he attempts to eat:
His patron's noble juice of purple hue,
Touch'd by his lips, a gilded cordial grew;
Unfit for drink, and wondrous to behold,
It trickles from his jaws a fluid gold.

   The rich poor fool, confounded with surprize,
Starving in all his various plenty lies:
Sick of his wish, he now detests the pow'r,
For which he ask'd so earnestly before;
Amidst his gold with pinching famine curst;
And justly tortur'd with an equal thirst.
At last his shining arms to Heav'n he rears,
And in distress, for refuge, flies to pray'rs.
O father *Bacchus*, I have sinn'd, he cry'd,
And foolishly thy gracious gift apply'd;
Thy pity now, repenting, I implore;
Oh! may I feel the golden plague no more.

  The hungry wretch, his folly thus confest,
Touch'd the kind deity's good-natur'd breast;
The gentle God annull'd his first decree,

And from the cruel compact set him free.
But then, to cleanse him quite from further harm,
And to dilute the relicks of the charm,
He bids him seek the stream that cuts the land
Nigh where the tow'rs of *Lydian Sardis* stand;
Then trace the river to the fountain head,
And meet it rising from its rocky bed;
There, as the bubling tide pours forth amain,
To plunge his body in, and wash away the stain.
The king instructed to the fount retires,
But with the golden charm the stream inspires:
For while this quality the man forsakes,
An equal pow'r the limpid water takes;
Informs with veins of gold the neighb'ring land,
And glides along a bed of golden sand.

Now loathing wealth, th' occasion of his woes,
Far in the woods he sought a calm repose;
In caves and grottos, where the nymphs resort,
And keep with mountain *Pan* their sylvan court.
Ah! had he left his stupid soul behind!
But his condition alter'd not his mind.

For where high *Tmolus* rears his shady brow,
And from his cliffs surveys the seas below,
In his descent, by *Sardis* bounded here,
By the small confines of *Hypaepa* there,
Pan to the nymphs his frolick ditties play'd,
Tuning his reeds beneath the chequer'd shade.
The nymphs are pleas'd, the boasting sylvan plays,
And speaks with slight of great *Apollo's* lays.
Tmolus was arbiter; the boaster still
Accepts the tryal with unequal skill.
The venerable judge was seated high
On his own hill, that seem'd to touch the sky.
Above the whisp'ring trees his head he rears,
From their encumbring boughs to free his ears;

A wreath of oak alone his temples bound,
The pendant acorns loosely dangled round.
In me your judge, says he, there's no delay:
Then bids the goatherd God begin, and play.
Pan tun'd the pipe, and with his rural song
Pleas'd the low taste of all the vulgar throng;
Such songs a vulgar judgment mostly please,
Midas was there, and *Midas* judg'd with these.

 The mountain sire with grave deportment now
To *Phoebus* turns his venerable brow:
And, as he turns, with him the listning wood
In the same posture of attention stood.
The God his own *Parnassian* laurel crown'd,
And in a wreath his golden tresses bound,
Graceful his purple mantle swept the ground.
High on the left his iv'ry lute he rais'd,
The lute, emboss'd with glitt'ring jewels, blaz'd
In his right hand he nicely held the quill,
His easy posture spoke a master's skill.
The strings he touch'd with more than human art,
Which pleas'd the judge's ear, and sooth'd his heart;
Who soon judiciously the palm decreed,
And to the lute postpon'd the squeaking reed.

 All, with applause, the rightful sentence heard,
Midas alone dissatisfy'd appear'd;
To him unjustly giv'n the judgment seems,
For *Pan's* barbarick notes he most esteems.
The lyrick God, who thought his untun'd ear
Deserv'd but ill a human form to wear,
Of that deprives him, and supplies the place
With some more fit, and of an ampler space:
Fix'd on his noddle an unseemly pair,
Flagging, and large, and full of whitish hair;
Without a total change from what he was,
Still in the man preserves the simple ass.

He, to conceal the scandal of the deed,
A purple turbant folds about his head;
Veils the reproach from publick view, and fears
The laughing world would spy his monstrous ears.
One trusty barber-slave, that us'd to dress
His master's hair, when lengthen'd to excess,
The mighty secret knew, but knew alone,
And, tho' impatient, durst not make it known.
Restless, at last, a private place he found,
Then dug a hole, and told it to the ground;
In a low whisper he reveal'd the case,
And cover'd in the earth, and silent left the place.

In time, of trembling reeds a plenteous crop
From the confided furrow sprouted up;
Which, high advancing with the ripening year,
Made known the tiller, and his fruitless care:
For then the rustling blades, and whisp'ring wind,
To tell th' important secret, both combin'd.

Phoebus, with full revenge, from Tmolus flies,
Darts thro' the air, and cleaves the liquid skies;
Near Hellespont he lights, and treads the plains
Where great Laomedon sole monarch reigns;
Where, built between the two projecting strands,
To Panomphaean Jove an altar stands.
Here first aspiring thoughts the king employ,
To found the lofty tow'rs of future Troy.
The work, from schemes magnificent begun,
At vast expence was slowly carry'd on:
Which Phoebus seeing, with the trident God
Who rules the swelling surges with his nod,
Assuming each a mortal shape, combine
At a set price to finish his design.
The work was built; the king their price denies,
And his injustice backs with perjuries.
This Neptune cou'd not brook, but drove the main,

A mighty deluge, o'er the *Phrygian* plain:
'Twas all a sea; the waters of the deep
From ev'ry vale the copious harvest sweep;
The briny billows overflow the soil,
Ravage the fields, and mock the plowman's toil.

 Nor this appeas'd the God's revengeful mind,
For still a greater plague remains behind;
A huge sea-monster lodges on the sands,
And the king's daughter for his prey demands.
To him that sav'd the damsel, was decreed
A set of horses of the Sun's fine breed:
But when *Alcides* from the rock unty'd
The trembling fair, the ransom was deny'd.
He, in revenge, the new-built walls attack'd,
And the twice-perjur'd city bravely sack'd.
Telamon aided, and in justice shar'd
Part of the plunder as his due reward:
The princess, rescu'd late, with all her charms,
Hesionè, was yielded to his arms;
For *Peleus*, with a Goddess-bride, was more
Proud of his spouse, than of his birth before:
Grandsons to *Jove* there might be more than one,
But he the Goddess had enjoy'd alone.

 For *Proteus* thus to virgin *Thetis* said,
Fair Goddess of the waves, consent to wed,
And take some spritely lover to your bed.
A son you'll have, the terror of the field,
To whom in fame, and pow'r his sire shall yield.

 Jove, who ador'd the nymph with boundless love,
Did from his breast the dangerous flame remove.
He knew the Fates, nor car'd to raise up one,
Whose fame and greatness should eclipse his own,
On happy *Peleus* he bestow'd her charms,
And bless'd his grandson in the Goddess' arms:

 A silent creek *Thessalia's* coast can show;

Two arms project, and shape it like a bow;
'Twould make a bay, but the transparent tide
Does scarce the yellow-gravell'd bottom hide;
For the quick eye may thro' the liquid wave
A firm unweedy level beach perceive.
A grove of fragrant myrtle near it grows,
Whose boughs, tho' thick, a beauteous grot disclose;
The well-wrought fabrick, to discerning eyes,
Rather by art than Nature seems to rise.
A bridled dolphin oft fair *Thetis* bore
To this her lov'd retreat, her fav'rite shore.
Here *Peleus* seiz'd her, slumbring while she lay,
And urg'd his suit with all that love could say:
But when he found her obstinately coy,
Resolv'd to force her, and command the joy;
The nymph, o'erpowr'd, to art for succour flies
And various shapes the eager youth surprize:
A bird she seems, but plies her wings in vain,
His hands the fleeting substance still detain:
A branchy tree high in the air she grew;
About its bark his nimble arms he threw:
A tyger next she glares with flaming eyes;
The frighten'd lover quits his hold, and flies:
The sea-Gods he with sacred rites adores,
Then a libation on the ocean pours;
While the fat entrails crackle in the fire,
And sheets of smoak in sweet perfume aspire;
'Till *Proteus* rising from his oozy bed,
Thus to the poor desponding lover said:
No more in anxious thoughts your mind employ,
For yet you shall possess the dear expected joy.
You must once more th' unwary nymph surprize,
As in her cooly grot she slumbring lies;
Then bind her fast with unrelenting hands,
And strain her tender limbs with knotted bands.

Still hold her under ev'ry different shape,
'Till tir'd she tries no longer to escape.
Thus he: then sunk beneath the glassy flood,
And broken accents flutter'd, where he stood.

  Bright *Sol* had almost now his journey done,
And down the steepy western convex run;
When the fair *Nereid* left the briny wave,
And, as she us'd, retreated to her cave.
He scarce had bound her fast, when she arose,
And into various shapes her body throws:
She went to move her arms, and found 'em ty'd;
Then with a sigh, Some God assists ye, cry'd,
And in her proper shape stood blushing by his side.
About her waiste his longing arms he flung,
From which embrace the great *Achilles* sprung.

  Peleus unmix'd felicity enjoy'd
(Blest in a valiant son, and virtuous bride),
'Till Fortune did in blood his hands imbrue,
And his own brother by curst chance he slew:
Then driv'n from *Thessaly*, his native clime,
Trachinia first gave shelter to his crime;
Where peaceful *Ceyx* mildly fill'd the throne,
And like his sire, the morning planet, shone;
But now, unlike himself, bedew'd with tears,
Mourning a brother lost, his brow appears.
First to the town with travel spent, and care,
Peleus, and his small company repair:
His herds, and flocks the while at leisure feed,
On the rich pasture of a neighb'ring mead.
The prince before the royal presence brought,
Shew'd by the suppliant olive what he sought;
Then tells his name, and race, and country right,
But hides th' unhappy reason of his flight.
He begs the king some little town to give,
Where they may safe his faithful vassals live.

Ceyx reply'd: To all my bounty flows,
A hospitable realm your suit has chose.
Your glorious race, and far-resounding fame,
And grandsire *Jove*, peculiar favours claim.
All you can wish, I grant; entreaties spare;
My kingdom (would 'twere worth the sharing) share.
  Tears stop'd his speech: astonish'd *Peleus* pleads
To know the cause from whence his grief proceeds.
The prince reply'd: There's none of ye but deems
This hawk was ever such as now it seems;
Know 'twas a heroe once, *Daedalion* nam'd,
For warlike deeds, and haughty valour fam'd;
Like me to that bright luminary born,
Who wakes *Aurora*, and brings on the morn.
His fierceness still remains, and love of blood,
Now dread of birds, and tyrant of the wood.
My make was softer, peace my greatest care;
But this my brother wholly bent on war;
Late nations fear'd, and routed armies fled
That force, which now the tim'rous pigeons dread.
A daughter he possess'd, divinely fair,
And scarcely yet had seen her fifteenth year;
Young *Chionè*: a thousand rivals strove
To win the maid, and teach her how to love.
Phoebus, and *Mercury* by chance one day
From *Delphi*, and *Cyllene* past this way;
Together they the virgin saw: desire
At once warm'd both their breasts with am'rous fire.
Phoebus resolv'd to wait 'till close of day;
But *Mercury's* hot love brook'd no delay;
With his entrancing rod the maid he charms,
And unresisted revels in her arms.
'Twas night, and *Phoebus* in a beldam's dress,
To the late rifled beauty got access.
Her time compleat nine circling moons had run;

To either God she bore a lovely son:
To *Mercury Autolycus* she brought,
Who turn'd to thefts and tricks his subtle thought;
Possess'd he was of all his father's slight,
At will made white look black, and black look white.
Philammon born to *Phoebus*, like his sire,
The Muses lov'd, and finely struck the lyre,
And made his voice, and touch in harmony conspire.
In vain, fond maid, you boast this double birth,
The love of Gods, and royal father's worth,
And *Jove* among your ancestors rehearse!
Could blessings such as these e'er prove a curse?
To her they did, who with audacious pride,
Vain of her own, *Diana's* charms decry'd.
Her taunts the Goddess with resentment fill;
My face you like not, you shall try my skill.
She said; and strait her vengeful bow she strung,
And sent a shaft that pierc'd her guilty tongue:
The bleeding tongue in vain its accents tries;
In the red stream her soul reluctant flies.
With sorrow wild I ran to her relief,
And try'd to moderate my brother's grief.
He, deaf as rocks by stormy surges beat,
Loudly laments, and hears me not intreat.
When on the fun'ral pile he saw her laid,
Thrice he to rush into the flames assay'd,
Thrice with officious care by us was stay'd.
Now, mad with grief, away he fled amain,
Like a stung heifer that resents the pain,
And bellowing wildly bounds along the plain.
O'er the most rugged ways so fast he ran,
He seem'd a bird already, not a man:
He left us breathless all behind; and now
In quest of death had gain'd *Parnassus'* brow:
But when from thence headlong himself he threw,

He fell not, but with airy pinions flew.
Phoebus in pity chang'd him to a fowl,
Whose crooked beak and claws the birds controul,
Little of bulk, but of a warlike soul.
A hawk become, the feather'd race's foe,
He tries to ease his own by other's woe.

 While they astonish'd heard the king relate
These wonders of his hapless brother's fate;
The prince's herdsman at the court arrives,
And fresh surprize to all the audience gives.
O *Peleus, Peleus*! dreadful news I bear,
He said; and trembled as he spoke for fear.
The worst, affrighted *Peleus* bid him tell,
Whilst *Ceyx* too grew pale with friendly zeal.
Thus he began: When *Sol* mid-heav'n had gain'd,
And half his way was past, and half remain'd,
I to the level shore my cattle drove,
And let them freely in the meadows rove.
Some stretch'd at length admire the watry plain,
Some crop'd the herb, some wanton swam the main.
A temple stands of antique make hard by,
Where no gilt domes, nor marble lure the eye;
Unpolish'd rafters bear its lowly height,
Hid by a grove, as ancient, from the sight.
Here *Nereus*, and the *Nereids* they adore;
I learnt it from the man who thither bore
His net, to dry it on the sunny shore.
Adjoyns a lake, inclos'd with willows round,
Where swelling waves have overflow'd the mound,
And, muddy, stagnate on the lower ground.
From thence a russling noise increasing flies,
Strikes the still shore; and frights us with surprize,
Strait a huge wolf rush'd from the marshy wood,
His jaws besmear'd with mingled foam, and blood,
Tho' equally by hunger urg'd, and rage,

His appetite he minds not to asswage;
Nought that he meets, his rabid fury spares,
But the whole herd with mad disorder tears.
Some of our men who strove to drive him thence,
Torn by his teeth, have dy'd in their defence.
The echoing lakes, the sea, and fields, and shore,
Impurpled blush with streams of reeking gore.
Delay is loss, nor have we time for thought;
While yet some few remain alive, we ought
To seize our arms, and with confederate force
Try if we so can stop his bloody course.
But *Peleus* car'd not for his ruin'd herd;
His crime he call'd to mind, and thence inferr'd,
That *Psamathè's* revenge this havock made,
In sacrifice to murder'd *Phocus'* shade.
The king commands his servants to their arms;
Resolv'd to go; but the loud noise alarms
His lovely queen, who from her chamber flew,
And her half-plaited hair behind her threw:
About his neck she hung with loving fears,
And now with words, and now with pleading tears,
Intreated that he'd send his men alone,
And stay himself, to save two lives in one.
Then *Peleus*: Your just fears, o queen, forget;
Too much the offer leaves me in your debt.
No arms against the monster I shall bear,
But the sea nymphs appease with humble pray'r.

The citadel's high turrets pierce the sky,
Which home-bound vessels, glad, from far descry;
This they ascend, and thence with sorrow ken
The mangled heifers lye, and bleeding men;
Th' inexorable ravager they view,
With blood discolour'd, still the rest pursue:
There *Peleus* pray'd submissive tow'rds the sea,
And deprecates the ire of injur'd *Psamathè*.

But deaf to all his pray'rs the nymph remain'd,
'Till *Thetis* for her spouse the boon obtain'd.
Pleas'd with the luxury, the furious beast,
Unstop'd, continues still his bloody feast:
While yet upon a sturdy bull he flew,
Chang'd by the nymph, a marble block he grew.
No longer dreadful now the wolf appears,
Bury'd in stone, and vanish'd like their fears.
Yet still the Fates unhappy *Peleus* vex'd;
To the *Magnesian* shore he wanders next.
Acastus there, who rul'd the peaceful clime,
Grants his request, and expiates his crime.

These prodigies affect the pious prince,
But more perplex'd with those that happen'd since,
He purposes to seek the *Clarian* God,
Avoiding *Delphi*, his more fam'd abode,
Since *Phlegyan* robbers made unsafe the road.
Yet could he not from her he lov'd so well,
The fatal voyage, he resolv'd, conceal;
But when she saw her lord prepar'd to part,
A deadly cold ran shiv'ring to her heart;
Her faded cheeks are chang'd to boxen hue,
And in her eyes the tears are ever new.
She thrice essay'd to speak; her accents hung,
And falt'ring dy'd unfinish'd on her tongue,
And vanish'd into sighs: with long delay
Her voice return'd, and found the wonted way.

Tell me, my lord, she said, what fault unknown
Thy once belov'd *Alcyonè* has done?
Whither, ah, whither, is thy kindness gone!
Can *Ceyx* then sustain to leave his wife,
And unconcern'd forsake the sweets of life?
What can thy mind to this long journey move?
Or need'st thou absence to renew thy love?
Yet, if thou go'st by land, tho' grief possess

My soul ev'n then, my fears will be the less.
But ah! be warn'd to shun the watry way,
The face is frightful of the stormy sea:
For late I saw a-drift disjointed planks,
And empty tombs erected on the banks.
Nor let false hopes to trust betray thy mind,
Because my sire in caves constrains the wind,
Can with a breath their clam'rous rage appease,
They fear his whistle, and forsake the seas:
Not so; for once indulg'd, they sweep the main;
Deaf to the call, or hearing, hear in vain;
But bent on mischief bear the waves before,
And not content with seas, insult the shore,
When ocean, air, and Earth, at once ingage,
And rooted forests fly before their rage:
At once the clashing clouds to battel move,
And lightnings run across the fields above:
I know them well, and mark'd their rude comport,
While yet a child within my father's court:
In times of tempest they command alone,
And he but sits precarious on the throne:
The more I know, the more my fears augment;
And fears are oft prophetick of th' event.
But if not fears, or reasons will prevail,
If Fate has fix'd thee obstinate to sail,
Go not without thy wife, but let me bear
My part of danger with an equal share,
And present, what I suffer only fear:
Then o'er the bounding billows shall we fly,
Secure to live together, or to die.

   These reasons mov'd her warlike husband's heart,
But still he held his purpose to depart:
For as he lov'd her equal to his life,
He would not to the seas expose his wife;
Nor could be wrought his voyage to refrain,

But sought by arguments to sooth her pain:
Nor these avail'd; at length he lights on one,
With which so difficult a cause he won:
My love, so short an absence cease to fear,
For by my father's holy flame I swear,
Before two moons their orb with light adorn,
If Heav'n allow me life, I will return.

This promise of so short a stay prevails;
He soon equips the ship, supplies the sails,
And gives the word to launch; she trembling views
This pomp of death, and parting tears renews:
Last with a kiss, she took a long farewel,
Sigh'd with a sad presage, and swooning fell:
While *Ceyx* seeks delays, the lusty crew,
Rais'd on their banks, their oars in order drew
To their broad breasts, the ship with fury flew.

The queen recover'd, rears her humid eyes,
And first her husband on the poop espies,
Shaking his hand at distance on the main;
She took the sign, and shook her hand again.
Still as the ground recedes, contracts her view
With sharpen'd sight, 'till she no longer knew
The much-lov'd face; that comfort lost supplies
With less, and with the galley feeds her eyes;
The galley born from view by rising gales,
She follow'd with her sight the flying sails:
When ev'n the flying sails were seen no more,
Forsaken of all sight she left the shore.

Then on her bridal bed her body throws,
And sought in sleep her wearied eyes to close:
Her husband's pillow, and the widow'd part
Which once he press'd, renew'd the former smart.

And now a breeze from shoar began to blow,
The sailors ship their oars, and cease to row;
Then hoist their yards a-trip, and all their sails

Let fall, to court the wind, and catch the gales:
By this the vessel half her course had run,
Both shoars were lost to sight, when at the close
Of day a stiffer gale at east arose:
The sea grew white, the rouling waves from far,
Like heralds, first denounce the watry war.

This seen, the master soon began to cry,
Strike, strike the top-sail; let the main-sheet fly,
And furl your sails: the winds repel the sound,
And in the speaker's mouth the speech is drown'd.
Yet of their own accord, as danger taught
Each in his way, officiously they wrought;
Some stow their oars, or stop the leaky sides,
Another bolder, yet the yard bestrides,
And folds the sails; a fourth with labour laves
Th' intruding seas, and waves ejects on waves.

In this confusion while their work they ply,
The winds augment the winter of the sky,
And wage intestine wars; the suff'ring seas
Are toss'd, and mingled, as their tyrants please.
The master would command, but in despair
Of safety, stands amaz'd with stupid care,
Nor what to bid, or what forbid he knows,
Th' ungovern'd tempest to such fury grows:
Vain is his force, and vainer is his skill;
With such a concourse comes the flood of ill;
The cries of men are mix'd with rattling shrowds;
Seas dash on seas, and clouds encounter clouds:
At once from east to west, from pole to pole,
The forky lightnings flash, the roaring thunders roul.

Now waves on waves ascending scale the skies,
And in the fires above the water fries:
When yellow sands are sifted from below,
The glittering billows give a golden show:
And when the fouler bottom spews the black

The *Stygian* dye the tainted waters take:
Then frothy white appear the flatted seas,
And change their colour, changing their disease,
Like various fits the *Trachin* vessel finds,
And now sublime, she rides upon the winds;
As from a lofty summit looks from high,
And from the clouds beholds the nether sky;
Now from the depth of Hell they lift their sight,
And at a distance see superior light;
The lashing billows make a loud report,
And beat her sides, as batt'ring rams a fort:
Or as a lion bounding in his way,
With force augmented, bears against his prey,
Sidelong to seize; or unapal'd with fear,
Springs on the toils, and rushes on the spear:
So seas impell'd by winds, with added pow'r
Assault the sides, and o'er the hatches tow'r.

   The planks (their pitchy cov'ring wash'd away)
Now yield; and now a yawning breach display:
The roaring waters with a hostile tide
Rush through the ruins of her gaping side.
Mean-time in sheets of rain the sky descends,
And ocean swell'd with waters upwards tends;
One rising, falling one, the Heav'ns and sea
Meet at their confines, in the middle way:
The sails are drunk with show'rs, and drop with rain,
Sweet waters mingle with the briny main.
No star appears to lend his friendly light;
Darkness, and tempest make a double night;
But flashing fires disclose the deep by turns,
And while the lightnings blaze, the water burns.

   Now all the waves their scatter'd force unite,
And as a soldier foremost in the fight,
Makes way for others, and an host alone
Still presses on, and urging gains the town;

So while th' invading billows come a-breast,
The hero tenth advanc'd before the rest,
Sweeps all before him with impetuous sway,
And from the walls descends upon the prey;
Part following enter, part remain without,
With envy hear their fellows' conqu'ring shout,
And mount on others' backs, in hopes to share
The city, thus become the seat of war.

   An universal cry resounds aloud,
The sailors run in heaps, a helpless crowd;
Art fails, and courage falls, no succour near;
As many waves, as many deaths appear.
One weeps, and yet despairs of late relief;
One cannot weep, his fears congeal his grief,
But stupid, with dry eyes expects his fate:
One with loud shrieks laments his lost estate,
And calls those happy whom their fun'rals wait.
This wretch with pray'rs and vows the Gods implores,
And ev'n the skies he cannot see, adores.
That other on his friends his thoughts bestows,
His careful father, and his faithful spouse.
The covetous worldling in his anxious mind,
Thinks only on the wealth he left behind.

   All *Ceyx* his *Alcyonè* employs,
For her he grieves, yet in her absence joys:
His wife he wishes, and would still be near,
Not her with him, but wishes him with her:
Now with last looks he seeks his native shoar,
Which Fate has destin'd him to see no more;
He sought, but in the dark tempestuous night
He knew not whither to direct his sight.
So whirl the seas, such darkness blinds the sky,
That the black night receives a deeper dye.

   The giddy ship ran round; the tempest tore
Her mast, and over-board the rudder bore.

One billow mounts, and with a scornful brow,
Proud of her conquest gain'd, insults the waves below;
Nor lighter falls, than if some giant tore
Pindus and *Athos* with the freight they bore,
And toss'd on seas; press'd with the pond'rous blow,
Down sinks the ship within th' abyss below:
Down with the vessel sink into the main
The many, never more to rise again.
Some few on scatter'd planks, with fruitless care,
Lay hold, and swim; but while they swim, despair.

Ev'n he who late a scepter did command,
Now grasps a floating fragment in his hand;
And while he struggles on the stormy main,
Invokes his father, and his wife's, in vain.
But yet his consort is his greatest care,
Alcyonè he names amidst his pray'r;
Names as a charm against the waves and wind;
Most in his mouth, and ever in his mind.
Tir'd with his toil, all hopes of safety past,
From pray'rs to wishes he descends at last;
That his dead body, wafted to the sands,
Might have its burial from her friendly hands,
As oft as he can catch a gulp of air,
And peep above the seas, he names the fair;
And ev'n when plung'd beneath, on her he raves,
Murm'ring *Alcyonè* below the waves:
At last a falling billow stops his breath,
Breaks o'er his head, and whelms him underneath.
That night, his heav'nly form obscur'd with tears,
And since he was forbid to leave the skies,
He muffled with a cloud his mournful eyes.

Mean-time *Alcyonè* (his fate unknown)
Computes how many nights he had been gone.
Observes the waining moon with hourly view,
Numbers her age, and wishes for a new;

Against the promis'd time provides with care,
And hastens in the woof the robes he was to wear:
And for her self employs another loom,
New-dress'd to meet her lord returning home,
Flatt'ring her heart with joys, that never were to come:
She fum'd the temples with an od'rous flame,
And oft before the sacred altars came,
To pray for him, who was an empty name.
All Pow'rs implor'd, but far above the rest
To *Juno* she her pious vows address'd,
Her much-lov'd lord from perils to protect,
And safe o'er seas his voyage to direct:
Then pray'd, that she might still possess his heart,
And no pretending rival share a part;
This last petition heard of all her pray'r,
The rest, dispers'd by winds, were lost in air.

But she, the Goddess of the nuptial bed,
Tir'd with her vain devotions for the dead,
Resolv'd the tainted hand should be repell'd,
Which incense offer'd, and her altar held:
Then *Iris* thus bespoke: Thou faithful maid,
By whom thy queen's commands are well convey'd,
Haste to the house of sleep, and bid the God
Who rules the night by visions with a nod,
Prepare a dream, in figure, and in form
Resembling him, who perish'd in the storm;
This form before *Alcyonè* present,
To make her certain of the sad event.

Indu'd with robes of various hue she flies,
And flying draws an arch (a segment of the skies):
Then leaves her bending bow, and from the steep
Descends, to search the silent house of sleep.

Near the *Cymmerians*, in his dark abode,
Deep in a cavern, dwells the drowzy God;
Whose gloomy mansion nor the rising sun,

Nor setting, visits, nor the lightsome noon;
But lazy vapours round the region fly,
Perpetual twilight, and a doubtful sky:
No crowing cock does there his wings display,
Nor with his horny bill provoke the day;
Nor watchful dogs, nor the more wakeful geese,
Disturb with nightly noise the sacred peace;
Nor beast of Nature, nor the tame are nigh,
Nor trees with tempests rock'd, nor human cry;
But safe repose without an air of breath
Dwells here, and a dumb quiet next to death.

An arm of *Lethe*, with a gentle flow
Arising upwards from the rock below,
The palace moats, and o'er the pebbles creeps,
And with soft murmurs calls the coming sleeps.
Around its entry nodding poppies grow,
And all cool simples that sweet rest bestow;
Night from the plants their sleepy virtue drains,
And passing, sheds it on the silent plains:
No door there was th' unguarded house to keep,
On creaking hinges turn'd, to break his sleep.

But in the gloomy court was rais'd a bed,
Stuff'd with black plumes, and on an ebon-sted:
Black was the cov'ring too, where lay the God,
And slept supine, his limbs display'd abroad:
About his head fantastick visions fly,
Which various images of things supply,
And mock their forms; the leaves on trees not more,
Nor bearded ears in fields, nor sands upon the shore.

The virgin ent'ring bright, indulg'd the day
To the brown cave, and brush'd the dreams away:
The God disturb'd with this new glare of light,
Cast sudden on his face, unseal'd his sight,
And rais'd his tardy head, which sunk again,
And sinking, on his bosom knock'd his chin;

At length shook off himself, and ask'd the dame,
(And asking yawn'd) for what intent she came.

To whom the Goddess thus: O sacred rest,
Sweet pleasing sleep, of all the Pow'rs the best!
O peace of mind, repairer of decay,
Whose balms renew the limbs to labours of the day,
Care shuns thy soft approach, and sullen flies away!
Adorn a dream, expressing human form,
The shape of him who suffer'd in the storm,
And send it flitting to the *Trachin* court,
The wreck of wretched *Ceyx* to report:
Before his queen bid the pale spectre stand,
Who begs a vain relief at *Juno's* hand.
She said, and scarce awake her eyes could keep,
Unable to support the fumes of sleep;
But fled, returning by the way she went,
And swerv'd along her bow with swift ascent.

The God, uneasy 'till he slept again,
Resolv'd at once to rid himself of pain;
And, tho' against his custom, call'd aloud,
Exciting *Morpheus* from the sleepy crowd:
Morpheus, of all his numerous train, express'd
The shape of man, and imitated best;
The walk, the words, the gesture could supply,
The habit mimick, and the mein bely;
Plays well, but all his action is confin'd,
Extending not beyond our human kind.
Another, birds, and beasts, and dragons apes,
And dreadful images, and monster shapes:
This demon, *Icelos*, in Heav'n's high hall
The Gods have nam'd; but men *Phobetor* call.
A third is *Phantasus*, whose actions roul
On meaner thoughts, and things devoid of soul;
Earth, fruits, and flow'rs he represents in dreams,
And solid rocks unmov'd, and running streams.

These three to kings, and chiefs their scenes display,
The rest before th' ignoble commons play.
Of these the chosen *Morpheus* is dispatch'd;
Which done, the lazy monarch, over-watch'd,
Down from his propping elbow drops his head,
Dissolv'd in sleep, and shrinks within his bed.

    Darkling the demon glides, for flight prepar'd,
So soft, that scarce his fanning wings are heard.
To *Trachin*, swift as thought, the flitting shade,
Thro' air his momentary journey made:
Then lays aside the steerage of his wings,
Forsakes his proper form, assumes the king's;
And pale, as death, despoil'd of his array,
Into the queen's apartment takes his way,
And stands before the bed at dawn of day:
Unmov'd his eyes, and wet his beard appears;
And shedding vain, but seeming real tears;
The briny waters dropping from his hairs.
Then staring on her with a ghastly look,
And hollow voice, he thus the queen bespoke.

    Know'st thou not me? Not yet, unhappy wife?
Or are my features perish'd with my life?
Look once again, and for thy husband lost,
Lo all that's left of him, thy husband's ghost!
Thy vows for my return were all in vain,
The stormy south o'ertook us in the main,
And never shalt thou see thy living lord again.
Bear witness, Heav'n, I call'd on thee in death,
And while I call'd, a billow stop'd my breath.
Think not, that flying fame reports my fate;
I present, I appear, and my own wreck relate.
Rise, wretched widow, rise; nor undeplor'd
Permit my soul to pass the *Stygian* ford;
But rise, prepar'd in black, to mourn thy perish'd lord.

    Thus said the player-God; and adding art

Of voice and gesture, so perform'd his part,
She thought (so like her love the shade appears)
That *Ceyx* spake the words, and *Ceyx* shed the tears;
She groan'd, her inward soul with grief opprest,
She sigh'd, she wept, and sleeping beat her breast;
Then stretch'd her arms t' embrace his body bare;
Her clasping arms inclose but empty air:
At this, not yet awake, she cry'd, O stay;
One is our fate, and common is our way!

So dreadful was the dream, so loud she spoke,
That starting sudden up, the slumber broke:
Then cast her eyes around, in hope to view
Her vanish'd lord, and find the vision true:
For now the maids, who waited her commands,
Ran in with lighted tapers in their hands.
Tir'd with the search, not finding what she seeks,
With cruel blows she pounds her blubber'd cheeks;
Then from her beaten breast the linnen tare,
And cut the golden caul that bound her hair.
Her nurse demands the cause; with louder cries
She prosecutes her griefs, and thus replies.

No more *Alcyonè*; she suffer'd death
With her lov'd lord, when *Ceyx* lost his breath:
No flatt'ry, no false comfort, give me none,
My shipwreck'd *Ceyx* is for ever gone:
I saw, I saw him manifest in view,
His voice, his figure, and his gestures knew:
His lustre lost, and ev'ry living grace,
Yet I retain'd the features of his face;
Tho' with pale cheeks, wet beard, and dropping hair,
None but my *Ceyx* could appear so fair:
I would have strain'd him with a strict embrace,
But thro' my arms he slipt, and vanish'd from the place:
There, ev'n just there he stood; and as she spoke,
Where last the spectre was she cast her look:

Fain would she hope, and gaz'd upon the ground,
If any printed footsteps might be found.

     Then sigh'd, and said: This I too well foreknew,
And my prophetick fears presag'd too true:
'Twas what I begg'd, when with a bleeding heart
I took my leave, and suffer'd thee to part;
Or I to go along, or thou to stay,
Never, ah never to divide our way!
Happier for me, that all our hours assign'd
Together we had liv'd; ev'n not in death disjoin'd!
So had my *Ceyx* still been living here,
Or with my *Ceyx* I had perish'd there:
Now I die absent, in the vast profound;
And me, without my self, the seas have drown'd.
The storms were not so cruel: should I strive
To lengthen life, and such a grief survive;
But neither will I strive, nor wretched thee
In death forsake, but keep thee company.
If not one common sepulchre contains
Our bodies, or one urn our last remains,
Yet *Ceyx* and *Alcyonè* shall join,
Their names remember'd in one common line.

     No farther voice her mighty grief affords,
For sighs come rushing in betwixt her words,
And stop'd her tongue; but what her tongue deny'd,
Soft tears, and groans, and dumb complaints supply'd.

     'Twas morning; to the port she takes her way,
And stands upon the margin of the sea:
That place, that very spot of ground she sought,
Or thither by her destiny was brought,
Where last he stood: and while she sadly said,
'Twas here he left me, lingring here delay'd
His parting kiss, and there his anchors weigh'd.

     Thus speaking, while her thoughts past actions trace,
And call to mind, admonish'd by the place,

Sharp at her utmost ken she cast her eyes,
And somewhat floating from afar descries:
It seems a corps a-drift to distant sight,
But at a distance who could judge aright?
It wafted nearer yet, and then she knew,
That what before she but surmis'd, was true:
A corps it was, but whose it was, unknown,
Yet mov'd, howe'er, she made the cause her own.
Took the bad omen of a shipwreck'd man,
As for a stranger wept, and thus began.

Poor wretch, on stormy seas to lose thy life,
Unhappy thou, but more thy widow'd wife;
At this she paus'd: for now the flowing tide
Had brought the body nearer to the side:
The more she looks, the more her fears increase,
At nearer sight; and she's her self the less:
Now driv'n ashore, and at her feet it lies,
She knows too much in knowing whom she sees:
Her husband's corps; at this she loudly shrieks,
'Tis he, 'tis he, she cries, and tears her cheeks,
Her hair, and vest; and stooping to the sands,
About his neck she cast her trembling hands.

And is it thus, o dearer than my life,
Thus, thus return'st thou to thy longing wife!
She said, and to the neighbouring mole she strode,
(Rais'd there to break th' incursions of the flood).

Headlong from hence to plunge her self she springs,
But shoots along, supported on her wings;
A bird new-made, about the banks she plies,
Not far from shore, and short excursions tries;
Nor seeks in air her humble flight to raise,
Content to skim the surface of the seas:
Her bill tho' slender, sends a creaking noise,
And imitates a lamentable voice.
Now lighting where the bloodless body lies,

She with a fun'ral note renews her cries:
At all her stretch, her little wings she spread,
And with her feather'd arms embrac'd the dead:
Then flick'ring to his palid lips, she strove
To print a kiss, the last essay of love.
Whether the vital touch reviv'd the dead,
Or that the moving waters rais'd his head
To meet the kiss, the vulgar doubt alone;
For sure a present miracle was shown.
The Gods their shapes to winter-birds translate,
But both obnoxious to their former fate.
Their conjugal affection still is ty'd,
And still the mournful race is multiply'd:
They bill, they tread; *Alcyonè* compress'd,
Sev'n days sits brooding on her floating nest:
A wintry queen: her sire at length is kind,
Calms ev'ry storm, and hushes ev'ry wind;
Prepares his empire for his daughter's ease,
And for his hatching nephews smooths the seas.

  These some old man sees wanton in the air,
And praises the unhappy constant pair.
Then to his friend the long-neck'd corm'rant shows,
The former tale reviving others' woes:
That sable bird, he cries, which cuts the flood
With slender legs, was once of royal blood;
His ancestors from mighty *Tros* proceed,
The brave *Laomedon*, and *Ganymede*
(Whose beauty tempted *Jove* to steal the boy),
And *Priam*, hapless prince! who fell with *Troy*:
Himself was *Hector's* brother, and (had Fate
But giv'n this hopeful youth a longer date)
Perhaps had rival'd warlike *Hector's* worth,
Tho' on the mother's side of meaner birth;
Fair *Alyxothoè*, a country maid,
Bare *Aesacus* by stealth in *Ida's* shade.

He fled the noisy town, and pompous court,
Lov'd the lone hills, and simple rural sport.
And seldom to the city would resort.
Yet he no rustick clownishness profest,
Nor was soft love a stranger to his breast:
The youth had long the nymph *Hesperiè* woo'd,
Oft thro' the thicket, or the mead pursu'd:
Her haply on her father's bank he spy'd,
While fearless she her silver tresses dry'd;
Away she fled: not stags with half such speed,
Before the prowling wolf, scud o'er the mead;
Not ducks, when they the safer flood forsake,
Pursu'd by hawks, so swift regain the lake.
As fast he follow'd in the hot career;
Desire the lover wing'd, the virgin fear.
A snake unseen now pierc'd her heedless foot;
Quick thro' the veins the venom'd juices shoot:
She fell, and 'scap'd by death his fierce pursuit;
Her lifeless body, frighted, he embrac'd,
And cry'd, Not this I dreaded, but thy haste:
O had my love been less, or less thy fear!
The victory, thus bought, is far too dear.
Accursed snake! yet I more curs'd than he!
He gave the wound; the cause was given by me.
Yet none shall say, that unreveng'd you dy'd.
He spoke; then climb'd a cliff's o'er-hanging side,
And, resolute, leap'd on the foaming tide.
Tethys receiv'd him gently on the wave;
The death he sought deny'd, and feathers gave.
Debarr'd the surest remedy of grief,
And forc'd to live, he curst th' unask'd relief.
Then on his airy pinions upward flies,
And at a second fall successless tries;
The downy plume a quick descent denies.
Enrag'd, he often dives beneath the wave,

And there in vain expects to find a grave.
His ceaseless sorrow for th' unhappy maid,
Meager'd his look, and on his spirits prey'd.
Still near the sounding deep he lives; his name
From frequent diving and emerging came.

The End of the Eleventh Book.

BOOK THE TWELTH

RIAM, to whom the story was unknown,
As dead, deplor'd his metamorphos'd son:
A cenotaph his name, and title kept,
And *Hector* round the tomb, with all his brothers, wept.
  This pious office *Paris* did not share;
Absent alone; and author of the war,
Which, for the *Spartan* queen, the *Grecians* drew
T' avenge the rape; and *Asia* to subdue.
  A thousand ships were mann'd, to sail the sea:
Nor had their just resentments found delay,
Had not the winds, and waves oppos'd their way.
At *Aulis*, with united pow'rs they meet,
But there, cross-winds or calms detain'd the fleet.
Now, while they raise an altar on the shore,
And *Jove* with solemn sacrifice adore;
A boding sign the priests and people see:
A snake of size immense ascends a tree,
And, in the leafie summit, spy'd a nest,
Which o'er her callow young, a sparrow press'd.
Eight were the birds unfledg'd; their mother flew,
And hover'd round her care; but still in view:
'Till the fierce reptile first devour'd the brood,
Then seiz'd the flutt'ring dam, and drunk her blood.
This dire ostent, the fearful people view;
Calchas alone, by *Phoebus* taught, foreknew
What Heav'n decreed; and with a smiling glance,
Thus gratulates to *Greece* her happy chance:
O *Argives*, we shall conquer: *Troy* is ours,
But long delays shall first afflict our pow'rs:
Nine years of labour, the nine birds portend;
The tenth shall in the town's destruction end.
  The serpent, who his maw obscene had fill'd,
The branches in his curl'd embraces held:
But, as in spires he stood, he turn'd to stone:

The stony snake retain'd the figure still his own.
    Yet, not for this, the wind-bound navy weigh'd;
Slack were their sails; and *Neptune* disobey'd.
Some thought him loth the town should be destroy'd,
Whose building had his hands divine employ'd:
Not so the seer; who knew, and known foreshow'd,
The virgin *Phoebe*, with a virgin's blood
Must first be reconcil'd: the common cause
Prevail'd; and pity yielding to the laws,
Fair *Iphigenia* the devoted maid
Was, by the weeping priests, in linnen-robes array'd;
All mourn her fate; but no relief appear'd;
The royal victim bound, the knife already rear'd:
When that offended Pow'r, who caus'd their woe,
Relenting ceas'd her wrath; and stop'd the coming blow.
A mist before the ministers she cast,
And, in the virgin's room, a hind she plac'd.
Th' oblation slain, and *Phoebe* reconcil'd,
The storm was hush'd, and dimpled ocean smil'd:
A favourable gale arose from shore,
Which to the port desir'd, the *Graecian* gallies bore.
    Full in the midst of this created space,
Betwixt Heav'n, Earth, and skies, there stands a place,
Confining on all three, with triple bound;
Whence all things, tho' remote, are view'd around;
And thither bring their undulating sound.
The palace of loud *Fame*, her seat of pow'r,
Plac'd on the summet of a lofty tow'r;
A thousand winding entries long and wide,
Receive of fresh reports a flowing tide.
A thousand crannies in the walls are made;
Nor gate, nor bars exclude the busie trade.
'Tis built of brass, the better to diffuse
The spreading sounds, and multiply the news:
Where eccho's in repeated eccho's play:

A mart for ever full, and open night and day.
Nor silence is within, nor voice express,
But a deaf noise of sounds, that never cease.
Confus'd, and chiding, like the hollow roar
Of tides, receding from th' insulted shore,
Or like the broken thunder heard from far,
When *Jove* at distance drives the rouling war.
The courts are fill'd with a tumultuous din
Of crouds, or issuing forth, or entring in:
A thorough-fare of news: where some devise
Things never heard, some mingle truth with lies;
The troubled air with empty sounds they beat,
Intent to hear, and eager to repeat.
Error sits brooding there, with added train
Of vain credulity, and joys as vain:
Suspicion, with sedition join'd, are near,
And rumours rais'd, and murmurs mix'd, and panique fear.
Fame sits aloft, and sees the subject ground,
And seas about, and skies above; enquiring all around.

    The Goddess gives th' alarm; and soon is known
The *Grecian* fleet descending on the town.
Fix'd on defence, the *Trojans* are not slow
To guard their shore, from an expected foe.
They meet in fight: by *Hector's* fatal hand
Protesilaus falls, and bites the strand:
Which with expence of blood the *Grecians* won;
And prov'd the strength unknown of *Priam's* son.
And to their cost the *Trojan* leaders felt
The *Grecian* heroes; and what deaths they dealt.

    From these first onsets, the *Sigaean* shore
Was strew'd with carcasses, and stain'd with gore:
Neptunian Cygnus troops of *Greeks* had slain;
Achilles in his carr had scour'd the plain,
And clear'd the *Trojan* ranks: where-e'er he fought,
Cygnus, or *Hector*, through the fields he sought:

Cygnus he found; on him his force essay'd:
For *Hector* was to the tenth year delay'd.
His white-main'd steeds, that bow'd beneath the yoke,
He chear'd to courage, with a gentle stroke;
Then urg'd his fiery chariot on the foe;
And rising shook his lance; in act to throw.
But first he cry'd, O youth, be proud to bear
Thy death, ennobled by *Pelides'* spear.
The lance pursu'd the voice without delay,
Nor did the whizzing weapon miss the way;
But pierc'd his cuirass, with such fury sent,
And sign'd his bosom with a purple dint.
At this the seed of *Neptune*: Goddess-born,
For ornament, not use, these arms are worn;
This helm, and heavy buckler, I can spare;
As only decorations of the war:
So *Mars* is arm'd for glory, not for need.
'Tis somewhat more from *Neptune* to proceed,
Than from a daughter of the sea to spring:
Thy sire is mortal; mine is ocean's king.
Secure of death, I shou'd contemn thy dart,
Tho' naked; and impassible depart:
He said, and threw: the trembling weapon pass'd
Through nine bull-hides, each under other plac'd,
On his broad shield; and stuck within the last.
Achilles wrench'd it out; and sent again
The hostile gift: the hostile gift was vain.
He try'd a third, a tough well-chosen spear;
Th' inviolable body stood sincere,
Though *Cygnus* then did no defence provide,
But scornful offer'd his unshielded side.

   Not otherwise th' impatient hero far'd,
Than as a bull incompass'd with a guard,
Amid the *Circus* roars, provok'd from far
By sight of scarlet, and a sanguine war:

They quit their ground, his bended horns elude;
In vain pursuing, and in vain pursu'd:
　Before to farther fight he wou'd advance,
He stood considering, and survey'd his lance.
Doubts if he wielded not a wooden spear
Without a point: he look'd, the point was there.
This is my hand, and this my lance, he said;
By which so many thousand foes are dead,
O whither is their usual virtue fled!
I had it once; and the *Lyrnessian* wall,
And *Tenedos*, confess'd it in their fall.
Thy streams, *Caïcus*, rowl'd a crimson-flood;
And *Thebes* ran red with her own natives' blood.
Twice *Telephus* employ'd their piercing steel,
To wound him first, and afterward to heal.
The vigour of this arm was never vain:
And that my wonted prowess I retain,
Witness these heaps of slaughter on the plain.
He said; and, doubtful of his former deeds,
To some new tryal of his force proceeds.
He chose *Menoetes* from among the rest;
At him he launch'd his spear, and pierc'd his breast:
On the hard earth the *Lycian* knock'd his head,
And lay supine; and forth the spirit fled.
　Then thus the hero: Neither can I blame
The hand, or jav'lin; both are still the same.
The same I will employ against this foe,
And wish but with the same success to throw.
So spoke the chief; and while he spoke he threw;
The weapon with unerring fury flew,
At his left shoulder aim'd: nor entrance found;
But back, as from a rock, with swift rebound
Harmless return'd: a bloody mark appear'd,
Which with false joy the flatter'd hero chear'd.
Wound there was none; the blood that was in view,

The lance before from slain *Menoetes* drew.

   Headlong he leaps from off his lofty car,
And in close fight on foot renews the war.
Raging with high disdain, repeats his blows;
Nor shield, nor armour can their force oppose;
Huge cantlets of his buckler strew the ground,
And no defence in his bor'd arms is found,
But on his flesh, no wound or blood is seen;
The sword it self is blunted on the skin.

   This vain attempt the chief no longer bears;
But round his hollow temples and his ears
His buckler beats: the son of *Neptune*, stunn'd
With these repeated buffets, quits his ground;
A sickly sweat succeeds, and shades of night;
Inverted Nature swims before his sight:
Th' insulting victor presses on the more,
And treads the steps the vanquish'd trod before,
Nor rest, nor respite gives. A stone there lay
Behind his trembling foe, and stopp'd his way:
Achilles took th' advantage which he found,
O'er-turn'd, and push'd him backward on the ground,
His buckler held him under, while he press'd,
With both his knees, above his panting breast.
Unlac'd his helm: about his chin the twist
He ty'd; and soon the strangled soul dismiss'd.

   With eager haste he went to strip the dead:
The vanish'd body from his arms was fled.
His sea-God sire, t' immortalize his frame,
Had turn'd it to a bird that bears his name.

   A truce succeeds the labours of this day,
And arms suspended with a long delay.
While *Trojan* walls are kept with watch and ward;
The *Greeks* before their trenches mount the guard;
The feast approach'd; when to the blue-ey'd maid
His vows for *Cygnus* slain the victor paid,

And a white heyfer on her altar laid.
The reeking entrails on the fire they threw,
And to the Gods the grateful odour flew.
Heav'n had its part in sacrifice: the rest
Was broil'd, and roasted for the future feast.
The chief-invited guests were set around!
And hunger first asswag'd, the bowls were crown'd,
Which in deep draughts their cares, and labours drown'd.
The mellow harp did not their ears employ:
And mute was all the warlike symphony:
Discourse, the food of souls, was their delight,
And pleasing chat prolong'd the summer's night.
The subject, deeds of arms; and valour shown,
Or on the *Trojan* side, or on their own.
Of dangers undertaken, fame atchiev'd,
They talk'd by turns; the talk by turns reliev'd.
What things but these could fierce *Achilles* tell,
Or what cou'd fierce *Achilles* hear so well?
The last great act perform'd, of *Cygnus* slain,
Did most the martial audience entertain:
Wondring to find a body free by Fate
From steel; and which cou'd ev'n that steel rebate:
Amaz'd, their admiration they renew;
And scarce *Pelides* cou'd believe it true.
    Then *Nestor* thus: what once this age has known,
In fated *Cygnus*, and in him alone,
These eyes have seen in *Caeneus* long before;
Whose body not a thousand swords cou'd bore.
Caeneus, in courage, and in strength, excell'd;
And still his *Othrys* with his fame is fill'd:
But what did most his martial deeds adorn
(Though since he chang'd his sex) a woman born.
    A novelty so strange, and full of Fate,
His list'ning audience ask'd him to relate.
Achilles thus commends their common sute:

O father, first for prudence in repute,
Tell, with that eloquence, so much thy own,
What thou hast heard, or what of *Caeneus* known:
What was he, whence his change of sex begun,
What trophies, join'd in wars with thee, he won?
Who conquer'd him, and in what fatal strife
The youth, without a wound, cou'd lose his life?

   Neleides then: Though tardy age, and time,
Have shrunk my sinews, and decay'd my prime;
Though much I have forgotten of my store,
Yet not exhausted, I remember more.
Of all that arms atchiev'd, or peace design'd,
That action still is fresher in my mind,
Than ought beside. If reverend age can give
To faith a sanction, in my third I live.

   'Twas in my second cent'ry, I survey'd
Young *Caenis*, then a fair *Thessalian* maid:
Caenis the bright, was born to high command;
A princess, and a native of thy land,
Divine *Achilles*; every tongue proclaim'd
Her beauty, and her eyes all hearts inflam'd.
Peleus, thy sire, perhaps had sought her bed,
Among the rest; but he had either led
Thy mother then; or was by promise ty'd;
But she to him, and all, alike her love deny'd.

   It was her fortune once to take her way
Along the sandy margin of the sea:
The Pow'r of ocean view'd her as she pass'd,
And, lov'd as soon as seen, by force embrac'd.
So Fame reports. Her virgin-treasure seiz'd,
And his new joys, the ravisher so pleas'd,
That thus, transported, to the nymph he cry'd;
Ask what thou wilt, no pray'r shall be deny'd.
This also Fame relates: the haughty fair,
Who not the rape ev'n of a God cou'd bear,

This answer, proud, return'd: To mighty wrongs
A mighty recompence, of right, belongs.
Give me no more to suffer such a shame;
But change the woman, for a better name;
One gift for all: she said; and while she spoke,
A stern, majestick, manly tone she took.
A man she was: and as the Godhead swore,
To *Caeneus* turn'd, who *Caenis* was before.

To this the lover adds, without request,
No force of steel shou'd violate his breast.
Glad of the gift, the new-made warrior goes;
And arms among the *Greeks*, and longs for equal foes.

Now brave *Perithous*, bold *Ixion's* son,
The love of fair *Hippodamè* had won.
The cloud-begotten race, half men, half beast,
Invited, came to grace the nuptial feast:
In a cool cave's recess the treat was made,
Whose entrance, trees with spreading boughs o'er-shade.
They sate: and summon'd by the bridegroom, came,
To mix with those, the *Lapythaean* name:
Nor wanted I: the roofs with joy resound:
And *Hymen*, *Io Hymen*, rung around.
Rais'd altars shone with holy fires; the bride,
Lovely her self (and lovely by her side
A bevy of bright nymphs, with sober grace),
Came glitt'ring like a star, and took her place.
Her heav'nly form beheld, all wish'd her joy;
And little wanted, but in vain, their wishes all employ.

For one, most brutal, of the brutal brood,
Or whether wine, or beauty fir'd his blood,
Or both at once, beheld with lustful eyes
The bride; at once resolv'd to make his prize.
Down went the board; and fastning on her hair,
He seiz'd with sudden force the frighted fair.
'Twas *Eurytus* began: his bestial kind

His crime pursu'd; and each as pleas'd his mind,
Or her, whom chance presented, took: the feast
An image of a taken town express'd.

The cave resounds with female shrieks; we rise,
Mad with revenge to make a swift reprise:
And *Theseus* first, What phrenzy has possess'd,
O *Eurytus*, he cry'd, thy brutal breast,
To wrong *Perithous*, and not him alone,
But while I live, two friends conjoyn'd in one?

To justifie his threat, he thrusts aside
The crowd of centaurs; and redeems the bride:
The monster nought reply'd: for words were vain,
And deeds cou'd only deeds unjust maintain;
But answers with his hand, and forward press'd,
With blows redoubled, on his face, and breast.
An ample goblet stood, of antick mold,
And rough with figures of the rising gold;
The hero snatch'd it up, and toss'd in air
Full at the front of the foul ravisher.
He falls; and falling vomits forth a flood
Of wine, and foam, and brains, and mingled blood.
Half roaring, and half neighing through the hall,
Arms, arms, the double-form'd with fury call;
To wreak their brother's death: a medley-flight
Of bowls, and jars, at first supply the fight,
Once instruments of feasts; but now of Fate;
Wine animates their rage, and arms their hate.

Bold *Amycus*, from the robb'd vestry brings
The chalices of Heav'n; and holy things
Of precious weight: a sconce that hung on high,
With tapers fill'd, to light the sacristy,
Torn from the cord, with his unhallow'd hand
He threw amid the *Lapythaean* band.
On *Celadon* the ruin fell; and left
His face of feature, and of form bereft:

So, when some brawny sacrificer knocks,
Before an altar led, an offer'd ox,
His eyes-balls rooted out, are thrown to ground;
His nose, dismantled, in his mouth is found;
His jaws, cheeks, front, one undistinguish'd wound.
    This, *Belates*, th' avenger, cou'd not brook;
But, by the foot, a maple board he took;
And hurl'd at *Amycus*; his chin it bent
Against his chest, and down the centaur sent:
Whom sputtring bloody teeth, the second blow
Of his drawn sword, dispatch'd to shades below.
    Grineus was near; and cast a furious look
On the side-altar, cens'd with sacred smoke,
And bright with flaming fires; The Gods, he cry'd,
Have with their holy trade our hands supply'd:
Why use we not their gifts? Then from the floor
An altar stone he heav'd, with all the load it bore:
Altar, and altar's freight together slew,
Where thickest throng'd the *Lapythaean* crew:
And, at once, *Broteas* and *Oryus* flew.
Oryus' mother, *Mycalè*, was known
Down from her sphere to draw the lab'ring moon.
    Exadius cry'd, Unpunish'd shall not go
This fact, if arms are found against the foe.
He look'd about, where on a pine were spread
The votive horns of a stag's branching head:
At *Grineus* these he throws; so just they fly,
That the sharp antlers stuck in either eye:
Breathless, and blind he fell; with blood besmear'd;
His eye-balls beaten out, hung dangling on his beard.
Fierce *Rhoetus*, from the hearth a burning brand
Selects, and whirling waves; 'till, from his hand
The fire took flame; then dash'd it from the right,
On fair *Charaxus'* temples, near the sight:
The whistling pest came on, and pierc'd the bone,

And caught the yellow hair, that shrivel'd while it shone.
Caught, like dry stubble fir'd; or like seerwood;
Yet from the wound ensu'd no purple flood;
But look'd a bubbling mass of frying blood.
His blazing locks sent forth a crackling sound;
And hiss'd, like red hot ir'n within the smithy drown'd.
The wounded warrior shook his flaming hair,
Then (what a team of horse could hardly rear)
He heaves the threshold stone, but could not throw;
The weight itself forbad the threaten'd blow;
Which dropping from his lifted arms, came down
Full on *Cometes*' head; and crush'd his crown.
Nor *Rhoetus* then retain'd his joy; but said,
So by their fellows may our foes be sped;
Then, with redoubled strokes he plies his head:
The burning lever not deludes his pains:
But drives the batter'd skull within the brains.

Thus flush'd, the conqueror, with force renew'd,
Evagrus, *Dryas*, *Corythus*, pursu'd:
First, *Corythus*, with downy cheeks, he slew;
Whose fall, when fierce *Evagrus* had in view,
He cry'd, What palm is from a beardless prey?
Rhoetus prevents what more he had to say;
And drove within his mouth the fi'ry death,
Which enter'd hissing in, and choak'd his breath.
At *Dryas* next he flew: but weary chance,
No longer wou'd the same success advance.
For while he whirl'd in fiery circles round
The brand, a sharpen'd stake strong *Dryas* found;
And in the shoulder's joint inflicts the wound.
The weapon stuck; which, roaring out with pain,
He drew; nor longer durst the fight maintain,
But turn'd his back, for fear; and fled amain.
With him fled *Orneus*, with like dread possess'd;
Thaumas, and *Medon* wounded in the breast;

And *Mermeros*, in the late race renown'd,
Now limping ran, and tardy with his wound.
Pholus, and *Melaneus* from fight withdrew,
And *Abas* maim'd, who boars encountring slew:
And *Augur Asbolos*, whose art in vain,
From fight dissuaded the four-footed train,
Now beat the hoof with *Nessus* on the plain;
But to his fellow cry'd, Be safely slow,
Thy death deferr'd is due to great *Alcides'* bow.
　Mean-time strong *Dryas* urg'd his chance so well,
That *Lycidas*, *Areos*, *Imbreus* fell;
All, one by one, and fighting face to face:
Crenaeus fled, to fall with more disgrace:
For, fearful, while he look'd behind, he bore,
Betwixt his nose, and front, the blow before.
Amid the noise, and tumult of the fray,
Snoring, and drunk with wine, *Aphidas* lay.
Ev'n then the bowl within his hand he kept,
And on a bear's rough hide securely slept.
Him *Phorbas* with his flying dart transfix'd;
Take thy next draught, with *Stygian* waters mix'd,
And sleep thy fill, th' insulting victor cry'd;
Surpriz'd with death unfelt, the centaur dy'd;
The ruddy vomit, as he breath'd his soul,
Repass'd his throat, and fill'd his empty bowl.
　I saw *Petraeus'* arms employ'd around
A well-grown oak, to root it from the ground.
This way, and that, he wrench'd the fibrous bands;
The trunk was like a sappling, in his hands,
And still obey'd the bent: while thus he stood,
Perithous' dart drove on; and nail'd him to the wood;
Lycus, and *Chromis* fell, by him oppress'd:
Helops, and *Dictis* added to the rest
A nobler palm: *Helops*, through either ear
Transfix'd, receiv'd the penetrating spear.

This *Dictis* saw; and, seiz'd with sudden fright,
Leapt headlong from the hill of steepy height;
And crush'd an ash beneath, that cou'd not bear his weight.
The shatter'd tree receives his fall; and strikes,
Within his full-blown paunch, the sharpen'd spikes.
Strong *Aphareus* had heav'd a mighty stone,
The fragment of a rock; and wou'd have thrown;
But *Theseus*, with a club of harden'd oak,
The cubit-bone of the bold centaur broke;
And left him maim'd; nor seconded the stroke.
Then leapt on tall *Bianor's* back (who bore
No mortal burden but his own, before);
Press'd with his knees his sides; the double man,
His speed with spurs increas'd, unwilling ran.
One hand the hero fastn'd on his locks;
His other ply'd him with repeated strokes.
The club rung round his ears, and batter'd brows;
He falls; and lashing up his heels, his rider throws.

 The same *Herculean* arms, *Nedymnus* wound;
And lay by him *Lycotas* on the ground,
And *Hippasus*, whose beard his breast invades;
And *Ripheus*, haunter of the woodland shades:
And *Thereus*, us'd with mountain-bears to strive,
And from their dens to draw th' indignant beasts alive.
 Demoleon cou'd not bear this hateful sight,
Or the long fortune of th' *Athenian* knight:
But pull'd with all his force, to disengage
From Earth a pine, the product of an age:
The root stuck fast: the broken trunk he sent
At *Theseus*; *Theseus* frustrates his intent,
And leaps aside; by *Pallas* warn'd, the blow
To shun (for so he said; and we believ'd it so).
Yet not in vain th' enormous weight was cast;
Which *Crantor's* body sunder'd at the waist:
Thy father's 'squire, *Achilles*, and his care;

Whom conquer'd in the *Polopeian* war,
Their king, his present ruin to prevent,
A pledge of peace implor'd, to *Peleus* sent.
    Thy sire, with grieving eyes, beheld his Fate;
And cry'd, Not long, lov'd *Crantor*, shalt thou wait
Thy vow'd revenge. At once he said, and threw
His ashen-spear; which quiver'd, as it flew;
With all his force, and all his soul apply'd;
The sharp point enter'd in the centaur's side:
Both hands, to wrench it out, the monster join'd;
And wrench'd it out; but left the steel behind;
Stuck in his lungs it stood: inrag'd he rears
His hoofs, and down to ground thy father bears.
Thus trampled under foot, his shield defends
His head; his other hand the lance portends.
Ev'n while he lay extended on the dust,
He sped the centaur, with one single thrust.
Two more his lance before transfix'd from far;
And two, his sword had slain, in closer war.
To these was added *Dorylas*, who spread
A bull's two goring horns around his head.
With these he push'd; in blood already dy'd,
Him fearless, I approach'd; and thus defy'd:
Now, monster, now, by proof it shall appear,
Whether thy horns are sharper, or my spear.
At this, I threw: for want of other ward,
He lifted up his hand, his front to guard.
His hand it pass'd; and fix'd it to his brow:
Loud shouts of ours attend the lucky blow.
Him *Peleus* finish'd, with a second wound,
Which thro' the navel pierc'd: he reel'd around;
And dragg'd his dangling bowels on the ground.
Trod what he drag'd; and what he trod, he crush'd:
And to his mother-Earth, with empty belly, rush'd.

Nor cou'd thy form, o *Cyllarus*, foreflow
Thy Fate (if form to monsters men allow):
Just bloom'd thy beard: thy beard of golden hue:
Thy locks, in golden waves, about thy shoulders flew.
Sprightly thy look: thy shapes in ev'ry part
So clean, as might instruct the sculptor's art;
As far as man extended: where began
The beast, the beast was equal to the man.
Add but a horse's head and neck; and he,
O *Castor*, was a courser worthy thee.
So was his back proportion'd for the seat:
So rose his brawny chest; so swiftly mov'd his feet.
Coal-black his colour, but like jett it shone;
His legs, and flowing tail were white alone.
Belov'd by many maidens of his kind;
But fair *Hylonomè* possess'd his mind;
Hylonomè, for features, and for face,
Excelling all the nymphs of double race:
Nor less her blandishments, than beauty, move;
At once both loving, and confessing love.
For him she dress'd: for him, with female care
She comb'd, and set in curls, her auburn hair.
Of roses, violets, and lillies mix'd,
And sprigs of flowing rosemary betwixt,
She form'd the chaplet, that adorn'd her front:
In waters of the *Pegasaean* fount,
And in the streams that from the fountain play,
She wash'd her face; and bath'd her twice a-day.
The scarf of furs, that hung below her side,
Was ermin, or the panther's spotted pride;
Spoils of no common beast: with equal flame
They lov'd: their silvan pleasures were the same:
All day they hunted: and when day expir'd,
Together to some shady cave retir'd:
Invited to the nuptials, both repair:

And, side by side, they both engage in war.
　　Uncertain from what hand, a flying dart
At *Cyllarus* was sent; which pierc'd his heart.
The jav'lin drawn from out the mortal wound,
He faints with stagg'ring steps; and seeks the ground:
The fair within her arms receiv'd his fall,
And strove his wand'ring spirits to recall:
And while her hand the streaming blood oppos'd,
Join'd face to face, his lips with hers she clos'd.
Stifled with kisses, a sweet death he dies;
She fills the fields with undistinguish'd cries;
At least her words were in her clamour drown'd;
For my stunn'd ears receiv'd no vocal sound.
In madness of her grief, she seiz'd the dart
New-drawn, and reeking from her lover's heart;
To her bare bosom the sharp point apply'd;
And wounded fell; and falling by his side,
Embrac'd him in her arms; and thus embracing dy'd.
　　Ev'n still methinks, I see *Phaeocomes*;
Strange was his habit, and as odd his dress.
Six lions' hides, with thongs together fast,
His upper part defended to his waist:
And where man ended, the continued vest,
Spread on his back, the houss and trappings of a beast.
A stump too heavy for a team to draw
(It seems a fable, tho' the fact I saw);
He threw at *Pholon*; the descending blow
Divides the skull, and cleaves his head in two.
The brains, from nose, and mouth, and either ear,
Came issuing out, as through a colendar
The curdled milk; or from the press the whey,
Driv'n down by weight above, is drain'd away.
　　But him, while stooping down to spoil the slain,
Pierc'd through the paunch, I tumbled on the plain.
Then *Chthonyus*, and *Teleboas* I slew:

A fork the former arm'd; a dart his fellow threw.
The jav'lin wounded me (behold the scar,
Then was my time to seek the *Trojan* war;
Then I was *Hector's* match in open field;
But he was then unborn; at least a child:
Now, I am nothing). I forbear to tell
By *Periphantas* how *Pyretus* fell;
The centaur by the knight: nor will I stay
On *Amphix*, or what deaths he dealt that day:
What honour, with a pointless lance, he won,
Stuck in the front of a four-footed man.
What fame young *Macareus* obtain'd in fight:
Or dwell on *Nessus*, now return'd from flight.
How prophet *Mopsus* not alone divin'd,
Whose valour equal'd his foreseeing mind.

    Already *Caeneus*, with his conquering hand,
Had slaughter'd five the boldest of their band.
Pyrachmus, Helymus, Antimachus,
Bromus the brave, and stronger *Stiphelus,*
Their names I number'd, and remember well,
No trace remaining, by what wounds they fell.

    Laitreus, the bulki'st of the double race,
Whom the spoil'd arms of slain *Halesus* grace,
In years retaining still his youthful might,
Though his black hairs were interspers'd with white,
Betwixt th' imbattled ranks began to prance,
Proud of his helm, and *Macedonian* lance;
And rode the ring around; that either hoast
Might hear him, while he made this empty boast:
And from a strumpet shall we suffer shame?
For *Caenis* still, not *Caeneus*, is thy name:
And still the native softness of thy kind
Prevails; and leaves the woman in thy mind;
Remember what thou wert; what price was paid
To change thy sex; to make thee not a maid:

And but a man in shew; go, card and spin;
And leave the business of the war to men.

  While thus the boaster exercis'd his pride,
The fatal spear of *Caeneus* reach'd his side:
Just in the mixture of the kinds it ran;
Betwixt the neather beast, and upper man:
The monster mad with rage, and stung with smart,
His lance directed at the hero's heart:
It struck; but bounded from his harden'd breast,
Like hail from tiles, which the safe house invest.
Nor seem'd the stroke with more effect to come,
Than a small pebble falling on a drum.
He next his fauchion try'd, in closer fight;
But the keen fauchion had no pow'r to bite.
He thrust; the blunted point return'd again:
Since downright blows, he cry'd, and thrusts are vain,
I'll prove his side; in strong embraces held
He prov'd his side; his side the sword repell'd:
His hollow belly eccho'd to the stroke,
Untouch'd his body, as a solid rock;
Aim'd at his neck at last, the blade in shivers broke.

  Th' impassive knight stood idle, to deride
His rage, and offer'd oft his naked side;
At length, Now monster, in thy turn, he cry'd,
Try thou the strength of *Caeneus*: at the word
He thrust; and in his shoulder plung'd the sword.
Then writh'd his hand; and as he drove it down,
Deep in his breast, made many wounds in one.

  The centaurs saw, inrag'd, th' unhop'd success;
And rushing on in crowds, together press;
At him, and him alone, their darts they threw:
Repuls'd they from his fated body flew.
Amaz'd they stood; 'till *Monichus* began,
O shame, a nation conquer'd by a man!
A woman-man! yet more a man is he,

Than all our race; and what he was, are we.
Now, what avail our nerves? th' united force,
Of two the strongest creatures, man and horse;
Nor Goddess-born; nor of *Ixion's* seed
We seem (a lover built for *Juno's* bed);
Master'd by this half man. Whole mountains throw
With woods at once, and bury him below.
This only way remains. Nor need we doubt
To choak the soul within; though not to force it out:
Heap weights, instead of wounds. He chanc'd to see
Where southern storms had rooted up a tree;
This, rais'd from Earth, against the foe he threw;
Th' example shewn, his fellow-brutes pursue.
With forest-loads the warrior they invade;
Othrys, and *Pelion* soon were void of shade;
And spreading groves were naked mountains made.
Press'd with the burden, *Caeneus* pants for breath;
And on his shoulders bears the wooden death.
To heave th' intolerable weight he tries;
At length it rose above his mouth and eyes:
Yet still he heaves; and, strugling with despair,
Shakes all aside, and gains a gulp of air:
A short relief, which but prolongs his pain;
He faints by fits; and then respires again:
At last, the burden only nods above,
As when an earthquake stirs th' *Idaean* grove.
Doubtful his death: he suffocated seem'd,
To most; but otherwise our *Mopsus* deem'd,
Who said he saw a yellow bird arise
From out the piles, and cleave the liquid skies:
I saw it too, with golden feathers bright;
Nor e'er before beheld so strange a sight.
Whom *Mopsus* viewing, as it soar'd around
Our troop, and heard the pinions' rattling sound,
All hail, he cry'd, thy country's grace and love!

Once first of men below, now first of birds above.
Its author to the story gave belief:
For us, our courage was increas'd by grief:
Asham'd to see a single man, pursu'd
With odds, to sink beneath a multitude,
We push'd the foe: and forc'd to shameful flight,
Part fell, and part escap'd by favour of the night.

This tale, by *Nestor* told, did much displease
Tlepolemus, the seed of *Hercules*:
For, often he had heard his father say,
That he himself was present at the fray;
And more than shar'd the glories of the day.

Old Chronicle, he said, among the rest,
You might have nam'd *Alcides* at the least:
Is he not worth your praise? The *Pylian* prince
Sigh'd ere he spoke; then made this proud defence.
My former woes in long oblivion drown'd,
I wou'd have lost; but you renew the wound:
Better to pass him o'er, than to relate
The cause I have your mighty sire to hate.
His fame has fill'd the world, and reach'd the sky
(Which, oh, I wish, with truth, I cou'd deny!);
We praise not *Hector*; though his name, we know,
Is great in arms; 'tis hard to praise a foe.

He, your great father, levell'd to the ground
Messenia's tow'rs: nor better fortune found
Elis, and *Pylos*; that a neighb'ring state,
And this my own: both guiltless of their fate.

To pass the rest, twelve, wanting one, he slew;
My brethren, who their birth from *Neleus* drew,
All youths of early promise, had they liv'd;
By him they perish'd: I alone surviv'd.
The rest were easie conquest: but the fate
Of *Periclymenos*, is wondrous to relate.
To him, our common grandsire of the main

Had giv'n to change his form, and chang'd, resume again.
Vary'd at pleasure, every shape he try'd;
And in all beasts, *Alcides* still defy'd:
Vanquish'd on Earth, at length he soar'd above;
Chang'd to the bird, that bears the bolt of *Jove*:
The new-dissembled eagle, now endu'd
With beak, and pounces, *Hercules* pursu'd,
And cuff'd his manly cheeks, and tore his face;
Then, safe retir'd, and tour'd in empty space.
Alcides bore not long his flying foe;
But bending his inevitable bow,
Reach'd him in air, suspended as he stood;
And in his pinion fix'd the feather'd wood.
Light was the wound; but in the sinew hung
The point, and his disabled wing unstrung.
He wheel'd in air, and stretch'd his vans in vain;
His vans no longer cou'd his flight sustain:
For while one gather'd wind, one unsupply'd
Hung drooping down, nor pois'd his other side.
He fell: the shaft that slightly was impress'd,
Now from his heavy fall with weight increas'd,
Drove through his neck, aslant, he spurns the ground,
And the soul issues through the weapon's wound.

Now, brave commander of the *Rhodian* seas,
What praise is due from me, to *Hercules*?
Silence is all the vengeance I decree
For my slain brothers; but 'tis peace with thee.

Thus with a flowing tongue old *Nestor* spoke:
Then, to full bowls each other they provoke:
At length, with weariness, and wine oppress'd,
They rise from table; and withdraw to rest.

The sire of *Cygnus*, monarch of the main,
Mean-time, laments his son, in battel slain,
And vows the victor's death; nor vows in vain.
For nine long years the smother'd pain he bore

(*Achilles* was not ripe for Fate before):
Then when he saw the promis'd hour was near,
He thus bespoke the God, that guides the year:
Immortal offspring of my brother *Jove*;
My brightest nephew, and whom best I love,
Whose hands were join'd with mine, to raise the wall
Of tott'ring *Troy*, now nodding to her fall,
Dost thou not mourn our pow'r employ'd in vain;
And the defenders of our city slain?
To pass the rest, could noble *Hector* lie
Unpity'd, drag'd around his native *Troy*?
And yet the murd'rer lives: himself by far
A greater plague, than all the wasteful war:
He lives; the proud *Pelides* lives, to boast
Our town destroy'd, our common labour lost.
O, could I meet him! But I wish too late:
To prove my trident is not in his Fate!
But let him try (for that's allow'd) thy dart,
And pierce his only penetrable part.

    Apollo bows to the superior throne;
And to his uncle's anger, adds his own.
Then in a cloud involv'd, he takes his flight,
Where *Greeks*, and *Trojans* mix'd in mortal fight;
And found out *Paris*, lurking where he stood,
And stain'd his arrows with plebeian blood:
Phoebus to him alone the God confess'd,
Then to the recreant knight, he thus address'd.
Dost thou not blush, to spend thy shafts in vain
On a degenerate, and ignoble train?
If fame, or better vengeance be thy care,
There aim: and, with one arrow, end the war.

    He said; and shew'd from far the blazing shield
And sword, which, but *Achilles*, none cou'd wield;
And how he mov'd a God, and mow'd the standing field.
The deity himself directs aright

Th' invenom'd shaft; and wings the fatal flight.
   Thus fell the foremost of the *Grecian* name;
And he, the base adult'rer, boasts the fame.
A spectacle to glad the *Trojan* train;
And please old *Priam*, after *Hector* slain.
If by a female hand he had foreseen
He was to die, his wish had rather been
The lance, and double ax of the fair warriour queen.
And now the terror of the *Trojan* field,
The *Grecian* honour, ornament, and shield,
High on a pile, th' unconquer'd chief is plac'd,
The God that arm'd him first, consum'd at last.
Of all the mighty man, the small remains
A little urn, and scarcely fill'd, contains.
Yet great in *Homer*, still *Achilles* lives;
And equal to himself, himself survives.

   His buckler owns its former lord; and brings
New cause of strife, betwixt contending kings;
Who worthi'st after him, his sword to wield,
Or wear his armour, or sustain his shield.
Ev'n *Diomede* sat mute, with down-cast eyes;
Conscious of wanted worth to win the prize:
Nor *Menelaus* presum'd these arms to claim,
Nor he the king of men, a greater name.
Two rivals only rose: *Laertes'* son,
And the vast bulk of *Ajax Telamon*:
The king, who cherish'd each with equal love,
And from himself all envy wou'd remove,
Left both to be determin'd by the laws;
And to the *Graecian* chiefs transferr'd the cause.

The End of the Twelfth Book.

BOOK THE THIRTEENTH

THE chiefs were set; the soldiers crown'd the field:
To these the master of the seven-fold shield
Upstarted fierce: and kindled with disdain.
Eager to speak, unable to contain
His boiling rage, he rowl'd his eyes around
The shore, and *Graecian* gallies hall'd a-ground.
Then stretching out his hands, O *Jove*, he cry'd,
Must then our cause before the fleet be try'd?
And dares *Ulysses* for the prize contend,
In sight of what he durst not once defend?
But basely fled that memorable day,
When I from *Hector's* hands redeem'd the flaming prey.
So much 'tis safer at the noisie bar
With words to flourish, than ingage in war.
By diff'rent methods we maintain our right,
Nor am I made to talk, nor he to fight.
In bloody fields I labour to be great;
His arms are a smooth tongue, and soft deceit:
Nor need I speak my deeds, for those you see,
The sun, and day are witnesses for me.
Let him who fights unseen, relate his own,
And vouch the silent stars, and conscious moon.
Great is the prize demanded, I confess,
But such an abject rival makes it less;
That gift, those honours, he but hop'd to gain,
Can leave no room for *Ajax* to be vain:
Losing he wins, because his name will be
Ennobled by defeat, who durst contend with me.
Were my known valour question'd, yet my blood
Without that plea wou'd make my title good:
My sire was *Telamon*, whose arms, employ'd
With *Hercules*, these *Trojan* walls destroy'd;
And who before with *Jason* sent from *Greece*,
In the first ship brought home the golden fleece.

Great *Telamon* from *Aeacus* derives
His birth (th' inquisitor of guilty lives
In shades below; where *Sisyphus*, whose son
This thief is thought, rouls up the restless heavy stone),
Just *Aeacus*, the king of Gods above
Begot: thus *Ajax* is the third from *Jove*.
Nor shou'd I seek advantage from my line,
Unless (*Achilles*) it was mix'd with thine:
As next of kin, *Achilles'* arms I claim;
This fellow wou'd ingraft a foreign name
Upon our stock, and the *Sisyphian* seed
By fraud, and theft asserts his father's breed:
Then must I lose these arms, because I came
To fight uncall'd, a voluntary name,
Nor shunn'd the cause, but offer'd you my aid?
While he long lurking was to war betray'd:
Forc'd to the field he came, but in the reer;
And feign'd distraction to conceal his fear:
'Till one more cunning caught him in the snare
(Ill for himself); and dragg'd him into war.
Now let a hero's arms a coward vest,
And he who shunn'd all honours, gain the best:
And let me stand excluded from my right,
Robb'd of my kinsman's arms, who first appear'd in fight,
Better for us, at home had he remain'd,
Had it been true the madness which he feign'd,
Or so believ'd; the less had been our shame,
The less his counsell'd crime, which brands the *Grecian*
Nor *Philoctetes* had been left inclos'd   [name;
In a bare isle, to wants and pains expos'd,
Where to the rocks, with solitary groans,
His suff'rings, and our baseness he bemoans:
And wishes (so may Heav'n his wish fulfill)
The due reward to him, who caus'd his ill.
Now he, with us to *Troy's* destruction sworn,

Our brother of the war, by whom are born
Alcides' arrows, pent in narrow bounds,
With cold and hunger pinch'd, and pain'd with wounds,
To find him food and cloathing, must employ
Against the birds the shafts due to the fate of *Troy*.
Yet still he lives, and lives from treason free,
Because he left *Ulysses'* company;
Poor *Palamede* might wish, so void of aid,
Rather to have been left, than so to death betray'd.
The coward bore the man immortal spight,
Who sham'd him out of madness into fight:
Nor daring otherwise to vent his hate,
Accus'd him first of treason to the state;
And then for proof produc'd the golden store,
Himself had hidden in his tent before:
Thus of two champions he depriv'd our host,
By exile one, and one by treason lost.
Thus fights *Ulysses*, thus his fame extends,
A formidable man, but to his friends:
Great, for what greatness is in words, and sound,
Ev'n faithful *Nestor* less in both is found:
But that he might without a rival reign,
He left this faithful *Nestor* on the plain;
Forsook his friend ev'n at his utmost need,
Who tir'd, and tardy with his wounded steed,
Cry'd out for aid, and call'd him by his name;
But cowardice has neither ears nor shame;
Thus fled the good old man, bereft of aid,
And, for as much as lay in him, betray'd:
That this is not a fable forg'd by me,
Like one of his, an *Ulyssean* lie,
I vouch ev'n *Diomede*, who tho' his friend,
Cannot that act excuse, much less defend:
He call'd him back aloud, and tax'd his fear;
And sure enough he heard, but durst not hear.

    The Gods with equal eyes on mortal look,
He justly was forsaken, who forsook:
Wanted that succour, he refus'd to lend,
Found ev'ry fellow such another friend:
No wonder, if he roar'd that all might hear;
His elocution was increas'd by fear:
I heard, I ran, I found him out of breath,
Pale, trembling, and half dead with fear of death.
Though he had judg'd himself by his own laws,
And stood condemn'd, I help'd the common cause:
With my broad buckler hid him from the foe
(Ev'n the shield trembled as he lay below);
And from impending Fate the coward freed:
Good Heav'n forgive me for so bad a deed!
If still he will persist, and urge the strife,
First let him give me back his forfeit life:
Let him return to that opprobrious field;
Again creep under my protecting shield:
Let him lie wounded, let the foe be near,
And let his quiv'ring heart confess his fear;
There put him in the very jaws of Fate;
And let him plead his cause in that estate:
And yet when snatch'd from death, when from below
My lifted shield I loos'd, and let him go;
Good Heav'ns, how light he rose, with what a bound
He sprung from earth, forgetful of his wound;
How fresh, how eager then his feet to ply;
Who had not strength to stand, had speed to fly!
    Hector came on, and brought the Gods along;
Fear seiz'd alike the feeble, and the strong:
Each *Greek* was an *Ulysses*; such a dread
Th' approach, and ev'n the sound of *Hector* bred:
Him, flesh'd with slaughter, and with conquest crown'd,
I met, and over-turn'd him to the ground;
When after, matchless as he deem'd in might,

He challeng'd all our host to single fight;
All eyes were fix'd on me: the lots were thrown;
But for your champion I was wish'd alone:
Your vows were heard; we fought, and neither yield;
Yet I return'd unvanquish'd from the field.
With *Jove* to friend, th' insulting *Trojan* came,
And menac'd us with force, our fleet with flame.
Was it the strength of this tongue-valiant lord,
In that black hour, that sav'd you from the sword?
Or was my breast expos'd alone, to brave
A thousand swords, a thousand ships to save?
The hopes of your return! And can you yield,
For a sav'd fleet, less than a single shield?
Think it no boast, o *Grecians*, if I deem
These arms want *Ajax*, more than *Ajax* them:
Or, I with them an equal honour share;
They honour'd to be worn, and I to wear.
Will he compare my courage with his sleight?
As well he may compare the day with night.
Night is indeed the province of his reign:
Yet all his dark exploits no more contain
Than a spy taken, and a sleeper slain;
A priest made pris'ner, *Pallas* made a prey:
But none of all these actions done by day:
Nor ought of these was done, and *Diomede* away.
If on such petty merits you confer
So vast a prize, let each his portion share;
Make a just dividend; and if not all,
The greater part to *Diomede* will fall.
But why for *Ithacus* such arms as those,
Who naked, and by night invades his foes?
The glitt'ring helm by moonlight will proclaim
The latent robber, and prevent his game:
Nor cou'd he hold his tott'ring head upright
Beneath that motion, or sustain the weight;

Nor that right arm cou'd toss the beamy lance;
Much less the left that ampler shield advance;
Pond'rous with precious weight, and rough with cost
Of the round world in rising gold emboss'd.
That orb would ill become his hand to wield,
And look as for the gold he stole the shield;
Which, shou'd your error on the wretch bestow,
It would not frighten, but allure the foe:
Why asks he, what avails him not in fight,
And wou'd but cumber, and retard his flight,
In which his only excellence is plac'd?
You give him death, that intercept his haste.
Add, that his own is yet a maiden-shield,
Nor the least dint has suffer'd in the field,
Guiltless of fight: mine batter'd, hew'd, and bor'd,
Worn out of service, must forsake his lord,
What farther need of words our right to scan?
My arguments are deeds, let action speak the man.
Since from a champion's arms the strife arose,
Go cast the glorious prize amid the foes;
Then send us to redeem both arms, and shield,
And let him wear, who wins 'em in the field.

He said: a murmur from a multitude,
Or somewhat like a stifled shout, ensu'd:
'Till from his seat arose *Laertes'* son,
Look'd down a while, and paus'd, e'er he begun;
Then, to th' expecting audience, rais'd his look,
And not without prepar'd attention spoke:
Soft was his tone, and sober was his face;
Action his words, and words his action grace.

If Heav'n, my lords, had heard our common pray'r,
These arms had caus'd no quarrel for an heir;
Still great *Achilles* had his own possess'd,
And we with great *Achilles* had been bless'd;
But since hard Fate, and Heav'n's severe decree,

Have ravish'd him away from you, and me
(At this he sigh'd, and wip'd his eyes, and drew,
Or seem'd to draw, some drops of kindly dew),
Who better can succeed *Achilles* lost,
Than he, who gave *Achilles* to your hoast?
This only I request, that neither he
May gain, by being what he seems to be,
A stupid thing; nor I may lose the prize,
By having sense, which Heav'n to him denies:
Since great or small, the talent I enjoy'd
Was ever in the common cause employ'd;
Nor let my wit, and wonted eloquence,
Which often has been us'd in your defense,
And in my own, this only time be brought
To bear against my self, and deem'd a fault.
Make not a crime, where Nature made it none;
For ev'ry man may freely use his own.
The deeds of long-descended ancestors
Are but by grace of imputation ours,
Theirs in effect; but since he draws his line
From *Jove*, and seems to plead a right divine;
From *Jove*, like him, I claim my pedigree,
And am descended in the same degree:
My sire *Laertes* was *Arcesius'* heir,
Arcesius was the son of *Jupiter*:
No parricide, no banish'd man, is known
In all my line: let him excuse his own.
Hermes ennobles too my mother's side,
By both my parents to the Gods ally'd.
But not because that on the female part
My blood is better, dare I claim desert,
Or that my sire from parricide is free;
But judge by merit betwixt him, and me:
The prize be to the best; provided yet
That *Ajax* for a while his kin forget,

And his great sire, and greater uncle's name,
To fortifie by them his feeble claim:
Be kindred and relation laid aside,
And honour's cause by laws of honour try'd:
For if he plead proximity of blood;
That empty title is with ease withstood.
Peleus, the hero's sire, more nigh than he,
And *Pyrrhus*, his undoubted progeny,
Inherit first these trophies of the field;
To *Scyros*, or to *Pthia*, send the shield:
And *Teucer* has an uncle's right; yet he
Waves his pretensions, nor contends with me.

  Then since the cause on pure desert is plac'd,
Whence shall I take my rise, what reckon last?
I not presume on ev'ry act to dwell,
But take these few, in order as they fell.

  Thetis, who knew the Fates, apply'd her care
To keep *Achilles* in disguise from war;
And 'till the threatning influence was past,
A woman's habit on the hero cast:
All eyes were cozen'd by the borrow'd vest,
And *Ajax* (never wiser than the rest)
Found no *Pelides* there: at length I came
With proffer'd wares to this pretended dame;
She, not discover'd by her mien, or voice,
Betray'd her manhood by her manly choice;
And while on female toys her fellows look,
Grasp'd in her warlike hand, a javelin shook;
Whom, by this act reveal'd, I thus bespoke:
O Goddess-born! resist not Heav'n's decree,
The fall of *Ilium* is reserv'd for thee;
Then seiz'd him, and produc'd in open light,
Sent blushing to the field the fatal knight.
Mine then are all his actions of the war;
Great *Telephus* was conquer'd by my spear,

And after cur'd: to me the *Thebans* owe,
Lesbos, and *Tenedos*, their overthrow;
Syros and *Cylla*: not on all to dwell,
By me *Lyrnesus*, and strong *Chrysa* fell:
And since I sent the man who *Hector* slew,
To me the noble *Hector's* death is due:
Those arms I put into his living hand,
Those arms, *Pelides* dead, I now demand.

   When *Greece* was injur'd in the *Spartan* prince,
And met at *Aulis* to avenge th' offence,
'Twas a dead calm, or adverse blasts, that reign'd,
And in the port the wind-bound fleet detain'd:
Bad signs were seen, and oracles severe
Were daily thunder'd in our gen'ral's ear;
That by his daughter's blood we must appease
Diana's kindled wrath, and free the seas.
Affection, int'rest, fame, his heart assail'd:
But soon the father o'er the king prevail'd:
Bold, on himself he took the pious crime,
As angry with the Gods, as they with him.
No subject cou'd sustain their sov'reign's look,
'Till this hard enterprize I undertook:
I only durst th' imperial pow'r controul,
And undermin'd the parent in his soul;
Forc'd him t' exert the king for common good,
And pay our ransom with his daughter's blood.
Never was cause more difficult to plead,
Than where the judge against himself decreed:
Yet this I won by dint of argument;
The wrongs his injur'd brother underwent,
And his own office, sham'd him to consent.

   'Tis harder yet to move the mother's mind,
And to this heavy task was I design'd:
Reasons against her love I knew were vain;
I circumvented whom I could not gain:

Had *Ajax* been employ'd, our slacken'd sails
Had still at *Aulis* waited happy gales.

    Arriv'd at *Troy*, your choice was fix'd on me,
A fearless envoy, fit for a bold embassy:
Secure, I enter'd through the hostile court,
Glitt'ring with steel, and crowded with resort:
There, in the midst of arms, I plead our cause,
Urge the foul rape, and violated laws;
Accuse the foes, as authors of the strife,
Reproach the ravisher, demand the wife.
Priam, *Antenor*, and the wiser few,
I mov'd; but *Paris*, and his lawless crew
Scarce held their hands, and lifted swords; but stood
In act to quench their impious thirst of blood:
This *Menelaus* knows; expos'd to share
With me the rough preludium of the war.

    Endless it were to tell, what I have done,
In arms, or council, since the siege begun:
The first encounter's past, the foe repell'd,
They skulk'd within the town, we kept the field.
War seem'd asleep for nine long years; at length
Both sides resolv'd to push, we try'd our strength.
Now what did *Ajax*, while our arms took breath,
Vers'd only in the gross mechanick trade of death?
If you require my deeds, with ambush'd arms
I trapp'd the foe, or tir'd with false alarms;
Secur'd the ships, drew lines along the plain,
The fainting chear'd, chastis'd the rebel-train,
Provided forage, our spent arms renew'd;
Employ'd at home, or sent abroad, the common cause

    The king, deluded in a dream by *Jove*,   [pursu'd.
Despair'd to take the town, and order'd to remove.
What subject durst arraign the Pow'r supream,
Producing *Jove* to justifie his dream?
Ajax might wish the soldiers to retain

From shameful flight, but wishes were in vain:
As wanting of effect had been his words,
Such as of course his thundring tongue affords.
But did this boaster threaten, did he pray,
Or by his own example urge their stay?
None, none of these: but ran himself away.
I saw him run, and was asham'd to see;
Who ply'd his feet so fast to get aboard, as he?
Then speeding through the place, I made a stand,
And loudly cry'd, O base degenerate band,
To leave a town already in your hand!
After so long expence of blood, for fame,
To bring home nothing, but perpetual shame!
These words, or what I have forgotten since
(For grief inspir'd me then with eloquence),
Reduc'd their minds; they leave the crowded port,
And to their late forsaken camp resort:
Dismay'd the council met: this man was there,
But mute, and not recover'd of his fear:
Thersites tax'd the king, and loudly rail'd,
But his wide opening mouth with blows I seal'd.
Then, rising, I excite their souls to fame,
And kindle sleeping virtue into flame.
From thence, whatever he perform'd in fight
Is justly mine, who drew him back from flight.

Which of the *Grecian* chiefs consorts with thee?
But *Diomede* desires my company,
And still communicates his praise with me.
As guided by a God, secure he goes,
Arm'd with my fellowship, amid the foes:
And sure no little merit I may boast,
Whom such a man selects from such an hoast;
Unforc'd by lots I went without affright,
To dare with him the dangers of the night:
On the same errand sent, we met the spy

Of *Hector*, double-tongu'd, and us'd to lie;
Him I dispatch'd, but not 'till undermin'd,
I drew him first to tell, what treach'rous *Troy* design'd:
My task perform'd, with praise I had retir'd,
But not content with this, to greater praise aspir'd:
Invaded *Rhesus*, and his *Thracian* crew,
And him, and his, in their own strength I slew;
Return'd a victor, all my vows compleat,
With the king's chariot, in his royal seat:
Refuse me now his arms, whose fiery steeds
Were promis'd to the spy for his nocturnal deeds:
Yet let dull *Ajax* bear away my right,
When all his days out-balance this one night.

  Nor fought I darkling still: the sun beheld
With slaughter'd *Lycians* when I strew'd the field:
You saw, and counted as I pass'd along,
Alastor, *Chromius*, *Ceranos* the strong,
Alcander, *Prytanis*, and *Halius*,
Noemon, *Charopes*, and *Ennomus*;
Coon, *Chersidamas*; and five beside,
Men of obscure descent, but courage try'd:
All these this hand laid breathless on the ground;
Nor want I proofs of many a manly wound:
All honest, all before: believe not me;
Words may deceive, but credit what you see.

  At this he bar'd his breast, and show'd his scars,
As of a furrow'd field, well plow'd with wars;
Nor is this part unexercis'd, said he;
That gyant-bulk of his from wounds is free:
Safe in his shield he fears no foe to try,
And better manages his blood, than I:
But this avails me not; our boaster strove
Not with our foes alone, but partial *Jove*,
To save the fleet: this I confess is true
(Nor will I take from any man his due):

But thus assuming all, he robs from you.
Some part of honour to your share will fall,
He did the best indeed, but did not all.
Patroclus in *Achilles'* arms, and thought
The chief he seem'd, with equal ardour fought;
Preserv'd the fleet, repell'd the raging fire,
And forc'd the fearful *Trojans* to retire.

But *Ajax* boasts, that he was only thought
A match for *Hector*, who the combat sought:
Sure he forgets the king, the chiefs, and me:
All were as eager for the fight, as he:
He but the ninth, and not by publick voice,
Or ours preferr'd, was only Fortune's choice:
They fought; nor can our hero boast th' event,
For *Hector* from the field unwounded went.

Why am I forc'd to name that fatal day,
That snatch'd the prop and pride of *Greece* away?
I saw *Pelides* sink, with pious grief,
And ran in vain, alas! to his relief;
For the brave soul was fled: full of my friend
I rush'd amid the war, his relicks to defend:
Nor ceas'd my toil, 'till I redeem'd the prey,
And, loaded with *Achilles*, march'd away:
Those arms, which on these shoulders then I bore,
'Tis just you to these shoulders should restore.
You see I want not nerves, who cou'd sustain
The pond'rous ruins of so great a man:
Or if in others equal force you find,
None is endu'd with a more grateful mind.

Did *Thetis* then, ambitious in her care,
These arms thus labour'd for her son prepare;
That *Ajax* after him the heav'nly gift shou'd wear!
For that dull soul to stare with stupid eyes,
On the learn'd unintelligible prize!
What are to him the sculptures of the shield,

Heav'n's planets, Earth, and Ocean's watry field?
The *Pleiads*, *Hyads*; less, and greater *Bear*,
Undipp'd in seas; *Orion's* angry star;
Two diff'ring cities, grav'd on either hand;
Would he wear arms he cannot understand?

    Beside, what wise objections he prepares
Against my late accession to the wars?
Does not the fool perceive his argument
Is with more force against *Achilles* bent?
For if dissembling be so great a crime,
The fault is common, and the same in him:
And if he taxes both of long delay,
My guilt is less, who sooner came away.
His pious mother, anxious for his life,
Detain'd her son; and me, my pious wife.
To them the blossoms of our youth were due,
Our riper manhood we reserv'd for you.
But grant me guilty, 'tis not much my care,
When with so great a man my guilt I share:
My wit to war the matchless hero brought,
But by this fool I never had been caught.

    Nor need I wonder, that on me he threw
Such foul aspersions, when he spares not you:
If *Palamede* unjustly fell by me,
Your honour suffer'd in th' unjust decree:
I but accus'd, you doom'd: and yet he dy'd,
Convinc'd of treason, and was fairly try'd:
You heard not he was false; your eyes beheld
The traytor manifest; the bribe reveal'd.

    That *Philoctetes* is on *Lemnos* left,
Wounded, forlorn, of human aid bereft,
Is not my crime, or not my crime alone;
Defend your justice, for the fact's your own:
'Tis true, th' advice was mine; that staying there
He might his weary limbs with rest repair,

From a long voyage free, and from a longer war.
He took the counsl, and he lives at least;
Th' event declares I counsell'd for the best:
Though faith is all in ministers of state;
For who can promise to be fortunate?
Now since his arrows are the Fate of *Troy*,
Do not my wit, or weak address, employ;
Send *Ajax* there, with his persuasive sense,
To mollifie the man, and draw him thence:
But *Xanthus* shall run backward; *Ida* stand
A leafless mountain; and the *Grecian* band
Shall fight for *Troy*; if, when my councils fail,
The wit of heavy *Ajax* can prevail.

   Hard *Philoctetes*, exercise thy spleen
Against thy fellows, and the king of men;
Curse my devoted head, above the rest,
And wish in arms to meet me breast to breast:
Yet I the dang'rous task will undertake,
And either die my self, or bring thee back.

   Nor doubt the same success, as when before
The *Phrygian* prophet to these tents I bore,
Surpriz'd by night, and forc'd him to declare
In what was plac'd the fortune of the war,
Heav'n's dark decrees, and answers to display,
And how to take the town, and where the secret lay:
Yet this I compass'd, and from *Troy* convey'd
The fatal image of their guardian-maid;
That work was mine; for *Pallas*, though our friend,
Yet while she was in *Troy*, did *Troy* defend.
Now what has *Ajax* done, or what design'd?
A noisie nothing, and an empty wind.
If he be what he promises in show,
Why was I sent, and why fear'd he to go?
Our boasting champion thought the task not light
To pass the guards, commit himself to night;

Not only through a hostile town to pass,
But scale, with steep ascent, the sacred place;
With wand'ring steps to search the cittadel,
And from the priests their patroness to steal:
Then through surrounding foes to force my way,
And bear in triumph home the heavn'ly prey;
Which had I not, *Ajax* in vain had held,
Before that monst'rous bulk, his sev'nfold shield.
That night to conquer *Troy* I might be said,
When *Troy* was liable to conquest made.

Why point'st thou to my partner of the war?
Tydides had indeed a worthy share
In all my toil, and praise; but when thy might
Our ships protected, did'st thou singly fight?
All join'd, and thou of many wert but one;
I ask'd no friend, nor had, but him alone:
Who, had he not been well assur'd, that art,
And conduct were of war the better part,
And more avail'd than strength, my valiant friend
Had urg'd a better right, than *Ajax* can pretend:
As good at least *Eurypilus* may claim,
And the more mod'rate *Ajax* of the name:
The *Cretan* king, and his brave charioteer,
And *Menelaus* bold with sword, and spear:
All these had been my rivals in the shield,
And yet all these to my pretensions yield.
Thy boist'rous hands are then of use, when I
With this directing head those hands apply.
Brawn without brain is thine: my prudent care
Foresees, provides, administers the war:
Thy province is to fight; but when shall be
The time to fight, the king consults with me:
No dram of judgment with thy force is join'd:
Thy body is of profit, and my mind.
By how much more the ship her safety owes

To him who steers, than him that only rows;
By how much more the captain merits praise,
Than he who fights, and fighting but obeys;
By so much greater is my worth than thine,
Who canst but execute, what I design.
What gain'st thou, brutal man, if I confess
Thy strength superior, when thy wit is less?
Mind is the man: I claim my whole desert,
From the mind's vigour, and th' immortal part.

But you, o *Grecian* chiefs, reward my care,
Be grateful to your watchman of the war:
For all my labours in so long a space,
Sure I may plead a title to your grace:
Enter the town, I then unbarr'd the gates,
When I remov'd their tutelary Fates.
By all our common hopes, if hopes they be
Which I have now reduc'd to certainty;
By falling *Troy*, by yonder tott'ring tow'rs,
And by their taken Gods, which now are ours;
Or if there yet a farther task remains,
To be perform'd by prudence, or by pains;
If yet some desp'rate action rests behind,
That asks high conduct, and a dauntless mind;
If ought be wanting to the *Trojan* doom,
Which none but I can manage, and o'ercome,
Award, those arms I ask, by your decree:
Or give to this, what you refuse to me.

He ceas'd: and ceasing with respect he bow'd,
And with his hand at once the fatal statue show'd.
Heav'n, air and ocean rung, with loud applause,
And by the gen'ral vote he gain'd his cause.
Thus conduct won the prize, when courage fail'd,
And eloquence o'er brutal force prevail'd.

He who cou'd often, and alone, withstand
The foe, the fire, and *Jove's* own partial hand,

Now cannot his unmaster'd grief sustain,
But yields to rage, to madness, and disdain;
Then snatching out his fauchion, Thou, said he,
Art mine; *Ulysses* lays no claim to thee.
O often try'd, and ever-trusty sword,
Now do thy last kind office to thy lord:
'Tis *Ajax* who requests thy aid, to show
None but himself, himself cou'd overthrow:
He said, and with so good a will to die,
Did to his breast the fatal point apply,
It found his heart, a way 'till then unknown,
Where never weapon enter'd, but his own.
No hands cou'd force it thence, so fix'd it stood,
'Till out it rush'd, expell'd by streams of spouting blood
The fruitful blood produc'd a flow'r, which grew
On a green stem; and of a purple hue:
Like his, whom unaware *Apollo* slew:
Inscrib'd in both, the letters are the same,
But those express the grief, and these the name.

  The victor with full sails for *Lemnos* stood
(Once stain'd by matrons with their husbands' blood),
Thence great *Alcides'* fatal shafts to bear,
Assign'd to *Philoctetes'* secret care.
These with their guardian to the *Greeks* convey'd,
Their ten years' toil with wish'd success repaid.
With *Troy* old *Priam* falls: his queen survives;
'Till all her woes compleat, transform'd she grieves
In borrow'd sounds, nor with an human face,
Barking tremendous o'er the plains of *Thrace*.
Still *Ilium's* flames their pointed columns raise,
And the red *Hellespont* reflects the blaze.
Shed on *Jove's* altar are the poor remains
Of blood, which trickl'd from old *Priam's* veins.
Cassandra lifts her hands to Heav'n in vain,
Drag'd by her sacred hair; the trembling train

Of matrons to their burning temples fly:
There to their Gods for kind protection cry;
And to their statues cling 'till forc'd away,
The victor *Greeks* bear off th' invidious prey.
From those high tow'rs *Astyanax* is thrown,
Whence he was wont with pleasure to look down.
When oft his mother with a fond delight
Pointed to view his father's rage in fight,
To win renown, and guard his country's right.

    The winds now call to sea; brisk northern gales
Sing in the shrowds, and court the spreading sails.
Farewel, dear *Troy*, the captive matrons cry;
Yes, we must leave our long-lov'd native sky.
Then prostrate on the shore they kiss the sand,
And quit the smoking ruines of the land.
Last *Hecuba* on board, sad sight! appears;
Found weeping o'er her children's sepulchres:
Drag'd by *Ulysses* from her slaughter'd sons,
Whilst yet she graspt their tombs, and kist their mouldring
Yet *Hector's* ashes from his urn she bore,   [bones.
And in her bosom the sad relique wore:
Then scatter'd on his tomb her hoary hairs,
A poor oblation mingled with her tears.

    Oppos'd to *Ilium* lye the *Thracian* plains,
Where *Polymestor* safe in plenty reigns.
King *Priam* to his care commits his son,
Young *Polydore*, the chance of war to shun.
A wise precaution! had not gold, consign'd
For the child's use, debauch'd the tyrant's mind.
When sinking *Troy* to its last period drew,
With impious hands his royal charge he slew;
Then in the sea the lifeless coarse is thrown;
As with the body he the guilt could drown.

    The *Greeks* now riding on the *Thracian* shore,
'Till kinder gales invite, their vessels moor.

Here the wide-op'ning Earth to sudden view
Disclos'd *Achilles*, great as when he drew
The vital air, but fierce with proud disdain,
As when he sought *Briseïs* to regain;
When stern debate, and rash injurious strife
Unsheath'd his sword, to reach *Atrides'* life.
And will ye go? he said. Is then the name
Of the once great *Achilles* lost to fame?
Yet stay, ungrateful *Greeks*; nor let me sue
In vain for honours to my *Manes* due.
For this just end, *Polyxena* I doom
With victim-rites to grace my slighted tomb.

    The phantom spoke; the ready *Greeks* obey'd,
And to the tomb led the devoted maid
Snatch'd from her mother, who with pious care
Cherish'd this last relief of her despair.
Superior to her sex, the fearless maid,
Approach'd the altar, and around survey'd
The cruel rites, and consecrated knife,
Which *Pyrrhus* pointed at her guiltless life,
Then as with stern amaze intent he stood,
"Now strike," she said; "now spill my genr'ous blood;
Deep in my breast, or throat, your dagger sheath,
Whilst thus I stand prepar'd to meet my death.
For life on terms of slav'ry I despise:
Yet sure no God approves this sacrifice.
O! cou'd I but conceal this dire event
From my sad mother, I should dye content.
Yet should she not with tears my death deplore,
Since her own wretched life demands them more.
But let not the rude touch of man pollute
A virgin-victim; 'tis a modest suit.
It best will please, whoe'er demands my blood,
That I untainted reach the *Stygian* flood.
Yet let one short, last, dying prayer be heard;

To *Priam's* daughter pay this last regard;
'Tis *Priam's* daughter, not a captive, sues;
Do not the rites of sepulture refuse.
To my afflicted mother, I implore,
Free without ransom my dead corpse restore:
Nor barter me for gain, when I am cold;
But be her tears the price, if I am sold:
Time was she could have ransom'd me with gold".

   Thus as she pray'd, one common shower of tears
Burst forth, and stream'd from ev'ry eye but hers.
Ev'n the priest wept, and with a rude remorse
Plung'd in her heart the steel's resistless force.
Her slacken'd limbs sunk gently to the ground,
Dauntless her looks, unalter'd by the wound.
And as she fell, she strove with decent pride
To hide, what suits a virgin's care to hide.
The *Trojan* matrons the pale corpse receive,
And the whole slaughter'd race of *Priam* grieve,
Sad they recount the long disastrous tale;
Then with fresh tears, thee, royal maid, bewail;
Thy widow'd mother too, who flourish'd late
The royal pride of *Asia's* happier state:
A captive lot now to *Ulysses* born;
Whom yet the victor would reject with scorn,
Were she not *Hector's* mother: *Hector's* fame
Scarce can a master for his mother claim!
With strict embrace the lifeless coarse she view'd;
And her fresh grief that flood of tears renew'd,
With which she lately mourn'd so many dead;
Tears for her country, sons, and husband shed.
With the thick gushing stream she bath'd the wound;
Kiss'd her pale lips; then weltring on the ground,
With wonted rage her frantick bosom tore;
Sweeping her hair amidst the clotted gore;
Whilst her sad accents thus her loss deplore.

"Behold a mother's last dear pledge of woe!
Yes, 'tis the last I have to suffer now.
Thou, my *Polyxena*, my ills must crown:
Already in thy Fate, I feel my own.
'Tis thus, lest haply of my numerous seed
One should unslaughter'd fall, even thou must bleed:
And yet I hop'd thy sex had been thy guard;
But neither has thy tender sex been spar'd.
The same *Achilles*, by whose deadly hate
Thy brothers fell, urg'd thy untimely fate!
The same *Achilles*, whose destructive rage
Laid waste my realms, has robb'd my childless age.
When *Paris'* shafts with *Phoebus'* certain aid
At length had pierc'd this dreaded chief, I said,
Secure of future ills, he can no more:
But see, he still pursues me as before.
With rage rekindled his dead ashes burn;
And his yet murd'ring ghost my wretched house must
This tyrant's lust of slaughter I have fed   [mourn.
With large supplies from my too-fruitful bed.
Troy's tow'rs lye waste; and the wide ruin ends
The publick woe; but me fresh woe attends.
Troy still survives to me; to none but me;
And from its ills I never must be free.
I, who so late had power, and wealth, and ease,
Bless'd with my husband, and a large encrease,
Must now in poverty an exile mourn;
Ev'n from the tombs of my dead offspring torn:
Giv'n to *Penelope*, who proud of spoil,
Allots me to the loom's ungrateful toil;
Points to her dames, and crys with scorning mien:
See *Hector's* mother, and great *Priam's* queen!
And thou, my child, sole hope of all that's lost,
Thou now art slain, to sooth this hostile ghost.
Yes, my child falls an offering to my foe!

Then what am I, who still survive this woe?
Say, cruel Gods! for what new scenes of death
Must a poor aged wretch prolong this hated breath?
Troy fal'n, to whom could *Priam* happy seem?
Yet was he so; and happy must I deem
His death; for O! my child, he saw not thine,
When he his life did with his *Troy* resign.
Yet sure due obsequies thy tomb might grace;
And thou shalt sleep amidst thy kingly race.
Alas! my child, such fortune does not wait
Our suffering house in this abandon'd state.
A foreign grave, and thy poor mother's tears
Are all the honours that attend thy herse.
All now is lost! — Yet no; one comfort more
Of life remains, my much-lov'd *Polydore*.
My youngest hope: here on this coast he lives,
Nurs'd by the guardian-king, he still survives.
Then let me hasten to the cleansing flood,
And wash away these stains of guiltless blood."

   Streit to the shore her feeble steps repair
With limping pace, and torn dishevell'd hair
Silver'd with age. "Give me an urn," she cry'd,
"To bear back water from this swelling tide":
When on the banks her son in ghastly hue
Transfix'd with *Thracian* arrows strikes her view.
The matrons shriek'd; her big-swoln grief surpast
The pow'r of utterance; she stood aghast;
She had nor speech, nor tears to give relief;
Excess of woe suppress'd the rising grief.
Lifeless as stone, on Earth she fix'd her eyes;
And then look'd up to Heav'n with wild surprise.
Now she contemplates o'er with sad delight
Her son's pale visage; then her aking sight
Dwells on his wounds: she varys thus by turns,
Wild as the mother-lion, when among

The haunts of prey she seeks her ravish'd young:
Swift flies the ravisher; she marks his trace,
And by the print directs her anxious chase.
So *Hecuba* with mingled grief, and rage
Pursues the king, regardless of her age.
She greets the murd'rer with dissembled joy
Of secret treasure hoarded for her boy.
The specious tale th' unwary king betray'd.
Fir'd with the hopes of prey: "Give quick," he said
With soft enticing speech, "the promis'd store:
Whate'er you give, you give to *Polydore*.
Your son, by the immortal Gods I swear,
Shall this with all your former bounty share."
She stands attentive to his soothing lyes,
And darts avenging horrour from her eyes.
Then full resentment fires her boyling blood:
She springs upon him, 'midst the captive crowd
(Her thirst of vengeance want of strength supplies):
Fastens her forky fingers in his eyes:
Tears out the rooted balls; her rage pursues,
And in the hollow orbs her hand imbrews.

The *Thracians*, fir'd, at this inhuman scene,
With darts, and stones assail the frantick queen.
She snarls, and growls, nor in an human tone;
Then bites impatient at the bounding stone;
Extends her jaws, as she her voice would raise
To keen invectives in her wonted phrase;
But barks, and thence the yelping brute betrays.
Still a sad monument the place remains,
And from this monstrous change its name obtains:
Where she, in long remembrance of her ills,
With plaintive howlings the wide desart fills.

Greeks, *Trojans*, friends, and foes, and Gods above
Her num'rous wrongs to just compassion move.
Ev'n *Juno's* self forgets her ancient hate,

And owns, she had deserv'd a milder fate.
    Yet bright *Aurora*, partial as she was
To *Troy*, and those that lov'd the *Trojan* cause,
Nor *Troy*, nor *Hecuba* can now bemoan,
But weeps a sad misfortune, more her own.
Her offspring *Memnon*, by *Achilles* slain,
She saw extended on the *Phrygian* plain:
She saw, and strait the purple beams, that grace
The rosie morning, vanish'd from her face;
A deadly pale her wonted bloom invades,
And veils the lowring skies with mournful shades.
But when his limbs upon the pile were laid,
The last kind duty that by friends is paid,
His mother to the skies directs her flight,
Nor cou'd sustain to view the doleful sight:
But frantick, with her loose neglected hair,
Hastens to *Jove*, and falls a suppliant there.
O king of Heav'n, o father of the skies,
The weeping Goddess passionately cries,
Tho' I the meanest of immortals am,
And fewest temples celebrate my fame,
Yet still a Goddess, I presume to come
Within the verge of your etherial dome:
Yet still may plead some merit, if my light
With purple dawn controuls the Pow'rs of night;
If from a female hand that virtue springs,
Which to the Gods, and men such pleasure brings.
Yet I nor honours seek, nor rites divine,
Nor for more altars, or more fanes repine;
Oh! that such trifles were the only cause,
From whence *Aurora's* mind its anguish draws!
For *Memnon* lost, my dearest only child,
With weightier grief my heavy heart is fill'd;
My warrior son! that liv'd but half his time,
Nipt in the bud, and blasted in his prime;

Who for his uncle early took the field,
And by *Achilles'* fatal spear was kill'd.
To whom but *Jove* shou'd I for succour come?
For *Jove* alone cou'd fix his cruel doom.
O sov'reign of the Gods accept my pray'r,
Grant my request, and sooth a mother's care;
On the deceas'd some solemn boon bestow,
To expiate the loss, and ease my woe.

   Jove, with a nod, comply'd with her desire;
Around the body flam'd the fun'ral fire;
The pile decreas'd, that lately seem'd so high,
And sheets of smoak roll'd upward to the sky:
As humid vapours from a marshy bog,
Rise by degrees, condensing into fog,
That intercept the sun's enliv'ning ray,
And with a cloud infect the chearful day.
The sooty ashes wafted by the air,
Whirl round, and thicken in a body there;
Then take a form, which their own heat, and fire
With active life, and energy inspire.
Its lightness makes it seem to fly, and soon
It skims on real wings, that are its own;
A real bird, it beats the breezy wind,
Mix'd with a thousand sisters of the kind,
That, from the same formation newly sprung,
Up-born aloft on plumy pinions hung.
Thrice round the pile advanc'd the circling throng,
Thrice, with their wings, a whizzing consort rung.
In the fourth flight their squadron they divide,
Rank'd in two diff'rent troops, on either side:
Then two, and two, inspir'd with martial rage,
From either troop in equal pairs engage.
Each combatant with beak, and pounces press'd,
In wrathful ire, his adversary's breast;
Each falls a victim, to preserve the fame

Of that great hero, whence their being came.
From him their courage, and their name they take,
And, as they liv'd, they dye for *Memnon's* sake.
Punctual to time, with each revolving year,
In fresh array the champion birds appear;
Again, prepar'd with vengeful minds, they come
To bleed, in honour of the souldier's tomb.

   Therefore in others it appear'd not strange,
To grieve for *Hecuba's* unhappy change:
But poor *Aurora* had enough to do
With her own loss, to mind another's woe;
Who still in tears, her tender nature shews,
Besprinkling all the world with pearly dews.

   Troy thus destroy'd, 'twas still deny'd by Fate,
The hopes of *Troy* should perish with the state.
His sire, the son of *Cytherea* bore,
And household-Gods from burning *Ilium's* shore,
The pious prince (a double duty paid)
Each sacred burthen thro' the flames convey'd.
With young *Ascanius*, and this only prize,
Of heaps of wealth, he from *Antandros* flies;
But struck with horror, left the *Thracian* shore,
Stain'd with the blood of murder'd *Polydore*.
The *Delian* isle receives the banish'd train,
Driv'n by kind gales, and favour'd by the main.

   Here pious *Anius*, priest, and monarch reign'd,
And either charge, with equal care sustain'd,
His subjects rul'd, to *Phoebus* homage pay'd,
His God obeying, and by those obey'd.

   The priest displays his hospitable gate,
And shows the riches of his church, and state
The sacred shrubs, which eas'd *Latona's* pain,
The palm, and olive, and the votive fane.
Here grateful flames with fuming incense fed,
And mingled wine, ambrosial odours shed;

Of slaughter'd steers the crackling entrails burn'd:
And then the strangers to the court return'd.

On beds of tap'stry plac'd aloft, they dine
With *Ceres'* gift, and flowing bowls of wine;
When thus *Anchises* spoke, amidst the feast:
Say, mitred monarch, *Phoebus'* chosen priest,
Or (e'er from *Troy* by cruel Fate expell'd)
When first mine eyes these sacred walls beheld,
A son, and twice two daughters crown'd thy bliss?
Or errs my mem'ry, and I judge amiss?

The royal prophet shook his hoary head,
With snowy fillets bound, and sighing, said:
Thy mem'ry errs not, prince; thou saw'st me then,
The happy father of so large a train;
Behold me now (such turns of chance befall
The race of man!), almost bereft of all.
For (ah!) what comfort can my son bestow,
What help afford, to mitigate my woe!
While far from hence, in *Andros'* isle he reigns,
(From him so nam'd) and there my place sustains.
Him *Delius* praescience gave; the twice-born God
A boon more wond'rous on the maids bestow'd.
Whate'er they touch'd, he gave them to transmute
(A gift past credit, and above their suit)
To *Ceres*, *Bacchus*, and *Minerva's* fruit.
How great their value, and how rich their use,
Whose only touch such treasures could produce!

The dire destroyer of the *Trojan* reign,
Fierce *Agamemnon*, such a prize to gain
(A proof we also were design'd by Fate
To feel the tempest, that o'erturn'd your state),
With force superior, and a ruffian crew,
From these weak arms, the helpless virgins drew:
And sternly bad them use the grant divine,
To keep the fleet in corn, and oil, and wine.

Each, as they could, escap'd: two strove to gain
Euboea's isle, and two their brother's reign.
The soldier follows, and demands the dames;
If held by force, immediate war proclaims.
Fear conquer'd Nature in their brother's mind,
And gave them up to punishment assign'd.
Forgive the deed; nor *Hector's* arm was there,
Nor thine, *Aeneas*, to maintain the war;
Whose only force upheld your *Ilium's* tow'rs,
For ten long years, against the *Grecian* pow'rs.
Prepar'd to bind their captive arms in bands,
To Heav'n they rear'd their yet unfetter'd hands,
Help, *Bacchus*, author of the gift, they pray'd;
The gift's great author gave immediate aid;
If such destruction of their human frame
By ways so wond'rous, may deserve the name;
Nor could I hear, nor can I now relate
Exact, the manner of their alter'd state;
But this in gen'ral of my loss I knew,
Transform'd to doves, on milky plumes they flew,
Such as on *Ida's* mount thy consort's chariot drew.

   With such discourse, they entertain'd the feast;
Then rose from table, and withdrew to rest.
The following morn, ere *Sol* was seen to shine,
Th' inquiring *Trojans* sought the sacred shrine;
The mystick Pow'r commands them to explore
Their ancient mother, and a kindred shore.
Attending to the sea, the gen'rous prince
Dismiss'd his guests with rich munificence,
In old *Anchises'* hand a sceptre plac'd,
A vest, and quiver young *Ascanius* grac'd,
His sire, a cup; which from th' *Aonian* coast,
Ismenian Therses sent his royal host.
Alcon of *Mylè* made what *Therses* sent,
And carv'd thereon this ample argument.

A town with sev'n distinguish'd gates was shown,
Which spoke its name, and made the city known;
Before it, piles, and tombs, and rising flames,
The rites of death, and quires of mourning dames,
Who bar'd their breasts, and gave their hair to flow,
The signs of grief, and marks of publick woe.
Their fountains dry'd, the weeping *Naiads* mourn'd,
The trees stood bare, with searing cankers burn'd,
No herbage cloath'd the ground, a ragged flock
Of goats half-famish'd, lick'd the naked rock,
Of manly courage, and with mind serene,
Orion's daughters in the town were seen;
One heav'd her chest to meet the lifted knife,
One plung'd the poyniard thro' the seat of life,
Their country's victims, mourns the rescu'd state,
The bodies burns, and celebrates their Fate.
To save the failure of th' illustrious line,
From the pale ashes rose, of form divine,
Two gen'rous youths; these, fame *Coronae* calls,
Who join the pomp, and mourn their mother's falls.

These burnish'd figures form'd of antique mold,
Shone on the brass, with rising sculpture bold;
A wreath of gilt *Acanthus* round the brim was roll'd.

Nor less expence the *Trojan* gifts express'd;
A fuming censer for the royal priest,
A chalice, and a crown of princely cost,
With ruddy gold, ond sparkling gems emboss'd.

Now hoisting sail, to *Crete* the *Trojans* stood,
Themselves remembring sprung from *Teucer's* blood;
But Heav'n forbids, and pestilential *Jove*
From noxious skies, the wand'ring navy drove.
Her hundred cities left, from *Crete* they bore,
And sought the destin'd land, *Ausonia's* shore;
But toss'd by storms at either *Strophas* lay,
'Till scar'd by *Harpies* from the faithless bay.

Then passing onward with a prosp'rous wind,
Left sly *Ulysses*' spacious realms behind;
Ambracia's state, in former ages known.
The strife of Gods, the judge transform'd to stone
They saw; for *Actian Phoebus* since renown'd,
Who *Caesar's* arms with naval conquest crown'd;
Next pass'd *Dodona*, wont of old to boast
Her vocal forest; and *Châonia's* coast,
Where king *Molossus'* sons on wings aspir'd,
And saw secure the harmless fewel fir'd.

Now to *Phaeacia's* happy isle they came,
For fertile orchards known to early fame;
Epirus past, they next beheld with joy
A second *Ilium*, and fictitious *Troy*;
Here *Trojan Helenus* the sceptre sway'd,
Who show'd their fate and mystick truths display'd.
By him confirm'd *Sicilia's* isle they reach'd,
Whose sides to sea three promontories stretch'd,
Pachynos to the stormy south is plac'd,
On *Lilybaeum* blows the gentle west,
Peloro's cliffs the northern bear survey,
Who rolls above, and dreads to touch the sea.
By this they steer, and favour'd by the tide,
Secure by night in *Zancle's* harbour ride.

Here cruel *Scylla* guards the rocky shore,
And there the waves of loud *Charybdis* roar:
This sucks, and vomits ships, and bodies drown'd;
And rav'nous dogs the womb of that surround,
In face a virgin; and (if ought be true
By bards recorded) once a virgin too.

A train of youths in vain desir'd her bed;
By sea-nymphs lov'd, to nymphs of seas she fled;
The maid to these, with female pride, display'd
Their baffled courtship, and their love betray'd.

When *Galatea* thus bespoke the fair

(But first she sigh'd), while *Scylla* comb'd her hair:
You, lovely maid, a gen'rous race pursues,
Whom safe you may (as now you do) refuse;
To me, tho' pow'rful in a num'rous train
Of sisters, sprung from Gods, who rule the main,
My native seas could scarce a refuge prove,
To shun the fury of the *Cyclops'* love,

    Tears choak'd her utt'rance here; the pity'ng maid
With marble fingers wip'd them off, and said:

    My dearest Goddess, let thy *Scylla* know,
(For I am faithful) whence these sorrows flow.

    The maid's intreaties o'er the nymph prevail,
Who thus to *Scylla* tells the mournful tale.

    Acis, the lovely youth, whose loss I mourn,
From *Faunus*, and the nymph *Symethis* born,
Was both his parents' pleasure; but, to me
Was all that love could make a lover be.
The Gods our minds in mutual bands did join:
I was his only joy, and he was mine.
Now sixteen summers the sweet youth had seen;
And doubtful down began to shade his chin:
When *Polyphemus* first disturb'd our joy;
And lov'd me fiercely, as I lov'd the boy.
Ask not which passion in my soul was high'r,
My last aversion, or my first desire:
Nor this the greater was, nor that the less;
Both were alike, for both were in excess.
Thee, *Venus*, thee both Heav'n, and Earth obey;
Immense thy pow'r, and boundless is thy sway.
The *Cyclops*, who defy'd th' aetherial throne,
And thought no thunder louder than his own,
The terror of the woods, and wilder far
Than wolves in plains, or bears in forests are,
Th' inhuman host, who made his bloody feasts
On mangl'd members of his butcher'd guests,

Yet felt the force of love, and fierce desire,
And burnt for me, with unrelenting fire.
Forgot his caverns, and his woolly care,
Assum'd the softness of a lover's air;
And comb'd, with teeth of rakes, his rugged hair.
Now with a crooked scythe his beard he sleeks;
And mows the stubborn stubble of his cheeks:
Now in the crystal stream he looks, to try
His simagres, and rowls his glaring eye.
His cruelty, and thirst of blood are lost;
And ships securely sail along the coast.

The prophet *Telemus* (arriv'd by chance
Where *Aetna's* summets to the seas advance,
Who mark'd the tracts of every bird that flew,
And sure presages from their flying drew)
Foretold the *Cyclops*, that *Ulysses'* hand
In his broad eye shou'd thrust a flaming brand.
The giant, with a scornful grin, reply'd,
Vain augur, thou hast falsely prophesy'd;
Already love his flaming brand has tost;
Looking on two fair eyes, my sight I lost,
Thus, warn'd in vain, with stalking pace he strode,
And stamp'd the margin of the briny flood
With heavy steps; and weary, sought agen
The cool retirement of his gloomy den.

A promontory, sharp'ning by degrees,
Ends in a wedge, and overlooks the seas:
On either side, below, the water flows;
This airy walk the giant lover chose.
Here on the midst he sate; his flocks, unled,
Their shepherd follow'd, and securely fed.
A pine so burly, and of length so vast,
That sailing ships requir'd it for a mast,
He wielded for a staff, his steps to guide:
But laid it by, his whistle while he try'd.

A hundred reeds of a prodigious growth,
Scarce made a pipe, proportion'd to his mouth:
Which when he gave it wind, the rocks around,
And watry plains, the dreadful hiss resound.
I heard the ruffian-shepherd rudely blow,
Where, in a hollow cave, I sat below;
On *Acis'* bosom I my head reclin'd:
And still preserve the poem in my mind.

   Oh lovely *Galatea*, whiter far
Than falling snows, and rising lillies are;
More flowry than the meads, as chrystal bright:
Erect as alders, and of equal height:
More wanton than a kid, more sleek thy skin,
Than orient shells, that on the shores are seen,
Than apples fairer, when the boughs they lade;
Pleasing, as winter suns, or summer shade:
More grateful to the sight, than goodly plains;
And softer to the touch, than down of swans;
Or curds new turn'd; and sweeter to the taste
Than swelling grapes, that to the vintage haste:
More clear than ice, or running streams, that stray
Through garden plots, but ah! more swift than they.

   Yet, *Galatea*, harder to be broke
Than bullocks, unreclaim'd, to bear the yoke,
And far more stubborn, than the knotted oak:
Like sliding streams, impossible to hold;
Like them, fallacious, like their fountains, cold.
More warping, than the willow, to decline
My warm embrace, more brittle, than the vine;
Immovable, and fixt in thy disdain:
Tough, as these rocks, and of a harder grain.
More violent, than is the rising flood;
And the prais'd peacock is not half so proud.
Fierce, as the fire, and sharp, as thistles are,
And more outragious, than a mother-bear:

Deaf, as the billows to the vows I make;
And more revengeful, than a trodden snake.
In swiftness fleeter, than the flying hind,
Or driven tempests, or the driving wind.
All other faults, with patience I can bear;
But swiftness is the vice I only fear.

Yet if you knew me well, you wou'd not shun
My love, but to my wish'd embraces run:
Wou'd languish in your turn, and court my stay;
And much repent of your unwise delay.

My palace, in the living rock, is made
By Nature's hand; a spacious pleasing shade:
Which neither heat can pierce, nor cold invade.
My garden fill'd with fruits you may behold,
And grapes in clusters, imitating gold;
Some blushing bunches of a purple hue:
And these, and those, are all reserv'd for you.
Red strawberries, in shades, expecting stand,
Proud to be gather'd by so white a hand.
Autumnal cornels latter fruit provide;
And plumbs, to tempt you, turn their glossy side:
Not those of common kinds; but such alone,
As in *Phaeacian* orchards might have grown:
Nor chestnuts shall be wanting to your food,
Nor garden-fruits, nor wildings of the wood;
The laden boughs for you alone shall bear;
And yours shall be the product of the year.

The flocks you see, are all my own; beside
The rest that woods, and winding vallies hide;
And those that folded in the caves abide.
Ask not the numbers of my growing store;
Who knows how many, knows he has no more.
Nor will I praise my cattle; trust not me,
But judge your self, and pass your own decree:
Behold their swelling dugs; the sweepy weight

Of ewes, that sink beneath the milky freight;
In the warm folds their tender lambkins lye;
Apart from kids, that call with human cry.
New milk in nut-brown bowls is duely serv'd
For daily drink; the rest for cheese reserv'd.
Nor are these household dainties all my store:
The fields, and forests will afford us more;
The deer, the hare, the goat, the savage boar.
All sorts of ven'son; and of birds the best;
A pair of turtles taken from the nest.
I walk'd the mountains, and two cubs I found
(Whose dam had left 'em on the naked ground),
So like, that no distinction could be seen:
So pretty, they were presents for a queen;
And so they shall; I took them both away;
And keep, to be companions of your play.

  Oh raise, fair nymph, your beauteous face above
The waves; nor scorn my presents, and my love.
Come, *Galatea*, come, and view my face;
I late beheld it, in the watry glass;
And found it lovelier, than I fear'd it was.
Survey my towring stature, and my size:
Not *Jove*, the *Jove* you dream, that rules the skies,
Bears such a bulk, or is so largely spread:
My locks (the plenteous harvest of my head)
Hang o'er my manly face; and dangling down,
As with a shady grove, my shoulders crown.
Nor think, because my limbs and body bear
A thick-set underwood of bristling hair,
My shape deform'd; what fouler sight can be,
Than the bald branches of a leafless tree?
Foul is the steed without a flowing mane:
And birds, without their feathers, and their train.
Wool decks the sheep; and Man receives a grace
From bushy limbs, and from a bearded face.

My forehead with a single eye is fill'd,
Round, as a ball, and ample, as a shield.
The glorious lamp of Heav'n, the radiant sun,
Is Nature's eye; and she's content with one.
Add, that my father sways your seas, and I,
Like you, am of the watry family.
I make you his, in making you my own;
You I adore; and kneel to you alone:
Jove, with his fabled thunder, I despise,
And only fear the lightning of your eyes.
Frown not, fair nymph; yet I cou'd bear to be
Disdain'd, if others were disdain'd with me.
But to repulse the *Cyclops*, and prefer
The love of *Acis* (Heav'ns!) I cannot bear.
But let the stripling please himself; nay more,
Please you, tho' that's the thing I most abhor;
The boy shall find, if e'er we cope in fight,
These giant limbs, endu'd with giant might.
His living bowels from his belly torn,
And scatter'd limbs shall on the flood be born:
Thy flood, ungrateful nymph; and fate shall find,
That way for thee, and *Acis* to be join'd.
For oh! I burn with love, and thy disdain
Augments at once my passion, and my pain.
Translated *Aetna* flames within my heart,
And thou, inhuman, wilt not ease my smart.

Lamenting thus in vain, he rose, and strode
With furious paces to the neighb'ring wood:
Restless his feet, distracted was his walk;
Mad were his motions, and confus'd his talk.
Mad, as the vanquish'd bull, when forc'd to yield
His lovely mistress, and forsake the field.

Thus far unseen I saw: when fatal chance,
His looks directing, with a sudden glance,
Acis and I were to his sight betray'd;

Where, nought suspecting, we securely play'd.
From his wide mouth a bellowing cry he cast,
I see, I see; but this shall be your last:
A roar so loud made *Aetna* to rebound:
And all the *Cyclops* labour'd in the sound.
Affrighted with his monstrous voice, I fled,
And in the neighbouring ocean plung'd my head.
Poor *Acis* turn'd his back, and Help, he cry'd,
Help, *Galatea*, help, my parent Gods,
And take me dying to your deep abodes.
The *Cyclops* follow'd; but he sent before
A rib, which from the living rock he tore:
Though but an angle reach'd him of the stone,
The mighty fragment was enough alone,
To crush all *Acis;* 'twas too late to save,
But what the Fates allow'd to give, I gave:
That *Acis* to his lineage should return;
And rowl, among the river Gods, his urn.
Straight issu'd from the stone a stream of blood;
Which lost the purple, mingling with the flood,
Then, like a troubled torrent, it appear'd:
The torrent too, in little space, was clear'd.
The stone was cleft, and through the yawning chink
New reeds arose, on the new river's brink.
The rock, from out its hollow womb, disclos'd
A sound like water in its course oppos'd,
When (wond'rous to behold), full in the flood,
Up starts a youth, and navel high he stood.
Horns from his temples rise; and either horn
Thick wreaths of reeds (his native growth) adorn.
Were not his stature taller than before,
His bulk augmented, and his beauty more,
His colour blue; for *Acis* he might pass:
And *Acis* chang'd into a stream he was,
But mine no more; he rowls along the plains

With rapid motion, and his name retains.

   Here ceas'd the nymph; the fair assembly broke,
The sea-green *Nereids* to the waves betook:
While *Scylla*, fearful of the wide-spread main,
Swift to the safer shore returns again.
There o'er the sandy margin, unarray'd,
With printless footsteps flies the bounding maid;
Or in some winding creek's secure retreat
She baths her weary limbs, and shuns the noonday's heat.
Her *Glaucus* saw, as o'er the deep he rode,
New to the seas, and late receiv'd a God.
He saw, and languish'd for the virgin's love;
With many an artful blandishment he strove
Her flight to hinder, and her fears remove.
The more he sues, the more she wings her flight,
And nimbly gains a neighb'ring mountain's height.
Steep shelving to the margin of the flood,
A neighb'ring mountain bare, and woodless stood;
Here, by the place secur'd, her steps she stay'd,
And, trembling still, her lover's form survey'd.
His shape, his hue, her troubled sense appall,
And dropping locks that o'er his shoulders fall;
She sees his face divine, and manly brow,
End in a fish's wreathy tail below:
She sees, and doubts within her anxious mind,
Whether he comes of God, or monster kind.
This *Glaucus* soon perceiv'd; and, Oh! forbear
(His hand supporting on a rock lay near),
Forbear, he cry'd, fond maid, this needless fear.
Nor fish am I, nor monster of the main,
But equal with the watry Gods I reign;
Nor *Proteus*, nor *Palaemon* me excell,
Nor he whose breath inspires the sounding shell.
My birth, 'tis true, I owe to mortal race,
And I my self but late a mortal was:

Ev'n then in seas, and seas alone, I joy'd;
The seas my hours, and all my cares employ'd,
In meshes now the twinkling prey I drew;
Now skilfully the slender line I threw,
And silent sat the moving float to view.
Not far from shore, there lies a verdant mead,
With herbage half, and half with water spread:
There, nor the horned heifers browsing stray,
Nor shaggy kids, nor wanton lambkins play;
There, nor the sounding bees their nectar cull,
Nor rural swains their genial chaplets pull,
Nor flocks, nor herds, nor mowers haunt the place,
To crop the flow'rs, or cut the bushy grass:
Thither, sure first of living race came I,
And sat by chance, my dropping nets to dry.
My scaly prize, in order all display'd,
By number on the greensward there I lay'd,
My captives, whom or in my nets I took,
Or hung unwary on my wily hook.
Strange to behold! yet what avails a lye?
I saw 'em bite the grass, as I sate by;
Then sudden darting o'er the verdant plain,
They spread their finns, as in their native main:
I paus'd, with wonder struck, while all my prey
Left their new master, and regain'd the sea.
Amaz'd, within my secret self I sought,
What God, what herb the miracle had wrought:
But sure no herbs have pow'r like this, I cry'd;
And strait I pluck'd some neighb'ring herbs, and try'd.
Scarce had I bit, and prov'd the wond'rous taste,
When strong convulsions shook my troubled breast;
I felt my heart grow fond of something strange,
And my whole Nature lab'ring with a change.
Restless I grew, and ev'ry place forsook,
And still upon the seas I bent my look.

Farewel for ever! farewel, land! I said;
And plung'd amidst the waves my sinking head.
The gentle Pow'rs, who that low empire keep,
Receiv'd me as a brother of the deep;
To *Tethys*, and to *Ocean* old, they pray
To purge my mortal earthy parts away.
The watry parents to their suit agreed,
And thrice nine times a secret charm they read,
Then with lustrations purify my limbs,
And bid me bathe beneath a hundred streams:
A hundred streams from various fountains run,
And on my head at once come rushing down.
Thus far each passage I remember well,
And faithfully thus far the tale I tell;
But then oblivion dark, on all my senses fell.
Again at length my thought reviving came,
When I no longer found my self the same;
Then first this sea-green beard I felt to grow,
And these large honours on my spreading brow;
My long-descending locks the billows sweep,
And my broad shoulders cleave the yielding deep;
My fishy tail, my arms of azure hue,
And ev'ry part divinely chang'd, I view.
But what avail these useless honours now?
What joys can immortality bestow?
What, tho' our *Nereids* all my form approve?
What boots it, while fair *Scylla* scorns my love?

Thus far the God; and more he wou'd have said;
When from his presence flew the ruthless maid.
Stung with repulse, in such disdainful sort,
He seeks *Titanian Circe's* horrid court.

The End of the Thirteenth Book.

BOOK THE FOURTEENTH

Now *Glaucus*, with a lover's haste, bounds o'er
The swelling waves, and seeks the *Latian* shore.
Messena, *Rhegium*, and the barren coast
Of flaming *Aetna*, to his sight are lost:
At length he gains the *Tyrrhene* seas, and views
The hills where baneful philters *Circe* brews;
Monsters, in various forms, around her press;
As thus the God salutes the sorceress.

O *Circe*, be indulgent to my grief,
And give a love-sick deity relief.
Too well the mighty pow'r of plants I know,
To those my figure, and new Fate I owe.
Against *Messena*, on th' *Ausonian* coast,
I *Scylla* view'd, and from that hour was lost.
In tend'rest sounds I su'd; but still the fair
Was deaf to vows, and pityless to pray'r.
If numbers can avail, exert their pow'r;
Or energy of plants, if plants have more.
I ask no cure; let but the virgin pine
With dying pangs, or agonies, like mine.

No longer *Circe* could her flame disguise,
But to the suppliant God marine, replies:
When maids are coy, have manlier aims in view;
Leave those that fly, but those that like, pursue.
If love can be by kind compliance won;
See, at your feet, the daughter of the Sun.

Sooner, said *Glaucus*, shall the ash remove
From mountains, and the swelling surges love;
Or humble sea-weed to the hills repair;
E'er I think any but my *Scylla* fair.

Strait *Circe* reddens with a guilty shame,
And vows revenge for her rejected flame.
Fierce liking oft a spight as fierce creates;
For love refus'd, without aversion, hates.

To hurt her hapless rival she proceeds;
And, by the fall of *Scylla*, *Glaucus* bleeds.

    Some fascinating bev'rage now she brews;
Compos'd of deadly drugs, and baneful juice.
At *Rhegium* she arrives; the ocean braves,
And treads with unwet feet the boiling waves.
Upon the beach a winding bay there lies,
Shelter'd from seas, and shaded from the skies:
This station *Scylla* chose; a soft retreat
From chilling winds, and raging *Cancer's* heat.
The vengeful sorc'ress visits this recess;
Her charm infuses, and infects the place.
Soon as the nymph wades in, her nether parts
Turn into dogs; then at her self she starts.
A ghastly horror in her eyes appears;
But yet she knows not, who it is she fears;
In vain she offers from her self to run,
And drags about her what she strives to shun.

    Oppress'd with grief the pitying God appears:
And swells the rising surges with his tears;
From the detested sorceress he flies;
Her art reviles, and her address denies:
Whilst hapless *Scylla*, chang'd to rocks, decrees
Destruction to those barques, that beat the seas.

    Here bulg'd the pride of fam'd *Ulysses'* fleet,
But good *Aeneas* 'scap'd the Fate he met.
As to the *Latian* shore the *Trojan* stood,
And cut with well-tim'd oars the foaming flood:
He weather'd fell *Charybdis*: but ere-long
The skies were darken'd, and the tempest strong.
Then to the *Libyan* coast he stretches o'er;
And makes at length the *Carthaginian* shore.
Here *Dido*, with an hospitable care,
Into her heart receives the wanderer.
From her kind arms th' ungrateful hero flies;

The injur'd queen looks on with dying eyes,
Then to her folly falls a sacrifice.

    Aeneas now sets sail, and plying gains
Fair *Eryx*, where his friend *Acestes* reigns:
First to his sire does fun'ral rites decree,
Then gives the signal next, and stands to sea;
Out-runs the islands where *Volcanos* roar;
Gets clear of *Syrens*, and their faithless shore:
But looses *Palynurus* in the way;
Then makes *Inarime*, and *Prochyta*.

    The gallies now by *Pythecusa* pass;
The name is from the natives of the place,
The father of the Gods detesting lies,
Oft, with abhorrence, heard their perjuries.
Th' abandon'd race, transform'd to beasts, began
To mimick the impertinence of Man.
Flat-nos'd, and furrow'd; with grimace they grin;
And look, to what they were, too near akin:
Merry in make, and busy to no end;
This moment they divert, the next offend:
So much this species of their past retains;
Tho' lost the language, yet the noise remains.

    Now, on his right, he leaves *Parthenope*:
His left, *Misenus* jutting in the sea:
Arrives at *Cuma*, and with awe survey'd
The grotto of the venerable maid:
Begs leave thro' black *Avernus* to retire;
And view the much-lov'd *Manes* of his sire.
Straight the divining virgin rais'd her eyes:
And, foaming with a holy rage, replies:

    O thou, whose worth thy wond'rous works proclaim;
The flames, thy piety; the world, thy fame;
Tho' great be thy request, yet shalt thou see
Th' *Elysian* fields, th' infernal monarchy;
Thy parent's shade: this arm thy steps shall guide:

To suppliant virtue nothing is deny'd.
   She spoke, and pointing to the golden bough,
Which in th' *Avernian* grove refulgent grew,
Seize that, she bids; he listens to the maid;
Then views the mournful mansions of the dead:
The shade of great *Anchises*, and the place
By Fates determin'd to the *Trojan* race.
   As back to upper light the hero came,
He thus salutes the visionary dame. —
   O, whether some propitious deity,
Or lov'd by those bright rulers of the sky!
With grateful incense I shall stile you one,
And deem no Godhead greater, than your own.
'Twas you restor'd me from the realms of night,
And gave me to behold the fields of light:
To feel the breezes of congenial air;
And Nature's blest benevolence to share.
   I am no deity, reply'd the dame,
But mortal, and religious rites disclaim.
Yet had avoided death's tyrannick sway,
Had I consented to the God of day.
With promises he sought my love, and said,
Have all you wish, my fair *Cumaean* maid.
I paus'd; then pointing to a heap of sand,
For ev'ry grain, to live a year, demand.
But ah! unmindful of th' effect of time,
Forgot to covenant for youth, and prime.
The smiling bloom, I boasted once, is gone,
And feeble age with lagging limbs creeps on.
Sev'n cent'ries have I liv'd; three more fulfil
The period of the years to finish still.
Who'll think, that *Phoebus*, drest in youth divine,
Had once believ'd his lustre less than mine?
This wither'd frame (so Fates have will'd) shall waste
To nothing, but prophetick words, at last.

The *Sibyll* mounting now from nether skies,
And the fam'd *Ilian* prince, at *Cuma* rise.
He sail'd, and near the place to anchor came,
Since call'd *Cajeta* from his nurse's name.
Here did the luckless *Macareus*, a friend
To wise *Ulysses*, his long labours end.
Here, wandring, *Achaemenides* he meets,
And, sudden, thus his late associate, greets.

Whence came you here, o friend, and whither bound?
All gave you lost on far *Cyclopean* ground;
A *Greek's* at last aboard a *Trojan* found.

Thus *Achaemenides* — With thanks I name
Aeneas, and his piety proclaim.
I 'scap'd the *Cyclops* thro' the hero's aid,
Else in his maw my mangled limbs had laid.
When first your navy under sail he found,
He rav'd, 'till *Aetna* labour'd with the sound.
Raging, he stalk'd along the mountain's side,
And vented clouds of breath at ev'ry stride.
His staff a mountain ash; and in the clouds
Oft, as he walks, his grisly front he shrouds.
Eyeless he grop'd about with vengeful haste,
And justled promontories, as he pass'd.
Then heav'd a rock's high summit to the main,
And bellow'd, like some bursting hurricane.

Oh! cou'd I seize *Ulysses* in his flight,
How unlamented were my loss of sight!
These jaws should piece-meal tear each panting vein,
Grind ev'ry crackling bone, and pound his brain.
As thus he rav'd, my joynts with horror shook;
The tide of blood my chilling heart forsook.
I saw him once disgorge huge morsels, raw,
Of wretches undigested in his maw.
From the pale breathless trunks whole limbs he tore,
His beard all clotted with o'erflowing gore.

My anxious hours I pass'd in caves; my food
Was forest fruits, and wildings of the wood.
At length a sail I wafted, and aboard
My fortune found an hospitable lord.

Now, in return, your own adventures tell,
And what, since first you put to sea, befell.

Then *Macareus* — There reign'd a prince of fame
O'er *Tuscan* seas, and *Aeolus* his name.
A largess to *Ulysses* he consign'd,
And in a steer's tough hide inclos'd a wind.
Nine days before the swelling gale we ran;
The tenth, to make the meeting land, began:
When now the merry mariners, to find
Imagin'd wealth within, the bag unbind.
Forthwith out-rush'd a gust, which backwards bore
Our gallies to the *Laestrigonian* shore,
Whose crown, *Antiphates* the tyrant wore.
Some few commission'd were with speed to treat;
We to his court repair, his guards we meet.
Two, friendly flight preserv'd; the third was doom'd,
To be by those curs'd cannibals consum'd.
Inhumanly our hapless friends they treat;
Our men they murder, and destroy our fleet.
In time the wise *Ulysses* bore away,
And drop'd his anchor in yon faithless bay.
The thoughts of perils past we still retain,
And fear to land, 'till lots appoint the men.
Polites true, *Elpenor* giv'n to wine,
Eurylochus, my self, the lots assign.
Design'd for dangers, and resolv'd to dare,
To *Circe's* fatal palace we repair.

Before the spacious front, a herd we find
Of beasts, the fiercest of the savage kind.
Our trembling steps with blandishments they meet,
And fawn, unlike their species, at our feet.

Within upon a sumptuous throne of state,
On golden columns rais'd, th' enchantress sate.
Rich was her robe, and amiable her mein,
Her aspect awful, and she look'd a queen.
Her maids not mind the loom, nor household care,
Nor wage in needle-work a *Scythian* war,
But cull in canisters disastrous flow'rs,
And plants from haunted heaths, and fairy bow'rs,
With brazen sickles reap'd at planetary hours.
Each dose the Goddess weighs with watchful eye;
So nice her art in impious pharmacy!
Entring she greets us with a gracious look,
And airs, that future amity bespoke.
Her ready nymphs serve up a rich repast;
The bowl she dashes first, then gives to taste.
Quick, to our own undoing, we comply;
Her pow'r we prove, and shew the sorcery.

　Soon, in a length of face, our head extends;
Our chine stiff bristles bears, and forward bends:
A breadth of brawn new burnishes our neck;
Anon we grunt, as we begin to speak.
Alone *Eurylochus* refus'd to taste,
Nor to a breast obscene the man debas'd.
Hither *Ulysses* hastes (so Fates command)
And bears the pow'rful *Moly* in his hand;
Unsheaths his scymitar, assaults the dame,
Preserves his species, and remains the same.
The nuptial right this outrage strait attends;
The dow'r desir'd is his transfigur'd friends.
The incantation backward she repeats,
Inverts her rod, and what she did, defeats.

　　And now our skin grows smooth, our shape upright;
Our arms stretch up, our cloven feet unite.
With tears our weeping gen'ral we embrace;
Hang on his neck, and melt upon his face,

Twelve silver moons in *Circe's* court we stay,
Whilst there they waste th' unwilling hours away.
'Twas here I spy'd a youth in *Parian* stone;
His head a pecker bore; the cause unknown
To passengers. A nymph of *Circe's* train
The myst'ry thus attempted to explain.

   Picus, who once th' *Ausonian* scpetre held,
Could rein the steed, and fit him for the field.
So like he was to what you see, that still
We doubt if real, or the sculptor's skill.
The graces in the finish'd piece, you find,
Are but the copy of his fairer mind.
Four lustres scarce the royal youth could name,
'Till ev'ry love-sick nymph confess'd a flame.
Oft for his love the mountain *Dryads* su'd,
And ev'ry silver sister of the flood:
Those of *Numicus, Albula,* and those
Where *Almo* creeps, and hasty *Nar* o'erflows:
Where sedgy *Anio* glides thro' smiling meads,
Where shady *Farfar* rustles in the reeds:
And those that love the lakes, and homage owe
To the chaste Goddess of the silver bow.

   In vain each nymph her brightest charms put on,
His heart no sov'reign would obey but one.
She whom *Venilia*, on Mount *Palatine*,
To *Janus* bore, the fairest of her line.
Nor did her face alone her charms confess,
Her voice was ravishing, and pleas'd no less.
When e'er she sung, so melting were her strains,
The flocks unfed seem'd list'ning on the plains;
The rivers would stand still, the cedars bend;
And birds neglect their pinions to attend;
The savage kind in forest-wilds grow tame;
And *Canens*, from her heav'nly voice, her name.

   Hymen had now in some ill-fated hour

Their hands united, as their hearts before.
Whilst their soft moments in delights they waste,
And each new day was dearer than the past;
Picus would sometimes o'er the forests rove,
And mingle sports with intervals of love.
It chanc'd, as once the foaming boar he chac'd,
His jewels sparkling on his *Tyrian* vest,
Lascivious *Circe* well the youth survey'd,
As simpling on the flow'ry hills she stray'd.
Her wishing eyes their silent message tell,
And from her lap the verdant mischief fell.
As she attempts at words, his courser springs
O'er hills, and lawns, and ev'n a wish outwings.

Thou shalt not 'scape me so, pronounc'd the dame,
If plants have pow'r, and spells be not a name.
She said — and forthwith form'd a boar of air,
That sought the covert with dissembled fear.
Swift to the thicket *Picus* wings his way
On foot, to chase the visionary prey.

Now she invokes the daughters of the night,
Does noxious juices smear, and charms recite;
Such as can veil the moon's more feeble fire,
Or shade the golden lustre of her sire.
In filthy fogs she hides the chearful noon;
The guard at distance, and the youth alone,
By those fair eyes, she cries, and ev'ry grace
That finish all the wonders of your face,
Oh! I conjure thee, hear a Queen complain;
Nor let the sun's soft lineage sue in vain.

Who-e'er thou art, reply'd the King, forbear,
None can my passion with my *Canens* share.
She first my ev'ry tender wish possest,
And found the soft approaches to my breast.
In nuptials blest, each loose desire we shun,
Nor time can end, what innocence begun.

Think not, she cry'd, to saunter out a life
Of form, with that domestick drudge, a wife;
My just revenge, dull fool, ere-long shall show
What ills we women, if refus'd, can do:
Think me a woman, and a lover too.
From dear successful spight we hope for ease,
Nor fail to punish, where we fail to please.

   Now twice to east she turns, as oft to west;
Thrice waves her wand, as oft a charm exprest.
On the lost youth her magick pow'r she tries;
Aloft he springs, and wonders how he flies.
On painted plumes the woods he seeks, and still
The monarch oak he pierces with his bill.
Thus chang'd, no more o'er *Latian* lands he reigns;
Of *Picus* nothing but the name remains.

   The winds from drisling damps now purge the air,
The mist subsides, the settling skies are fair:
The court their sovereign seek with arms in hand,
They threaten *Circe*, and their lord demand.
Quick she invokes the spirits of the air,
And twilight elves, that on dun wings repair
To charnels, and th' unhallow'd sepulcher.

   Now, strange to tell, the plants sweat drops of blood,
The trees are toss'd from forests where they stood;
Blue serpents o'er the tainted herbage slide,
Pale glaring spectres on the *Aether* ride;
Dogs howl, Earth yawns, rent rocks forsake their beds,
And from their quarries heave their stubborn heads.
The sad spectators, stiffen'd with their fears
She sees, and sudden ev'ry limb she smears;
Then each of savage beasts the figure bears.

   The Sun did now to western waves retire,
In tides to temper his bright world of fire.
Canens laments her royal husband's stay;
Ill suits fond love with absence, or delay,

Where she commands, her ready people run;
She wills, retracts; bids, and forbids anon.
Restless in mind, and dying with despair,
Her breasts she beats, and tears her flowing hair.
Six days, and nights she wanders on, as chance
Directs, without or sleep, or sustenance.
Tiber at last beholds the weeping fair;
Her feeble limbs no more the mourner bear;
Stretch'd on his banks, she to the flood complains,
And faintly tunes her voice to dying strains.
The sick'ning swan thus hangs her silver wings,
And, as she droops, her elegy she sings,
Ere-long sad *Canens* wastes to air; whilst Fame
The place still honours with her hapless name.

    Here did the tender tale of *Picus* cease,
Above belief the wonder, I confess.
Again we sail, but more disasters meet,
Foretold by *Circe*, to our suff'ring fleet.
My self unable further woes to bear,
Declin'd the voyage, and am refug'd here.

    Thus *Macareus* — Now with a pious aim
Had good *Aeneas* rais'd a fun'ral flame,
In honour of his hoary nurse's name.
Her epitaph he fix'd; and setting sail,
Cajeta left, and catch'd at ev'ry gale.

    He steer'd at distance from the faithless shore
Where the false Goddess reigns with fatal pow'r;
And sought those grateful groves, that shade the plain,
Where *Tyber* rouls majestick to the main,
And fattens, as he runs, the fair campain.

    His kindred Gods the hero's wishes crown
With fair *Lavinia*, and *Latinus*' throne:
But not without a war the prize he won.
Drawn up in bright array the battel stands:
Turnus with arms his promis'd wife demands.

Hetrurians, *Latians* equal fortune share;
And doubtful long appears the face of war.
Both pow'rs from neighb'ring princes seek supplies,
And embassies appoint for new allies.
Aeneas, for relief, *Evander* moves;
His quarrel he asserts, his cause approves.
The bold *Rutilians*, with an equal speed,
Sage *Venelus* dispatch to *Diomede*.
The King, late griefs revolving in his mind,
These reasons for neutrality assign'd. —
  Shall I, of one poor dotal town possest,
My people thin, my wretched country waste;
An exil'd prince, and on a shaking throne;
Or risk my patron's subjects, or my own?
You'll grieve the harshness of our hap to hear;
Nor can I tell the tale without a tear.
  After fam'd *Ilium* was by *Argives* won,
And flames had finish'd, what the sword begun;
Pallas, incens'd, pursu'd us to the main,
In vengeance of her violated fane.
Alone *Oilëus* forc'd the *Trojan* maid,
Yet all were punish'd for the brutal deed.
A storm begins, the raging waves run high,
The clouds look heavy, and benight the sky;
Red sheets of light'ning o'er the seas are spread,
Our tackling yields, and wrecks at last succeed.
'Tis tedious our disast'rous state to tell;
Ev'n *Priam* wou'd have pity'd, what befell.
Yet *Pallas* sav'd me from the swallowing main;
At home new wrongs to meet, as Fates ordain.
Chac'd from my country, I once more repeat
All suff'rings seas could give, or war compleat.
For *Venus*, mindful of her wound, decreed
Still new calamities should past succeed.
Agmon, impatient thro' successive ills,

With fury, love's bright Goddess thus reviles: —
These plagues in spight to *Diomede* are sent;
The crime is his, but ours the punishment.
Let each, my friends, her puny spleen despise,
And dare that haughty harlot of the skies.

   The rest of *Agmon's* insolence complain,
And of irreverence the wretch arraign.
About to answer; his blaspheming throat
Contracts, and shrieks in some disdainful note.
To his new skin a fleece of feather clings,
Hides his late arms, and lengthens into wings.
The lower features of his face extend,
Warp into horn, and in a beak descend.
Some more experience *Agmon's* destiny,
And wheeling in the air, like swans they fly:
These thin remains to *Daunus'* realms I bring,
And here I reign, a poor precarious king.

   Thus *Diomedes*. *Venulus* withdraws;
Unsped the service of the common cause.
Puteoli he passes, and survey'd
A cave long honour'd for its awful shade.
Here trembling reeds exclude the piercing ray,
Here streams in gentle falls thro' windings stray,
And with a passing breath cool zephyrs play.
The goatherd God frequents the silent place,
As once the wood-nymphs of the sylvan race,
'Till *Appulus* with a dishonest air,
And gross behaviour, banish'd thence the fair.
The bold buffoon, when-e'er they tread the green,
Their motion mimicks, but with gest obscene.
Loose language oft he utters; but ere-long
A bark in filmy net-work binds his tongue.
Thus chang'd, a base wild olive he remains;
The shrub the coarseness of the clown retains.

Mean-while the *Latians* all their pow'r prepare,
'Gainst Fortune, and the foe to push the war.
With *Phrygian* blood the floating fields they stain;
But, short of succours, still contend in vain.
Turnus remarks the *Trojan* fleet ill mann'd,
Unguarded, and at anchor near the strand;
He thought; and strait a lighted brand he bore,
And fire invades, what 'scap'd the waves before.
The billows from the kindling prow retire;
Pitch, rosin, searwood on red wings aspire,
And *Vulcan* on the seas exerts his attribute of fire.

This when the mother of the Gods beheld,
Her towry crown she shook, and stood reveal'd;
Her brindl'd lions rein'd, unveil'd her head,
And hov'ring o'er her favour'd fleet, she said:

Cease *Turnus*, and the heav'nly Pow'rs respect,
Nor dare to violate, what I protect.
These gallies, once fair trees on *Ida* stood,
And gave their shade to each descending God.
Nor shall consume; irrevocable Fate
Allots their being no determin'd date.

Strait peals of thunder Heav'n's high arches rend,
The hail-stones leap, the show'rs in spouts descend.
The winds with widen'd throats the signal give;
The cables break, the smoking vessels drive.
Now, wondrous, as they beat the foaming flood,
The timber softens into flesh, and blood;
The yards, and oars new arms, and legs design;
A trunk the hull; the slender keel, a spine;
The prow a female face; and by degrees
The gallies rise green daughters of the seas.
Sometimes on coral beds they sit in state,
Or wanton on the waves they fear'd of late.
The barks, that beat the seas are still their care,
Themselves remembring what of late they were;

To save a *Trojan* sail in throngs they press,
But smile to see *Alcinous* in distress.

    Unable were those wonders to deter
The *Latians* from their unsuccessful war.
Both sides for doubtful victory contend;
And on their courage, and their Gods depend.
Nor bright *Lavinia*, nor *Latinus'* crown,
Warm their great soul to war, like fair renown.
Venus at last beholds her godlike son
Triumphant, and the field of battel won;
Brave *Turnus* slain, strong *Ardea* but a name,
And bury'd in fierce deluges of flame.
Her tow'rs, that boasted once a sov'reign sway,
The fate of fancy'd grandeur now betray.
A famish'd heron from the ashes springs,
And beats the ruin with disastrous wings.
Calamities of towns distrest she feigns,
And oft, with woful shrieks, of war complains.

    Now had *Aeneas*, as ordain'd by Fate,
Surviv'd the period of *Saturnia's* hate:
And by a sure irrevocable doom,
Fix'd the immortal majesty of *Rome*.
Fit for the station of his kindred stars,
His mother Goddess thus her suit prefers.

    Almighty Arbiter, whose pow'rful nod
Shakes distant Earth, and bows our own abode;
To thy great progeny indulgent be,
And rank the Goddess born a deity.
Already has he view'd, with mortal eyes,
Thy brother's kingdoms of the nether skies.

    Forthwith a conclave of the godhead meets,
Where *Juno* in the shining senate sits,
Remorse for past revenge the Goddess feels;
Then thund'ring *Jove* th' almighty mandate seals;
Allots the prince of his celestial line

An *Apothëosis*, and rights divine.
 The crystal mansions eccho with applause,
And, with her graces, love's bright Queen withdraws;
Shoots in a blaze of light along the skies,
And, born by turtles, to *Laurentum* flies.
Alights, where thro' the reeds *Numicius* strays,
And to the seas his watry tribute pays.
The God she supplicates to wash away
The parts more gross, and subject to decay,
And cleanse the Goddess-born from seminal allay.
The horned flood with glad attention stands,
Then bids his streams obey their sire's commands.

 His better parts by lustral waves refin'd,
More pure, and nearer to aetherial mind;
With gums of fragrant scent the Goddess strews,
And on his features breathes ambrosial dews.
Thus deify'd, new honours *Rome* decrees,
Shrines, festivals; and styles him *Indiges*.

 Ascanius now the *Latian* sceptre sways;
The *Alban* nation, *Sylvius*, next obeys.
Then young *Latinus*: next an *Alba* came,
The grace, and guardian of the *Alban* name.
Then *Epitus*; then gentle *Capys* reign'd;
Then *Capetis* the regal pow'r sustain'd.
Next he who perish'd on the *Tuscan* flood,
And honour'd with his name the river God.
Now haughty *Remulus* begun his reign,
Who fell by thunder he aspir'd to feign.
Meek *Acrota* succeeded to the crown;
From peace endeavouring, more than arms, renown,
To *Aventinus* well resign'd his throne.
The mount on which he rul'd, preserves his name,
And *Procas* wore the regal diadem.

 A *Hama-Dryad* flourish'd in these days,
Her name *Pomona*, from her woodland race.

In garden culture none could so excell,
Or form the pliant souls of plants so well;
Or to the fruit more gen'rous flavours lend,
Or teach the trees with nobler loads to bend.

The nymph frequented not the flatt'ring stream,
Nor meads, the subject of a virgin's dream;
But to such joys her nurs'ry did prefer,
Alone to tend her vegetable care.
A pruning-hook she carry'd in her hand,
And taught the straglers to obey command;
Lest the licentious, and unthrifty bough,
The too-indulgent parent should undo.
She shows, how stocks invite to their embrace
A graft, and naturalize a foreign race
To mend the salvage teint; and in its stead
Adopt new nature, and a nobler breed.

Now hourly she observes her growing care,
And guards their nonage from the bleaker air:
Then opes her streaming sluices, to supply
With flowing draughts her thirsty family.

Long had she labour'd to continue free
From chains of love, and nuptial tyranny;
And in her orchard's small extent immur'd,
Her vow'd virginity she still secur'd.
Oft would loose *Pan*, and all the lustful train
Of Satyrs, tempt her innocence in vain.
Silenus, that old dotard, own'd a flame;
And he, that frights the thieves with stratagem
Of sword, and something else too gross to name.
Vertumnus too pursu'd the maid no less;
But, with his rivals, shar'd a like success.
To gain access a thousand ways he tries;
Oft, in the hind, the lover would disguise.
The heedless lout comes shambling on, and seems
Just sweating from the labour of his teams.

Then, from the harvest, oft the mimick swain
Seems bending with a load of bearded grain.
Sometimes a dresser of the vine he feigns,
And lawless tendrils to their bounds restrains.
Sometimes his sword a soldier shews; his rod,
An angler; still so various is the God.
Now, in a forehead-cloth, some crone he seems,
A staff supplying the defect of limbs;
Admittance thus he gains; admires the store
Of fairest fruit; the fair possessor more;
Then greets her with a kiss: th' unpractis'd dame
Admir'd a grandame kiss'd with such a flame.
Now, seated by her, he beholds a vine
Around an elm in am'rous foldings twine.
If that fair elm, he cry'd, alone should stand,
No grapes would glow with gold and tempt the hand;
Or if that vine without her elm should grow,
'Twould creep a poor neglected shrub below.

   Be then, fair nymph, by these examples led;
Nor shun, for fancy'd fears, the nuptial bed.
Not she for whom the *Lapithites* took arms,
Nor *Sparta's* queen, could boast such heavenly charms.
And if you would on woman's faith rely,
None can your choice direct so well, as I.
Tho' old, so much *Pomona* I adore,
Scarce does the bright *Vertumnus* love her more.
'Tis your fair self alone his breast inspires
With softest wishes and unsoyl'd desires.
Then fly all vulgar followers, and prove
The God of seasons only worth your love:
On my assurance well you may repose;
Vertumnus scarce *Vertumnus* better knows.
True to his choice, all looser flames he flies;
Nor for new faces fashionably dies.
The charms of youth, and ev'ry smiling grace

Bloom in his features, and the God confess.
Besides, he puts on ev'ry shape at ease;
But those the most, that best *Pomona* please.
Still to oblige her is her lover's aim;
Their likings and aversions are the same.
Nor the fair fruit your burthen'd branches bear;
Nor all the youthful product of the year,
Could bribe his choice; your self alone can prove
A fit reward for so refin'd a love.
Relent, fair nymph, and with a kind regret,
Think 'tis *Vertumnus* weeping at your feet.
A tale attend, thro' *Cyprus* known, to prove
How *Venus* once reveng'd neglected love.

   Iphis, of vulgar birth, by chance had view'd
Fair *Anaxaretè* of *Teucer's* blood.
Not long had he beheld the royal dame,
Ere the bright sparkle kindled into flame.
Oft did he struggle with a just despair,
Unfix'd to ask, unable to forbear.
But love, who flatters still his own disease,
Hopes all things will succeed, he knows will please.
Where-e'er the fair one haunts, he hovers there;
And seeks her confident with sighs, and pray'r,
Or letters he conveys, that seldom prove
Successless messengers in suits of love.

   Now shiv'ring at her gates the wretch appears,
And myrtle garlands on the columns rears,
Wet with a deluge of unbidden tears.
The nymph more hard than rocks, more deaf than seas,
Derides his pray'rs; insults his agonies;
Arraigns of insolence th' aspiring swain;
And takes a cruel pleasure in his pain.
Resolv'd at last to finish his despair,
He thus upbraids th' inexorable fair. —

   O *Anaxaretè*, at last forget

The licence of a passion indiscreet.
Now triumph, since a welcome sacrifice
Your slave prepares, to offer to your eyes.
My life, without reluctance, I resign;
That present best can please a pride, like thine.
But, o! forbear to blast a flame so bright,
Doom'd never to expire, but with the light.
And you, great Pow'rs, do justice to my name;
The hours, you take from life, restore to Fame.

Then o'er the posts, once hung with wreaths, he throws
The ready cord, and fits the fatal noose;
For death prepares; and bounding from above,
At once the wretch concludes his life, and love.

Ere-long the people gather, and the dead
Is to his mourning mother's arms convey'd.
First, like some ghastly statue, she appears;
Then bathes the breathless coarse in seas of tears,
And gives it to the pile; now as the throng
Proceed in sad solemnity along,
To view the passing pomp, the cruel fair
Hastes, and beholds her breathless lover there.
Struck with the sight, inanimate she seems;
Set are her eyes, and motionless her limbs:
Her features without fire, her colour gone,
And, like her heart, she hardens into stone.
In *Salamis* the statue still is seen
In the fam'd temple of the *Cyprian* Queen.
Warn'd by this tale, no longer then disdain,
O nymph belov'd, to ease a lover's pain.
So may the frosts in Spring your blossoms spare,
And winds their rude autumnal rage forbear.

The story oft *Vertumnus* urg'd in vain,
But then assum'd his heav'nly form again.
Such looks, and lustre the bright youth adorn.
As when with rays glad *Phoebus* paints the morn,

The sight so warms the fair admiring maid,
Like snow she melts: so soon can youth persuade.
Consent, on eager winds, succeeds desire;
And both the lovers glow with mutual fire.

　Now *Procas* yielding to the Fates, his son
Mild *Numitor* succeeded to the crown.
But false *Amulius*, with a lawless pow'r,
At length depos'd his brother *Numitor*.
Then *Ilia's* valiant issue, with the word,
Her parent re-inthron'd, the rightful lord.
Next *Romulus* to people *Rome* contrives;
The joyous time of *Pales'* feast arrives;
He gives the word to seize the *Sabine* wives.
The sires enrag'd take arms, by *Tatius* led,
Bold to revenge their violated bed.
A fort there was, not yet unknown to fame,
Call'd the *Tarpeian*, its commander's name.
This by the false *Tarpeia* was betray'd,
But death well recompens'd the treach'rous maid.
The foe on this new-bought success relies,
And silent, march; the city to surprize.
Saturnia's arts with *Sabine* arms combine;
But *Venus* countermines the vain design;
Intreats the nymphs that o'er the springs preside,
Which near the fane of hoary *Janus* glide,
To send their succours; ev'ry urn they drain,
To stop the *Sabines'* progress, but in vain.

　The *Naiads* now more stratagems essay;
And kindling sulphur to each source convey.
The floods ferment, hot exhalations rise,
'Till from the scalding ford the army flies.
Soon *Romulus* appears in shining arms,
And to the war the *Roman* legions warms:
The battel rages, and the field is spread
With nothing, but the dying, and the dead.

Both sides consent to treat without delay,
And their two chiefs at once the sceptre sway.
But *Tatius* by *Lavinian* fury slain;
Great *Romulus* continu'd long to reign.

   Now warrior *Mars* his burnish'd helm puts on,
And thus addresses Heav'n's imperial throne.

   Since the inferior world is now become
One vassal globe, and colony to *Rome*,
This grace, o *Jove*, for *Romulus* I claim,
Admit him to the skies, from whence he came.
Long hast thou promis'd an aetherial state
To *Mars's* lineage; and thy word is Fate.

   The sire, that rules the thunder, with a nod,
Declar'd the *Fiat*, and dismiss'd the God.

   Soon as the Pow'r armipotent survey'd
The flashing skies, the signal he obey'd;
And leaning on his lance, he mounts his car,
His fiery coursers lashing thro' the air.
Mount *Palatine* he gains, and finds his son
Good laws enacting on a peaceful throne;
The scales of heav'nly justice holding high,
With steady hand, and a discerning eye.
Then vaults upon his carr, and to the spheres,
Swift, as a flying shaft, *Rome's* founder bears.
The parts more pure, in rising are refin'd,
The gross, and perishable lag behind.
His shrine in purple vestments stands in view;
He looks a God, and is *Quirinus* now.

   Ere-long the Goddess of the nuptial bed,
With pity mov'd, sends *Iris* in her stead
To sad *Hersilia* — Thus the meteor maid: —

   Chast relict! in bright truth to Heav'n ally'd,
The *Sabines'* glory, and the sex's pride;
Honour'd on Earth, and worthy of the love
Of such a spouse, as now resides above,

Some respite to thy killing griefs afford;
And if thou wouldst once more behold thy lord,
Retire to yon steep mount, with groves o'er-spread,
Which with an awful gloom his temple shade.

  With fear the modest matron lifts her eyes,
And to the bright embassadress replies: —

  O Goddess, yet to mortal eyes unknown,
But sure thy various charms confess thee one:
O quick to *Romulus* thy votress bear,
With looks of love he'll smile away my care:
In what-e'er orb he shines, my Heav'n is there.

  Then hastes with *Iris* to the holy grove,
And up the Mount *Quirinal* as they move,
A lambent flame glides downward thro' the air,
And brightens with a blaze *Hersilia's* hair.
Together on the bounding ray they rise,
And shoot a gleam of light along the skies.
With op'ning arms *Quirinus* met his bride,
Now *Ora* nam'd, and press'd her to his side.

The End of the Fourteenth Book.

BOOK THE FIFTEENTH

A KING is sought to guide the growing state,
　　One able to support the publick weight
　　And fill the throne where *Romulus* had sate.
Renown, which oft bespeaks the publick voice,
Had recommended *Numa* to their choice:
A peaceful, pious prince; who not content
To know the *Sabine* rites, his study bent
To cultivate his mind; to learn the laws
Of Nature, and explore their hidden cause.
Urg'd by this care, his country he forsook,
And to *Crotona* thence his journey took.
Arriv'd, he first enquir'd the founder's name
Of this new colony; and whence he came.
Then thus a senior of the place replies
(Well read, and curious of antiquities):
'Tis said, *Alcides* hither took his way
From *Spain*, and drove along his conquer'd prey;
Then, leaving in the fields his grazing cows,
He sought himself some hospitable house:
Good *Croton* entertain'd his godlike guest;
While he repair'd his weary limbs with rest.
The hero, thence departing, bless'd the place;
And here, he said, in time's revolving race,
A rising town shall take his name from thee.
Revolving time fulfill'd the prophecy:
For *Myscelos*, the justest man on Earth,
Alemon's son, at *Argos* had his birth:
Him *Hercules*, arm'd with his club of oak,
O'ershadow'd in a dream, and thus bespoke:
Go, leave thy native soil, and make abode,
Where *Aesaris* rowls down his rapid flood:
He said; and sleep forsook him, and the God.
Trembling he wak'd, and rose with anxious heart;
His country laws forbad him to depart:

What shou'd he do? 'Twas death to go away,
And the God menac'd, if he dar'd to stay.
All day he doubted, and when night came on,
Sleep, and the same forewarning dream, begun:
Once more the God stood threatning o'er his head;
With added curses if he disobey'd.
Twice warn'd, he study'd flight; but wou'd convey,
At once, his person, and his wealth away:
Thus while he linger'd, his design was heard;
A speedy process form'd, and death declar'd.
Witness there needed none of his offence;
Against himself the wretch was evidence:
Condemn'd, and destitute of human aid,
To him, for whom he suffer'd, thus he pray'd.

  O Pow'r, who hast deserv'd in Heav'n a throne,
Not giv'n, but by thy labours made thy own,
Pity thy suppliant, and protect his cause,
Whom thou hast made obnoxious to the laws.

  A custom was of old, and still remains,
Which life, or death by suffrages ordains:
White stones, and black within an urn are cast;
The first absolve, but Fate is in the last.
The judges to the common urn bequeath
Their votes, and drop the sable signs of death;
The box receives all black, but, pour'd from thence,
The stones came candid forth; the hue of innocence.
Thus *Alemonides* his safety won,
Preserv'd from death by *Alcumena's* son:
Then to his kinsman-God his vows he pays,
And cuts with prosp'rous gales th' *Ionian* seas:
He leaves *Tarentum* favour'd by the wind,
And *Thurine* bays, and *Temises*, behind;
Soft *Sybaris*, and all the capes that stand
Along the shore, he makes in sight of land;
Still doubling, and still coasting, 'till he found

The mouth of *Aesaris*, and promis'd ground;
Then saw, where, on the margin of the flood,
The tomb, that held the bones of *Croton* stood:
Here, by the Gods' command, he built, and wall'd
The place predicted; and *Crotona* call'd.
Thus Fame, from time to time, delivers down
The sure tradition of th' *Italian* town.

Here dwelt the man divine, whom *Samos* bore,
But now self-banish'd from his native shore,
Because he hated tyrants, nor cou'd bear
The chains, which none but servile souls will wear.
He, tho' from Heav'n remote, to Heav'n cou'd move,
With strength of mind, and tread th' abyss above;
And penetrate, with his interior light,
Those upper depths, which Nature hid from sight:
And what he had observ'd, and learnt from thence,
Lov'd in familiar language to dispence.

The crowd with silent admiration stand,
And heard him, as they heard their God's command;
While he discours'd of Heav'n's mysterious laws,
The world's original, and Nature's cause;
And what was God; and why the fleecy snows
In silence fell, and rattling winds arose;
What shook the stedfast Earth, and whence begun
The dance of planets round the radiant sun;
If thunder was the voice of angry *Jove*,
Or clouds, with nitre pregnant, burst above:
Of these, and things beyond the common reach,
He spoke, and charm'd his audience with his speech.

He first the taste of flesh from tables drove,
And argu'd well, if arguments cou'd move:
O mortals, from your fellows' blood abstain,
Nor taint your bodies with a food profane:
While corn, and pulse by Nature are bestow'd,
And planted orchards bend their willing load;

While labour'd gardens wholesom herbs produce,
And teeming vines afford their gen'rous juice;
Nor tardier fruits of cruder kind are lost,
But tam'd with fire, or mellow'd by the frost;
While kine to pails distended udders bring,
And bees their hony redolent of Spring;
While Earth not only can your needs supply,
But, lavish of her store, provides for luxury;
A guiltless feast administers with ease,
And without blood is prodigal to please.
Wild beasts their maws with their slain brethren fill;
And yet not all, for some refuse to kill;
Sheep, goats, and oxen, and the nobler steed,
On browz, and corn, and flow'ry meadows, feed.
Bears, tygers, wolves, the lyon's angry brood,
Whom Heav'n endu'd with principles of blood,
He wisely sundred from the rest, to yell
In forests, and in lonely caves to dwell;
Where stronger beasts oppress the weak by might,
And all in prey, and purple feasts delight.

O impious use! to Nature's laws oppos'd,
Where bowels are in other bowels clos'd:
Where fatten'd by their fellow's fat, they thrive;
Maintain'd by murder, and by death they live.
'Tis then for nought, that Mother Earth provides
The stores of all she shows, and all she hides,
If men with fleshy morsels must be fed,
And chaw with bloody teeth the breathing bread:
What else is this, but to devour our guests,
And barb'rously renew *Cyclopean* feasts!
We, by destroying life, our life sustain;
And gorge th' ungodly maw with meats obscene.

Not so the Golden Age, who fed on fruit,
Nor durst with bloody meals their mouths pollute.
Then birds in airy space might safely move,

And tim'rous hares on heaths securely rove:
Nor needed fish the guileful hooks to fear,
For all was peaceful; and that peace sincere.
Whoever was the wretch (and curs'd be he)
That envy'd first our food's simplicity,
Th' essay of bloody feasts on brutes began,
And after forg'd the sword to murder Man.
Had he the sharpen'd steel alone employ'd
On beasts of prey; that other beasts destroy'd,
Or Man invaded with their fangs and paws,
This had been justify'd by Nature's laws,
And self-defence: but who did feasts begin
Of flesh, he stretch'd necessity to sin.
To kill man-killers, Man has lawful pow'r,
But not th' extended licence, to devour.

 Ill habits gather by unseen degrees,
As brooks make rivers, rivers run to seas.
The sow, with her broad snout, for rooting up
Th' intrusted seed, was judg'd to spoil the crop,
And intercept the sweating farmer's hope:
The covetous churl, of unforgiving kind,
Th' offender to the bloody priest resign'd:
Her hunger was no plea: for that she dy'd.
The goat came next in order to be try'd:
The goat had cropt the tendrils of the vine:
In vengeance laity, and clergy join,
Where one had lost his profit, one his wine.
Here was, at least, some shadow of offence;
The sheep was sacrific'd on no pretence,
But meek, and unresisting innocence.
A patient, useful creature, born to bear
The warm, and wooly fleece, that cloath'd her murderer;
And daily to give down the milk she bred,
A tribute for the grass on which she fed.
Living, both food and rayment she supplies,

And is of least advantage, when she dies.
 How did the toyling ox his death deserve,
A downright simple drudge, and born to serve?
O tyrant! with what justice canst thou hope
The promise of the year, a plenteous crop;
When thou destroy'st thy lab'ring steer, who till'd,
And plough'd with pains, thy else ungrateful field?
From his yet reeking neck, to draw the yoke,
That neck, with which the surly clods he broke;
And to the hatchet yield thy husbandman,
Who finish'd Autumn, and the Spring began!
 Nor this alone! but Heav'n it self to bribe,
We to the Gods our impious acts ascribe:
First recompence with death their creatures' toil;
Then call the bless'd above to share the spoil:
The fairest victim must the Pow'rs appease
(So fatal 'tis sometimes too much to please!),
A purple fillet his broad brows adorns,
With flow'ry garlands crown'd, and gilded horns:
He hears the murd'rous pray'r the priest prefers,
But understands not, 'tis his doom he hears:
Beholds the meal betwixt his temples cast
(The fruit and product of his labours past);
And in the water views perhaps the knife
Uplifted, to deprive him of his life;
Then broken up alive, his entrails sees
Torn out, for priests t' inspect the Gods' decrees.
 From whence, o mortal men, this gust of blood
Have you deriv'd, and interdicted food?
Be taught by me this dire delight to shun,
Warn'd by my precepts, by my practice won:
And when you eat the well-deserving beast,
Think, on the lab'rour of your field you feast!
 Now since the God inspires me to proceed,
Be that, whate'er inspiring Pow'r, obey'd.

For I will sing of mighty mysteries,
Of truths conceal'd before, from human eyes,
Dark oracles unveil and open all the skies.
Pleas'd as I am to walk along the sphere
Of shining stars, and travel with the year,
To leave the heavy Earth, and scale the height
Of *Atlas*, who supports the heav'nly weight;
To look from upper light, and thence survey
Mistaken mortals wand'ring from the way,
And wanting wisdom, fearful for the state
Of future things, and trembling at their Fate!
    Those I would teach; and by right reason bring
To think of death, as but an idle thing.
Why thus affrighted at an empty name,
A dream of darkness, and fictitious flame?
Vain themes of wit, which but in poems pass,
And fables of a world, that never was!
What feels the body, when the soul expires,
By time corrupted, or consum'd by fires?
Nor dies the spirit, but new life repeats
In other forms, and only changes seats.
    Ev'n I, who these mysterious truths declare,
Was once *Euphorbus* in the *Trojan* war;
My name, and lineage I remember well,
And how in fight by *Sparta's* king I fell.
In *Argive Juno's* fane I late beheld
My buckler hung on high, and own'd my former shield.
    Then, death, so call'd, is but old matter dress'd
In some new figure, and a vary'd vest:
Thus all things are but alter'd, nothing dies;
And here, and there th' unbody'd spirit flies.
By time, or force, or sickness dispossest,
And lodges, where it lights, in man or beast;
Or hunts without, 'till ready limbs it find,
And actuates those according to their kind;

From tenement to tenement is toss'd,
The soul is still the same, the figure only lost:
And, as the soften'd wax new seals receives,
This face assumes, and that impression leaves;
Now call'd by one, now by another name;
The form is only chang'd, the wax is still the same:
So death, so call'd, can but the form deface;
Th' immortal soul flies out in empty space,
To seek her fortune in some other place.

    Then let not piety be put to flight,
To please the taste of glutton appetite;
But suffer inmate souls secure to dwell,
Lest from their seats your parents you expel;
With rabid hunger feed upon your kind,
Or from a beast dislodge a brother's mind.

    And since, like *Typhis* parting from the shore,
In ample seas I sail, and depths untry'd before,
This let me further add, that Nature knows
No stedfast station, but, or ebbs, or flows:
Ever in motion; she destroys her old,
And casts new figures in another mold.
Ev'n times are in perpetual flux, and run,
Like rivers from their fountain, rowling on,
For time, no more than streams, is at a stay;
The flying hour is ever on her way:
And as the fountain still supplies her store,
The wave behind impels the wave before;
Thus in successive course the minutes run,
And urge their predecessor minutes on,
Till moving, ever new: for former things
Are set aside, like abdicated kings:
And every moment alters what is done,
And innovates some act, 'till then unknown.

    Darkness we see emerges into light,
And shining suns descend to sable night;

Ev'n Heav'n it self receives another dye,
When weary'd animals in slumbers lie
Of midnight ease: another, when the gray
Of morn preludes the splendor of the day.
The disk of *Phoebus*, when he climbs on high,
Appears at first but as a bloodshot eye;
And when his chariot downwards drives to bed.
His ball is with the same suffusion red;
But mounted high in his meridian race
All bright he shines, and with a better face:
For there, pure particles of *Aether* flow,
Far from th' infection of the world below.

Nor equal light th' unequal Moon adorns,
Or in her waxing, or her waning horns,
For ev'ry day she wanes, her face is less;
But gath'ring into globe, she fattens at increase.

Perceiv'st thou not the process of the year,
How the four seasons in four forms appear,
Resembling human life in ev'ry shape they wear?
Spring first, like infancy, shoots out her head,
With milky juice requiring to be fed:
Helpless, tho' fresh, and wanting to be led.
The green stem grows in stature, and in size,
But only feeds with hope the farmer's eyes;
Then laughs the childish year with flowrets crown'd,
And lavishly perfumes the fields around,
But no substantial nourishment receives;
Infirm the stalks, unsolid are the leaves.

Proceeding onward whence the year began,
The Summer grows adult, and ripens into Man.
This season, as in men, is most repleat
With kindly moisture, and prolifick heat.

Autumn succeeds, a sober tepid age,
Not froze with fear, nor boiling into rage;
More than mature, and tending to decay,

When our brown locks repine to mix with odious gray.
   Last, Winter creeps along with tardy pace,
Sour is his front, and furrow'd is his face;
His scalp if not dishonour'd quite of hair,
The ragged fleece is thin; and thin is worse than bare.
   Ev'n our own bodies daily change receive,
Some part of what was theirs before, they leave;
Nor are to-day, what yesterday they were;
Nor the whole same to-morrow will appear.
   Time was, when we were sow'd, and just began,
From some few fruitful drops, the promise of a man:
Then Nature's hand (fermented as it was)
Moulded to shape the soft, coagulated mass;
And when the little man was fully form'd,
The breathless embrio with a spirit warm'd;
But when the mother's throws begin to come,
The creature, pent within the narrow room,
Breaks his blind prison, pushing to repair
His stifled breath, and draw the living air;
Cast on the margin of the world he lies,
A helpless babe, but by instinct he cries.
He next essays to walk, but downward press'd
On four feet imitates his brother beast:
By slow degrees he gathers from the ground
His legs, and to the rowling chair is bound;
Then walks alone; a horseman now become,
He rides a stick, and travels round the room.
In time he vaunts among his youthful peers,
Strong-bon'd, and strung with nerves, in pride of years,
He runs with mettle his first merry stage,
Maintains the next, abated of his rage,
But manages his strength, and spares his age.
Heavy the third, and stiff, he sinks apace,
And tho' tis down hill all, but creeps along the race.
Now sapless on the verge of death he stands,

Contemplating his former feet and hands;
And, *Milo*-like, his slacken'd sinews sees,
And wither'd arms, once fit to cope with *Hercules*,
Unable now to shake, much less to tear, the trees.

So *Helen* wept, when her too faithful glass
Reflected on her eyes the ruins of her face:
Wondring, what charms her ravishers cou'd spy,
To force her twice, or ev'n but once t' enjoy!

Thy teeth, devouring time, thine, envious age,
On things below still exercise your rage:
With venom'd grinders you corrupt your meat,
And then, at lingring meals, the morsels eat.

Nor those, which elements we call, abide,
Nor to this figure, nor to that are ty'd;
For this eternal world is said, of old,
But four prolifick principles to hold,
Four different bodies; two to Heav'n ascend,
And other two down to the center tend:
Fire first with wings expanded mounts on high,
Pure, void of weight, and dwells in upper sky;
Then air, because unclog'd in empty space,
Flies after fire, and claims the second place:
But weighty water, as her nature guides,
Lies on the lap of Earth; and Mother Earth subsides.

All things are mix'd of these, which all contain,
And into these are all resolv'd again:
Earth rarifies to dew; expanded more,
The subtil dew in air begins to soar;
Spreads, as she flies, and weary of her name
Extenuates still, and changes into flame;
Thus having by degrees perfection won,
Restless they soon untwist the web, they spun,
And fire begins to lose her radiant hue,
Mix'd with gross air, and air descends to dew;
And dew condensing, does her form forego,

And sinks, a heavy lump of Earth below.

   Thus are their figures never at a stand,
But chang'd by Nature's innovating hand;
All things are alter'd, nothing is destroy'd,
The shifted scene for some new show employ'd.

   Then, to be born, is to begin to be
Some other thing we were not formerly:
And what we call to die, is not t' appear,
Or be the thing, that formerly we were.
Those very elements, which we partake
Alive, when dead some other bodies make:
Translated grow, have sense, or can discourse;
But death on deathless substance has no force.

   That forms are chang'd, I grant; that nothing can
Continue in the figure it began:
The golden age, to silver was debas'd:
To copper that; our metal came at last.

   The face of places, and their forms, decay;
And that is solid Earth, that once was sea:
Seas in their turn retreating from the shore,
Make solid land, what ocean was before;
And far from strands are shells of fishes found,
And rusty anchors fix'd on mountain-ground:
And what were fields before, now wash'd and worn
By falling floods from high, to valleys turn,
And crumbling still descend to level lands;
And lakes, and trembling bogs, are barren sands.
And the parch'd desart floats in streams unknown;
Wondring to drink of waters not her own.

   Here Nature living fountains opes; and there
Seals up the wombs, where living fountains were;
Or earthquakes stop their ancient course, and bring
Diverted streams to feed a distant spring.
So *Licus*, swallow'd up, is seen no more,
But far from thence knocks out another door.

Thus *Erasinus* dives; and blind in Earth
Runs on, and gropes his way to second birth,
Starts up in *Argos'* meads, and shakes his locks
Around the fields, and fattens all the flocks.
So *Mysus* by another way is led,
And, grown a river, now disdains his head:
Forgets his humble birth, his name forsakes,
And the proud title of *Caïcus* takes.
Large *Amenane*, impure with yellow sands,
Runs rapid often, and as often stands,
And here he threats the drunken fields to drown;
And there his dugs deny to give their liquor down.

   Anigros once did wholsome draughts afford,
But now his deadly waters are abhorr'd:
Since, hurt by *Hercules*, as Fame resounds,
The centaurs in his current wash'd their wounds.
The streams of *Hypanis* are sweet no more,
But brackish lose the taste they had before.
Antissa, *Pharos*, *Tyre*, in seas were pent,
Once isles, but now increase the continent;
While the *Leucadian* coast, main land before,
By rushing seas is sever'd from the shore.
So *Zancle* to th' *Italian* earth was ty'd,
And men once walk'd, where ships at anchor ride.
'Till *Neptune* overlook'd the narrow way,
And in disdain pour'd in the conqu'ring sea.

   Two cities that adorn'd th' *Achaian* ground,
Buris, and *Helice*, no more are found,
But whelm'd beneath a lake, are sunk and drown'd;
And boatsmen through the crystal water show,
To wond'ring passengers, the walls below.

   Near *Trazen* stands a hill, expos'd in air
To winter-winds, of leafy shadows bare:
This once was level ground: but (strange to tell)
Th' included vapours, that in caverns dwell,

Lab'ring with cholick pangs; and close confin'd,
In vain sought issue for the rumbling wind:
Yet still they heav'd for vent, and heaving still
Inlarg'd the concave, and shot up the hill;
As breath extends a bladder, or the skins
Of goats are blown t' inclose the hoarded wines:
The mountain yet retains a mountain's face,
And gather'd rubbish heals the hollow space.

Of many wonders, which I heard, or knew,
Retrenching most, I will relate but few:
What, are not springs with qualities oppos'd,
Endu'd at seasons, and at seasons lost?
Thrice in a day thine, *Ammon*, change their form,
Cold at high noon, at morn, and evening warm:
Thine, *Athaman*, will kindle wood, if thrown
On the pil'd earth, and in the waning moon.
The *Thracians* have a stream, if any try
The taste, his harden'd bowels petrify;
Whate'er it touches, it converts to stones,
And makes a marble pavement, where it runs.

Crathis, and *Sybaris* her sister flood,
That slide through our *Calabrian* neighbour wood,
With gold, and amber dye the shining hair,
And thither youth resort (for who would not be fair?).

But stranger virtues yet in streams we find,
Some change not only bodies, but the mind:
Who has not heard of *Salmacis* obscene,
Whose waters into women soften men?
Or *Aethiopian* lakes, which turn the brain
To madness, or in heavy sleep constrain?
Clytorian streams the love of wine expel
(Such is the virtue of th' abstemious well),
Whether the colder nymph that rules the flood
Extinguishes, and balks the drunken God;
Or that *Melampus* (so have some assur'd)

When the mad *Proetides* with charms he cur'd,
And pow'rful herbs, both charms, and simples cast
Into the sober spring, where still their virtues last.

Unlike effects *Lyncestis* will produce;
Who drinks his waters, tho' with mod'rate use,
Reels as with wine, and sees with double sight:
His heels too heavy, and his head too light.
Ladon, once *Pheneos*, an *Arcadian* stream
(Ambiguous in th' effects, as in the name),
By day is wholsome bev'rage; but is thought
By night infected, and a deadly draught.

Thus running rivers, and the standing lake,
Now of these virtues, now of those partake:
Time was (and all things time, and Fate obey)
When fast *Ortygia* floated on the sea;
Such were *Cyanean* isles, when *Typhis* steer'd
Betwixt their streights, and their collision fear'd;
They swam, where now they sit; and firmly join'd
Secure of rooting up, resist the wind.
Nor *Aetna* vomiting sulphureous fire
Will ever belch; for sulphur will expire
(The veins exhausted of the liquid store):
Time was, she cast no flames; in time will cast no more.

For whether Earth's an animal, and air
Imbibes; her lungs with coolness to repair,
And what she sucks remits; she still requires
Inlets for air, and outlets for her fires;
When tortur'd with convulsive fits she shakes,
That motion choaks the vent, 'till other vent she makes:
Or when the winds in hollow caves are clos'd,
And subtle spirits find that way oppos'd,
They toss up flints in air; the flints that hide
The seeds of fire, thus toss'd in air, collide,
Kindling the sulphur, 'till the fewel spent
The cave is cool'd, and the fierce winds relent.

Or whether sulphur, catching fire, feeds on
Its unctuous parts, 'till all the matter gone
The flames no more ascend; for Earth supplies
The fat that feeds them; and when Earth denies
That food, by length of time consum'd, the fire
Famish'd for want of fewel must expire.

A race of men there are, as Fame has told,
Who shiv'ring suffer *Hyperborean* cold,
'Till nine times bathing in *Minerva's* lake,
Soft feathers, to defend their naked sides, they take.
'Tis said, the *Scythian* wives (believe who will)
Transform themselves to birds by magick skill;
Smear'd over with an oil of wond'rous might,
That adds new pinions to their airy flight.

But this by sure experiment we know,
That living creatures from corruption grow:
Hide in a hollow pit a slaughter'd steer,
Bees from his putrid bowels will appear;
Who, like their parents, haunt the fields, and bring
Their hony-harvest home, and hope another Spring.
The warlike-steed is multiply'd, we find,
To wasps, and hornets of the warrior kind.
Cut from a crab his crooked claws, and hide
The rest in Earth, a scorpion thence will glide,
And shoot his sting, his tail in circles toss'd
Refers the limbs his backward father lost:
And worms, that stretch on leaves their filmy loom,
Crawl from their bags, and butterflies become.
Ev'n slime begets the frog's loquacious race:
Short of their feet at first, in little space
With arms, and legs endu'd, long leaps they take
Rais'd on their hinder part, and swim the lake,
And waves repel: for Nature gives their kind,
To that intent, a length of legs behind.

The cubs of bears a living lump appear,

When whelp'd, and no determin'd figure wear.
Their mother licks 'em into shape, and gives
As much of form, as she her self receives.

　　The grubs from their sexangular abode
Crawl out unfinish'd, like the maggot's brood:
Trunks without limbs; 'till time at leisure brings
The thighs they wanted, and their tardy wings.

　　The bird who draws the carr of *Juno*, vain
Of her crown'd head, and of her starry train;
And he that bears th' Artillery of *Jove*,
The strong-pounc'd eagle, and the billing dove;
And all the feather'd kind, who cou'd suppose
(But that from sight, the surest sense, he knows)
They from th' included yolk, not ambient white, arose.

　　There are, who think the marrow of a man,
Which in the spine, while he was living, ran;
When dead, the pith corrupted will become
A snake, and hiss within the hollow tomb.

　　All these receive their birth from other things;
But from himself the *Phoenix* only springs:
Self-born, begotten by the parent flame
In which he burn'd, another, and the same;
Who not by corn, or herbs his life sustains,
But the sweet essence of *Amomum* drains:
And watches the rich gums *Arabia* bears,
While yet in tender dew they drop their tears.
He (his five centuries of life fulfill'd)
His nest on oaken boughs begins to build,
Or trembling tops of palm, and first he draws
The plan with his broad bill, and crooked claws,
Nature's artificers; on this the pile
Is form'd, and rises round, then with the spoil
Of *Casia*, *Cynamon*, and stems of *Nard*
(For softness strew'd beneath) his fun'ral bed is rear'd:
Fun'ral and bridal both; and all around

The borders with corruptless myrrh are crown'd,
On this incumbent; 'till aetherial flame
First catches, then consumes the costly frame:
Consumes him too, as on the pile he lies;
He liv'd on odours, and in odours dies.

An infant *Phoenix* from the former springs,
His father's heir, and from his tender wings
Shakes off his parent dust, his method he pursues,
And the same lease of life on the same terms renews.
When grown to manhood he begins his reign,
And with stiff pinions can his flight sustain,
He lightens of its load the tree that bore
His father's royal sepulcher before,
And his own cradle: this (with pious care
Plac'd on his back) he cuts the buxome air,
Seeks the Sun's city, and his sacred church,
And decently lays down his burden in the porch.

A wonder more amazing wou'd we find?
Th' *Hyaena* shows it, of a double kind,
Varying the sexes in alternate years,
In one begets, and in another bears.
The thin *Camelion* fed with air, receives
The colour of the thing, to which he cleaves.

India when conquer'd, on the conqu'ring God
For planted vines the sharp-ey'd *Lynx* bestow'd,
Whose urine, shed before it touches Earth,
Congeals in air, and gives to gems their birth.
So *Coral* soft, and white in ocean's bed,
Comes harden'd up in air, and glows with red.

All changing species should my song recite;
Before I ceas'd, wou'd change the day to night.
Nations, and empires flourish, and decay,
By turns command, and in their turns obey;
Time softens hardy people, time again
Hardens to war a soft, unwarlike train.

Thus *Troy* for ten long years her foes withstood,
And daily bleeding bore th' expence of blood:
Now for thick streets it shows an empty space,
Or only fill'd with tombs of her own perish'd race,
Her self becomes the sepulcher of what she was.

  Mycenè, *Sparta*, *Thebes* of mighty fame,
Are vanish'd out of substance into name.
And *Dardan Rome* that just begins to rise,
On *Tiber's* banks, in time shall mate the skies:
Widening her bounds, and working on her way;
Ev'n now she meditates imperial sway:
Yet this is change, but she by changing thrives,
Like moons new-born, and in her cradle strives
To fill her infant-horns; an hour shall come,
When the round world shall be contain'd in *Rome*.

  For thus old saws foretel, and *Helenus*
Anchises' drooping son enliven'd thus:
When *Ilium* now was in a sinking state;
And he was doubtful of his future fate:
O Goddess-born, with thy hard fortune strive,
Troy never can be lost, and thou alive.
Thy passage thou shalt free through fire, and sword,
And *Troy* in foreign lands shall be restor'd.
In happier fields a rising town I see
Greater, than what e'er was, or is, or e'er shall be:
And Heav'n yet owes the world a race deriv'd from thee.
Sages, and chiefs, of other lineage born,
The city shall extend, extended shall adorn:
But from *Iülus* he must draw his breath,
By whom thy *Rome* shall rule the conquer'd Earth:
Whom Heav'n will lend Mankind on Earth to reign,
And late require the precious pledge again.
This *Helenus* to great *Aeneas* told,
Which I retain, e'er since in other mould
My soul was cloath'd; and now rejoice to view

My country walls rebuilt, and *Troy* reviv'd anew,
Rais'd by the fall, decreed by loss to gain;
Enslav'd but to be free, and conquer'd but to reign.
 'Tis time my hard-mouth'd coursers to controul,
Apt to run riot, and transgress the goal:
And therefore I conclude, Whatever lies,
In Earth, or flits in air, or fills the skies,
All suffer change; and we, that are of soul
And body mix'd, are members of the whole.
Then when our sires, or grandsires, shall forsake
The forms of men, and brutal figures take,
Thus hous'd, securely let their spirits rest,
Nor violate thy father in the beast,
Thy friend, thy brother, any of thy kin,
If none of these, yet there's a man within:
O spare to make a *Thyestaean* meal,
T' inclose his body, and his soul expel.
 Ill customs by degrees to habits rise,
Ill habits soon become exalted vice:
What more advance can mortals make in sin
So near perfection, who with blood begin?
Deaf to the calf, that lyes beneath the knife,
Looks up, and from her butcher begs her life:
Deaf to the harmless kid, that ere he dies
All methods to procure thy mercy tries,
And imitates in vain thy children's cries.
Where will he stop, who feeds with houshold bread,
Then eats the poultry, which before he fed?
Let plough thy steers; that when they lose their breath,
To Nature, not to thee, they may impute their death.
Let goats for food their loaded udders lend,
And sheep from winter-cold thy sides defend;
But neither sprindges, nets, nor snares employ,
And be no more ingenious to destroy.
Free as in air, let birds on Earth remain,

Nor let insidious glue their wings constrain;
Nor opening hounds the trembling stag affright,
Nor purple feathers intercept his flight:
Nor hooks conceal'd in baits for fish prepare,
Nor lines to heave 'em twinkling up in air.

Take not away the life you cannot give,
For all things have an equal right to live.
Kill noxious creatures, where 'tis sin to save;
This only just prerogative we have:
But nourish life with vegetable food,
And shun the sacrilegious taste of blood.

These precepts by the *Samian* sage were taught,
Which God-like *Numa* to the *Sabines* brought,
And thence transferr'd to *Rome*, by gift his own:
A willing people, and an offer'd throne.
O happy monarch, sent by Heav'n to bless
A salvage nation with soft arts of peace,
To teach religion, rapine to restrain,
Give laws to lust, and sacrifice ordain:
Himself a saint, a Goddess was his bride,
And all the Muses o'er his acts preside.

Advanc'd in years he dy'd; one common date
His reign concluded, and his mortal state.
Their tears plebeians, and patricians shed,
And pious matrons wept their monarch dead.
His mournful wife, her sorrows to bewail,
Withdrew from *Rome*, and sought th' *Arician* vale.
Hid in thick woods, she made incessant moans,
Disturbing *Cinthia's* sacred rites with groans.
How oft the nymphs, who rul'd the wood and lake,
Reprov'd her tears, and words of comfort spake!
How oft (in vain) the son of *Theseus* said,
Thy stormy sorrows be with patience laid;
Nor are thy fortunes to be wept alone,
Weigh others' woes, and learn to bear thine own,

Be mine an instance to asswage thy grief:
Would mine were none! — yet mine may bring relief.
    You've heard, perhaps, in conversation told,
What once befel *Hippolytus* of old;
To death by *Theseus'* easie faith betray'd,
And caught in snares his wicked step-dame laid.
The wondrous tale your credit scarce may claim,
Yet (strange to say) in me behold the same,
Whom lustful *Phaedra* oft had press'd in vain,
With impious joys, my father's bed to stain;
'Till seiz'd with fear, or by revenge inspir'd,
She charg'd on me the crimes herself desir'd.
Expell'd by *Theseus*, from his home I fled
With heaps of curses on my guiltless head.
Forlorn, I sought *Pitthëan Troezen's* land,
And drove my chariot o'er *Corinthus'* strand;
When from the surface of the level main
A billow rising, heav'd above the plain;
Rolling, and gath'ring, 'till so high it swell'd,
A mountain's height th' enormous mass excell'd;
Then bellowing, burst; when from the summit cleav'd,
A horned bull his ample chest upheav'd.
His mouth, and nostrils, storms of briny rain,
Expiring, blew. Dread horror seiz'd my train.
I stood unmov'd. My father's cruel doom
Claim'd all my soul, nor fear could find a room.
Amaz'd, awhile my trembling coursers stood
With prick'd up ears, contemplating the flood;
Then starting sudden, from the dreadful view,
At once, like lightning, from the seas they flew,
And o'er the craggy rocks the rattling chariot drew.
In vain to stop the hot-mouth'd steeds I try'd,
And bending backward all my strength apply'd;
The frothy foam in driving flakes distains
The bits, and bridles, and bedews the reins.

But tho', as yet untam'd they run, at length
Their heady rage had tir'd beneath my strength,
When in the spokes, a stump intangling, tore
The shatter'd wheel, and from its axle bore.
The shock impetuous tost me from the seat,
Caught in the reins beneath my horse's feet.
My reeking guts drag'd out alive, around
The jagged strump, my trembling nerves were wound,
Then stretch'd the well-knit limbs, in pieces hal'd,
Part stuck behind, and part the chariot trail'd;
'Till, midst my cracking joints, and breaking bones,
I breath'd away my weary'd soul in groans.
No part distinguish'd from the rest was found,
But all my parts an universal wound.

Now say, self-tortur'd nymph, can you compare
Our griefs as equal, or in justice dare?
I saw besides the darksome realms of woe,
And bath'd my wounds in smoking streams below.
There I had staid, nor second life injoy'd,
But *Poean's* son his wondrous art imploy'd.
To light restor'd, by medicinal skill,
In spight of Fate, and rigid *Pluto's* will,
Th' invidious object to preserve from view,
A misty cloud around me *Cynthia* threw;
And lest my sight should stir my foes to rage,
She stamp'd my visage with the marks of age.
My former hue was chang'd, and for it shown
A set of features, and a face unknown.
A-while the *Goddess* stood in doubt, or *Crete*,
Or *Delos'* isle, to chuse for my retreat.
Delos, and *Crete* refus'd, this wood she chose,
Bad me my former luckless name depose,
Which kept alive the mem'ry of my woes;
Then said, Immortal life be thine; and thou,
Hippolytus once call'd, be *Virbius* now.

Here then a God, but of th' inferior race,
I serve my Goddess, and attend her chace.

But others' woes were useless to appease
Egeria's grief, or set her mind at ease.
Beneath the hill, all comfortless she laid,
The dropping tears her eyes incessant shed,
'Till pitying *Phoebe* eas'd her pious woe,
Thaw'd to a spring, whose streams for ever flow.

The nymphs, and *Virbius*, like amazement fill'd,
As seiz'd the swains, who *Tyrrhene* furrows till'd;
When heaving up, a clod was seen to roll,
Untouch'd, self-mov'd, and big with human soul.
The spreading mass in former shape depos'd,
Began to shoot, and arms and legs disclos'd,
'Till form'd a perfect man, the living mold
Op'd its new mouth, and future truths foretold;
And *Tages* nam'd by natives of the place,
Taught arts prophetic to the *Tuscan* race.

Or such as once by *Romulus* was shown,
Who saw his lance with sprouting leaves o'er-grown,
When fix'd in Earth the point began to shoot,
And growing downward turn'd a fibrous root;
While spread aloft the branching arms display'd,
O'er wondring crowds, an unexpected shade.

Or as when *Cippus* in the current view'd
The shooting horns that on his forehead stood,
His temples first he feels, and with surprize
His touch confirms th' assurance of his eyes.
Streight to the skies his horned front he rears,
And to the Gods directs these pious pray'rs.

If this portent be prosp'rous, O decree
To *Rome* th' event; if otherwise, to me.
An altar then of turf he hastes to raise,
Rich gums in fragrant exhalations blaze;
The panting entrails crackle as they fry,

And boding fumes pronounce a mystery,
Soon as the augur saw the holy fire,
And victims with presaging signs expire,
To *Cippus* then he turns his eyes with speed,
And views the horny honours of his head:
Then cry'd, Hail conqueror! thy call obey,
Those omens I behold presage thy sway.
Rome waits thy nod, unwilling to be free,
And owns thy sov'reign pow'r as Fate's decree.

    He said — and *Cippus*, starting at th' event,
Spoke in these words his pious discontent.

    Far hence, ye Gods, this execration send,
And the great race of *Romulus* defend.
Better that I in exile live abhorr'd,
Than e'er the Capitol shou'd style me lord.

    This spoke, he hides with leaves his omen'd head.
Then prays, the senate next convenes, and said:

    If augurs can foresee, a wretch is come,
Design'd by destiny the bane of *Rome*.
Two horns (most strange to tell) his temples crown;
If e'er he pass the walls, and gain the town,
Your laws are forfeit, that ill-fated hour;
And liberty must yield to lawless pow'r.
Your gates he might have enter'd; but this arm
Seiz'd the usurper, and with-held the harm.
Haste, find the monster out, and let him be
Condemn'd to all the senate can decree;
Or ty'd in chains, or into exile thrown;
Or by the tyrant's death prevent your own.

    The crowd such murmurs utter as they stand,
As swelling surges breaking on the strand;
Or as when gath'ring gales sweep o'er the grove,
And their tall heads the bending cedars move.
Each with confusion gaz'd, and then began
To feel his fellow's brows, and find the man.

Cippus then shakes his garland off, and cries,
The wretch you want, I offer to your eyes.
    The anxious throng look'd down, and sad in thought,
All wish'd they had not found the sign they sought:
In haste with laurel wreaths his head they bind;
Such honour to such virtue was assign'd.
Then thus the senate — Hear, o *Cippus*, hear;
So god-like is thy tutelary care,
That since in *Rome* thy self forbids thy stay,
For thy abode those acres we convey
The plough-share can surround, the labour of a day.
In deathless records thou shalt stand inroll'd,
And *Rome's* rich posts shall shine with horns of gold.
    Melodious maids of *Pindus*, who inspire
The flowing strains, and tune the vocal lyre;
Tradition's secrets are unlock'd to you,
Old tales revive, and ages past renew;
You, who can hidden causes best expound,
Say, whence the isle, which *Tiber* flows around,
Its altars with a heav'nly stranger grac'd,
And in our shrines the God of physic plac'd.
    A wasting plague infected *Latium's* skies;
Pale, bloodless looks were seen, with ghastly eyes;
The dire disease's marks each visage wore,
And the pure blood was chang'd to putrid gore:
In vain were human remedies apply'd;
In vain the pow'r of healing herbs was try'd:
Weary'd with death, they seek celestial aid,
And visit *Phoebus* in his *Delphic* shade;
In the world's centre sacred *Delphos* stands,
And gives its oracles to distant lands:
Here they implore the God, with fervent vows,
His salutary pow'r to interpose,
And end a great afflicted city's woes.
The holy temple sudden tremors prov'd;

The laurel grove and all its quivers mov'd;
In hollow sounds the priestess, thus, began,
And thro' each bosom thrilling horrors ran.
"Th' assistance, *Roman*, which you here implore,
Seek from another, and a nearer shore;
Relief must be implor'd, and succour won,
Not from *Apollo*, but *Apollo's* son;
My son, to *Latium* born, shall bring redress:
Go with good omens, and expect success."

When these clear oracles the senate knew;
The sacred tripod's counsels they pursue,
Depute a pious and a chosen band,
Who sail to *Epidaurus'* neighb'ring land:
Before the *Graecian* elders when they stood,
They pray 'em to bestow the healing God:
"Ordain'd was he to save *Ausonia's* state;
So promis'd *Delphi*, and unerring Fate."

Opinions various their debates enlarge:
Some plead to yield to *Rome* the sacred charge;
Others, tenacious of their country's wealth,
Refuse to grant the pow'r, who guards its health.

While dubious they remain'd, the wasting light
Withdrew before the growing shades of night;
Now, *Roman*, clos'd in sleep were mortal eyes,
When health's auspicious God appears to thee,
And thy glad dreams his form celestial see:
In his left hand, a rural staff preferr'd,
His right is seen to stroke his decent beard.
"Dismiss," said he, with mildness all divine,
"Dismiss your fears; I come, and leave my shrine;
This serpent view, that with ambitious play
My staff encircles, mark him ev'ry way;
His form, tho' larger, nobler, I'll assume,
And chang'd, as Gods should be, bring aid to *Rome*."
Here fled the vision, and the vision's flight

Was follow'd by the chearful dawn of light.
   Now was the morn with blushing streaks o'erspread,
And all the starry fires of Heav'n were fled;
The chiefs perplex'd, and fill'd with doubtful care,
To their protector's sumptuous roofs repair,
By genuin signs implore him to express,
What seats he deigns to chuse, what land to bless:
Scarce their ascending pray'rs had reach'd the sky;
Lo, the serpentine God, erected high!
Forerunning hissings his approach confest;
Bright shone his golden scales, and wav'd his lofty crest;
The trembling altar his appearance spoke;
The marble floor, and glittering ceiling shook;
The doors were rock'd; the statue seem'd to nod;
And all the fabric own'd the present God:
His radiant chest he taught aloft to rise,
And round the temple cast his flaming eyes:
Struck was th' astonish'd crowd; the holy priest,
His temples with white bands of ribbon drest,
With rev'rent awe the Power divine confest!
The God! the God! he cries; all tongues be still!
Each conscious breast devoutest ardour fill!
O beauteous! O divine! assist our cares,
And be propitious to thy vot'ries prayers!
All with consenting hearts, and pious fear,
The words repeat, the deity revere:
The *Romans* in their holy worship join'd,
With silent awe, and purity of mind:
Gracious to them, his crest is seen to nod,
And, as an earnest of his care, the God,
Thrice hissing, vibrates thrice his forked tongue;
And now the smooth descent he glides along:
Still on the ancient seats he bends his eyes,
In which his statue breaths, his altars rise;
His long-lov'd shrine with kind concern he leaves,

And to forsake th' accustom'd mansion grieves:
At length, his sweeping bulk in state is born
Thro' the throng'd streets, which scatter'd flowers adorn;
Thro' many a fold he winds his mazy course,
And gains the port and moles, which break the ocean's force.
'Twas here he made a stand, and having view'd
The pious train, who his last steps pursu'd,
Seem'd to dismiss their zeal with gracious eyes,
While gleams of pleasure in his aspect rise.

  And now the *Latian* vessel he ascends;
Beneath the weighty God the vessel bends:
The *Latins* on the strand great *Jove* appease,
Their cables loose, and plough the yielding seas:
The high-rear'd serpent from the stern displays
His gorgeous form, and the blue deep surveys;
The ship is wafted on with gentle gales,
And o'er the calm *Ionian* smoothly sails;
On the sixth morn th' *Italian* coast they gain,
And touch *Lacinia*, grac'd with *Juno's* fane;
Now fair *Calabria* to the sight is lost,
And all the cities on her fruitful coast;
They pass at length the rough *Sicilian* shore,
The *Brutian* soil, rich with metalic ore,
The famous isles, where *Aeolus* was king,
And *Paestum* blooming with eternal Spring:
Minerva's cape they leave, and *Capreae's* isle,
Campania, on whose hills the vineyards smile,
The city, which *Alcides'* spoils adorn,
Naples, for soft delight and pleasure born;
Fair *Stabiae*, with *Cumean* Sibyl's seats,
And *Baia's* tepid baths, and green retreats;
Linternum next they reach, where balmy gums
Distil from mastic trees, and spread perfumes:
Caieta, from the nurse so nam'd, for whom
With pious care *Aeneas* rais'd a tomb,

Vulturne, whose whirlpools suck the numerous sands,
And *Trachas*, and *Minturnea's* marshy lands,
And *Formia's* coast is left, and *Circe's* plain,
Which yet remembers her enchanting reign;
To *Antium*, last, his course the pilot guides.

    Here, while the anchor'd vessel safely rides
(For now the rufled deep portends a storm),
The spiry God unfolds his spheric form,
Thro' large indentings draws his lubric train,
And seeks the refuge of *Apollo's* fane;
The fane is situate on the yellow shore:
When the sea smil'd, and the winds rag'd no more,
He leaves his father's hospitable lands,
And furrows, with his rattling scales, the sands
Along the coast; at length the ship regains,
And sails to *Tibur*, and *Lavinum's* plains.
Here mingling crowds to meet their patron came,
Ev'n the chast guardians of the *Vestal* flame,
From every part tumultuous they repair,
And joyful acclamations rend the air:
Along the flowry banks, on either side,
Where the tall ship floats on the swelling tide,
Dispos'd in decent order altars rise,
And crackling incense, as it mounts the skies,
The air with sweets refreshes; while the knife,
Warm with the victim's blood, lets out the streaming life.

    The world's great mistress, *Rome*, receives him now;
On the mast's top reclin'd he waves his brow,
And from that height surveys the great abodes,
And mansions, worthy of residing Gods.
The land, a narrow neck, it self extends,
Round which his course the stream divided bends;
The stream's two arms, on either side, are seen,
Stretch'd out in equal length; the land between.
The isle, so call'd from hence derives its name:

'Twas here the salutary serpent came;
Nor sooner has he left the *Latian* pine,
But he assumes again his form divine,
And now no more the drooping city mourns,
Joy is again restor'd, and health returns.

But *Aesculapius* was a foreign power:
In his own city *Caesar* we adore:
Him arms, and arts alike renown'd beheld,
In peace conspicuous, dreadful in the field;
His rapid conquest, and swift-finish'd wars,
The hero justly fix'd among the stars;
Yet is his progeny his greatest fame:
The son immortal makes the father's name.
The sea-girt *Britons*, by his courage tam'd,
For their high rocky cliffs, and fierceness fam'd;
His dreadful navies, which victorious rode
O'er *Nile's* affrighted waves and seven-sourc'd flood;
Numidia, and the spacious realms regain'd;
Where *Cinyphis* or flows, or *Juba* reign'd;
The powers of titled *Mithridates* broke,
And *Pontus* added to the *Roman* yoke;
Triumphal shows decreed, for conquests won,
For conquests, which the triumphs still outshone;
These are great deeds; yet less, than to have giv'n
The world a lord, in whom, propitious Heav'n,
When you decreed the sov'reign rule to place,
You blest with lavish bounty human race.

Now lest so great a prince might seem to rise
Of mortal stem, his sire much reach the skies;
The beauteous Goddess, that *Aeneas* bore,
Foresaw it, and foreseeing did deplore;
For well she knew her hero's fate was nigh,
Devoted by conspiring arms to die.
Trembling, and pale, to every God, she cry'd,
Behold, what deep and subtle arts are try'd,

To end the last, the only branch that springs
From my *Iülus*, and the *Dardan* kings!
How bent they are! how desp'rate to destroy
All that is left me of unhappy *Troy*!
Am I alone by Fate ordain'd to know
Uninterrupted care, and endless woe!
Now from *Tydides'* spear I feel the wound:
Now *Ilium's* tow'rs the hostile flames surround:
Troy laid in dust, my exil'd son I mourn,
Thro' angry seas, and raging billows born;
O'er the wide deep his wandring course he bends;
Now to the sullen shades of *Styx* descends,
With *Turnus* driv'n at last fierce wars to wage,
Or rather with unpitying *Juno's* rage.
But why record I now my ancient woes?
Sense of past ills in present fears I lose;
On me their points the impious daggers throw;
Forbid it, Gods, repel the direful blow:
If curs'd weapons *Numa's* priest expires,
No longer shall ye burn, ye Vestal fires.

　　While such complainings *Cypria's* grief disclose;
In each celestial breast compassion rose:
Not Gods can alter Fate's resistless will;
Yet they foretold by signs th' approaching ill.
Dreadful were heard, among the clouds, alarms
Of ecchoing trumpets, and of clashing arms;
The Sun's pale image gave so faint a light,
That the sad Earth was almost veil'd in night;
The *Aether's* face with fiery meteors glow'd;
With storms of hail were mingled drops of blood;
A dusky hue the morning star o'erspread,
And the Moon's orb was stain'd with spots of red;
In every place portentous shrieks were heard,
The fatal warnings of th' infernal bird;
In ev'ry place the marble melts to tears;

While in the groves, rever'd thro' length of years,
Boding, and awful sounds the ear invade;
And solemn music warbles thro' the shade;
No victim can attone the impious age,
No sacrifice the wrathful Gods asswage;
Dire wars and civil fury threat the state;
And every omen points out *Caesar's* fate:
Around each hallow'd shrine, and sacred dome,
Night-howling dogs disturb the peaceful gloom;
Their silent seats the wandring shades forsake,
And fearful tremblings the rock'd city shake.

Yet could not, by these prodigies, be broke
The plotted charm, or staid the fatal stroke;
Their swords th' assassins in the temple draw;
Their murth'ring hands nor Gods nor temples awe;
This sacred place their bloody weapons stain,
And Virtue falls, before the altar slain.
'Twas now fair *Cypria*, with her woes opprest,
In raging anguish smote her heav'nly breast;
Wild with distracting fears, the Goddess try'd
Her hero' in th' etherial cloud to hide,
The cloud, which youthful *Paris* did conceal,
When *Menelaus* urg'd the threatning steel;
The cloud, which once deceiv'd *Tydides'* sight,
And sav'd *Aeneas* in th' unequal fight.

When *Jove* — In vain, fair daughter, you assay
To o'er-rule destiny's unconquer'd sway:
Your doubts to banish, enter *Fate's* abode;
A privilege to heav'nly powers allow'd;
There shall you see the records grav'd, in length,
On ir'n and solid brass, with mighty strength;
Which Heav'n's and Earth's concussion shall endure,
Maugre all shocks, eternal, and secure:
There, on perennial adamant design'd,
The various fortunes of your race you'll find:

Well I have mark'd 'em, and will now relate
To thee the settled laws of future Fate.
He, Goddess, for whose death the Fates you blame,
Has finish'd his determin'd course with Fame:
To thee 'tis giv'n at length, that he shall shine
Among the Gods, and grace the worship'd shrine:
His son to all his greatness shall be heir,
And worthily succeed to empire's care:
Our self will lead his wars, resolv'd to aid
The brave avenger of his father's shade:
To him its freedom *Mutina* shall owe,
And *Decius* his auspicious conduct know;
His dreadful powers shall shake *Pharsalia's* plain,
And drench in gore *Philippi's* fields again:
A mighty leader, in *Sicilia's* flood,
Great *Pompey's* warlike son, shall be subdu'd:
Aegypt's soft queen, adorn'd with fatal charms,
Shall mourn her soldier's unsuccessful arms:
Too late shall find her swelling hopes were vain,
And know, that *Rome* o'er *Memphis* still must reign:
What name I *Afric*, or *Nile's* hidden head?
Far as both oceans roll, his power shall spread:
All the known Earth to him shall homage pay,
And the seas own his universal sway:
When cruel war no more disturbs Mankind;
To civil studies shall he bend his mind,
With equal justice guardian laws ordain,
And by his great example vice restrain:
Where will his bounty or his goodness end?
To times unborn his gen'rous views extend;
The virtues of his heir our praise engage,
And promise blessings to the coming age:
Late shall he in his kindred orbs be placed,
With *Pylian* years, and crowded honours graced.
Mean-time, your hero's fleeting spirit bear,

Fresh from his wounds, and change it to a star:
So shall great *Julius* rites divine assume,
And from the skies eternal smile on *Rome*.

  This spoke, the Goddess to the senate flew;
Where, her fair form conceal'd from mortal view,
Her *Caesar's* heav'nly part she made her care,
Nor left the recent soul to waste to air;
But bore it upwards to its native skies:
Glowing with new-born fires she saw it rise;
Forth springing from her bosom up it flew,
And kindling, as it soar'd, a comet grew:
Above the lunar sphere it took its flight,
And shot behind it a long trail of light.

  Thus rais'd, his glorious off-spring *Julius* view'd,
Beneficently great, and scattering good,
Deeds, that his own surpass'd, with joy beheld,
And his large heart dilates to be excell'd.
What tho' this prince refuses to receive
The preference, which his juster subjects give;
Fame uncontroll'd, that no restraint obeys,
The homage, shunn'd by modest virtue, pays,
And proves disloyal only in his praise.
Tho' great his sire, him greater we proclaim:
So *Atreus* yields to *Agamemnon's* fame;
Achilles so superior honours won,
And *Peleus* must submit to *Peleus'* son;
Examples yet more noble to disclose,
So *Saturn* was eclips'd, when *Jove* to empire rose;
Jove rules the Heav'ns, the Earth *Augustus* sways;
Each claims a monarch's, and a father's praise.

  Celestials, who for *Rome* your cares employ;
Ye Gods, who guarded the remains of *Troy*;
Ye native Gods, here born, and fix'd by Fate;
Quirinus, founder of the *Roman* state;
O parent *Mars*, from whom *Quirinus* sprung;

Chaste *Vesta*, *Caesar's* household Gods among,
Most sacred held; domestic *Phoebus*, thou,
To whom with *Vesta* chaste alike we bow;
Great guardian of the high *Tarpeian* rock;
And all ye Pow'rs, whom poets may invoke;
O grant, that day may claim our sorrows late,
When lov'd *Augustus* shall submit to Fate,
Visit those seats, where Gods and heroes dwell,
And leave, in tears, the world he rul'd so well!

    The work is finish'd, which nor dreads the rage
Of tempests, fire, or war, or wasting age;
Come, soon or late, death's undetermin'd day,
This mortal being only can decay;
My nobler part, my fame, shall reach the skies,
And to late times with blooming honours rise:
Whate'er th' unbounded *Roman* power obeys,
All climes and nations shall record my praise:
If 'tis allow'd to poets to divine,
One half of round eternity is mine.

FINIS

WORDSWORTH CLASSICS
OF WORLD LITERATURE

The Koran

The Newgate Calendar

Njal's Saga

*Sir Gawain and the Green
Knight*

The Upanishads

APULEIUS
The Golden Ass

ARISTOTLE
The Nicomachean Ethics

MARCUS AURELIUS
Meditations

FRANCIS BACON
Essays

JAMES BOSWELL
The Life of Samuel Johnson
(ABRIDGED)

JOHN BUNYAN
The Pilgrim's Progress

CATULLUS
Poems

CERVANTES
Don Quixote

CARL VON CLAUSEWITZ
On War
(ABRIDGED)

CONFUCIUS
The Analects

DANTE
The Inferno

CHARLES DARWIN
The Origin of Species
The Voyage of the Beagle

RENÉ DESCARTES
Key Philosophical Writings

ERASMUS
Praise of Folly

SIGMUND FREUD
The Interpretation of Dreams

EDWARD GIBBON
*The Decline and Fall of the
Roman Empire*
(ABRIDGED)

KAHLIL GIBRAN
The Prophet

HERODOTUS
Histories

THOMAS HOBBES
Leviathan

HORACE
The Odes